IN THE SHADOW OF POWERS

Black Lives and Liberation

Brandon Byrd, Vanderbilt University
Zandria F. Robinson, Rhodes College
Christopher Cameron, University of North Carolina, Charlotte
series editors

Black Lives Matter. What began as a Twitter hashtag after the 2013 acquittal of George Zimmerman for the murder of Trayvon Martin has since become a widely recognized rallying cry for black being and resistance. The series aims are twofold: 1) to explore social justice and activism by black individuals and communities throughout history to the present, including the Black Lives Matter movement and the evolving ways it is being articulated and practiced across the African Diaspora; and 2) to examine everyday life and culture, rectifying well-worn "histories" that have excluded or denied the contributions of black individuals and communities or recast them as entirely white endeavors. Projects draw from a range of disciplines in the humanities and social sciences and will first and foremost be informed by "peopled" analyses, focusing on everyday actors and community folks.

IN THE SHADOW OF POWERS

DANTÈS BELLEGARDE IN HAITIAN SOCIAL THOUGHT
SECOND EDITION

PATRICK BELLEGARDE-SMITH
FOREWORD BY BRANDON R. BYRD

Vanderbilt University Press | Nashville

© 2019 by Vanderbilt University Press
Nashville, Tennessee 37235
All rights reserved.

This book is printed on acid-free paper.
Manufactured in the United States of America

Library of Congress Cataloging-in-Publication Data
Names: Bellegarde-Smith, Patrick, author. | Byrd, Brandon R., writer of
    preface.
Title: In the shadow of powers : Dantès Bellegarde in Haitian social thought
    / Patrick Bellegarde-Smith ; foreword by Brandon R. Byrd.
Description: Second edition. | Nashville : Vanderbilt University Press, 2019.
    | Series: Black lives and liberation | Includes bibliographical references
    and index.
Identifiers: LCCN 2018046156| ISBN 9780826522269 (pbk. ; alk. paper) | ISBN
    9780826522276 (ebook)
Subjects: LCSH: Bellegarde, Dantès, 1877–1966—Political and social views. |
    Haiti—Intellectual life.
Classification: LCC F1927.B413 B45 2019 | DDC 972.94/05092—dc23 LC record
    available at https://lccn.loc.gov/2018046156

ISBN 978-0-8265-2226-9 (paperback)
ISBN 978-0-8265-2227-6 (ebook)

For the twenty-two great-grand- and
great-great-grandchildren of Dantès Bellegarde:

Sasha Hagen, Myesha Gosselin, Brandon Bernier, Heaven Bernier,
Marie-Christine Ravix, Christelle Ravix, Alvin Wayne Smith, Jr.,
Ashlei Dolen, Gilbert Ravix, Karim Ravix, Keira Ravix, Loic Ravix,
Fritz Duroseau, Victoria Duroseau, Jean-Bernard Duroseau,
Louis-Philippe Duroseau, Thierry Malebranche, Sonia Malebranche,
Beatrice Malebranche, Kloe Chavannes, and Ailee Chavannes.

CONTENTS

ACKNOWLEDGMENTS

Earlier versions of portions of several chapters appeared variously in *Caribbean Quarterly*, 20, 304 (September-December 1974), 21–35, "Haiti: Perspectives of Foreign Policy; An Essay on the International Relations of a Small State"; *Caribbean Studies* 20, 1 (March 1980), 5–33, "Haitian Social Thought in the Nineteenth Century: Class Formation and Westernization"; *Phylon* 42, 3 (Fall 1981), 233–244, "Dantès Bellegarde and Pan-Africanism"; *The Americas: A Quarterly Review of Inter-American Cultural History* 39, 2 (October 1982), 167–184, "International/Social Theory in a Small State: An Analysis of the Thought of Dantès Bellegarde."

Dantès Bellegarde in full diplomatic regalia. The official portrait taken in 1921 for the embassy of the Republic of Haiti, Paris, France. Author's personal collection.

FOREWORD

I couldn't help saying to myself that that man would have brought $1,500 at auction in New Orleans in 1860 for stud purposes.
—John Avery McIlhenny, 1917

Haiti has a great man whose years do not as yet number fifty but who has in that comparatively brief space of time become Haitian minister to France, Member of the Permanent Court of Arbitration of the Hague, Member of the Commission of Experts on Slavery and Forced Labor operating in connection with the Council of the League of Nations, Commander of the French Legion of Honor and international spokesman of the Negroes of the World.
—W. E. B. Du Bois, *The Crisis*, April 1926

John Avery McIlhenny was the oldest son of the Confederate whose black workers invented Tabasco.[1] He also was a well-known Democrat from Louisiana and the prototype of what passed for a southern gentleman. Schooled. White. Rich. All of which meant that he needn't mind his manners. Not around black people, at least.

In 1917, McIlhenny, then on his way to becoming the most powerful civilian official in U.S.-occupied Haiti,[2] ignored his plate of food and glared at the Haitian politicians seated across a dining table in Port-au-Prince. In particular, his eyes were fixed on the Haitian Minister of Public Instruction and Agriculture. "I couldn't help saying to myself," McIlhenny was not ashamed to later admit, "that that man would have brought $1,500 at auction in New Orleans in 1860 for stud purposes."[3]

That man was Dantès Bellegarde.[4]

To McIlhenny, the educated Haitian was as impossible as a sovereign Haiti. As the United States occupied the latter,[5] he forced the former into his narrow ontological framework rooted in racial capitalism, U.S. slavery, and Jim Crow. Haitians, black people, McIlhenny thought he knew, were only as valuable as their bodies and manual labor, as the price that the market assigned or the profits they could produce. So, rather than engaging his Haitian counterpart in polite conversation, McIlhenny imagined him far removed from freedom and that moment and his seat at that table. He reduced Bellegarde from a superior black intellect to a blank canvas on which to paint his desires of racial domination.

The discursive enslavement of Dantès Bellegarde was, in many ways, preordained by the histories of slavery and race that molded the American mind. Indeed, it was symptomatic of the history of Haiti, the black nation birthed in a slave revolution that had "the peculiar characteristic of being unthinkable even as it happened."[6]

It's almost trite to cite Michel-Rolph Trouillot's now-famous argument about the conceptual impossibility of the Haitian Revolution. Nonetheless, it bears some repeating here. As Trouillot wrote more than two decades ago,[7] the U.S. and European intellectuals who articulated lofty ideas of universalism, human freedom, and representative government while enslaving millions of Africans could not understand a slave revolution that pushed those ideas to their most profound conclusion. It was impossible for them to conceive of a revolution initiated by black people who, although believed to lack will, history, or an understanding of freedom, had succeeded in dismantling colonialism *and* slavery in one fell swoop.[8]

But categories did not exist to comprehend Haitians, either. By the nineteenth-century, most Europeans and Americans shared a worldview that associated whiteness with dominance and blackness with subordination.[9] Their mental organization of the world emerged from and reinforced the geopolitical hierarchies made by the Transatlantic Slave Trade. It supported slavery, colonialism, and white imperialism. It did not account for the existence of Haitians, a black people who possessed their own country at a time when they were not meant to own their own bodies.

Put simply, the silencing of the Haitian Revolution entailed the erasure of Haitians. It encouraged the denial of Haitians' agency as revolutionaries, statesmen, scholars, and soldiers—as people, thinkers and doers, not commodities subject to the will of white buyers, sellers, and auctioneers.

Thomas Hart Benton was one of many who admitted as much. In defending the United States' refusal to grant diplomatic recognition to Haiti, a policy that lasted from the end of the Haitian Revolution in 1804 until 1862, the U.S. senator from slaveholding Missouri insisted that his country would "not permit black Consuls and Ambassadors to establish themselves in our cities, and to parade through our country, and give their fellow blacks in the United States, proof in hand of the honors which await them, for a like successful effort on their part."[10] He rationalized the disavowal of Haitians as a matter of national security and psychological ease. Benton knew that to find comfort in the myth of white supremacy, it was best not to acknowledge the reality of Haitians, those embodiments of black independence, black intelligence, and even black pride.[11]

So the discursive enslavement of Dantès Bellegarde was, in a way, preordained *and* predictive. It, of course, predated the U.S. military occupation that stripped Haiti of its sovereignty from 1915 to 1934.[12] But it also eroded any meaningful distinction between Benton and McIlhenny; between the racial ideologies that could and did arise from racial slavery and Jim Crow, white imperialism and the neocolonial order that Bellegarde would live to see become ascendant.

To be sure, the occupation that McIlhenny enforced as the financial adviser to the Haitian government did not just cement old ideas about Haiti as a violent and regressive nation of a savage and superstitious people. Instead, it produced new expressions of anti-blackness meant to make palatable an unthinkable people. U.S. travel writers, journalists, and Marines, too many of them unapologetic apostles of the Jim Crow South, exported sensationalized stories of "Voodoo" rituals and brain-dead "zombies" from Haiti to the United States. Their compatriots were more than happy to then displace their anxieties about race, modernization, and masculinity onto Haitians, a people imagined as the exotic foil to normative Americans long after they ostensibly won back their sovereignty.[13]

The continued exploitation of Haiti's resources and the manipulation of its people in the long wake of occupation raises questions related to those that Trouillot once asked.[14] If Haitians are assumed to exist only as antagonists or dependents in the U.S. imagination, how can they be understood or appreciated on their own terms? Put another way, can our narratives be true to a people who remain unthinkable in the same world in which these narratives are made? How *does* one write a history of an impossible people? Of subjects made the objects but not the authors of history and ideas?

The questions must be asked in order to understand Patrick Bellegarde-Smith's answer. And that's exactly what *In the Shadow of Powers* was and remains. Published in a moment when new tropes reinforced older ones that had long obscured Haiti's realities,[15] it is an enduring and urgent response to a call produced and reproduced from the deafening silences of our histories.

By 1985, when Bellegarde-Smith wrote his groundbreaking book on his grandfather and Haitian social thought, Haiti had gone from occupation to dictatorship. Haitian President Jean-Claude Duvalier, the playboy turned heir to his father's murderous regime, stole hundreds of millions of dollars from the Haitian treasury and foreign aid.[16] Much of that money came from the U.S. government because it could bend Duvalier to its political and economic interests. From its perspective, endemic violence and corruption in Haiti were small costs of doing business in the context of the Cold War. There were, it was assumed, bound to be casualties of neocolonial rule.

U.S. and European elites profited. The international image of Haitians deteriorated. Again. While Duvalier embraced an export-oriented development strategy that benefited foreign investors at the expense of Haitian workers,[17] the U.S. press reported that he used "Voodoo" to control the Haitian masses. When Haitian refugees belied that stereotype and sought asylum in the United States, the U.S. Centers for Disease Control claimed that they were principal carriers of AIDS.[18] Discursive violence and social stigmatization were offered as substitutes for brutal dictatorship and political oppression. Caught between an untenable rock and an unforgiving hard place, said to possess diseased minds and infectious bodies, Haitians were regarded as aberrant or impossible subjects of a free democratic society. In U.S. minds, they became or remained zombies, not people, forever enslaved to their vices, their gods, and the whims of U.S. empire.

The silences of academic scholarship were no help at all. Before Bellegarde-Smith finished his foundational text, during the five decades in which the U.S. occupation gave way to the U.S.-sponsored dictatorship that then accelerated the formation of the modern Haitian Diaspora, the number of scholars who published Anglophone works on Haitian thought and thinkers could be counted on one hand with fingers to spare. David Nicholls. J. Michael Dash. You could even count C. L. R. James's incredible account of the Haitian Revolution, perhaps.[19] Beyond that lay a fertile field of Haitian intellectual history left fallow by Americans and Europeans who were clearly capable of seeing Haitians as slaves or even revolutionaries but rarely intellectuals.

In other words, the historiographical redemption of Dantès Bellegarde was, in many ways, unthinkable. It was, at the very least, without sufficient precedent. *In the Shadow of Powers* was the rare work to position Haitians as self-conscious and influential actors in the world of global politics and as producers rather than objects of meaningful thought. It was the first book to recover Bellegarde as an intellectual who demanded for Haitians an equal place in the geopolitical order and who claimed for all black people and black nations a seat at the table.

Of course, Bellegarde-Smith knew all of this. He explained in the introduction to *In the Shadow of Powers* that no "effort [had] been expended outside Haiti in studying the pattern of Haitian intellectual development." He noted that U.S. and European scholarship had "overwhelmingly reflected the racialist ideologies then in vogue."[20] And that the erasure of Haitian intellectuals who promoted ideas of human equality mirrored the silencing and disavowal of the Haitian Revolution that destabilized global politics, colonial economics, and widespread theories of black irrationality.

He suggested, too, the real necessity of making visible the Haitian intellectuals who inherited *and* advanced the egalitarian principles of an unthinkable revolution. For Bellegarde-Smith, his grandfather had to be understood as a product of an age of imperialism when the United States and Europe stopped treating Haiti as a pariah and came to covet it as a prize.[21] Bellegarde was driven by a subversive, racially-inclusive vision of civilized progress. He believed and continued to push for Haiti to establish an existence for itself, black people, and the colonized world independent of the considerable shadow cast by the world's military, economic, and industrial powers.

Bellegarde's dream was powerful, but there was no clear path toward its realization. While the occupation encouraged some Haitian intellectuals including Jean Price-Mars and Jacques Roumain to fight for Haiti's existence outside of Western structures and position African culture or Communism as the basis for Haitian national identity and social organization,[22] Bellegarde continued to argue that Haitians had to make the case for their sovereignty through cultural assimilation. He concluded that Westernization was the only road to take. For Bellegarde, capitalism was a progressive force and Communism had no promise. He believed, too, that French and Catholicism were modern while Kreyòl and Vodou were backward, African, and thus vulnerable to attack. "What would befall a small Dahomean island in the heart of the Americas?" Bellegarde once asked his compatriots.[23] Of course, intervention was possible. Perhaps extinction was, too.

For such views, Bellegarde fell out of favor with peers who espoused more radical demands for black economic and cultural self-determination amidst the international struggles for desegregation and decolonization. And yet, as Bellegarde-Smith suggested, many lessons can be gained from Bellegarde when he's brought back into view. These include invaluable insights into the ideas of liberation that emerge among occupied and colonized people, the inter-sections of enduring concepts of race and culture, progress and civilization, the limits and possibilities of political and economic sovereignty throughout the Global South, and the continued struggle for universal emancipation that began more than two centuries ago during the Haitian Revolution.

To be sure, more than five decades since Bellegarde's death, the consid-erable threats to and persistent strivings for human freedom that emerged during his time have yet to pass. Amidst a massive refugee crisis caused, in part, by the West's commitment to an unending "War on Terror," fascism and authoritarianism are ascendant everywhere from the Philippines and Turkey to Hungary and the United States.[24] Xenophobia is the norm rather than the exception. While white nationalists in Western Europe and the White House promote policies that would make John McIlhenny and the other architects of the occupation proud, international income inequality has reached levels unseen since the days of unchecked industrial capitalism, Jim Crow, and imperialism.[25] Now as then, black intellectuals and activists across the African Diaspora have to proclaim that their lives—and minds—matter.[26] That they possess a right to their bodies, their labor, and even their nations still striving for freedom beyond the shadow of the world's powers.

In short, the need for the historiographical resurrection of Dantès Bellegarde is clear. The second life of *In the Shadow of Powers,* realized in a moment when the U.S. president has revived the stereotype that all Haitians have AIDS and called Haiti a "shithole," answers the never-ending call to abolish old narratives of Haiti and Haitians produced from the prejudices of the U.S. mind.[27] Moreover, it advances the recent "Haitian turn" in Anglophone scholarship that has enhanced our understanding of the Haitian Revolution but offered less analysis of the rich intellectual his-tory of post-independence Haiti.[28] Most importantly, it re-introduces our generation of scholars, students, and activists to Bellegarde, the author and diplomat who W. E. B. Du Bois rightly celebrated as the "international spokesman of the Negroes of the World," not the commodified object of his white contemporaries' imagination.[29]

And so, *In the Shadow of Powers* is a timely inspiration for those who dare imagine or write histories disavowed, silenced, and thought unthink-able. It is a reminder of the power of black minds amid the devaluation of black life. It is a testament to the humanity of impossible people.

Brandon R. Byrd

INTRODUCTION TO
THE SECOND EDITION

More than half a century has passed since the death of Haiti's best-known diplomat, my grandfather, Dantès Bellegarde, yet he remains an iconic and legendary figure. Gone are the days when, strolling in the streets of Port-au-Prince, people would recognize me by my profile, singularly similar to that of my grandfather, a profile shared by many family members. Yet just ten years ago, far from the town of Leogane, half-way to the provincial capital of Jacmel, a young man who had just completed his secondary schooling asked if I was related to "the" Dantès Bellegarde. We were both attending a Vodou religious ceremony deep in the countryside, and he spoke of the mandatory course on Haitian literature where he had studied Bellegarde's life and oeuvre.

The last half century saw the rise of the Haitian middle-classes to power, an expansion of the body politic that then reached into the urban working class and the peasantry. Power was wrestled away from the control of the effete upper-class, an aristocracy of sorts, that had not shared power since the early nineteenth century. From Haiti's origins as a dangerously rogue state in the most complete revolution the world had experienced 1791–1806, the country had hewed closely to the orthodoxy of the nineteenth century in an attempt to gain international acceptance. That never came.

The Bellegardes and the families to which they were related by blood or marriage had provided some 150 years of continuous service to the republic. Dantès Bellegarde's maternal great-grandfather had served as Haiti's first minister of justice, while his paternal grandfather, as a young man, had sought to overthrow President Jean-Pierre Boyer for acquiescing to French demands for reparations to French slave-owners for the loss of their slaves, in the Franco-Haitian Treaty of 1825. His paternal aunt, Argentine Bellegarde, is celebrated as the major figure in early women's education, and two of his five daughters, Fernande and Marie Bellegarde, helped establish the country's first feminist organization in the 1930s. As president of the Constitutional Assembly that wrote Haiti's Constitution in 1950, Bellegarde insisted that it grant women the right to vote. There was stubborn resistance, and, in a compromise, that right became effective in 1957.

This is the legacy I found, growing up in the Bellegarde household, in the late 1940s until mid-1964. In that household, discussions of history and politics were a daily occurrence, unending and "bothersome" in the mind of my younger siblings. The family compound at 88 Avenue John Brown was an urban *lakou*—a foundational feature of the Haitian cultural landscape in which the matriarch, but in this case the patriarch, ruled. There, I had the benefit of my grandfather's massive library, and I did use his help in my schoolwork, in difficult translations of ancient Greek and Latin—*thèmes d'imitation* and *versions*—languages that proved arduous in my early teens. Yes, I cheated! He had taught both these ancient languages at the Lycée Pétion in the 1890s.

The Haitian philosopher Beaubrun Ardouin (1796–1865) had argued in the mid-nineteenth century, that the past was never absent in the present. My small hand in the fragile hand of my great-grandmother's "Nanne," Marie-Noëlle Boisson (1858–1952), was the linkage between past and present, between her parents and myself. There were four generations of Bellegardes living simultaneously in that house in the neighborhood of Lalue until 1952, when my great-grandmother died. She remains still a powerful presence for me. As a child, I felt in my flesh the burden of an "embodied" tradition; in essence, I was trapped.

The truth be told, the Bellegardes had become poor, the family having suffered what is called a *"revers de fortune,"* a tragic reversal of luck—from good to bad, from riches to rags—which fueled my understanding at an early age of social classes and their fragility. We had become, as it were, impoverished aristocracy, a category that does indeed exist. We lived in a shaded oasis in central Port-au-Prince, among the lower middle-class. Dantès Bellegarde had been content to remain in the neighborhood that saw his birth in 1877. He would die in that same house, eighty-nine years later. But though poor, he was light-skinned, the Haitian version of "white privilege," and that status would serve him well.

The Haitian Revolution of 1791 had expressed a tragic misunderstanding between social groups who might have been political allies, the white slave-owning plantation owners, and the *affranchis*, as the freed blacks and mulattoes were called. Many in that latter grouping had bought into the peculiar psychology that developed in every European colonial enterprise, a sacrosanct class system and an evolving capitalist system. The egalitarian spirit of the French Revolution of 1789 was deeply troublesome to the *grands seigneurs* who formed the colony's bourgeoisie. Hence, the colonial struggle acquired the aspect of a race war, which it was, though it need not have been. The white owners rejected the entreaties of the colored affranchi slave-owners and landowners for a common front, and the insurrections that ensued led to the Revolution and to Haitian independence, while ensuring the opprobrium and resentment of white nations for the next two centuries. The international system established by Western Europe was shaken to its foundation and never recovered. Haiti was despised and isolated. It was seen as the original terrorist state.

The Haitian Revolution, the most far-reaching of all such revolutions, in that it brought forth the concept of universal freedom, clearly not a goal in the earlier American movement nor in the French Revolution, remains the least studied of any revolutions in modern or contemporary history. Throughout the nineteenth and well into the twentieth century, Western European and American scholarship reflected the racialist ideologies in vogue, in all disciplines, including the emerging field of anthropology. The birth of liberalism via the Enlightenment that had accompanied the French and the American Revolutions, gave way to the forces of conservatism in Western Europe, into the worldwide empires it controlled, and racialist views actually worsened, and Haiti suffered some more.

Latin America and the Caribbean, including Haiti, share elements of a common history. The rise of empires, the impact of colonization, the subjugation and the genocide of indigenous groups, slavery as a system that pervaded all other systems, policies of cultural assimilation, intended or not, and presently neocolonialism, were all factors that compelled the wretchedness of contemporary life in these nations. After "race" is factored in, economic factors find their own "level of significance" as the engine of growth for development of some countries and the underdevelopment of many more. In the European empires, race and color divisions became highly correlated with class, a necessity for further wealth accumulation by small but dominant minorities.

If "Haiti was born without a head,"[1] to use Dantès Bellegarde's expression, since the Revolution had turned the system upside down, *tête en bas*, as we say, the country soon acquired that head when former affranchis and war-heroes sought to fill the vacuum created by the physical elimination of colonial whites from the territory. The elites that arose in Haiti, as elsewhere in Latin America, were hard at work in justifying their leadership through the elaboration of theories and ideologies of national development. The documentation for probing studies of Haitian social thought has always existed, found in the numerous works written by Haitian intellectuals over more than two centuries of an abundant literary production. But most of these written works remain untranslated from the French, obscuring the motivations of these elites and the similarities they shared with other similarly situated groups abroad.

Because of its historical positioning as the first independent nation in the Americas after the United States, Haiti pioneered Pan-Americanism. And because Haiti is "black," it also pioneered in early-forms of Pan-Africanism, and the worldwide literary Négritude movement. Haitian intellectuals were deeply conflicted nonetheless, and Pan-Americanism, Pan-Africanism, and Négritude signified different awarenesses in the body politic, while coexisting side by side. Collaboration with imperial forces and bursts of racial pride simultaneously defined much of elite behavior in Haiti. Liberian and Sierra Leonean elites showed some of the same patterns, also having arose early from the colonial cauldron.

But for African-descended people worldwide, Haiti had remained a beacon, particularly when it achieved a modicum of success in various fields. It was not, then, the "poorest country in the Western hemisphere." Not then, not yet.

Dantès Bellegarde expressed in his flesh the "angst," what Haitians would label the "*tiraillements*," the pulling asunder of two unreconciled souls reminiscent of W. E. B. Du Bois's felicitous formulation. When accused of cultural "bovarysm" by his friend and antagonist Jean Price-Mars—that other giant in Haitian letters—his response, etched with his fingernail on the margins of that statement in Price-Mars's book, was simply that he was not black, but a proud *mulâtre*, a mulatto. Yet abroad, he had little choice but to bathe in his blackness, proud of Du Bois's description of him as an international spokesman of the Negroes of the world. That angst and behavior reflected the tenuous position of other light-skinned Haitians when traveling abroad. Other Latin American leaders also found themselves to be "white" at home, but "colored" as they traveled north or northeast.

Bellegarde's sincerity, however, could not be doubted. His pre-scriptions for what ailed Haiti were predicated on the realities of early twentieth-century conditions and what the powers would allow. He was an internationalist because small states had no other good choices. "The South" had yet to be invented in scholarship, though it had always existed. The Third World was not a category, when just three independent black states had embassies in Washington, DC: Haiti, Liberia, and Ethiopia. But Bellegarde's diplomatic successes in Paris and in Geneva, and his accep-tance by European intellectuals, reinforced his views, and his vision for his country remained consistent. In "adult" conversations I had with my grandfather in the late 1950s and early 1960s, he expressed the thought that his own evolution, from a poor child from an illiterate and poor creo-lophone mother, with a live-in cousin who was a *manbo* (a female Vodou priest), was a harbinger of the changes Haiti could itself undertake. Thus, he had avoided the cost of being called a "savage" in a civilized world, and Haiti could undertake the same transformation that he himself had undergone. He held himself as an exemplar and a harbinger of what else was possible.

Even Jean Price-Mars (1875–1969), the Father of the Négritude move-ment, had been flattered by the statement that Haiti had been "the for-ward beacon of Latinity in America," according to French Senator Henri Béranger. Bellegarde had simply misread the cultural revolution that had taken place under the leadership of his friend Jean Price-Mars, in which a wholesale reassessment of Haiti's African roots had fueled a political revolu-tion of sort, with the middle-classes reaching power with the governments of Presidents Dumarsais Estimé, François Duvalier, and their successors. But anthropologists Anténor Firmin (1850–1911) and Louis-Joseph Janvier (1885–1911) had earlier laid the groundwork for such a revolutionary change, disputing European racial superiority.

In the final analysis, the francophone element in Haiti consists of per-haps 5 percent of the population, and social philosophers on either side of the cultural divide presented *"une littérature à tendances"* rather than full-fledged ideological differences, as these men reflected prevalent Western views as social Darwinists or as adherent of Herbert Spencer, Henri Bergson, Karl Marx, and all the others.

At the very end of Bellegarde's diplomatic career in 1957, P. W. Buck and M. B. Travis, Jr., also writing in 1957, had envisioned a unique role for Haiti within the scope of Latin American diplomatic action:

Haiti, by reason of its special character and history, is almost a unique link in the fabric of international society. Its people being Negro, its culture French, its political and geographic situation American, Haiti may well interpret America to Europe, and both to Africa.[2]

Without entering into a dispute over the specific elements and assumptions of this declaration, one can accept the overall premise and its intent, in acknowledging that social and foreign policy is the prerogative of elites everywhere, and this is particularly true in countries where nonliterate populations subsist.

Ideologies are challenging. Part of the complexity is the effort one must make assessing their impact on society, broadly, in the economic and social life of a given polity. The history of ideas, and more generally, the development of social philosophies in emerging states, is the concern and the preserve of a small coterie of intellectuals, while the impact is not attenuated by their relatively small numbers in the polity. It is especially true in a context in which social philosophers and those in actual power at all levels of the state are the same individuals. These are part of the "social realities," as understood by Karl Marx to affect social development. Ideology, together with other social realities such as "race" or religious beliefs, helps us understand a complex reality that, in the case of Haiti, is dominated by obdurate negative international conditions outside of the country's control.

An analysis of social thought is further justified whether it is practiced by an inbred elite based on its social prerogatives, or by a vanguard party on the left. In either case, elitism persists, but ideas retain their influence.

Dantès Bellegarde was the quasi-official ideologue of the Haitian state over successive governments, offering a key to understanding the evolution of social thought in Haiti. He was, additionally, the best synthesizer of much of nineteenth-century thinking, in what was the adaptation of liberalism in a Latin American context. His nineteen books published between 1904 and 1962, together with hundreds of journal and newspaper articles, made of him—and Jean Price-Mars—one of two major social philosophers in the first half of the twentieth century. In the meanderings of his thought, one finds the path of the evolution of Haitian social philosophy. Humans, indeed, do not exist in a vacuum, but within a social context, and individuals live lives of conditioned reflexes; they respond to contemporaries and to society. In the final analysis, modes of thought and personality emerge from sociocultural situations that are a part of the collective.

Bellegarde contributed substantially to the formulation of foreign policy, usually a presidential prerogative in Haiti, particularly by his bold presence at the League of Nations, at the Pan-American Union, and later, at the Organization of American States and at the United Nations. At the League of Nations in 1930, while American military forces were occupying Haiti, he critiqued severely U.S. foreign policy toward Latin America. This action forced his recall by the Haitian government at the insistance of the United States. Latin American states were like sardines swimming in seas infested by sharks. Bellegarde was also instrumental in the development of financial and fiscal policies whose effects were felt in Haiti over several decades. But another major contribution was Bellegarde's participation at several Pan-African Congresses, starting in 1921, and the great friendships he maintained with major African-American personalities. His connection with the African-American intelligentsia ensured the enmity of the United States government. No previous attempts have been made to analyze Bellegarde's contributions in these various fields, within the dynamics of both international conditions and domestic realities facing the Haitian state. The first of these dimensions includes the climate in which only three black states existed, a world in which the Caribbean and African nations were still colonized; the second incorporates Haiti's chronic political instability, bearing the impact of colonialism lingering after a century of independent life.

Because a pillar that establishes states and societal systems is an ideological armature, and because the impact of a well-placed individual upon a society in transition can be almost as great as the impact of the milieu upon that person, a study of Bellegardian thought was warranted. This was understood by Secretary of State Paul Blanchet when he eulogized Bellegarde at the Port-au-Prince cemetery, on behalf of the Haitian government: "The work to which he dedicated his entire life remains a testimony whose worth will be assessed by the historian after a lapse of time, through resurrecting the psychology of the men and events of that era."[3] Blanchet had introduced the elements that would be considered to appraise the political life and the literary career Bellegarde had maintained for more than half a century. His "death's majesty renders to Dantès Bellegarde his true place,"[4] was more than a literary flourish, suggesting that an evaluation of a man's life and oeuvre could only now be undertaken.

This book evaluates the contribution of Dantès Bellegarde through his writings to the general pattern of Haitian intellectual development

throughout the nineteenth century and examines critically the consistency
of these writings in relation to his public career, in his role as a foremost
exponent of the rights of small states during the years that witnessed the
emergence of a vibrant black cultural awareness on the world stage.[5]

The man who had told his countrymen of an impending American
military invasion in February 1907, "God is too far, and the United States
is too close,"[6] and had warned the world in 1922, in a celebrated formula,
that "the League of Nations must be audaciously prudent or, if you will,
prudently audacious,"[7] remained after his death the subject of some con-
troversy. The letters received and the interviews undertaken by me revealed,
within the usual courtesy, the rancor and the disagreements that sur-
rounded Bellegarde throughout his life. He was seen as an internationalist
and an ardent nationalist. He was a patriot. He was chiefly the pre-eminent
Francophile who fought American cultural influence, yet collaborated with
the U.S. occupying forces. He defended the Roman Catholic Church as a
factor of civilization against the encroachment of American Protestantism,
though he eschewed any religious sensibility in private. Hegemonic
Christianity and French, along with other European languages, had been
instruments for continued colonial control over indigenous populations,
and remained so after independence, in a form of cultural neocolonialism.
Bellegarde remains one of the most debated Haitian scholars, but also one
of the least read. Over the past two decades, however, small Haitian presses
have republished some of his works, but never sought permission from the
family in doing so.

My mentor Harold E. Davis, a pioneer of the study of Latin American
philosophy in the United States, did not include Haiti in any of his texts,
despite acknowledging Haiti's sustained help to the revolutionary movements that led to the freedom of several Latin American states. But he urged
me to fill the gap.[8]

Lucian W. Pye argued that "Quite different methods of research
are called for in the study of [elite and mass] cultures. Work on the elite
political culture involves skills in interpreting ideologies, in characterizing
operational codes, and in defining the spirit and calculations that lie behind
high-risk political behavior."[9] Between studies attempting to explicate the
psychology or the psychic needs of eminent personalities, such as those of
Erik H. Erikson, and studies of "opinion" that usually delve into transient
questions, lies an important middle ground that delineates ideological orientation. In the United States, up to the present, ideologies are usually

defined narrowly as more style than essence.[10] Perhaps the same can be said of Haiti where elites remained true to themselves.[11]

The point of intersection between ideology and elites would be self-evident, since, in the words of T. B. Bottomore, "there is a profound association between changes in social structure and the rise and fall of elites."[12] The activities of elites themselves, their guiding social thought as part of social reality, become worthy of study, and crucial in the analysis of a society in its totality.

Gaetano Mosca, in his defense of elitism, believed that: "The dominion of an organized minority, obeying a single impulse, over the unorganized majority is inevitable."[13] I interpret "impulse" as ideology that allows for the concentration and the uniformity of effort. This would seem to apply whether one writes of advanced industrial systems or so-called "backward" polities that share the planet. Indeed, the First and the Third World are part of the same capitalist system.

Because an individual cannot be divorced from his or her milieu, Chapter 1, "The Context of the Cultural Crisis: Haiti Social Policy and Foreign Relations," paints in broad strokes what political scientists may define as the linkage between domestic and foreign policy and its impact upon an evolving national state. Chapter 2, "The Basis for Haitian Social Policy: Social Thought in the Nineteenth Century," specifies Dantès Bellegarde's intellectual antecedents, via the consolidation of the Haitian bourgeoisie. Chapter 3, "Milieu, Moment, Interest: The Career and Life of Dantès Bellegarde," details the career and the influences suffered by Bellegarde, as reflected through the macroanalysis undertaken in the first two chapters. Chapter 4, "Synthesis of an Approach: History and Culture," analyses the creative thought of Bellegarde as it relates nationally and internationally to other social theorists, in his understanding of history and vision of cultural phenomena. Chapter 5, "Synthesis of an Approach: Education and Commerce," analyses the means for achieving the goals envisioned by Bellegarde. Chapter 6, "Perspective on Social Conflict and Culture," places Bellegarde's internal reality as it evolved, as the citizen of a small nation state.

There were difficulties encountered in elaborating this study. At one level, I had to take into account the suspicions of those interviewed and the paucity of available resources and documentation. Due to the dearth of financial resources in Haiti, libraries, archives, and research centers have complicated stories. At another level, I had to remain alert of the shifting definitions of left, right, and center in the political spectrum, in Haiti and abroad, and as they evolve over time. Similarly, the shift over more than two centuries of the definition of socioeconomic classes presented an additional complication in a work that portrays the development and the evolution of Haitian intellectual thought: The affranchis displaced the colonial bourgeoisie of grand planteurs in 1804, acquiring supremacy in the 1820s, forming an aristocracy of sorts. A post-independence petite bourgeoisie (into which Dantès Bellegarde was born) was incorporated into an expanded ruling oligarchy at century's end. A new middle class was forged by new educational possibilities, partly due to the efforts of Bellegarde, in the first quarter of the twentieth century, and from the expansion of economic growth, was strengthened. Political upheavals in the early 1940s led to middle-class governments assuming power, semi-permanently, with a new moneyed and emergent bourgeoisie. And we have observed the rise of an urban working class and a peasantry that refuses its subaltern status, but that has fought for change since the 1840s, explicating the unsettled and unstable conditions in Haiti from the beginning.

Primary data for this work included the books and articles published by Dantès Bellegarde in Haiti, in Western Europe, and in North and South America, as well as unpublished material that had been preserved by his descendants in Port-au-Prince and abroad. I have also made use of his extensive correspondence. Other sources include articles in the Haitian and foreign press and academic journals that have mentioned his action in some capacity. Memoirs and work by contemporaries have been sifted for their details.

I have conducted interviews in Haiti and in the United States and maintained a correspondence with personalities in Europe who knew Dantès Bellegarde well and who had interacted with him at various levels. In this second edition, I note that all these individuals, bar none, are now deceased. These were Jacques Antoine, Hebert Aptheker, Roger N. Baldwin, Mercer Cook, Léon-Gontran Damas, Ulrick Duvivier, Kenneth Holland, Ghislain Gouraige, Léon Laleau, Rayford W. Logan, Maurice A. Lubin, Leslie Manigat, Sidney W. Mintz, Luis Muñoz-Marin, Gaston Monnerville, Teodoro Moscoso, Jean Piaget, Max Bissainthe, Auguste Viatte, Dilia Vieux-Briere, Max Wilson, Paulette Poujol-Oriol, Harold E. Davis, Arthur C. Breycha-Vauthier, Jaime Benitez, Richard Pattee, Auguste Bellegarde, Argentine (Titine) Bellegarde, Fernande Nicolas (née Bellegarde), Marie (Mayotte) Bellegarde, Simone Bellegarde-Smith, and Jean Bellegarde. The memory of warm and lengthy conversations lingers on . . .

My heartfelt thanks go to Brandon Byrd for his foreword and to Beth Kressel Itkin and the other Vanderbilt University Press staff members who worked on this project, including Dariel Mayer, Joell Smith-Borne, Zachary Gresham, and Silvia Benvenuto.

It is always difficult to write about a friend, or a grandparent, or about someone who was both. There is always the dilemma of saying too much or too little. When too much is said, one runs the risk of violating the individual's right to some privacy and the secrets entrusted to a confidant; if too little is said, one wonders if justice was done. This imperative applies whether one speaks of an unknown or of a celebrity.

Justice requires a fair representation of the individual's thought within the context of the varied and many experiences that have shaped a life. The difficulty seems to increase when one writes of a man who, by his work and his influence, belongs to a whole nation.

I have agonized plenty while sifting through the details of my grandfather's actions, weighing them for their significance, and painfully questioning old ideas and assumptions. I have received the opinions of family members and old friends with suspicion, all the while fearing their disappointment and embarrassment in the end. I have attempted to specify a man's internal reality and the contributive impact of his milieu. If done properly, the work restores a man; his ideals and words give him life.

CHAPTER 1

THE CONTEXT OF
THE CULTURAL CRISIS

HAITIAN SOCIAL POLICY AND FOREIGN RELATIONS

*Our past has not yet become a real past; it is still a
present which does not choose to become history.*

—Leopoldo Zea

An encounter, heavy in symbolism, occurred in the foothills of the
Massif-du-Nord on February 9, 1802. Isaac and Placide Louverture,
accompanied by their tutor, Abbé Coisnon, were the emissaries of Napoleon
Bonaparte. Their mission was to convince Toussaint Louverture to abandon
the struggle for freedom. The French army had to be freed from entangle-
ments in Saint Domingue before the Napoleonic dream for North American
conquest could be undertaken.[1] Toussaint agreed to meet the ambassadors
at his headquarters at Ennery.

Isaac was Toussaint's legitimate son; Placide was the son of his wife
Suzanne Simon and a white slave master. Both had been pursuing their
studies in France when ordered back with the Leclerc expedition. This diplomatic appeal could have been an afterthought in view of the virtual cer-
tainty of continued warfare. Toussaint did not retreat from his position.
Instead, he demanded reluctantly that his sons choose between his cause
and France. Isaac responded that France had made him a man by giving
him dignity of thought; he could not fight against it. Placide, his stepson,
answered, "I cannot abandon the one who made me a man by giving me
my freedom. Father, my place is at your side."[2] Moved by their sincerity,
Toussaint pressed both his sons against him, appreciating their choices while
agonizing over them.

Toussaint understood the dilemma. He himself had found sustenance in the ideals of revolutionary France, and had personally benefited from the French political upheavals, rising to the rank of commander-in-chief of the French army in Saint Domingue and governor-general of the colony.[3] The events in Saint Domingue were sparked by the French Revolution, but local economic and political circumstances had made these developments possible in the colony.[4]

The Economic Dimension

Economically, Saint Domingue became the most lucrative colony of the French crown.[5] Politically, as a result of a revolt against the inhuman efficiency of the plantation economic system and the influence of the French Revolution, Haiti became the first independent state in Latin America, the first modern state of African origin, the first ministate of modern times, (followed by Belgium in 1830), and the only state in history that arose from a successful slave rebellion. The war that gave birth to the state was significantly different from other slave upheavals in the Western hemisphere. It distinguished itself as a war that sought the universal realization of black emancipation, while other movements usually advocated freedom only for their proponents, but maintenance of the status quo. This impulse toward universalism created a "modern" state rather than a West-African protostate.

Some historians have seen in Haiti the first real and successful confrontation arising from a conflict between European and American local bourgeois interests. Indeed, the Haitian movement was the result of internal pressures in the colony as well as the product of European forces and rivalry.[6] This view is further supported by the influential position that France held at this moment of world history, which placed Haiti in the midst of the revolutionary ferment. Of France's position, the historian Charles A. Hale wrote, in reference to Mexican political evolution:

> Any attempt to uncover the structure of political liberalism in the Atlantic world must center on France. Obviously, John Locke, Edmund Burke, and Jeremy Bentham were not Frenchmen. English thought and English institutions were crucial to liberals everywhere. Yet France provided the classic situation in which liberalism as a body of theory was directed toward political and ultimately social change. By definition, liberal theory was elaborated with reference to an *ancien* regime; the model was France.[7]

Furthermore, the Caribbean basin had served as a prototype for economic experimentation. The earliest example of modern colonialism and of westernization took place within its confines, starting with Spanish expansion in the sixteenth century. Capital formation in the region, without which European industrialization would have been delayed,[8] was at the base of West Indian societal development. Capitalism, through the plantation system, was a social and economic system that exploited local resources in a systematic fashion, and fashioned minds (assimilation) and body (miscegenation) irreversibly.

These factors, in all their complexities, are the key to social reality in the region, as well as to the variables defining the foreign relations and social policies of Caribbean states ever since.

The conditions found in slavery had eliminated tribal distinctions among slaves; the adoption of the plantation economy, however, with its social and psychological implications was of greater significance. Unlike the South American *hacienda*, the plantation was geared to external markets. Therefore, the institution must be viewed in the context of a wider system whose financial and industrial centers were located elsewhere.[9] Locally, its implications were far-reaching, as it permeated the fabric of colonial life. Far from acting as a preserver of cultures, the plantation originated its own by restructuring the human element into a society built for economic gain; survival and control were but two sides of a coin.

"Plantation" *was* culture insofar as it helped eradicate whole cultural systems and acted to build a new structure rather than to assimilate the newcomer slaves into the mainstream of the dominant European cultures. The new cultural entity was based on the economic purpose the capitalists sought to impart to their colonies. The economic system was thus determining the manner of interaction between European and African cultures and the means that the latter would use to penetrate New World cultures. From the reality of colonial conditions, one deduces that the ruling group exercised inordinate leverage on the development of society, more so than any other segment of the population. All this occurred where there had previously been a "demographic void": African influences would be felt through the plantation.

Since plantation was a capitalistic organization, its owner was not a farmer, but a businessman, usually absent from the scene[10] whose intense labor requirements created the necessity for slavery. If many conditions found in slavery were conducive to rapid westernization, the economic goals of the enterprise retarded that process by fostering rigid class and color stratifications. Once the economic aims were set, however, the mass of slaves were relatively free to develop around established rules any cultural traits they chose. There were contradictory forces at work: some were willing and able to claim the Western gods as theirs, while others retained a potential for symbiotic innovation by merging the Western and the African traditions.

The construct that emerged from the interaction of economic structure, race, and locale, was given the name "Creole culture." Several scholars have noted, however, that the dismantling of the plantation economy in Haiti after independence was not accompanied by a similar breakdown in cultural behavioral patterns. Creole culture handily survived the Revolution and reappeared bolstered after the consolidation of the Haitian bourgeoisie in the period 1820–1865. Thus, it was upon the foundation of that Creole culture that later Haitian cultural developments, such as the elite policy of assimilation and emulation of Western norms, were to take place.[11]

The Social Dimension

Colonial conditions had fostered three major social groupings in society, with appropriate subgroups. The white colonists were at the apex. The slaves constituted a teeming and rebellious mass, largely abandoned to itself. In between existed a level intermediate in color and aspirations. Class and individual interests dictated that the *affranchis* would lend weight to one side or another in the hope of strengthening their insecure social position.

The French Revolution was slowly disclosing its full implications for the French colonial empire. The revolution in which Saint Domingue was immersed was a response to the overall aspirations of that period. The slaves' hatred for their bondage had in the past erupted in countless rebellions. These uprisings had been independent of the upheavals taking place in Europe. The *affranchis*, on the other hand, had been anxious to partake of the new heralded liberties; the French Revolution provided an impetus from which a concerted effort took form.

Dissatisfaction was widespread. The more conservative colonists, as distinct from the *petits blancs* who formed an urban proletariat,[12] were fearful of the events taking place in metropolitan France, and attempted coups that would take Saint Domingue away from the influences of French revolutionary politics. The *affranchis*, on the other hand wished to remove the petty vexations of daily life and gain the status of *citoyens actifs*, or fullfledged citizens. A major slave revolt that erupted in 1791 was followed by a temporary restoration of order brought about partially through a general emancipation of slaves in 1793. This was ordered by Léger-Félicité Sonthonax and then confirmed by the French parliament.

In Haiti, an alliance was formed, following a formula adopted in France by the Revolution, against the colonists, *les grands seigneurs*, who were a sort of local aristocracy. The *affranchis* had achieved an imposing economic position despite racial prejudice: one-fourth to one-third of all plantations were owned by them, as well as one-fourth of the half-million slaves. They had had access to education and to certain artisan professions as well as membership in the armed colonial militias, the *maréchaussée*.[13] Only the upper level of the colonial administration had remained closed to this group, but abo to the white Creoles in a parallel to Spanish America. The revolutionary mood in France and social discrimination at home was sufficient to explode colonial strictures. The *affranchis* entered into an alliance with the mass of slaves— the colonial *sans-culottes*—not at first, but after they repeatedly failed to attain an agreement with the colonial establishment.[14]

The historian Harold E. Davis has stated that every phase of the Haitian Revolution was closely linked with its French counterpart.[15] From this standpoint, there are sociological as well as ideological similarities between the Haitian Revolution and other Latin American movements. Although the Haitian situation seemed more complicated ethnically, the *affranchis* had achieved a similar economic position to that realized by the Spanish-American *criollos*. My assessment is based upon the class ascription of the leadership of movements that pitted *criollos* against *peninsulares* "ideologically," rather than upon the "shock troops" of slaves and *peones* that carried these countries to independence. Traditional Western historiography has been pleased to demonstrate the differences that existed between Haiti and the rest of Latin America, basing its argument on the racial criterion, rather than on similar economic and ideological interests between the ruling groups in formation.

But nowhere in the Western hemisphere, including the United States, was independence rousing more popular support than in the Haitian wars. French racial policy and the respective numerical strength of the warring groups ensured from the beginning that emancipation would be a primary goal. A full-fledged war emerged in response to the ill-timed measures taken by the French government and the plantocracy, particularly the repeal of the French Assembly's Emancipation decree in 1802. The strength of the slave leadership ensured the inclusion of that group's grievances in the agenda.

The slaves' strength was felt in the exodus of most whites and of some *affranchis* to France, Louisiana, Maryland, Cuba, and to the Lesser Antilles, as they grew fearful about their ultimate position in society once independence was achieved.[16]

If the Haitian Revolution occurred before most other Latin American independence movements, it was because of the unique position of Saint Domingue as the most prosperous European colony at the time, because of the ratio of slaves to masters, which facilitated insurrections and instability, and because of the timing of the French Revolution. Haiti belonged thoroughly to its age, the modern world, through its integration in the French economy; it had become all that it was capable of becoming, short of threatening the colonial relationship. Its economic growth was to serve the interests of the colonizing power, never its own.[17]

The Political Dimension

The formal declaration of Haitian independence, which followed the fait accompli since the goal was realized in November 1803, was proclaimed January 1, 1804. Dantès Bellegarde summarized the situation as critical: "Amongst them [the Haitians, there is] no cohesion, no true hierarchy." He furthered his thought by specifying, "latent hostility was demonstrated in a Creole saying still in use among the masses, 'since Guinea, Negroes hate Negroes.'"[18]

Haiti was politically independent. There had been no public schools built in Saint Domingue under French rule, thus there was practically no formally trained cadre available to lead the new nation. The exodus of black and mulatto *affranchis* had further contributed to this dearth of educated individuals. The first minister of finance, General Vernet, was an illiterate.[19] Many former *affranchis* would stake their claims to political leadership and property confiscated from the white colonists on the argument that they were literally the descendants and the heirs of the French *colons*. Governor-General Jean-Jacques Dessalines is said to have exclaimed in anguish to such preposterous claims, "And the poor blacks whose fathers are in Africa, won't they inherit anything?"

Elite political culture may be defined as the set of beliefs, values, and patterns of behavior of the economically and politically prominent group in society. Ideologies are comprehensive, explicit, and biased guidelines, espoused by the power structure for application to everyday issues arising in government. Ideology, more than political style, although it is also that, has eminent integrative functions as it attempts to wed the "ought to be" to the "is." It provides further a method for achieving goals and relates the understanding by the political elite of its own economic and social interests. In a sense, it is philosophy *remis en enfance*, brought to long-term developmental strategy and everyday tactics; it is the practice and the simplification of a complex philosophical *donnée*. Philosophy thus becomes the texture and the infrastructure of existence as understood by the individual within his or her group, while ideology derives its strength primarily from the application of these perceptions.

Colonial societies, in which a segment of the population was formed from the "union" between the master and the colonized, have adopted as the most salient element of their daily psychology the "rape" that was accomplished and the resultant self-hatred. One finds in this respect the sublimation of rape that explains in these societies all human interrelationships and all existing relations between the governed and their institutions. By forcibly depriving peoples of their cultural heritage, colonialism had undertaken a restructuring of social alliances and instituted its domination over the colonized norms and values; this resulted in a sort of internalized feeling of inferiority.[20]

The vanquished, in a sense, exhibited a form of idolatry vis-à-vis the conqueror. In Haiti, due to the social policies adopted by a westernizing elite after independence, the new victors, as will be seen later, still exhibited that idolatry in regards to the vanquished whites, as is illustrated in their social thought. This sort of psychological violence inherent in colonialism, together with the administrative practices encountered in every colonial system, go a long way toward explaining the spirit of authoritarianism still found in neocolonial societies today.'[21]

The International Dimension

In Haiti, the *affranchis*-derived elite adopted what they felt to be a sensible and pragmatic ideology that was nonthreatening to the existing international system. The use of the French language, for instance, as an instrument of socialization, was never seriously challenged after independence.[22] The Haitian leadership chose westernization deliberately as the only "practical" path to modernization. A reflection of this domestic social policy is found in the foreign policy of the new state, which opted, as will be seen later, for nonintervention in the affairs of other Caribbean countries and for an accommodation with all nations. It would then appear to a casual observer of the Haitian scene that in the violent wars that accompanied the birth of the nation, all revolutionary energies were spent.[23]

By declaring its independence, Haiti had defied the international system. The country was ostracized. Not only was no help forthcoming, but no sympathy was apparent. Ostracism, as distinct from self-imposed isolation, may be a strong and negative instrument on those against whom it is used. It is the word that best described the period immediately following Haitian independence. Whereas the Netherlands, the United Kingdom, and the Scandinavian countries engaged in trade relations with the black state, the United States refrained from commercial intercourse, despite intense lobbying by the Haitian government to regularize the situation. All withheld diplomatic recognition. The officially acknowledged reason for the United States, lack of a similar diplomatic recognition by France, ran counter to Monroe Doctrine pronouncements on hemispheric solidarity. Peace in eleven slave states of the union hung in the balance. France, which had renounced the liberation of slaves in its West Indian colonies, artfully fanned these fears of the United States in appealing to the "good sense" of the Americans. In a plea addressed in July 1805 to Secretary of State James Madison, Charles Talleyrand wrote:

> The existence of a black people in arms, occupying a country it has soiled by the most criminal acts, is a horrible spectacle for all white nations. These must understand that in accepting the continuation of this state of affairs, they would be supporting pyromaniacs and assassins. There is no valid reason that holds for individuals, citizens of a loyal and generous government to grant support to these brigands who have declared themselves the enemies of all governments.[24]

United States trade with Haiti was prohibited during the Jefferson administration in 1806 by act of congress. This prohibition was renewed in 1807 and 1809.[25] The Haitian government, through Secretary of State Joseph-Balthazar Inginac, appealed to United States Secretary of State John Quincy Adams, in July 1822. He argued in reply to the discriminating measures levied against Haiti:

> The Government of the United States is the first to which Haiti feels compelled to address a report on its political situation, soliciting that a regular act of congress from her older sister would recognize her

independence which already dates of nineteen years. . . . If there is a difference of color between the sons of the United States and those of the Haitian Republic, there is amongst them similarity in sentiment and will power.[26]

Despite the hopes of the Haitian government, the Monroe Doctrine was not construed by the United States government to be a doctrine of collective security.[27] Under direct and effective pressure from the United States, an invitation to attend the Panama Congress in 1826 was not extended to Haiti, despite the aid it gave to Francisco Miranda and Simón Bolívar in their efforts to achieve South American independence. Opinion in the United States was divided in respect to the wave of liberalism sweeping over the continent. Thus, about Latin American social customs, South Carolina Senator Robert Y. Hayne declared in 1825:

Those governments have proclaimed the principles of "liberty and equality," and have marched to victory under the banner of "universal emancipation." You find men of color at the head of their armies, in their Legislative Halls, and in their Executive Departments. They are looking to Hayti, even now, with feelings of the strongest confraternity, and show, by the very documents before us, that they acknowledge her to be independent. . . . There is not a nation on the globe with whom I would consult on that subject, least of all, the new Republics.[28]

And Missouri Senator Thomas Hart Benton echoed this statement: "And I would not go to Panama to '*determine the rights of Hayti and the Africans*' in the United States."[29] According to Andrew Cleven, congressional opposition to United States participation in the Panama Congress was based primarily on the Haitian question.[30]

The United Kingdom had engaged early in trade relations with Haiti. English military invasions of Saint Domingue in 1792 in support of the plantocracy had contributed to the rise to power of Toussaint Louverture. The latter, called upon by the French colonial administration to defeat the English, had arranged for skillful military and economic negotiations, the Haitians' first diplomatic victory.[31] However, it was through its citizenry that Great Britain was to achieve its greatest impact on early Haitian political development, rather than through regular diplomatic channels. Abolitionists Thomas Clarkson and William Wilberforce maintained a lasting friendship with Haiti's Henry Christophe and attempted to create a favorable climate of opinion in Europe for the new country.

France presented a different challenge. Under the reign of Charles X, France promised, in 1825, to recognize the de facto independence of Haiti. But it demanded and received a promise of payment of an indemnity of 150 million francs for the dispossessed colonists. The economic and political repercussions of this debt, which Haiti found difficult to pay, loomed large in Haitian politics for the next century.[32] Neither the Ordinance of 1825 nor the Treaty of 1838 negotiated under Louis-Philippe and recognizing Haitian independence by the French government, softened the United States attitude, however. John Quincy Adams, in a new argument based on the terms and spirit of the French Ordinance of 1825, held that Haitian independence was a "legal fiction."[33]

United States' reluctance to recognize Haiti after 1838 could be understood largely as a reaction to American domestic pressures, since the last great obstacle, French nonrecognition of Haiti, had been removed. But these domestic pressures were both social and economic, and resulted principally from the reluctance of the United States to enter into contact with a black people on a basis of equality, and from the objections of Southern agricultural interests, which could suffer from foreign tropical competition.[34]

Both the newly created African state of Liberia (1847) and Haiti had to await the election of Abraham Lincoln and the ensuing Civil War to gain United States recognition, which was granted in 1862. This recognition of Haiti was instrumental in alleviating some international hostility, and regularized Haiti's foreign relations. Another action that decreased Haiti's isolation was the signing, in 1860, of a Concordat between the Holy See and the government of President Fabre-Nicolas Geffrard. This Concordat stabilized the role of the Roman Catholic church in Haiti and subsequently heightened the power of the Haitian bourgeoisie by augmenting its prestige.[35] But this increased international acceptance and the parallel increase in external trade also led Haiti into a phase of neocolonialism, that of increased economic dependence on a few powers.

The Cultural Dimension

Haiti's small ruling elite of mulattoes and blacks had not desired the ostracism by Western powers that had befallen the country, nor had it directed a policy of isolation. But the decline of isolation and the new role of the Roman Catholic church in the field of Haitian national education, both contributed significantly to the development of the hegemony of the Haitian upper stratum. That elite, which in the mid-nineteenth century may have constituted no more than 1 percent of the population, arose essentially from the cultural and sexual interaction between the two major groupings of the colonial era, the Europeans and the Africans. That "middle-group" had had an important role during the colonial era. It had emerged from the tensions of colonial life and from the clash of cultures. The cultural outcome, as this intensely "pragmatic" group emerged, was a foregone conclusion.

Cultural assimilation, as an ideal, had emerged formally in France at the time of the French Revolution. But, however imprecisely defined it may have been at that time, assimilation had nonetheless a powerful impact on early colonial upheavals because of the philosophical assumption that people, whatever their racial stock, could aspire to equality. The concept, which had been secularized from an earlier period—when it more than likely meant religious "integration" of slaves into the Christian mold, came to encompass mental and cultural assimilation into a French-Western mold. Later, as in the case of Senegal and Algeria, its meaning was to be extended further, signifying political fusion with the metropolitan power.[36]

To the intuitive French colonial philosophy, the psychological facts of slavery and of the plantation, both geared to economic efficiency, were added. The uprooted individuals from varied African backgrounds clearly and objectively realized the personal gain found in westernization. The stimuli of uprootedness and a strange environment, together with the gradual addition of relatively small numbers of individuals to the dominant culture, contributed to assimilation. Assimilation, as it reflected a sincere French ideological outlook, was first and foremost a powerful instrument of persuasion.[37] It was this outlook that was to lead blacks in the Francophonie areas to look on France favorably over an extended period.

Centuries earlier, assimilation had become conspicuous as an imperial policy, an "assimilative impulse," in the expansion of the Roman Empire. That system, with its concomitant individual psychological trauma implied by colonialism, was to be perfected by the French, themselves the victims of the Latinization of Cisalpine Gaul in an earlier period. To an earlier religious dimension, new philosophical and legal elements were added in the seventeenth century, when the Cardinal de Richelieu decreed that the neophytes in the colonized areas were to have the rights of natural Frenchmen.

But it was in the French Revolution that the principle emerged fully developed as an egalitarian doctrine.[38]

French cultural domination over subaltern cultures was taken for granted by France. Ideally, it was believed, these archaic cultures would wither away under the spell of the genial Gallic civilization. The justification for assimilation accompanied every French liberal movement. Assimilation sprang from the tenets of French intellectualism, which maintained the universality and persuasiveness of reason and the perfectibility of the individual. Writing in 1966, Dimitri Georges Lavroff concluded:

> The partisans of the policy of assimilation of the colonies to the mother country were generally animated by a revolutionary and Jacobin spirit . . . socialists particularly, with Jean-Jaurès, were favorable to such a policy. . . .[39]

Traditionally, these mother country radicals had been the colonized's "best friends," since their attitude was based on a humanist ideal.[40] A primary distinction between European colonial systems was made by the French writer Eugène Aubin, who posited that the British conversely considered themselves "an imperial race, made for essential domination . . . and too disdainful to initiate inferior races in the secret of their superiority."[41]

It must be noted that the power of France in the capitalist hierarchy was waning in the nineteenth century, in contrast to that of Great Britain and the United States, and that challenges to the policy of assimilation were now being made in the name of the natural sciences and positivism, as the liberal impulse gave way to a more conservative world order.

The policy of assimilation had created the means for an individual's transcendence over his or her non-Western values; it had resulted in the formation of a westernized intermediary group of individuals with considerably less power than that of the "civilizing" group, but more powerful than the "natives" from whom it arose. This group, destined to give colonial society its managers and its intellectuals, was an elite in formation.

Non-Western nations, emerging out of the experience of Western European and American colonial undertakings, had largely accepted a Western view of themselves. Haiti was not exempt from this characteristic. Some argue that this may well be a reflection of a "popular" acceptance of the intellectual's power in determining societal values in modernizing societies.[42] It may be the recognition of an underdeveloped status as defined by Western sociological standards, which allow as a matter of definitional necessity, for minimal differentiation within elite groups.[43]

Elites in non-Western states, in their drive for development, have emulated Western culture in defense of their class interests, and in response to international conditions. Their ambition has been to effect innovation that would diminish the gap that presumably exists between developed nations and non-Western entities in all fields of endeavors. But even in responding to the international conditions that have given elites their raison d'être, they could hardly exercise a role antagonistic to Western interests, since they owed their very formation and their ambivalent social position to an economic and cultural clash. Even when they lacked the solid credentials that spring from "grass-root support," the political leadership of these elites remained inescapable.

The words *culture* and *intellectual* have acquired new meaning, distinct from that accorded in traditional society or in Euro-American society, a meaning to which one must remain alert.[44] Edward Shils argued that the gestation and life of new states are unequivocally the creation of the intellectual.[45] He is only partially right insofar as these intellectuals provide an ideological framework that justifies statehood and establish policies for national development. And although the argument downplays the economic basis of elite power within a worldwide context, it is valid at least to the extent that three useful points can be deduced from it: first, that the intellectual is usually the only "educated" element in the community; second, that, as a result, the degree of his or her involvement in political institutional life is inordinately high; and, third, that the possession of his or her culture—in itself a cultural transformation at a personal level and already serving as a prototype—came from prolonged contact with Western intellectual culture and economic interests. Thus, the intellectual had internalized the ways of the invader and attempted to create conditions for his or her nation's survival based on class interests disguised as the national interest, in accord with the changes he or she perceived to be occurring in the international system.

The intellectual's impact on society upon entering politics would seem parallel in scope to his or her individual transformation. The emergence of an intelligentsia and the development of "bourgeois" nationalism are linked, as the individual expresses a personal ambivalence as he/she recognizes the cultural crisis that, in a way, symbolizes the malaise of the entire society. But because of the situation of the intellectual within his or her nation at the forefront of the cultural clash, the crisis seems more acute and the alienation more severe.[46] Western-style education became the vector for modernization seen as integration into the modern world, and the spark for societal transformation was given by the intelligentsia, viewed as the avant-garde.

In small societies, however seemingly isolated they may be, external factors play a preponderant role in determining much of domestic social policy. Haiti's social development and cultural policy were largely the result of circumstances brought about by the colonial and neocolonial situation imposed upon it by more powerful states. An overview of these external factors is necessary in order to place Haitian internal developments in perspective.

Early Foreign Policy: Nonintervention

Haitian political independence did not alter ultimately the inherent structure of society nor its development along lines whose seeds had been sown during the colonial period. It did, however, effect a displacement of social groups through the elimination of the white upper stratum. Once the dust had settled on the Haitian Revolution and the counterrevolution was victorious—since the incremental decisions that could have led to momentous change had not been taken—the future social and political direction was almost certain. The incipient Haitian bourgeoisie answered the call of nationalism sweeping through Europe and the Americas in the wake of the Napoleonic military and political victories.[47]

If nation building demanded that a national cultural identity be formally recognized, another priority was added for the nascent state. An ideology of government, with directions and powers to be defined, needed to be translated into institutions and practices. A new nation-state exercises new roles as it assumes the formal trappings granted by independence. It fills a gap at the highest level of organization, exercising its new sovereignty in selecting a form of government. In order to function in the international system, it must and does create a more sophisticated organization than it had hitherto needed in the economic, military, and diplomatic spheres. But historical facts establish precedents and define the particularity of a nation, thus becoming crucial in latter development. Hence, an early shift in policy, however slight, has portents for future choices that become increasingly limited as time passes, since institutions can be said to be in their infancy and therefore, more malleable.

Haitian independence may have been an afterthought to the achievement of liberation for the slave, and freedom from petty social vexation for the *affranchi*, rather than an early deliberate goal. After independence, in any case, the urgency of consolidating the gains won by war reflected the compromises that the leadership was anxious to make. Since it was felt that France could not live down the humiliation of its military defeat at the hands of the Haitians and would attempt to reconquer its colony, the quest for legitimacy through international acceptance was the sine qua non of continued Haitian independence. This need gave rise to a paradoxical domestic and foreign policy problem for a black state that had suddenly appeared in the European international system where none previously existed.

The major aspects of foreign policy formulation are interlocked with decisions in the domestic arena. In the small state, as various scholars have pointed out, external factors have a special tendency to limit domestic freedom of action.[48] In Haiti, since the number of decision makers was small and because the bourgeoisie was dependent on the export-import trade for its livelihood, the domestic and the foreign policy sectors fused into one. Toussaint Louverture's decision to maintain the plantation system, after he had established his hold over an autonomous Saint Domingue, may be viewed partly as an attempt to alleviate the fears of foreign powers as much as to maintain a viable economy. Henry Christophe would seek similar overall aims with many of the same methods. Jean-Jacques Dessalines—who declared by constitutional fiat all Haitians officially "black," regardless of skin color or race, in an attempt to forestall internal division—pronounced a foreign policy of strict nonintervention on the first day of independence:

> Let us take care that the proselytist spirit does not destroy our work; let us allow our neighbors to breathe in peace, to live peacefully under the laws which they have made, and let us not, firebrand revolutionaries, erect ourselves as the legislators for the Antilles, and to give consistency to our glory, disturb the tranquility of the islands that surround us; they have not been, as the one we inhabit, washed by the innocent blood of their population; they have no vengeance to extract against the authority that protects them.[49]

This unequivocal statement, which flies in the face of reality, for slavery existed throughout the region, was destined primarily to placate English fears that Jamaica would follow the Haitian example and that unrest would erupt in other European colonies. Actually, Haiti was in no position to provide naval support for slave insurrections anywhere in the Caribbean, and was well aware of the weaknesses of its own defenses against an expected offensive return by the French."[50] Because of European and American racial prejudice, the Haitian bourgeoisie felt the necessity to prepare for war.[51] The organization of the state remained militaristic under successive Haitian governments, and military leaders retained full control of the state apparatus. This militaristic tradition remained active for the next century.

The Haitian leadership was anxious that the diplomatic signals it sent, showing Haiti's willingness to cooperate with all nations, should be well received. It had inscribed in the country's first constitution therefore, the following provision: "The Emperor will never take any measures with the view of making conquests, or to disturb the peace and internal regime of foreign colonies."[52]

Christophe similarly laid the foundation of his noninterventionist foreign policy in Article Nine of the Constitution of 1807 promulgated when he assumed power in the secessionist North. He later reiterated these tenets in a letter, dated November 1816, addressed to the British abolitionist Thomas Clarkson:

> For a long time past my ships of war have been used only along the coast and have never travelled any distance from our own shores. The Government of His Britannic Majesty cannot, I am certain, ignore this fact; it surely cannot give credit to the false allegations of the planters. . . . Why then should it suppose that we intend to deviate from the principles which we have always professed? How can anyone do us the injury of suggesting that we, who have so much reason to be grateful to the Government and to the people of England for the interest which they have always taken in our welfare, should ever seek to upset the regime of the British colonies? Is it because these same colonies have experienced troubles and internal commotions? But these have nothing in common with the cause which we defended for more than twenty-seven years.[53]

While Christophe adhered to this policy of strict nonintervention, partly on the advice of his English mentors, President Alexandre Pétion[54] had adopted a different course of action. He accorded substantial aid to

Simón Bolívar who, during several years of unsuccessful challenge to Spanish authority, had been twice driven out of Venezuela. In December 1815, Bolivar disembarked at the southern port of Les Cayes, seeking support for a new expedition against the Spanish Crown. Pétion contributed rifles, munitions, and a printing press, from which a proclamation of South American slave emancipation (1816) was to be issued, in return for this aid. Pétion permitted Haitian soldiers to join the expeditionary force. After a second visit of six months to the southern port of Jacmel, Bolivar launched a series of attacks that eventually resulted in the independence of Venezuela, Colombia, Peru, Ecuador, and Bolivia.[55]

The schism in the Haitian leadership between Pétion and Christophe was perhaps more than a symbol of their personal differences. Pétion represented the rising bourgeois element in an almost "pure" European form; he stood for a significant segment of the leadership that understood how similar its political interests were to those of the new Spanish-American *independentistas.* Christophe, on the other hand, had achieved a somewhat more "nationalistic" approach to Haitian development. Although his approach borrowed heavily from the ideologies of Western Europe, he did not seem to perceive as strongly a common Latin American interest. As the successor to Toussaint Louverture and Dessalines, he attempted to counteract initiatives for the restoration of French power in Haiti by favoring the British, whose pragmatism and utilitarianism he genuinely admired. Christophe's policies indicated a utilitarian frame of mind and as will be seen, this theoretical orientation did not end with his death.

Pétion had the reputation of a philosopher-president. As a product of the Enlightenment, he attempted to pursue liberal policies like those of Western Europe. And although he was an elitist who saw little good in the common person, and a misogynist, he was nonetheless easygoing by temperament, adored by the Haitian masses, and elicited great praise from Bolivar. He is also remembered for the first widespread Latin American agrarian reform (1807–18), one that eventually transformed Haiti into a land of small peasant landholdings, in contrast to other countries in Latin America. His assistance to the Bolivarian armies and his idealism also made him a precursor of what became Pan-Americanism.

Haitian interventions in the Spanish-American independence movement, despite formal pledges not to interfere abroad, indicated a pragmatic approach to international relations and the problem of Haitian national security.[56] The difficult task of aiding slave rebellions elsewhere in the West

Indies had to be weighed against the more attainable goal of placating England. The French colonies were relatively distant and insignificant, and France had recognized Haiti before emancipating its slaves in 1843; these factors made France relatively nonthreatening to Haiti. Another Caribbean power, Spain, still presented a clear danger to the survival of the black republic. Spain had regained the eastern portion of the island of Haiti at the fall of Napoleon (1814). Furthermore, Spain had maintained slavery in its remaining American colonies and was in possession of the neighboring territory where the mulatto element, well incorporated into the life of the colony and antagonistic to Haiti, predominated.[57]

The United States Occupation, 1915–1934

The United States, so enamored of its own liberties, is already less fond of the liberties of others. Quite the contrary: it has made of this liberty an instrument for causing other people misery.[58]

—Simón Bolívar

There had been constant friction in the relations between Haiti and the United States after Haitian independence. Shortly after the Dominican Republic was restored to independent status in 1865, after a brief annexation to Spain, proposals for annexation by the United States were made by a coalition of American economic interests and a segment of the Dominican bourgeoisie led by President Buenaventura Báez. In the same period, bilateral negotiations with the Danish government for the acquisition of Danish Caribbean territory by the United States were started by Secretary of State William Seward.

The failure of these efforts signified renewed interest on the part of the United States for a coaling station in the northwestern part of Haiti at Môle Saint-Nicolas, one of the finest natural harbors in the West Indies. United States efforts at gaining the Môle, and the Haitian government's efforts to stall for time, dominated the relations between the two nations throughout the late 1800s.[59] These attempts seemed to have been made principally for American business interests, at times against the better judgment of United States' diplomats accredited in Port-au-Prince.[60]

The rights of Haiti as successor to Spain and France, to the one-square-mile islet of La Navase had been challenged by American guano prospectors since 1856. This island has remained a source of contention to the present.[61] Between 1857 and the turn of the century, United States Navy warships successfully intervened in Haiti nineteen times on behalf of American business interests.[62] As late as 1915, United States investments in Haiti only amounted to $4 million in U.S. dollars, while German commercial interests in Cuba, Haiti, and the Dominican Republic amounted to $1 million in U.S. dollars in 1918.[63] But Haiti's economic potential for development was said to be immense. An American writer, William MacCorkle, wrote in 1915, after having commented on the country's strategic position: "This island has within its shores more natural wealth than any other territory of similar size in the world."[64]

In addition to intervening in Cuba and Puerto Rico (1898), the Dominican Republic (1906), and in Nicaragua (1909), the United States sought at the same period to control Haitian customhouses, whose collections constituted the only revenue of the Haitian government. As late as 1915, 80 percent of these customs revenues were pledged to servicing the external debt owed France.[65] In the hope of averting foreign intervention,[66] Haiti had always met its debt obligations unlike several other Latin American nations.

The immediate cause of the United States occupation in 1915 was a dispute between the Haitian government and the Banque Nationale together with the National Railroad Company. The Banque's chief stockholders were the Banque de l'Union Parisienne and the National City Bank of New York, which had acquired 20 percent of the stock. Under United States pressure, German interests in the Banque had been limited to 5 percent.[67]

A report to the Department of State by the United States envoy to Haiti gives a succinct, yet flavorful rendition of the background of events in 1914:

> If then, at the end of the fiscal year . . . the Bank shall not have renewed the Convention,[68] the government will find it most difficult to operate. The statement that the government, in the absence of a budget convention, will be without income is based upon the fact that under the terms of the Loan Contract of 1910, the Bank is designated as the sole treasury of the government, and as such receives all moneys of the government, and further is empowered to hold such moneys intact until the end of the fiscal year. . . .
>
> It is just this condition that the Bank desires, for it is the belief of the Bank that the government when confronted by such a crisis, would be forced to ask the assistance of the United States in adjusting its financial tangle and that American supervision of the customs would result.[69]

In furtherance of United States financial aims, the Banque impounded all Haitian government revenues in 1914. Then, at the Banque's request, the U.S.S. *Machias* landed a contingent of United States Marines and seized $500,000 of Haiti's gold reserves from the coffers of the bank for "safe-keeping" in New York, on December 7, 1914.[70]

The Compagnie des Chemins de Fer de la Plaine du-Cul-de-Sac (National Railroad) provided another reason for the occupation of Haiti by American forces in 1915. In 1910 the company had secured a concession to build twenty-one sections of rails from Port-au-Prince to Cap Haitien. The Haitian government guaranteed 6 percent interest on the construction cost, up to the maximum of $32,000 a mile in U.S. dollars. The company built only three unconnected segments, alleging that political unrest was interfering with its work. The staggering cost was (U.S.) $3.6 million. Because the company had defaulted on the construction of seventeen segments, the Haitian government refused to meet the promised payments.[71]

According to John H. Allen, United States Secretary of State William Jennings Bryan revealed an appalling ignorance of Caribbean conditions when he is said to have exclaimed, after being briefed on the developing Haitian crisis: "Dear me, think of it! Niggers speaking French."[72]

Following a massacre of political prisoners in Port-au-Prince, on orders from President Vilbrun Guillaume Sam—who had received strong United States support in his quest for the presidency a year earlier[73]—the U.S.S. *Washington*, in July 1915, came within view of the city. An angry crowd of relatives, fearing that revenge for the assassinations would never be forthcoming because of the impending United States military landing, stormed the French legation in which the president had sought refuge and brutally murdered him. In the afternoon of July 28, 1915, the *Washington* landed its contingent of Marines and the U.S. occupation began.

The United States decision to intervene was made far in advance of the date it occurred.[74] The alleged reason for the occupation, according to U.S. officials, was to protect Haiti from a Franco-German financial coalition. Admiral William Caperton said he had landed to "protect property and preserve order."[75] At hearings on the United States intervention, held by U.S. Senator Medill McCormick in 1922, Secretary of State Robert Lansing expressed the fear that a German naval base would be established in Haiti. The disguises of the real motives for the invasion were thin, since France and Germany were then at war and, by the summer of 1915, virtually all German cruisers had been swept from the seas.[76] As Professor Mercer Cook expressed it later in an article analyzing this period: "The true cause of the intervention—the [U.S.] ambition to dominate the economic resources of the little country—soon became apparent."[77]

In keeping with the tenor of the times, the administrative commander of the United States occupying forces, who was also a former military governor of the Dominican Republic, in an official document to the secretary of the navy, revealed an element of racial prejudice:

> The people of Haiti have had no immediate contact with a superior cultivation and intelligence such as the Negroes of the United States have had since their emancipation. . . . The same traits of negro [*sic*] character that are found in the United States exist in Haiti, both good and bad; but I consider that the bad traits are more in evidence in Haiti than in the United States, where they are under better control.[78]

To this factor of racial prejudice was added an element of cultural conflict.[79] Several years later, in 1930, the United States chargé d'affaires in Port-au-Prince reported to Secretary of State Henry L. Stimson:

> In general, while the Anglo-Saxon has a deep sense of the value of social organization and of the obligation of democratic government to assume a large share of responsibility for the social welfare of the masses, and has in addition a profound conviction of the value of democratic government, the Latin mind, on the contrary, is apt to scorn democracy and neglect activities looking to the health and educational welfare of the masses. . . . The Anglo-Saxon, who excels in collective action is apt to be impatient with the Haitian characteristic of intense individualism inherited from the French regime. . . . The action of the Haitian, in common with the Latin in general, is in the main directed by emotion rather than by reason, which in the main dictates the action of the Anglo-Saxon.[80]

In 1915, however, several powerful elements within Haiti were willing to collaborate with the United States. These were that segment of the population that had a partial foreign composition, the Roman Catholic church hierarchy, and the merchants. The Haitian bourgeoisie, in contrast to some land-owning traditional elites of the rest of Latin America, depended almost exclusively on commerce and external trade for its livelihood. As a group, the bourgeoisie seemed to have accepted the United States occupation as a necessary evil. Arthur C. Millspaugh, in his *Haiti under American Control, 1915–1930*, wrote:

> There were, of course, a few of this class who were prompted by their conception of patriotism to favor American control as necessary for the good of the country. Personal interests of others were in one way or another furthered by American activities and aims. But in general the politicians were against the occupation because it deprived them of their former opportunities for power and profit.[81]

Who were these "politicians" whose patriotism is put in doubt in this statement? They were, according to this author, members of the old "militaristic and nationalistic" *caudillos* who had seized the presidency through coup d'état. They will be discussed more fully in the later discussion of the opposition to the United States invasion.

The *engouement* of the Roman Catholic church for the goals of the Occupation is readily explained.[82] Its hierarchy and much of the clergy was French, and the loftier goals of the United States "civilizing" mission were also those it had pursued with limited success since 1860. From the moment that the invasion took place, the clergy collaborated from the pulpit.[83] Foreign merchants, especially the Arab Levantine and Italian merchants, who had settled in large numbers in Haiti at the turn of the century, were, likewise, effective in their support for the United States.[84]

Members of the Haitian bourgeoisie were often tied to the foreign merchants by bonds of marriage, particularly to the French and German[85] merchants. As a class, they responded favorably to the law and order that augured progress and enrichment. President Sténio Vincent, a nationalist under whose term of office the United States troops departed from Haiti, wrote in his characteristically diplomatic language in 1939:

> The conditions under which the American government intervened in Haiti, opened an easy path for its altruistic action and its civilizing influence. There was, in general, among the Haitians, a sort

of discreet understanding to excuse the intervention, hoping that it would liquidate the chaotic situation that existed in the country, substituting an organized life of peace and work. The most intransigent patriots, those who were obstinately refusing to accept the *fait accompli*, came to consider it as a necessary evil, albeit temporary, faced with the evidence of the results.[86]

Resistance to the United States occupation occurred at two levels. It came in part from the intellectual elite, but mostly from the peasantry. Resistance in other forms came from what one might call, for lack of a more adequate term the traditional *caudillos*. For the most part, they were nonbourgeois blacks who tended to be "nationalists." They had often abrogated political power through military force and were on a collision course with the "more progressive" bourgeois civilians. They were the remnants of Haiti's militaristic past, and they commanded the respect of segments of the peasantry. They in particular were to feel one of the fundamental changes brought about by the American intervention, the creation of a constabulary which, in the words of Sidney W. Mintz, "may have ended forever the possibility of an agrarian revolt against the central authority."[87] Through their nationalism, these *caudillos* opposed the intervention as they pursued the so-called black tradition in Haitian history.

The first civilian to be elected to the Haitian presidency was legislator and lawyer Michel Oreste in 1913; Dantès Bellegarde's first major political appointment as that of Oreste's Chef de cabinet, chief of the president's staff, dated from this period. The United States authorities favored this group.

Intellectual resistance emerged in a nationalistic outcry as *le choc*,[88] the shock of the occupation, set in. This shock seemed to be primarily a reaction to the racial and cultural antagonism of the North Americans. The elite was awakened from its snug *bien-être*. But no collaboration seems to have resulted between this resistance and the broader peasant movement.

Between the intellectual and the peasant movements, however, a special cultural relationship arose. Persistent racial prejudice, as illustrated by the positivist social Darwinism prevalent abroad, together with the trauma of foreign occupation, provided the impetus for a cultural realignment. Négritude—as the movement became known internationally—as an instrument of social and foreign policy, must be understood within the context of the international scene and the evolution of these Haitian cultural phenomena.

Négritude—a movement for cultural independence from Western behavioral norms—crowned a process began when Haiti obtained its political independence in 1804. A similar conception had been incipient for over a century throughout Latin America, where race, class, and culture converged. Tupac Amaru in Peru and Miguel Hidalgo and José Maria Morelos in Mexico had sought far-reaching changes in social and political relations between classes, a goal that was denied them. Much later, Indigenismo, in which a new awareness of Indian cultural roots developed, was one of the theoretical bases for the Mexican Revolution of 1910. It became a basic ingredient in the Aprista political philosophy in Peru, and in the Bolivian National Revolutionary Movement (MNR) which triumphed briefly in 1952. Negrismo in Cuba, and a new black cultural awareness in the literatures of the Dominican Republic and Puerto Rico in the twentieth century indicated an important break with the past. Harold E. Davis expressed the radicalism of these ideas when he wrote:

> Such a theory makes of indigenous cultures and their influence much more than a social political problem. It introduces cultural value concepts to condition the science which seeks to analyze and ameliorate these twentieth century problems. It is also accompanied by a profound disquietude, not limited by any means to America, but which in this continent had prompted philosophical inquiry into the meaning of the term American and the concept of Man which has developed in America.[89]

In Haiti the relationship between intellectual and peasant was wanting. It was a gap that had persisted over time and was difficult to bridge, even when the two groups were faced with the immediacy of a foreign occupation of Haitian soil. Such a cultural bond, though in formation, could not be readily translated into joint political action.

The peasant resistance movement to the United States occupation had as an immediate cause the reestablishment of an old French colonial law, the *corvée*, which required citizens to give several days of free labor a year for road construction in their district of residence. This system, reinstituted by the Americans, rapidly degenerated into forced labor. The peasantry felt that the whites were reinstituting slavery, and peasant insurrections against the system developed throughout the country.

In response to guerrilla activity in the countryside, United States reprisals were swift and drastic. Hans Schmidt related that the "first recorded instance of coordinated air-ground combat, in March, 1919" took place in Haiti.[90] Tens of thousands of Haitian peasants were massacred, a fact revealed in population statistics for the period,[91] according to Georges Anglade. Thousands more peasants were interned at the concentration camp at Chabert,[92] and Haitian immigration to Cuba and to the Dominican Republic increased dramatically.[93]

For a timely picture, it is useful to quote *in extenso*, from the United States Senate Committee investigation of the occupation of Haiti (1922), headed by Senator Medill McCormick, and prompted by denunciations of the occupation by the American liberal press. The Senate report described the Haitian situation as follows:

> The guerrilla outbreak was opposed first of all by the Gendarmerie, which was recruited principally from the same class of the population as the bandits and officered by the United States Marines holding commissions in the Gendarmerie, but by March 1919, it became clear that the Gendarmerie could not suppress the outlawry without assistance, and thereupon the Marine Corps took over the greater part of the burden, although the Gendarmerie remained in active service. The enemy knew their country perfectly. When arms were not in their hands they could not be distinguished at sight from other inhabitants. The transformation from peasant to bandit and vice-versa could be made at an instant's warning. There was reason to suspect almost any male adult of being from time to time engaged in active lawlessness and habituated to guerrilla warfare. . . .
>
> Each patrol was necessarily commanded by an American. . . . Many of them were commanded by sergeants, corporals, or even privates. . . . To the credit of our country nearly all of these men performed their duties admirably. Their courage sustained them in the face of danger and hardship, and their common sense and justice slowly won the confidence of the inhabitants. . . .
>
> The campaign continued through the year 1919. . . . It is impossible to give the exact number of engagements, but it is accurate to say that in one place or another armed encounters occurred daily. Late in 1919 Charlemagne [Peralte] was killed in the field. This broke the

back of the uprising, but another principal leader, Benoît [Batraville], remained in the bush for several months until he was killed in May, 1920. . . .[94]

Under the title "Illegal Executions," the Senate committee report continued:

> The Committee has heard a number of complaints of the burning of homes of innocent inhabitants by the Marines. . . . The times and places alleged . . . seem, however, to indicate that the houses burned were palm and wattle huts in settlements infested by bandits. The bandits were either there or nearby in camps or were resting in the guise of innocent inhabitants, and the huts were burned by the patrols. In some cases this was a necessary military measure. It is also quite possible that some habitations were burned without substantial justification on this ground, but the Committee has not learned of any that were burned at places and times where and when there were not grounds to suspect that they were used as a shelter for the enemy.

In a report published in 1927, the Women's International League for Peace and Freedom, the oldest international women's organization, headquartered in Philadelphia, described atrocities that were ignored in official United States documentation. The main author of that report, Emily Greene Balch, was later nominated for the Nobel Peace Prize by Dantès Bellegarde, in his official capacity as a member of the Administrative Council of the International Bureau of Peace (Geneva).[95] Among the atrocities described by the League were the following:

> We may cite a signed memorial presented to our party in Haiti which refers to the burning alive of Cazo Noël, and of Médard Bélony and his wife, the summary execution of the three children of Hergéné, and of the twin sisters Athélia and Cloraine Etienne, the beating and torturing with fire of the widow of Romain Brégarde, the beating to death of the notary, Mr. Garnier, Jr., the burning alive of one Vixina in broad daylight in the court of Gendarmerie of Maissade, the execution by beating of Dorléan Joseph, the execution by machine gun of the daughters of the widow Célicour Rosier in the yard of their house, when their mother, aged 84, received two bullets in her thigh; the

daily shooting down of cattle, the many burnings of fields full of crops, distilleries, mills and houses.[96]

And although the reports from that period are mute on the subject, rape must have occurred as it does in all wartime situations, as evidenced by the increase of mulattoes in the Haitian peasant population.

The men and women guerrillas commanded by Charlemagne Peralte and Benoit Batraville were labeled "gooks" by the Americans.[97] The insurrectionists' goal was to "drive the Americans from Haiti," and through their uprising render the situation politically untenable for the United States.[98] At the height of the struggle their number was estimated at 40,000, as few as 5,000 being armed with machetes and old rifles.[99] The others seem to have been unarmed. The American writer Harold P. Davis commented on the peasant uprising as follows:

> This outbreak was in character as much organized banditry as it was revolutionary, acts of violence being committed against innocent natives, and whole districts being systematically looted. There was, however, a distinct anti-American feeling which, intensified by propaganda from the cities and highly exaggerated accounts of oppression by the Americans, soon led to a very serious situation.[100]

Davis noted that Haitian peasant women, under the disguise of supplying the cities with produce, carried ammunition and useful information back to the hills.[101] He concluded as follows: "Regardless of material benefits which might possibly result, the Haitians did not want to be governed by Americans and by a President supported by the armed forces of the United States."[102] Davis nonetheless commended the marines who "suffered cheerfully hardships" in order to put down the insurrection.[103] The killing of "civilian" bystanders was the price that had to be paid for such military operations.[104] Many other American writers of the time, including Arthur C. Millspaugh, felt similarly. The latter had estimated the "bandits" to account for one-fifth of the Haitian population in numbers.[105]

The author has insisted on quoting extensively from the available documentation since neither American history as usually taught in the United States nor official Haitian historiography mentions the atrocities committed by the United States in Haiti. The full picture has not yet emerged, despite a few recent attempts by American revisionist historians.

At the governmental level, all executive departments of the Haitian state had been seized outright by the occupying forces, except for Education and Justice. These two ministries were left in Haitian hands some say, by sheer oversight of the American authorities.[106] The Haitian parliament was dismissed permanently because it had proven particularly resistant to American desires to change some Haitian laws not to the invader's liking, and the president [Dartiguenave] himself was molested publicly.[107] According to official American sources, plebiscites that legalized the United States intervention were fraudulent.[108] The Haitian press was muzzled; journalists were incarcerated and subjected to the jurisdiction of United States military courts if they were critical of any aspect of the American occupation.[109] Mail censorship was instituted. The *gendarmerie*'s intelligence network kept a dossier on all prominent Haitians.[110] Samuel Guy Inman, an American critic of the occupation, reported that the local American *gendarme* exercised totalitarian control over all details in his district.[111] Whatever the cost, Haiti would learn to be democratic under United States tutelage.

A most damaging change, however, was that brought about by the new American-drafted constitution. That document, which is said to have been written entirely by the then young Assistant Secretary of the Navy, Franklin Delano Roosevelt, was referred to by presidential candidate Warren G. Harding in 1920, as having been "jammed down the throat of helpless neighbors at the points of bayonets borne by the U.S. Marines."[112] It must be noted, however, that once elected, President Harding did not alter Wilson's Haitian policy, nor did his successors Presidents Coolidge and Hoover.[113]

Article five of the new constitution granted land-ownership rights to foreigners for the first time in Haitian history.[114] The denial of this right to foreign persons had risen out of the independence movement in the early part of the nineteenth century, as the Haitian government sought to establish small independent farmers as a bulwark against foreign invasion, and from a spirit of economic self-preservation on the part of the Haitian bourgeoisie, which would have had to compete for scarce economic resources. The Americans, on the other hand, envisioned large-scale capital investments in scientifically managed large plantations for profits and for Haiti's own "agricultural salvation."[115] Seemingly irrelevant was the fact that, according to Celso Furtado, the Haitian land tenure pattern had given the peasant the highest standard of living among peasantries in Latin America in the nineteenth century.[116] Some Americans even bemoaned the absence of a "planter class" that had contributed so handsomely to the wealth of other West Indian countries.[117]

In summary, the United States occupation of Haiti had occurred under pressures from American businesses that had had some investments in the county. But despite this factor, American investments did not substantially grow during the Occupation. And even the building of highways and bridges, an infrastructural realization that would tend to boost commerce, was accomplished partly because of its military significance in crushing the peasant insurrection.[118] The United States record was equally unenviable in other fields, such as that of education, as shall be seen in subsequent chapters, that analyze Dantès Bellegarde's actions at the head of the Ministry for Public Instruction.

The United States occupation provided the background for Dantès Bellegarde's rise in Haitian politics. The nineteen years it lasted encompassed the bulk of Bellegarde's intellectual production; his thought acquired its definitive form on the major questions concerning national development. That period also witnessed his major political and diplomatic successes and failures.

CHAPTER 2

THE BASIS FOR HAITIAN SOCIAL POLICY

SOCIAL THOUGHT IN THE NINETEENTH CENTURY

Le passé est le régulateur du présent comme de l'avenir.
—Beaubrun Ardouin

The Brazilian anthropologist Darcy Ribeiro synthesized the conditions of colonial existence, which were based on violent European expansion, with its single-minded purpose of acquiring wealth. He specified the impact of the colonial enterprise on the individual: "Each people, even each human being, was affected and caught up in the European economic system or in the ideals of wealth, power, justice, or health inspired by it."[1]

Generally speaking, two groups counted significantly in colonial Latin America. In Ibero-America, the first group, the *peninsulares*, as representatives of the Crown and of the Church, were in command. The second, the *criollos*, although they were a significant group in acquired wealth and education, were barred from exercising the highest political functions; nevertheless, they became the heirs to metropolitan ideals in the sequel to societal upheaval. Because they were essentially transplanted Europeans, the thought that animated early *pensadores* was European in origin, owing little to aboriginal social concepts.

Thus, the study of Latin American thought, being the expression of *criollo* elites, is a variant of European philosophy.[2] The other human groups, either *indios* or blacks were slaves, or in a condition akin to slavery; although their presence was felt, whatever theories of social organization they had could not have been influential in state organizational concepts, judging from the results. This entire state of affairs was as true of Haiti as of Latin America.

Early political distinctions were those between two broad European concepts of "power," the liberal and the conservative; the protagonists were the descendants of the *conquistadores*. Radical cultural shifts that may have heralded a radical political course as well, had not been anticipated, and the break between Spain and its American colonies or between Portugal and Brazil had been merely political. In Haiti, although the conservative link was entirely missing after independence, as shall be seen in the course of this chapter, the liberal forces in charge of the state showed character- istics similar to those found in Spanish America. French colonization had been rejected, but development was to occur within French philosophical traditions.

Charles A. Hale admirably summarized the dilemma faced by Latin American elites after independence:

> By asking the liberals to choose between Hidalgo and Iturbide, [Lucas] Alaman hit at the liberals' most vulnerable point, the social basis for their liberalism. When the liberals were faced with a stirring of the Indian masses . . . they recoiled from egalitarianism. In this they were no different from contemporary liberals throughout the Atlantic world when confronted with the "social question." Mexican liberals could talk of the need for a society of the free property holders or of an "aris- tocracy of talent" without facing the real condition of two-thirds of the population. Theirs was a social question, though, which presented unique problems, because this two-thirds majority was an ethnically distinct group.[3]

As shall be seen, this description of the Mexican dilemma applied equally well to Haiti, for the conditions of French colonial rule had led to the creation of two groups, the *affranchis* and the slaves, separated by the criterion of "culture," a gulf as deep as any ethnic differences. These two groups were left in contention after the European segment of the popula- tion was eliminated in the wars of independence.

French political influences, English political thinking, and the example of the North American rebellion aided in the formulation of rationalistic social thought and in the establishment of a sense of social optimism at the time of Latin American independence.[4] In the New World, the sentiment of a historic destiny was readily translated by a Utopian mood, and was concerned with defining a "new man," a founder of "new" societies.[5] If a new effort were to be made, however, it would be vis-à-vis Europe. Latin America was to be an improvement on European society; by definitional necessity this implied a continuation of the parent culture.

But as with the patterns seen in the French Revolution of 1789, the Latin American movements were a mixture of conflicting and often contradictory movements. In Mexico for instance, Miguel Hidalgo and José Maria Morelos represented a popular, egalitarian ideal that, in its demands, transcended the narrow constituencies based on the *hombres honrados* of the *ayuntamientos* established by the *criollos*. Between this incipient revolutionary *indigenismo* and the *criollo* rebellion there was a link; and, "both conceptions could subsist jointly at the same time, [since] they are two stages of the same historical attitude. . . ."[6] The incipient power of the masses could not be ignored; the social basis of the newly established states was to consist of these large "incult" populations.

The Preindependence Period: The Colonial Class Struggle

Haitian social thought of any consequence starts in the years of turmoil surrounding the French Revolution, and in Haiti's own revolutionary period, 1788–1806. The beginning date of this period is the year that saw the *grands seigneurs* demand adequate representation for Saint Domingue as a French province in the French parliament; 1806 was the year of Jean-Jacques Dessalines's assassination, which seemed to have ended the possibility of social organization divergent from the Western model.

Economics has been the dominant factor in the historical development of Saint Domingue. During the colonial era, interaction between colonizer and metropolis was primarily economic, and the grievances, as in North America, took on the coloration of an economic bill of rights. Gabriel Debien wrote, "Saint Domingue looks at the war as a passive witness. It buys dearly European goods, and sells its own cheaply."[7] Paraphrasing an anonymous white colonist writing in 1750, Debien summarized, "the colonist baulk under the direction of the metropolis so far away which only thinks of its own interests because it understands only those, and which controls the colonial interest by agents not chosen among the colonists. The tutelage is too strong, too visible."[8] The colonial economy was made to favor France to the detriment of the plantocracy.

But a contradiction more apparent than real seemed to exist within this colonial haute bourgeoisie. Liberal in economics and trade policies, and chafing politically under nonenlightened local metropolitan representatives, it was hopelessly conservative socially. Its wealth depended on the exploitation of agricultural resources and semimanufactured products made possible by slavery. Desiring incorporation with the mother country with which it shared a common liberal fervor, the colonial haute bourgeoisie clashed with the metropolitan haute bourgeoisie whose interests favored the continuation of the colonial pact unchanged.

The groups against which the haute bourgeoisie's social conservatism was directed were the remainder of society, and its efforts were directed at maintaining the status quo domestically. The divisions of the colonial society were deep. The metropolitan authorities were hated outsiders. The haute bourgeoisie had little need for the *petits blancs*, who constituted an urban proletariat and were seen as the enemies of the plantocracy. Both these groups, however, were united in their hatred for the *affranchis*, many of whom had achieved a higher level of education than the whites and had acquired vast wealth in plantations and slaves.

Thinking that its interests would prevail in France, the colonial haute bourgeoisie hoped to have Saint Domingue recognized as a French province,[9] and sent delegates to the Etats-Généraux in 1788. Terrified, however, by the implications of the *Déclaration des droits de l'homme* (1789) for the colonial social structure, these delegates returned to Saint-Domingue "as much to maintain the colony safely away from the revolutionary contagion as to organize their own movement against metropolitan oppression," in the words of Gérard M. Laurent.[10] This paralleled events in Spanish America.

But internal dissension forestalled the formation of a coalition favoring the position of the haute bourgeoisie, as was soon illustrated by the composition of two warring factions, the *pompons blancs* and the *pompons rouges*. The first group, consisting of *affranchis*, among others, were royalists organized by Governor du Peynier. The second group, made up of individuals from the haute bourgeoisie, considered itself to be "revolutionary." Because of this alignment, and the expressed social conservatism of the plantocracy, later slave uprisings were made under the white royalist banner of the Bourbons. The association of *the grands seigneurs* with revolutionary France made "royalists" out of the Haitian (slave) freedom fighters, until this association was reversed by Toussaint Louverture as he took command of the movement. Laurent summarized the plantocracy's dilemma:

They did not want to associate their movement with any other social category. According to them, these must not know any social and economic evolution. They condemned the *petits blancs* to their economic domination, the *affranchis* to suffer color discrimination, [and] the blacks to bend to infamous life conditions. Like the bourgeois of France, they practiced human exploitation.[11]

The *affranchis'* acquisition of property and their educational achievement exacerbated prejudices against them. Discriminatory measures and social prejudice increased in direct relation to that group's increasing economic power. They were restricted in the bearing of arms, prohibited from wearing European dress, barred from the medical profession and from the priesthood. They had to submit to separate accommodations in restaurants, at church, and in theaters. The colonial prohibition against marrying whites, commonly ignored in the early years of the colony, was extended in 1778 to France.[12] It was, however, within this group that the ideals of the French Revolution were to take hold most significantly.

The *affranchis* in Saint Domingue were almost as numerous as the whites—28,000 to 30,000—and their economic interests were similar to those of the white planters. Their wealth also depended on the liberalization of French colonial trade policy and on the continuation of slavery. In social terms, their demands were moderate. They hoped for the dismantling of discriminatory measures taken against them and, as a corollary, they hoped to exercise their full civil rights as *citoyens actifs*. But, culturally, the *affranchis* were largely assimilated into French culture, even though they shared at least one ancestor with the black and mulatto slaves who constituted the colony's lower caste. They had not wished to overturn the social structure, only to share in the power; slavery was to continue unimpaired—*affranchis'* prejudice against slaves was as severe, if not actually stronger, than anti-*affranchi* feelings among the whites.[13]

Faced with the haute bourgeoisie's refusal to apply the French Assembly's law of March 8, 1791, which granted the *affranchis* their rights, the latter divided into two factions—one, led by Jacques Ogé, that favored violence to implement these rights, and another that advocated a nonviolent course based on exemplary citizenship and loyalty to the colonial order. This route was personified by Julien Raimond, a longtime resident of France who had married a French woman.

Jean-Baptiste Chavannes, who had been a member of the Saint Domingue contingent to the United States war of independence, was the first to suggest that the slaves be enlisted in support of the *affranchi* cause, and armed for combat. These men, considered today precursors of Haiti's independence, were wealthy, and owned property and slaves. The abolition of slavery was anathema to them.[14]

In a letter addressed to the Saint Domingue Northern Provincial Assembly in 1790, Jacques Ogé wrote:

My prepossessions are correct and I hope that you will regard them as such. I will not rouse the workshops, this means would be undignified. Learn to appreciate the merits of a man whose intentions are pure. When I solicited from the National Assembly a decree I later obtained in favor of the American colonists previously known by the insulting epithet of mixed-bloods, I had not included in my demands the fate of the Negroes who live in slavery. . . . We have only claimed for a class of free men who were under the yoke of oppression for the last two centuries. We want the application of the decree of March 28th [*sic*]. We persist in asking that it be promulgated and we do not cease repeating to our friends that our adversaries are unjust, and that they do not know how to reconcile their interests to ours. Because [I am] employing the means at my disposition, I am using sweetness [in my approach]. But if, contrary to what I expect, you do not satisfy my demands, I will no longer answer for the disorder to which my vengeance may carry me.[15]

And to the white planters in general, Ogé addressed these words:

If we do not take prompt and efficacious measures, if firmness, courage, and steadfastness do not unify us all, if we do not rapidly join into a sheaf all our lights, our means, and our efforts, if we slumber a moment on the brink of the abyss, let us shudder upon awakening. Behold the blood that runs, behold our invaded landholdings, . . . our burnt homes; our friends, our neighbors, our women, and our children, butchered and mutilated, behold the slave who raises the flag of revolt. . . .[16]

The slave insurrection foreseen by Ogé, and instigated by hundreds of chieftains erupted on August 22, 1791, following a Vodou ceremony held a week earlier. Fifty thousand slaves took part in the initial uprising. And because their masters were *pompons rouges*, they fought under the white flag of the king of France.

Faced with a growing slave insurrection and with a liberal French government that seemed to threaten the colony's economic interests, the plantocracy called upon English military forces to occupy Saint Domingue. Gabriel Debien cited an anonymous source that concluded: "The colony must no longer regard France as the mother country. It must take common cause with the mulattoes, place itself under the protection of England, and open its ports to all foreign powers."[17] But with the exception of the second clause, that concerning the mulattoes, the haute bourgeoisie proved ready for foreign intervention.

The study of the economic dimension of the struggle has persisted in the best analyses to date. The foremost West Indian historian, the Marxist C. L. R. James, has analyzed the history of the seventeenth and eighteenth century from the standpoint of the preponderance of economic forces, seeing the colony as "the instrument in the hands of economic destiny."[18] Aimé Césaire of Martinique has placed Haiti in a slightly different perspective in respect to the "colonial problem," generalizing its experience as follows:

> Saint Domingue is the first country of modern times that has posed
> to reality and has proposed to the reflection of humankind, and this
> in all its social, economic, and racial complexity, the question the 20th
> century has endeavored to solve, the colonial problem. The first country
> where this question had arisen. The first county where it was resolved.[19]

Like James, Eric Williams has developed a convincing argument that economic forces alone were ultimately significant in the international emancipation movement.[20] But mainstream scholars, in a time-honored tradition spanning two centuries, have wished to study Saint Domingue in terms of color and race, to the near exclusion of other factors.[21] Among these are T. Lothrop Stoddard, Edward Long, Bryan Edwards, Pierre Victor de Malouet, Moreau de Saint-Méry, and a number of contemporary scholars who have espoused a bias for race and ethnicity over class analysis.[22]

Although racial prejudice played a significant role in Haitian diplomatic relations with Western Europe and the United States, and *color* was a code word in Haiti masking a virulent class struggle with cultural overtones, race and color cannot satisfactorily explain Haitian (and for that matter, West Indian) historical development. Indeed, race and color as part of what Marx would call "social realities," partly explain the aborted development of a national Haitian bourgeoisie, able to compete in the international setting at a time when strong racialism blanketed Western culture in the nineteenth and early twentieth century. But race and color were never sufficient to explain internal Haitian societal dynamics. More to the point is Professor Ghislain Gouraige's assessment of the colonial "dislocation" that led to an independent Haiti. He wrote:

> This war was indeed that of the French colonial army divided in two, one faction having come from Europe, the other, trained locally. The very same French flag had served the belligerents in both camps until 1803. The triumph of the indigenous army was that of French methods and military disciplines.[23]

Thus, the independence movement had truncated the bourgeoisie along racial lines. But this fact did not impede the development or the continuation of social thought in Haiti that may well be characterized as bourgeois.

After Haitian independence in 1804, many individuals, white, mulatto, and some black, had fled Haiti for an exile that proved permanent, reinforcing the middle classes wherever they went. These individuals were in the extreme right of the political spectrum. Often writing against the new state, they represented a forceful opinion in France and in the United States that could not be underestimated. Their exile helps to explain the lack of a traditional conservative "alternative" in Haiti, just as bourgeois hegemony, even as late as the mid-twentieth century, mitigated against the development of a socialist alternative in Haitian social thought.

The victorious *affranchis*, in their task of writing or of rewriting history—a task taken up by all elites in power—blurred the power struggle that occurred in the quest for national unity and for bourgeois hegemony. Much of the original slave leadership had been decimated by the successful leaders of the Haitian Revolution so that they could assume full control of the movement. Such early leaders as Georges Biassou, Dutty Boukman, Bélair, Jean-Francois Papillon, Petit Noël, Prieur Sans-Souci, Larose, and Lamour Dérance had been pushed aside, usually by assassination. It may be significant to note that even the first names of many of these figures went unrecorded. Especially neglected were Haitian women such as Sanite Bélair and Marie-Jeanne Lamartinière.

The Postindependence Period:
The Consolidation of Bourgeois Hegemony

The first formal piece in Haitian literature was the *Acte d'indépendance* written by Félix Boisrond-Tonnerre, on the eve of the proclamation of independence, December 31, 1803. That the "Jacobin" spirit was still present is revealed by the words of Boisrond-Tonnerre who, upon hearing an uninspiring first draft of the *Acte*, inspired by the United States' Declaration of Independence, exclaimed: "To write the *Acte de l'Indépendance*, we need the skin of a white man for parchment, his skull for an inkstand, his blood for ink, and a bayonet for a pen."[24]

The *Acte* that celebrated the separation of Haiti from its metropolis was written in French. Similarly, the thought on the social organization of the fledging state is expressed in the mother country's tongue. The style, the substance, the tone were heavily borrowed from France. African modes of thinking had had no noticeable impact on the leadership just as Incaic and Aztec thought had had little or no influence on the Spanish American leadership. Preliterate civilizations that formed the intellectual heritage of the masses had not permeated the culture of those in power, except in rare circumstances and late.[25]

During the war of independence, and for two years after it had been won, Jean-Jacques Dessalines had been the dominant leader of the mass of former slaves whose participation in the struggle had been necessary for achieving freedom. Although Dessalines was a general in the French army, his sympathies were clearly with the masses; he had been the slave of a black *affranchi*, and often exhibited the marks, imprinted on his back, of the slave driver's whip. His forceful character and the direction he seemed to have planned for Haiti may explain his short reign. Moderates rapidly replaced such "extremists."

The other Haitian leaders had not been as ignorant of Western thought as Dessalines had been. Toussaint, who became literate at age forty while still a slave, had read Caesar's *Commentaries*, Marshall Maurice de Saxe's *Rêveries*, Herodotus's *Histoire des guerres*, and with special interest, Abbé Guillaume Raynal's *Histoire philosophique*, edited by Diderot, a work that is said to have been found at the bedside of several other Latin American leaders, including Bolívar.[26]

President Alexandre Pétion—who had as his bedside reading Fénelon's *Télémaque*, a book that advocated the need for a powerful and beneficent aristocracy—had been a major influence in the drafting of the nation's constitution in 1806. That first document defined the cardinal principles of the new republic along the lines of the *Philosophes'* thought:

> Liberty, which consists of being able to do what does not hinder another person's rights; equality, which consists in that the law is the same for all and which admits no distinction of birth, no hereditary powers; safety, which results from the aid of all to insure the rights of all; property which, inviolable and sacred, is the right to enjoy and to dispose of one's property, of one's income, of the fruits of one's work and industry.[27]

The thought that animated the Haitian leadership was not the "democratic" ideal of Jean-Jacques Rousseau. Rather, it was the more moderate thought of Condorcet who, in his *De l'influence de la révolution d'Amérique*, clamored for a constitutional monarchy as the guarantor of property rights in a "well-ordered democracy." Analyzing Condorcet's thought, Jacques Droz wrote, "Condorcet is not disposed to recognize, despite his affirmations the fact of equal political rights for all citizens; only the propertied can participate in public life. . . ."[28] In fact, President Pétion's far-reaching agrarian reform, (1807–18), the first such reform to be undertaken in Latin America, met stiff resistance from the Haitian Senate composed of former *affranchis*.[29]

By 1806, in Haiti after the assassination of Dessalines, and by 1813, in Mexico, after the military defeat of José Maria Morelos before Valladolid, the *criollo* elites had gained a substantial victory. By 1820 in both nations, the "middle-sectors," transmogrified into a local aristocracy, had consolidated their position. In 1805, before Gran Colombian independence, the learned Francisco Miranda had visited Haiti, receiving from Dessalines, who favored the scorched-earth policy, the advice: *"Koupé tets, boulé cayes,"* ("behead the enemy and burn down the plantations"), a piece of advice unlikely to be heeded by the suave friend of Jeremy Bentham. Miranda departed after enlisting some Haitians into his army.[30]

Later, in 1815 and 1816, when Simón Bolívar visited President Pétion, the climate had already changed appreciably in Haiti. The ascendency of the *affranchis* was being completed. The Haitian constitution of 1816, with its provision for a lifetime presidency, later became the model for the South American *libertador*'s proposed constitution for Bolivia.[31] But sentiments of brotherhood between the Spanish-American *criollos* and the Haitian *affranchis* arose in part from economic interests and the social status shared by these two elites.

The Haitian military men in power after 1806 possessed the spirit if not the talents of their civilian predecessors, Jean-Baptiste Chavannes, Jacques Ogé, and Julien Raimond.[32] The hopes for a liberal democracy did not accord with the harsh realities of an ex-colonial milieu in which the overwhelming majority of the population had been black or mulatto slaves scarcely a generation removed from Africa. The political absolutism that came to prevail in Haiti derived from a colonial tradition transposed as the hereditary model of the new state.[33] Moreover, the form of political organization had to be geared to the restoration of economic order as a precondition for the state's survival. Finally, considerations of an ideological nature demanded the quick imposition of bourgeois rule if Haiti was to reenter the orthodox circle of the mid-nineteenth century.

National bourgeoisies were now in power throughout the "civilized" world and Haiti could ill-afford to be an exception. The bourgeois alliance with the slaves had given Haiti a reputation of radicalism that made it difficult for the country to gain international acceptance. On the other hand, the aspirations of the former slaves were, it appeared, contrary to continued bourgeois hegemony. At that time, the pamphleteers who doubled as secretaries of state, seemed almost as powerful as the chiefs they served, be they Dessalines's Félix Boisrond Tonnerre, Juste Chanlatte and Etienne-Victor Mentor, Henry Christophe's Pompée-Valentin de Vastey (the brother-in-law of General Alexandre Dumas) and the brilliant Julien Prévost, or Pétion's Guy-Joseph Bonnet and Joseph-Balthazar Inginac.[34]

President Jean Pierre Boyer's long reign (1818–43), which consolidated the Haitian bourgeoisie by giving it its characteristic shape for the next century, was overthrown by two separate movements. The first originated in the bourgeoisie itself, among individuals who felt that their social class was strong enough to liberalize the government; the second was a popular uprising that also originated in the south and had a strong impact in

Haitian social thought, since it fostered stronger rationalizations for bourgeois power, as shall be seen later in this chapter.

Central to the first movement was the secret Société des droits de l'homme et du citoyen, founded by gentlemen from the south of Haiti, the bastion of *affranchi* power. The society exploited the general dissatisfaction that had developed after twenty-five years of the Boyer presidency. The *Manifeste de Praslin* ("Praslin Manifesto") of April 1843, expressed two basic grievances: the lack of a program for national development and the lack of a rational plan for public education. Other lesser grievances included Boyer's poor legislative record, the suppression of the freedom of the press and of public debate, and the abuses of the executive vis-à-vis the legislative branch.[35] The very liberal constitution enacted that same year by the victorious rebels introduced a civilian government to the republic for the first time. The president was to be elected by a wider electoral assembly rather than by the legislature; a chamber of deputies was to supplement the unicameral Senate; judges were to be elected to their positions by each underlying layer of the judicial branch.

Writing about this agitated period in Haitian history, the social thinker Justin-Chrysostome Dorsainvil commented: "Many bourgeois could not conceive of the idea that a people that could neither read nor write would be called upon to itself choose its mayors, deputies, senators, and judges."[36] These were socially conservative bourgeois who felt that any liberalization of the government was detrimental to their economic interests and to their social supremacy.

Ralph L. Woodward has argued that as successors of the Latin American independence movements, "the liberals had welcomed foreign ideas, adopted foreign constitutions, and legal codes, [and] promoted foreign trade. . . ."[37] Is this judgment warranted in the light of the ethnic composition of the Latin American leadership and of conditions in the international system? Leopoldo Zea made a more discerning comment on the half-hearted attempt at cultural differentiation by successive generations of *pensadores*, declaring: "The problem seemed insoluble: Spanish America endeavored to present itself, as in the past, divided into two great parts, one with its head still turned toward a colonial past, and with another head oriented toward a future void of reality."[38]

Nineteenth-century political history was dominated by the rise of liberalism. Triumphant in Western Europe, it had spread to the Far East, Eastern

Europe, and Latin America on the wings of Western European increased commercial activity. From the beginning, it acquired a vision of irreversible moral and technological progress that made it the ideological foundation of an entrenched bourgeoisie. French liberalism, for its part, was able to incorporate the romantic *literati* into politics, for romanticism, too, was a global vision of the universe. By the close of the nineteenth century, the victory of the bourgeoisie assured, such liberal romantics as Victor Hugo dreamed of a more conservative universe.[39] Jacques Droz would conclude, "Liberalism is, in the final analysis, the expression of the economic interests of the bourgeoisie."[40]

The combination of philosophic universalism and European economic expansion led to imperialism. The dominant ideology of the nineteenth century was the successor of the ideas of the Enlightenment. Edouard Herriot would name as patron saints of the French Parti Radical, Denis Diderot, Voltaire, Benjamin Constant, Alphonse de Lamartine, and Léon Bourgeois; the latter was Dantès Bellegarde's colleague and ally at the League of Nations in 1921.[41]

As could be seen from Herriot's list, the interaction between literature and politics is too profound to be missed. In France, political romanticism led to the election to parliament of Lamartine, Béranger, and Hugo among others. In Haiti, similarly, *literati* in contact with European politics and intellectual development acquired increased authority in a milieu whose literate population amounted to perhaps one or two percent. As shall be seen later in this chapter, these developments were critical in Haitian history because they led to the first serious attempts at historical research and to bourgeois philosophical rationalization of its own power. This period acquires further importance for our inquiry because the social thought that resulted remained a most significant influence on Dantès Bellegarde's own intellectual development.

In the Haitian bourgeois Revolution of 1843 and the French Revolution of 1848, the idea of "social class" emerged in intellectual circles, popularized and strengthened. But, as with Dantès Bellegarde later, this thought was not carried to its logical conclusion. These social classes were declared by intellectuals not to be in conflict but as necessary to a healthy state. Fraternity, the spirit of 1789, was resurrected, while conciliation and harmony between classes was expected. The people were now considered to be "the human race," a romanticized concept in which social distinctions were purposefully blurred.[42] National unity was stressed.

Haitian romanticism in social thought had begun in 1835, with the creation of a *cénacle* (a literary society or coterie) on the model of the Cénacle de l'arsenal of Paris. Members of this society included the Ardouin brothers, the Nau brothers, and Lespinasse, among others.[43] This group had been largely responsible for laying the intellectual groundwork for the Revolution of 1843.

But the Haitian Revolution of 1843, which preceded the revolutions of 1848 in Europe, some Haitians proudly note, as the height of political romanticism, came too late to stem an open revolt by the peasantry. The goals of the Piquets—the insurrectionists carried pikes, hence their name—in 1844 were twofold: to dispossess the rich, effecting a widespread reform in the agrarian sector, starting with state lands,[44] and to suppress the domination of the mulatto bourgeoisie by installing a "black" in the presidency.[45]

In 1844, the *armée souffrante* (the suffering army) as the Piquets called themselves, under the leadership of Jean-Jacques Acaau, Dugué Zamor, and Jean Claude, penetrated the important towns of Les Cayes, Jérémie, and l'Anse-à-Veau before being defeated by Generals Fabre-Nicolas Geffrard (mulatto) and Jean-Baptiste Riche (black). The administration of President Charles-Rivière Hérard, a leader of the bourgeois Revolution of 1843, was soon replaced by that of a succession of three black octogenarians, Philippe Guerrier, (1844–45), Louis Pierrot (1845–46), and Jean-Baptiste Riche (1846–47). The Piquets were forced into submission. The admitted policy of the bourgeoisie became known as the *politique de doublure*, an almost untranslatable Haitian expression indicating the willingness of the power elite to rule through black military men, illiterate veterans of the wars of independence, in order to assuage the populace.

It is during this period that the writing of Haitian history took on a definitive character. Following the lead of such French historians as Augustin Thierry and Adolphe Thiers, both romantic historians, the Haitian elite sought to give a strong armature to its claim of continued elite leadership for Haiti.[46]

One of the early Haitian historians was Thomas Madiou (1814–84), who had studied in France; he became an important political figure in the government and in Haitian diplomacy. His four volumes on the history of Haiti appeared in 1847, 1848, and 1904; a fifth volume was written, but has not been published to date. His viewpoint is the most balanced among the writers of his time; like the others, he believed that a knowledge of history served to "direct a society in the ways of progress."[47] With other Haitian historians of his time, he declared that the globe belonged to all humans, regardless of race, and that civilization was achieved through the "fusion" of the various racial stocks.[48] Beaubrun Ardouin (1796–1865), who published an eleven-volume work, *Etudes sur l'histoire d'Haiti*, between 1853 and 1860, stated that Toussaint was a despot and that his deportation was "an extremely useful action for the complete freedom of the black race."[49] Ardouin also wrote that Dessalines's assassination had been a "fatal necessity,"[50] and that Christophe, Toussaint's true heir in his hypocrisy (being pro-white and anti-mulatto), was a tyrant of the worst sort.[51] To the black despotic north, Ardouin opposed the mulatto democratic south; he further claimed the West Indies as a whole for the mulatto who had nowhere to go.[52] In the first volume of his *Etudes*, Ardouin summarized his views of history and elitism as follows:

> And so proceeds humanity in its ascending march toward civilization. When nations tire of the abuses of their governments, it will always be the superior classes that will be the first to place themselves on the firing line to attack and reform these governments. Often insufficiently strong to obtain victory, these superior classes do not hesitate in calling the inferior classes of society to the rescue. The latter pose their condition for support and usually act as if they had no hidden motives; but they, in the final analysis, equally benefit from the victory obtained if they do not substitute themselves, because of their numbers and their strength during the momentary disorganization of constituted authority, to the social position of the superior classes which had hoped to impart to them a beneficial direction.[53]

Joseph Saint-Rémy (1815–58), a Paris-trained lawyer and the author of a five-volume biography of Pétion, believed that racial differences were superficial and due primarily to climatic factors.[54] He agreed with Ardouin that "humanity is a great family of brothers."[55] All these early historians denied the factor of color prejudice inside Haiti and argued that, based on the laws Haiti had enacted, equal opportunities existed for blacks and mulattoes alike. A fourth historian, Beauvais Lespinasse (1811–63), added that the spirit of freedom was a mulatto gift to the Negroes; the former had acquired the spirit of independence from the latter, he argued, and all Haitians must unite for the interest of the state.[56]

Madiou, Ardouin, Saint-Rémy, and Lespinasse were diplomats as well as historians. They were also powerful figures in Haitian politics; yet their historical works addressed themselves as much to a foreign public as they did to Haitians. Their histories and memoirs express concerns for national unity and a quest for societal development as generally understood in the nineteenth century. Furthermore, these historians also hoped to address race prejudice outside Haiti by showing the world that Haiti was capable of the kind and level of intellectual achievement they themselves demonstrated.

Development, economic and politico-social, was a primary concern of the men at the helm. This concept explains why social thought, rather than more esoteric branches of philosophy, took hold in Haiti and the rest of Latin America in the nineteenth century. This concern for rapid development, rather than the newness of the continent—for the Americas, two centuries after discovery and benefiting from the heritage of Western culture could not be considered new—justified this turn toward social thought.[57]

But differences in the views as well as the ambitions of groups within the dominant elite partly militated against governmental stability.[58] The forces of liberalism, representing a younger movement, and the older represented in the *independentistas*, were locked in battle throughout the continent, over the issues of economic policies, secularization, federalism. The older political forces that had emerged at the time of the Latin American independence movement were socially conservative. The Spanish liberal movement of 1820 had done much to introduce an element of disquietude in Spanish America; the Napoleonic invasion of Spain precipitated Spanish-American political independence in its wake.

In a sense, some of these earlier Latin American leaders, such as the Mexican Iturbide, held ideas that preceded those of the Enlightenment. Because of this, the struggle for power in the Latin American states acquired a bitterness that otherwise could have been avoided, for between nineteenth-century liberalism and eighteenth-century Enlightenment there existed a generational difference and differing emphases rather than full-fledged differences in kind. And although liberalism had declared itself to be "new," its true origin lay in the Enlightenment.

In France proper, which had developed as the bastion of European liberalism in the 1820s and 1830s, contemporary goals dictated that distance be established from the creed and the excesses of the 1789 French Revolution. The Revolution was thought to have led to excesses in the name of "reason" and "equality." Because much of eighteenth-century philosophy had insisted on natural rights independently of individual rights, and because it was felt that this view could easily lead to unreasonable demands by the untutored masses, liberalism sought to emphasize the "individual" rather than the "people," adopting a policy that much later would be defined as justifying "tokenism" while absolving the system of guilt for those who did not succeed.

But liberalism nevertheless gave the nineteenth century its distinguishing mark, that of a broad social optimism paralleling the scientific and technological discoveries of the age. Irene Collins has summarized this aspect of liberalism in these felicitous phrases:

> To embrace all the variations of liberalism throughout the century a complicated definition would be required, yet liberals themselves, certainly up to 1860 and 1870, saw nothing complicated in their creed. Whatever twists and turns were demanded of them by circumstances, they held at heart a simple faith: a belief that progress, leading to final perfection, could be achieved by means of free institutions.[59]

But Louis-Philippe's rise to the French throne in 1830, and his subsequent "reactionary" policies, forced liberals to turn away from the French model and to draw strength from their own national aspirations.[60]

After 1830, conservative parties were in the ascendance throughout Latin America, but by mid-century, acceptance of Comtian and Spencerian evolutionary thought by liberals fostered a more conservative trend in the liberal parties, making possible reconciliation and consensus between these two groups.[61] Writing about the 1821 to 1853 period, a student of Mexican liberalism, Charles A. Hale, has remarked, "in numerous ways liberals and conservatives were not always far apart. They shared many common assumptions, especially on social questions."[62] It is symptomatic that, once in power, the group surrounding Porfirio Diaz, who dominated Mexico from 1876 to 1911 labeled itself "liberal-conservative."

Indeed, toward the end of the nineteenth century, following the "anarchy" of earlier romanticism and the disillusion that had accompanied it, the consolidation of a new bourgeois order had occurred. This new order incorporated newly enfranchised members, widening the circle of the oligarchy to include the new industrialists. In this development, one perceives the ability of each national bourgeoisie to recreate the instrument of its own survival with minimal support from outside sources. Haiti showed no marked differences from this trend as will later be seen. As Latin America passed through the evolution from utilitarianism[63] to positivism, one must conclude, as Alberto Zum Felde does, that "Saint-Simon as a replacement for Bentham gives no guaranty of a greater awareness of and control over American politico-social phenomenon; all that it means is that the actors are the same men in a change of clothes."[64]

Positivism, whose influence remains to this date in Latin and North America—though modified to conform to new notions in psychology, to a philosophy of existentialism and relativism, to new sociological terms— swept the area (including Haiti) and transformed its intellectual landscape. The acceptance of positivism, as well as of the later neopositivism, in Latin America was enthusiastic. Positivism was a logical outcome in the evolution of liberal Western thought. Blessed with hindsight, one is tempted to con- clude with Leopoldo Zea that "positivism was thus only a new expression of triumphant liberalism, its constructive image, once its combative mission had been concluded."[65]

This positivism held that order and stability, established through legal and moral constraints, must rule. Thus, in Mexico, Gabino Barreda declared that moral education "must prepare Mexicans to be good servants of society. . . ."[66] Since wealth is the indicator of societal health, it was argued, no obstacle must be placed in the way of those apt individuals who understand the laws of its development.

By the end of the century, Herbert Spencer and John Stuart Mill loomed larger in Latin American thought than Comte.[67] Evolution became a handy concept expressing at the same time, the hope of Latin America for sustained economic progress, within the same old social strictures, and the inevitability of progress that would guarantee the eventually successful transformation of society into one of greater freedom under law. What may have started as a liberal rationalization for impending social change had now become the justification for the status quo. This socially conservative aspect of positivism is nowhere clearer than in Brazil, where a more orthodox Comtian positivism, supported by Comtian religious humanism, allowed for the hope of steady development in an evolutionary manner.[68]

Differences from the pattern of adaptation of European thought in Spanish-America may be observed in Luso-America and also in French-America. The colonial pattern established in sixteenth-century mercantilism persisted in the realm of Latin American thought as long as Europe remained preponderant there. The cross-fertilization among Latin American nations seemed to have been minimal, even in the nineteenth century. Hence, Arturo Ardao correctly assessed the main differences between the Latin American and the European variants of positivism, arguing that in Latin America the movement "anticipated and precipitated scientific culture instead of resulting from scientific thought as in Europe."[69] And Thomas E. Skidmore declared in a similar vein: "In Brazil . . . liberalism came as a result of intellectual trends per se rather than any profound economic change. . . . The Brazilians were applying liberal ideas . . . in a context not significantly different from the world of their fathers."[70] The undeniable link between social thought and ideology was again apparent as they became fused in an indissoluble alloy.[71] This phenomenon was equally true of the Haitian bourgeoisie, which turned to Europe for its intellectual sustenance and owed little to "traditional" Haitian culture.

With the growth of positivism in Haiti, two political parties came to dominate the political scene, the Liberal party and the National party. Both grew out of a rift within the intelligentsia. In 1876, a year before the birth of Dantès Bellegarde, throughout Latin America, liberal parties were in the ascendant.[72] The principal Haitian spokesmen of these parties were two educated mulattoes, both members of Parliament, Boyer Bazelais (1833–83) and Jean-Demesvar Delorme (1831–1901).

In his *Histoire du peuple haitien*, Bellegarde argued the basic lack of differences to be found in the platforms of the two parties. Pursuing his analysis, he stated that: "a political program in Haiti is only worth as much as the man who proposed it. More often than not, one does not ask the party chief about his ideas: his name suffices, or his skin color, or his birthplace."[73] Earlier, Jean Price-Mars had attempted to establish Boyer Bazelais in the proper intellectual context. He was an example, said Price-Mars, "of this generation of men who felt that it was the right moment to oppose to the oldish system of authoritarian government, the more adequate system of parliamentary control. . . ."[74]

Demesvar Delorme, a friend of such French political and literary leaders as Alphonse de Lamartine, Victor Hugo, and Jules Michelet, had demanded "*le gouvernement de la pensée*."[75] He dreamed of constitutional monarchies, but worked at establishing educational policies for his country: "This civilization we want to introduce in the country will penetrate through public education. These are lights which . . . will spread throughout the republic the healthy notions of order, of law, and of progress."[76]

The civilization he proposed was French:

It is by language that civilization spreads. Commerce and other materialistic interests tend to propagate the practical influence of languages of Anglo-Saxon origin. Great Britain and the United States are taking over the world. But materialistic interests are not the only ones sought after by humankind, and it behooves the French nation to counterbalance this materialistic tendency by the expansion of its tongue, which is expansive and civilizing, in the very best interest of its social and political influence.[77]

From its inception, as we have noted, Haitian social thought had been prejudiced in favor of Western European norms of social organization, thereby giving its rationale to Haiti's westernized elite. Of the interaction between ideology and educational policy, Jean Price-Mars wrote:

All Haitian education has had but one objective, a latent rather than a formal objective, dimly felt rather than clearly expressed; an objective which consists in producing highly educated men so that by their very existence and great culture, they can refute the thesis upheld by others that the Negro is inferior.[78]

Baron de Vastey had defended the European colonization of Africa.[79] Madiou and Saint-Rémy, in their historical studies, had hoped for an intermixture of the races as the vector of civilization and progress. Ardouin had declared that men issued from miscegenation were the ones fit to rule Haiti, "as these citizens formed the most enlightened class in the nation. . . ."[80]

The declarations had prepared Haitian minds for the belief that Bellegarde was to present, that although there were no inherently superior races, there were superior cultures and classes. Haitian social thinkers, according to essayist Frédéric Marcelin, writing in 1878, "heralded the solidarity of intelligence for all times and in all countries."[81]

During the late nineteenth century, when doctrines of racial inequality based on social Darwinism and positivism were gaining ground in Europe and in the United States, the number of Haitian students abroad was steadily increasing. In a statement commenting indirectly on the Haitian bourgeoisie's financial means at this time, Marcelin wrote: "The time was not distant when each year in April, the bourgeois would discuss whether or not he would spend his summer in Paris or in one of these mountain villages that surround Port-au-Prince."[82]

By 1880 the Haitian intellectual elite was divided into bourgeois and petit-bourgeois components. Both groups agreed that the task at hand was to provide a scientific preparation to a population of illiterate former slaves. Thus Professor Max Wilson, speaking of this period, stated to the author: "The new team's formula, of young men recently arrived from Paris . . . had degenerated into dogma. The paradox is that these positivists had instituted a political party [Liberal], and that their "enemy" was the National party, headed by Demesvar Delorme who was every bit as "European" as they themselves were."[83] He added that Haitian political circumstances inherited from the colonial period, color prejudice, petty personal hatreds, and the bickering within a small polity had all been incorporated into "the accepted definition of a scientific elite."

These quotations, in this author's view, well summarize the intellectual situation of Haiti at the turn of the century. The arrival on the local scene at this time of men who were the proud possessors of the newest French and Western European social ideas clashed with the social environment in which these ideas were to operate. Social prejudice and family quarrels were to illustrate the limitations of imported social thought upon the Haitian milieu.[84]

Louis-Joseph Janvier (1855–1911), had pursued his studies of philosophy with Auguste Comte's disciple, Pierre Lafitte, as well as with Paul Janet and other philosophers in Paris.[85] He spent thirty out of the fifty-six years of his life in Europe, first as a student, then as a Haitian diplomat. Janvier was a positivist, but as a member of the National party clique, he faced personal opposition from the Liberal party, that other stronghold of enlightened positivism. The National party was predominantly, but not exclusively, black in its membership, while the Liberal party tended to include a higher proportion of mulattoes. The latter were better established socially—Boyer Bazelais was related to former president Boyer—while the National party tended to accommodate members of the petite bourgeoisie and other individuals who were "upwardly mobile."

Comtian positivism, which established a "synthesis" of previous social and political thought, had an inherently conservative core through its emphasis on stability and order. Originally, it had focused on deflecting the criticism levied by the *Philosophes* of the Enlightenment against the institutions of the ancien regime.[86] Similarly, romanticism, as it emerged in

Europe in the first quarter of the nineteenth century, was an individualistic statement of those fearful of the widespread technological and industrial changes occurring at the time. Early liberalism, on the other hand, as it evolved out of the Enlightenment, had had, according to the positivists, an unsettling quality that had menaced the political order.

But neither romanticism nor Comtianism truly applied to Haiti in the mid and late nineteenth century. The Haitian economy was neocolonial in the sense of being dependent on its Western European trade partners. Haiti's bourgeoisie was relatively powerless in international terms; its industrial proletariat was less than embryonic. Thus, the emulation of Western culture alone could explain the Haitian intellectual developments of the nineteenth century that are seemingly divorced from Haitian social realities. But this factor was reinforced by the internal Haitian bourgeois desire to apply the scientific message in order to "modernize" the country.

In the last quarter of the nineteenth century, and in the first years of the twentieth, many men (but few women it seems) animated the scene of Haitian intellectual life. Two of these men predominated in the intellectual formation of Dantès Bellegarde. They were Anténor Firmin (1850–1911), and Justin Dévot (1857–1921), the first influential in politics, the other primarily as an academician.

In politics, Bellegarde was a *firministe*, a follower of Firmin, and his allegiance to that leader had cost him in 1907, his house and his library, lost to arson, his job, and almost his life and that of his young son, Auguste. Later, he wrote lovingly of this black leader of the Liberal party, who had adopted the "political, economic, and social program of Boyer Bazelais."[87]

Firmin was a "self-made" man and a poor man. He had abandoned the study of law in France to rebut Western European sociologists on the issue of race in a massive but now dated work, *De l'égalité des races humaines.* Firmin argued in favor of the use of the French language in Haiti, just as Bellegarde later did and for the adoption of French civilization rather than Anglo-Saxonism: "The Haitian who needs to evolve mentally, could not have conceived of a better linguistic tool," Firmin had said.[88] He had added, just as Bellegarde did, that foreigners had an important role to play in Haitian social development, as settlers, preaching by their example.[89]

Justin Dévot, a Paris-trained jurist who with Solon Ménos founded the law school, the Ecole Libre de Droit, was named to the Cour de Cassation (The Haitian Supreme Court) in 1911. Having studied under the master of positivism himself, Auguste Comte, Dévot was the most prestigious, and one of the ablest positivists in the country. His books and pamphlets indicate the range of his interests. They include, among others, *La Nationalité, Acta et verba, Cours d'instruction civique, Le Travail intellectuel et la mémoire sociale, Le Positivisme.*

Dantès Bellegarde owed Justin Dévot a great intellectual debt. In a chapter of his *Pour une Haiti heureuse* entitled, *"Justin Dévot, directeur spirituel du peuple haitien,"* he recognized that debt in a lyrical passage:

> The philosopher observes and notes, but in his fingers run, it seems, a shudder which is like the prolongation of an emotion . . . he employs the resources of his spirit to satisfy the needs of his heart from which emerges the impulse. Because he has been able in realizing from within him, this unity of the moral person obtained by the harmonious equilibrium of all faculties, the reasons of the heart always are found to be those of the spirit. . . .[90]

Dantès Bellegarde agreed with Dévot that the primary task for Haiti was to transform "little by little, and without violent shocks whatever, society itself, to attune mores to institutions, to prepare free men for a free country."[91]

In view of the internal Haitian conditions, including its lack of adequate natural resources and its nonwesternized mass, as well as its upper-stratum more aristocratic in mentality than bourgeois, Max Wilson in the aforementioned interview, concluded that "it is obvious that once transposed to such a context, [Haitian] positivism would become the thing of a quasi-ethnic and neocolonialist elite. How does one base democracy under such conditions?"[92] But the attempts of these sincere proponents of positivism, both those cited and such others as Hannibal Price, Solon Ménos, Dantès Destouches, Léon Audain, Frédéric Doret, Frédéric Marcelin, Georges Sylvain, Massilon Coicou, Horace-Pauléus Sannon, Camille Lhérisson—some of whom preceded Bellegarde, while others were his contemporaries—did not bring the anticipated happy results.

Later, when Henri Bergson made his mark on Western thought, and his ideas were introduced into the Haitian intellectual scene, they heralded a transition in Haitian social thought, as well as in that of Latin America in general. Bergsonism was "the logical conclusion of historical positivism, meaning a correction of naive materialism," according to Wilson. His concepts of *élan vital* and of creative evolution would appear to justify literature, imagination, religion, and faith from within an empirical, scientific base. The Bergsonian message offered to some cultured Haitians the option of integrating the spiritual values of Vodou into their studies, while to others, such as Bellegarde, it offered an invigorated Western culture, removed from the stale materialism of earlier positivistic thought. In Haiti, this logical progression of positivism produced Professor Justin-Chrysostome Dorsainvil (1880–1942), a positivist and a Bergsonian, a professor of philosophy for seventeen years at the Lycée Pétion, and the author of *Vodou et névrose* (1931), as well as of history manuals still in use in all classrooms in Haiti.

Thus, Haitian liberal thought had run its course. It had been centrist, or "liberal" due to the social origin of its exponents, and because of the international system that had found it difficult enough to accept a black intelligentsia without having to tolerate further a leftist intelligentsia. Because of history, a right-wing alternative, similar to the French reactionary traditionalism of Joseph de Maistre, had not flourished. Because of contemporary economics, a left-wing social thought had been improbable. But Haitian social thought as a variant of Western philosophical trends, was nonetheless anchored at one end to Jeremy Bentham of utilitarian fame, to James Mill and, at the pinnacle, to Adam Smith and Jean-Jacques Rousseau. The first of these was, of course, the father of Capitalism, the second of romanticism.

Dantès Bellegarde studied exclusively at Haitian schools, yet he was the bearer of the Western tradition. In comparison to Haitians who had travelled abroad for their education, he was a "self-educated man." Nonetheless, he was cognizant enough of Haitian history and of the philosophical trends that had gained acceptance in that nation's history to become the major heir to Haitian nineteenth-century thought and its most gifted synthesizer.

CHAPTER 3

MILIEU AND MOMENT

THE CAREER AND LIFE OF DANTÈS BELLEGARDE

*Les philosophes n'ont fait qu'interpréter le monde de différentes manières,
mais il s'agit de le transformer "Philosophers have only interpreted
the world in various ways; the point is to transform it."*

— Karl Marx, *Thèses sur Feuerback*

The Republic of Haiti was seventy-three years old when Dantès Bellegarde was born in 1877; at his death in 1966, it was a hundred and sixty-two. Thus, his public career of fifty-three years duration, coming at the dawn of the modern era, sheds light on the contemporary history of Haiti. Moreover, his thought and actions, as we shall see in this chapter, helped to shape that history.

In 1933 the literary historian Duraciné Vaval commented that Bellegarde was the quasi-official ideologue of the state;[1] in 1926, W. E. B. Du Bois had graced him with the title, "International Spokesman of the Negroes of the World."[2] Later, in 1951, Adolf A. Berle, Jr., noted on a trip to Haiti: "Dantès Bellegarde was kind enough to delay his trip [to the U.N. Sixth General Assembly, held in Paris] so that he could talk with me. I gave him the best briefing I could on the state of politics in the United States. . . . A very interesting and heartwarming talk. . . ."[3]

In the domestic arena, the anthropologist Sidney W. Mintz praised the educational reforms of the 1920s, without which, as he wrote, "those modifications in the class structure for which [President] Estimé is sometimes given credit might not have occurred. . . ."[4] This period of the 1920s was that of Bellegarde's tenure as minister of public instruction and cults. Historian Edner Brutus, writing in 1948, declared him one of the country's most outstanding ministers in that portfolio.[5] Commenting on Bellegarde's

54

thought and action as a diplomat, the poet and former foreign minister Léon Laleau wrote in 1966:

> The first amongst us, he placed audaciously at international gatherings, Race before Nationality, Man before citizen. Today, one does his best to ignore the fact that it is he who dared imprint this decisive direction to our foreign policy, as one holds a grudge against him for having— without denying our African origins—boasted of our equally strong European origins. . . .[6]

These commentaries on the political action of Dantès Bellegarde suggest the various elements to be taken into account in assessing his impact on Haitian thought and social development. In this and the following two chapters, the particulars of his domestic and international positions will be examined.

The Formative Years

Louis Dantès Bellegarde was born in the middle-class neighborhood of Lalue in Port-au-Prince, on May 18, 1877. The conditions of his birth made him a member of the impoverished petite bourgeoisie. His mother, Marie Boisson, a "white" mulatto[7] of great beauty, gave birth out of wedlock to two sons of Jean-Louis Bellegarde. She was poor and illiterate, unilingual in Creole, and a seamstress by training. With her older sister Louise Boisson[8] and her two brothers, Pétion and Jules Boisson, she had assumed the burden of raising her two sons.[9]

Despite her poverty, Marie Boisson had descended from a prestigious individual of early Haitian history. Her maternal grandfather was Jacques-Ignace Fresnel, a white man recognized for his probity, who, according to the historian Thomas Madiou,[10] was appointed to a judgeship by Dessalines and subsequently became Haiti's first *Grand Juge*, or minister of justice, in the cabinet of President Boyer.

According to Charles Mackenzie, the United Kingdom's envoy to Haiti in 1826, Fresnel was a military man who presided in the Supreme Court of Justice and exercised jurisdiction over all other courts, as well as over law officers throughout the island of Haiti (Hispaniola).[11] He was also known as the founder of Haitian Freemasonry. The author has been unable to discover the reasons for the Fresnel/Boisson family's poverty.[12]

Dantès Bellegarde's father, Jean-Louis Bellegarde, a black, had been the director of the botanical gardens at the Faculté de Médecine, according to the young Dantès.[13] Jean-Louis Bellegarde's father (the grandfather of Dantès Bellegarde), was Jean-Louis de Bellegarde, who had fought as a young boy in the wars of independence.[14] Later, in 1827, he had led a rebellion against President Boyer when the latter agreed to pay a heavy indemnity to former French planters as part of the settlement for recognition of Haitian independence by France. Of this episode Mackenzie wrote in his *Notes on Haiti*:

On the 26th June three black officers were arrested on a charge of having tampered with a soldier, to join them in assassinating the President. The ostensible prime mover of the plan, Captain Bellegarde, also a Negro, escaped.

The prisoners were charged with conspiring to murder the President, to expel or murder all Europeans, and to alter the government. They denied the intention to murder the President, or any of the foreigners; but avowed their wish to put an end to the existing system of government, which they treated as oppressive, and to break off all connexion with France—a connexion which they considered to be maintained merely to extort the last of their miserable pittance.[15]

Jean-Louis de Bellegarde escaped execution by firing squad by hiding out in the hills of Turgeau surrounding Port-au-Prince; he lived to become the duke of Saint-Louis du Nord, marshall of the Second [Haitian] Empire, and commandant of the Port-au-Prince military *arrondissement* during the reign of Faustin I (1849–1859).[16] It is a family legend that Jean-Louis de Bellegarde's father was a "mulatto" officer of Toussaint Louverture's entourage.

Windsor Bellegarde (1872–1930), a half-brother of Dantès Bellegarde, and also an "illegitimate" child,[17] was a graduate in history and philosophy of the prestigious Ecole Normale Supérieure of Paris. He became a noted historian and a member of the Haitian parliament.[18] Windsor's relationship to Dantès was always close. Dantès's uterine brother, Clément Bellegarde (1878—1907), became a professor of geography and history at the Lycée Pétion, but later abandoned teaching for a military career. At the time of his death, he had risen to the rank of first captain, commandant of the French-trained army's elite corps, the Bataillon d'Instruction du Centenaire.[19]

A paternal aunt, Argentine Bellegarde Foureau (1852–1901), was a powerful influence in the early development of Dantès Bellegarde.[20] A woman of great character and strength, she had pioneered in the field of women's education and had been appointed by President Lysius-Félicité Salomon to be director of the venerable Pensionnat National de Demoiselles, a girls' boarding school founded by President Pétion. Argentine Bellegarde's educational achievements made her a model to be emulated by the young Dantès, in part because education was the foremost avenue for social mobility in Haitian society. Her influence would later be seen in Bellegarde's espousal of political rights for women. He recognized his debt to her in a moving article published at her death and named his first-born daughter after her.[21]

At the time of Dantès Bellegarde's childhood, Lalue was already a poor "middle-class" neighborhood as it is today. Then it was virtually on the outskirts of the capital, now it is at the very center of town. Stories that have filtered down to the present in the family circle relate the tensions, based on differences in skin color, that existed among the poor families of the area. Marie Boisson was seemingly troubled and often fearful of the "negative" impact of the neighborhood on the development of her light-skinned sons Dantès and Clément.[22] These "ethnic" problems were faced by almost any mulatto child who was immersed in predominantly "black" surroundings. An inhibitive social distance vis-à-vis darker neighbors seems to have been adopted. The fact that the mulattoes inherited a culture that happens to rule the world made them often anxious to set limits to their social interaction with individuals darker than they were.

Dantès Bellegarde was able to take advantage of the free public school system begun in Haiti in 1816.[23] He first attended the neighborhood elementary school at Lalue. Later, in 1891, he went to the free Lycée Pétion from which he graduated six years later with a baccalauréat ès-lettres and ès-sciences, as well as with the top honor prize.[24] He later would justify his interest in public life in terms of repaying the Haitian people for the sacrifices it had made in financing the school system.

At the age of fifteen, Bellegarde volunteered to teach illiterate soldiers and workers from the slums.[25] During his school years, Bellegarde advanced from being unilingual in the Creole language, to mastering French, English, Spanish, Latin, and Greek.[26] He learned Spanish with the Cuban journalist Bartolomé Maso, at the turn of the century when many Cubans had fled to Haiti to escape Spanish oppression.[27]

After graduation, Dantès Bellegarde taught successively French in *septième* and *quatrième*, Latin in *troisième*, and then the class of *philosophie*.[28] During that time, he contributed articles or managed various newspapers and journals, including *La Ronde, Le Soir, Le Nouvelliste, L'Appel*, and later (in 1923), the *Revue de l'Association Internationale des Hommes d'Affaires*.

In February 1902, Dantès married a schoolteacher and colleague two years his senior, Cécile Savain (1875–1965).[29] Of this union were born Auguste, Argentine, Jeanne, Marie, Simone, Fernande, and Jean Bellegarde. Cécile Savain, the granddaughter of a white Englishman named Richards, was a magazine writer and was considered a feminist. After her marriage, and particularly when her husband started gaining notoriety, Cécile Bellegarde seemed to have drifted away from her own family, perhaps simply because her family belonged to the petite bourgeoisie, and she was outgrowing that status as a result of her husband's rise in politics.[30]

Despite the heavy schedule of his early public life, Dantès Bellegarde succeeded in being an affectionate father who, in the evenings, helped his children complete their homework as they sat, each on a step of the staircase leading to the second story of their home. In the mornings, he enjoyed several hours of gardening before walking over to the ministry for his day's work as a cabinet officer, usually arriving at his destination before his employees. He rejected the offer of an official motor car, once they became available in Haiti, and acquired an automobile only in the late 1950s. Sunday afternoon is remembered by his children as a day when Dantès Bellegarde, his spouse, and his brood of seven children would pile into the horse-drawn buggy and go for rides in the country.[31]

After high school, Dantès Bellegarde's ambition had been to study architectural engineering, but there were no schools teaching this subject in the country. Consequently, he would later help found, and taught at, the Ecole Libre des Sciences Appliquées (circa 1907). At the time, however, he enrolled at the Faculté de Droit, received his *licence*, and was admitted to the Port-au-Prince bar in 1901.[32]

By the time Bellegarde received his education, historically significant educational efforts made earlier had had important effects. These reforms had been instituted by President Geffrard, in tandem with the negotiations he undertook with the Holy See, negotiations that culminated in a Concordat (1860) and that introduced the Roman Catholic teaching orders into Haiti.[33] President Salomon reinforced the westernizing impact of this education by welcoming French lay teachers. They were to strengthen the public schools, thereby completing reforms in all schools, both public and religious.

The Church-connected schools, *collèges* and *pensionnats*, through superior organization and financing (and also through charging a small fee) became the preserve of the Haitian upper classes. Consequently, the (public) *lycées* were but slowly transformed, catering to individuals of the petite bourgeoisie and, as space allowed, to other urbanites aspiring to elite status. In several of his works, Dantès Bellegarde paid tribute to these French teaching missions and to the intellectual influence that such professors as Jules Moll and Henri Villain had on his generation.

The Generation de La Ronde

Shortly after graduation from the *lycée*, Dantès Bellegarde became the secretary of *La Ronde*, a literary publication that was to greatly influence the course of Haitian literature. The publication gave its name to the entire turn-of-the-century historical period, a period that became known as *la génération de la Ronde*. Literary movements had traditionally rallied around such newspapers and journals; most of them had been short-lived, but their impact lasting.[34]

Literary organs such as *La Ronde* fulfilled several functions. They created a forum for expressing ideas, lending them an ideological armature. And they tended to parallel events in the political arena, one perhaps existing as a reaction against a dictatorship, another representing a reaction to a period of liberalization.[35] In Haiti, politics and literature were interwoven, partly because of the country's low rate of literacy. These publications also served as publishing outlets, pooling scant financial resources to publish within their pages the works of authors who would otherwise remain unknown. Authors of great fame often had their only printed work scattered in numerous such publications. But despite these limitations in publication, Haitian literature towers over that of other Caribbean states; as late as 1951 it appeared that Haiti had produced more books on a per capita basis than any other Latin American nation.[36]

La Ronde, "the greatest literary movement Haiti has known. . . ."[37] occurred at the eve of the centenary of independence. Its goal was no less than the rejuvenation of society through literature, to paraphrase an early leader of the movement, Pétion Gérome. He added:

We live in troubled times: literature can regenerate the masses, by its ideals and the glorious memories of the past; it will act on the environment sooner than the latter can shape it; it will give the joys of the strong odors of the land, of the lusty smells of our virgin forests. . . .[38]

Since the *génération de la Ronde* encompassed diverse literary traditions, it cannot accurately be called a school, although it deserves in some degree the label of movement. The tenor of that movement was the creation of a bridge between those intellectuals who imitated French literary genres and those who were beginning to accept the bolder characteristics seen in literary négritude. Dantès Bellegarde, then aged twenty-one, explained the spirit of tolerance that animated his peers when he wrote in an editorial in *La Ronde*'s first issue on May 5, 1898—

Our sympathetic understanding will go to all those who, despite railleries, contribute to the richness of our literature. Our admiration will be especially forthcoming to the writers who . . . will have rendered in an original form the beauties of our nature and marked their works with a truly national imprint.[39]

This statement was to be one of the few "nationalistic" utterances made by Dantès Bellegarde. Because he deviated so early and strongly from the position he advocated here, as will be seen in the course of this work, one must either explain the statement as a *péché de jeunesse* or as confusion on his part as to what constituted a "national imprint."

Perhaps more to the point, *La Ronde* was a logical continuation of the policies of the nineteenth century, although it embraced at the same time a wider humanistic or universal approach to literature, an increasing amount of nationalistic fervor as expressed through the Haitian novel of the period, as well as a maturity of thought hitherto unrivaled. *La Ronde* was eclectic, appearing at the century's end after romanticism had had a protracted sway in Haitian letters. It must be viewed as an important phase in the history of Haitian intellectual development, especially in the sense that it strengthened and disseminated further positivistic ideas. The political ferment of that period, as illustrated by ephemeral presidencies, together with the strengthening of the national bourgeoisie gives us further social and economic understanding of the movement.

In an unguarded moment, Dantès Bellegarde candidly expressed the dreams his generation had for the country:

Our group in 1900 was most candid and even romantic, of that social romanticism that disposed it to be favorably fond of the humble. We were all, blacks and mulattoes, without any personal wealth. We had been educated in the public schools that were maintained by the people's money. We loved that people from which we differed only by our education [*culture* in the text]. We wanted to be of use to it rather than to use it [*le servir et non nous servir de lui*] to satisfy our ambitions. Our candor and our romanticism were such that we dreamt of making Haiti a small American Switzerland, with a joyous population basking in freedom's light and in the peace accorded by fecund labor.[40]

In the Service of Haiti

The subtitle above, the title of Bellegarde's last published work, well expressed his public career. It began in 1904 when Murville Férère, the minister for foreign affairs and public instruction named him to a joint German-Haitian commission. This commission was to investigate alleged damages suffered by some German commercial enterprises during a recent political upheaval. While serving on this commission, Dantès Bellegarde was recalled to the capital and appointed Chef de division at the Ministry of Foreign Affairs and Public Instruction in replacement of Sténio Vincent.[41] He acquired this position in lieu of his brother Windsor Bellegarde. Windsor had been slated for the office, but had been denounced to President Nord Alexis as politically dangerous. The first names were adroitly switched at the last moment by Minister Férère.

Because the ministry was divided into the two broad areas of foreign affairs and education, Dantès Bellegarde was, at twenty-seven, almost solely in charge of national education.[42] Within twenty-four hours of his installation, he submitted extensive plans for educational reforms to be implemented throughout the system. He also advocated that the teaching staff and technicians at the department be insulated against political crises and be given tenure. At his initiative, textbooks on civics, history, geography, and literature were prepared.[43] In addition, while he was Chef de division, Bellegarde contributed his teaching services gratis to various schools.

Bellegarde was dismissed in 1907 by President Alexis, and threatened with execution by firing squad because he had favored presidential aspirant Anténor Firmin, and because he had formed the Cercle d'Etudes Sociales for the study of reform outside governmental action. To the president, both actions bordered on treason. Furthermore, Bellegarde had warned the nation, on February 25, 1907, of the dangers that the lack of necessary reforms could bring about exclaiming: "God is too far, and the United States is too close."[44] After several days under house arrest, and having briefly sought asylum at the French legation, Bellegarde lost his house and all its contents to arson.[45] In 1908, however, he was appointed professor of civil law at the Faculté de Droit.

Disillusioned by his brief experience in politics, Dantès Bellegarde became an accountant and worked in several business firms. In 1907, he transferred to the Banque Nationale as the *sous-chef* of accounting services, later becoming secretary to the directorate, and chief of correspondence and statistical services. Here he made valuable contacts in the business sector and in the foreign community. Several years later, in 1916, when he was still at the Banque, he was sent on his first trip abroad, a three-month visit to New York.[46]

The election of Michel Oreste to the presidency in 1913 was heralded by Bellegarde as a victory for the civilian over the military element. This election may well be described as a struggle between a dying militarism, represented by the aging traditional *caudillo*, and bourgeois "progressivism." Michel Oreste had been an honest parliamentarian, steeped in the liberal tenets of Boyer Bazelais, founder of the Liberal party in the nineteenth century.[47] Bellegarde served the Oreste regime as the president's Chef du cabinet particulier, chief of staff of the president's official household, a vital position in such a centralized government as that of Haiti. He remained at this post until the overthrow of the Oreste government eight months later.

In 1918, after a five-year interlude spent at the Banque, Bellegarde was persuaded to reenter politics as the minister of public instruction and agriculture in a new Phillippe-Sudre Dartiguenave cabinet. President Dartiguenave, formerly the president of the Senate, had owed his election to his pragmatism in dealing with United States demands, soon after the United States occupation of Haiti was effected in 1915. In accepting the ministry, Bellegarde had insisted on adding the agriculture portfolio to his functions, because he considered education and agriculture as complementary. Berthoumieux Danache,

Chef du cabinet particulier for President Dartiguenave, in commenting favorably on Bellegarde's role in that government, said that although Bellegarde could have taken either the portfolio of finances or that of external affairs, he had opted for the relative obscurity of the ministry of public instruction. Danache argued, however, that despite Bellegarde's choice of this relatively obscure ministry, he had made a real contribution in the field of international finance and in foreign affairs.

> Later, when the law concerning the reevaluation of the Haitian Gourde [currency] came to be discussed in the Council of State, the President, who knew well Bellegarde's glib eloquence, asked him to shoulder [*sic*] Fleury Féquière. . . . Without being able to judge personally of the accuracy of the thesis which was opposed by Emile Elie, a specialist in financial matters, I do not think I am venturing too far when saying that Dantès Bellegarde gleaned the honors of this memorable session which reminded one—by the breadth of the discussion and the merit of those who participated—of the oratorical jousts of the best epochs of Haitian parliamentary life.[48]

Dantès Bellegarde's knowledge of finances seemed considerable indeed, as appeared later in his discussions of the subject at various international gatherings. Yet relatively little is known of his activities in this realm of finance during the early part of his career. The record of his achievements in the field of education and agriculture is more complete. He himself wrote at length about his efforts at this ministry. Others have also written about his work during his tenure in this department.[49] The American literary critic Edmund Wilson described him later: "I met M. Bellegarde in Port-au-Prince—a very polished and upright old gentleman, a Mulatto almost white, with his stiff hair worn *en brosse* like a Frenchman. . . ."[50] Samuel Guy Inman, returning from a trip to the Dominican Republic and Haiti, wrote in 1919:

> The brilliancy of the cultured classes is most remarkable, equalling such circles in European capitals. Some of the most intellectual of foreign ministers sent to Washington have been Haitians. One seldom meets finer gentleman than the Minister of Education [Bellegarde] and some other present government officials than I met at Port-au-Prince.[51]

At that time, Haitian cabinet ministers discussed surrealistic poetry before the formal openings of cabinet meetings, to the great hilarity of Americans in Haiti who proudly reflected on the lack of literary achievements of United States presidents and cabinet members.

Faced with the enormous difficulties in implementing the constitutional provisions that instituted free and compulsory education at the elementary level in 1816, and free education at the secondary and university levels in 1879, Dantès Bellegarde applied his efforts to restructuring the educational system. The major defect of the existing system, as he saw it, was the dangerous politicization of the staff. This characteristic made the staff incapable of functioning as a technical and professional body, and of assuring continuity in policy. In dealing with the problem, he established strict rules for tenure and promotions, established clear criteria for appointment, and increased salaries considerably.[52] Edner Brutus, commenting on these actions of Bellegarde, in his *Instruction publique en Haiti, 1492–1945*, wrote: "His law of July 28 [1918] remains the most important he has signed, and one of the most significant [laws] ever voted upon, [and] introduced by our ministers. . . ."[53]

Because United States authorities favored an emphasis on vocational training, this field took on increased importance under Bellegarde's leadership. There was strenuous opposition to the introduction of any new development in the field of education by the United States, however, partly because government revenues were being diverted to service the foreign debt in an accelerated fashion.[54] The general result was far from favorable. According to Mercer Cook: "When the Americans had finished their bunglesome experiments on the Haitian schools, Haiti was obliged to call in a Belgian expert. The latter reports: 'after eighteen years of American occupation, the Haitian peasant has remained just where he was [before]'."[55]

A typical account of United States opposition to Haitian-sponsored reforms is that of the historian Rayford W. Logan. In discussing the Haitian medical school, he wrote:

This school, founded in 1823 and enjoying a continuous if somewhat changing existence, has been a source of great pride to the Haitians. . . . In 1918 six of the best professors of the Medical School were dismissed because they had voted against the American-made constitution in the plebiscite of that year. On the insistence of the then minister of public instruction, M. Dantès Bellegarde, President Dartiguenave ordered their reinstatement. But Mr. McClean, the American Chief of Hygiene, had openly demanded the suppression of the Medical School which he looked upon as a farce and which he intended to replace by an American school. In order to accomplish his purpose he shortly afterward prevented Haitian students from entering the hospital, had the apparatus thrown into the yard, and set up a school for nurses in the building. The minister had the apparatus transferred to the old *Palais de l'Exposition*; several Haitian doctors placed their laboratories at the disposal of the students and continued the school with the aid of other doctors who contributed their services [as was most likely customary, gratis].[56]

Moreover, Haitians viewed United States opposition to their developmental schemes as racist. The fact that vocational training was allowed to proceed and that classical education was deemphasized provided ammunition to those holding that view. Thus, Professor Logan concluded an article on Haitian education in the *Journal of Negro History*, stating: "Haitians are particularly resentful because in the adjoining country of Santo Domingo, which has essentially the same problems as Haiti, we have pursued a different policy. . . . Before 1915 Haitians considered vocational training as beneath them. The apparent attempt is now being made to convince them that vocational training is the only kind for them."[57]

American policy for Haiti was similar to that it adopted for blacks in the United States. Ready acceptance of Booker T. Washington's practical ideas on Negro development through the acquisition of manual skills was within the broad framework of "scientific" progress as perceived in the United States in the late nineteenth century. On the United States scene, however, such ideas had been opposed strenuously by such black leaders as W. E. B. Du Bois.[58] But these policies, which passed for progress and liberalism toward American blacks in the United States, seemed to have been adopted abroad either to maximize economic profits or as a psychological weapon to be used against educated blacks; they translated as United States-sponsored authoritarianism. The United States was neither as generous nor as magnanimous as it claimed.[59]

Dantès Bellegarde had visualized the problem of agriculture as an extension of a larger educational crisis. Within the developmental schemes he dreamed to implement, rural schools were to answer the needs of the local populace rather than those of some ideal theoretical formulation that would make them identical to the urban school network. Consequently, he believed that rural school districts should be decentralized and run by educational advisory boards in each locality. The schools would also provide agricultural training and hygiene as part of their routine instruction. The ministry's main job would then be teaching and advising the peasantry in the latest agricultural techniques. That ministerial task would ensure a measure of physical well-being and financial security to the peasants. At the same time, it would ensure the economic development of the nation.[60] (See Chapter 5 for the theory behind Dantès Bellegarde's actions to these ends as minister of education and agriculture.)

In August 1918, Dantès Bellegarde presented the Council of State with a bill for rural and agricultural organization that would replace the Rural Code in operation since 1863. He also presented a second bill making credit available to small peasant farmers. The objectives of this new rural code were no less than the establishment of local government, according to Bellegarde, with encouragement from the central government and favoring a leadership role by the local elite. The local councils he advocated would comprise large landowners, "important" farmers, and the heads of industrial and agricultural enterprises, both Haitian and foreign.[61] Furthermore, under his proposed law, a uniformly applied head tax would displace the *corvée*—the ancient French system of forced labor that the Americans had reinstituted.

The United States authorities in Haiti were not pleased by Bellegarde's new rural code, nor by his project for agricultural credit. The unspoken policy of the United States authorities was to deny Haitians credit for any ideas they had, even if it meant resurrecting the same plans under American patronage at a later date. As was customary, without making their objections known, the occupation authorities buried the projects.[62]

Missions Abroad

It is a tradition of long standing in Haitian politics to send abroad as diplomatic envoys those individuals who might "embarrass" the president politically, if they remained on the local scene, by restricting his freedom of action. The American civil libertarian Roger N. Baldwin, in a letter addressed to this author, mused that this may have been a factor in Bellegarde's long service abroad.[63] Whether this consideration entered into Bellegarde's first appointment cannot be readily determined. One may seriously doubt this insinuation in the case of Bellegarde, however, because no evidence seems to support it.[64] Whatever the political reasons may have been, however, Bellegarde presented his credential letters to French President Alexandre Millerand in April 1921, and later that year to Pope Benedict XV in Rome.

The Haitian foreign service consists of individuals appointed by the president and serving at his pleasure. Ghislain Gouraige implicitly acknowledged what he believed was a major criterion for the success of Haitian envoys, stating that the primary, albeit unspoken, directive to all those sent abroad is that they should not "bring shame [*faire honte*] to the country."[65] Léon-Gontran Damas, in a similar vein, credited the astuteness of the Haitian leadership that sought diplomatic representatives of the caliber of Dantès Bellegarde, Jean Price-Mars, and Léon Laleau, all men of great personal merit and impressive education.[66] Indeed, internal strife in Haiti was not allowed to interfere with the quality of Haitian diplomatic representation, as all sides assumed the necessity for "brilliant" delegates.

Relative stability in terms of bourgeois hegemony for more than a century (1830–1940), *le besoin de paraître*, the emphasis on appearance rather than being, ensured a high level of foreign representation. The diplomats were well educated (and often light-skinned). The experience of the United States occupation, which lasted until 1934, had been an irritant reinforcing color prejudice; it resulted in favoring the light-skinned element for diplomatic assignment well into the 1940s.[67]

But a strict "color" analysis of government policies would be both simplistic and inaccurate. The economic and social interests of the traditional client-elite, in the final analysis, were probably more significant in the defense of the status quo. The Haitian diplomatic offensive, in view of the ever-present simmering class and color conflict at home, and racial prejudice abroad, became little more than an *"acte de présence"* in the sense that a bolder course of action was hopelessly hindered.

Dantès Bellegarde's diplomatic successes illustrated the conditions that became the accepted criteria for success in developing societies in a neocolonial situation. Through his father's lineage he had inherited a connection with the old militaristic and nationalistic guard. From his mother he had inherited a light complexion that served him well.[68] Through his marriage he had reinforced his position within the petite bourgeoisie. Like other nonbourgeois who strove for status, he was able only through education and international recognition to transcend his origins and break through the strictures of the Haitian social establishment. Both these factors became for him, as for others of his class, the avenue for social mobility in a society in which illiteracy was the norm, but also a society that craved status among nations.

The Republic of Haiti came to be represented at all important international forums in the twentieth century. Haiti signed the Treaty of Versailles in 1919 as a belligerent power. It was a member of the League of Nations, of the Pan American Union (later, the Organization of American States), and of the United Nations from their inceptions. Prestige accompanied the fact that black representation was being assumed by Haiti, through this *acte de présence*. This prestige was temporary, however, for it was diluted in the 1960s, by the emergence of numerous states of African origin in Africa and the Caribbean.

Dantès Bellegarde's appointment to the Permanent Court of Arbitration (Hague Court) in December 1920, and to the prestigious post of Haitian minister to France, had come during the military occupation of Haiti by American troops. After 1913, the United States had increased its share of the Haitian external market to 60 percent, displacing France from its previously preeminent position.[69] Bellegarde therefore attempted to resurrect the Franco-Haitian commerce that had been disrupted by the war, tying this objective with the goal of national self-determination for Haiti.[70] France was no longer feared politically, he believed, and so could now play the role of a rival paramount power, counterbalancing the United States in the Haitian political equation. Bellegarde was to be an activist in his new diplomatic functions, as he had been previously in the Dartiguenave cabinet. His activities in favor of closer economic and financial relations with France, Sweden, and Belgium, based partly on his personal acquaintance with Raymond Poincaré, Hyalmar Branting, and Henri LaFontaine, were largely unsuccessful, however.[71] He also endeavored to create a favorable climate of opinion for Haiti within the "Latin block" of nations at the League. The "block" was a group comprised of the nations of Latin America, France, Italy, Spain, Portugal, Belgium, and Romania (whose people spoke a Romance language). In this latter enterprise, the creation of favorable opinions, he was more successful.[72]

Dantès Bellegarde left Paris in January 1923, carrying with him the ribbon of the *Legion d'honneur*, with the grade of *Commandeur*. He was the only Haitian to have received this honor from the French government up to that time.

Haitian representation to the Vatican increased in significance after the American occupation of Haiti. In a letter to Bellegarde dated August 30, 1921, President Dartiguenave stated:

> I am basing some hope on our beginning contacts with the Vatican. If the cost of living in Paris allows you this sacrifice, I will take it upon myself to have you reimbursed for the expenses necessitated by your travel upon your return to France.[73]

The President's wish was not granted. The American financial advisor declared that since Bellegarde's assignment to the Vatican had been honorary, his expenses would be considered . . . honorary as well.[74]

Another major center of Haitian foreign policy was the League of Nations. To the traditional *acte de présence* in diplomatic intercourse, *la volonté d'agir*, the desire to take action, had been added in the wake of the occupation of the country. In 1920, the sum of four thousand dollars had been authorized by the American financial advisor for the Haitian delegation in Paris to attend the League's first assembly in Geneva. The American official refused to credit any funds for the second assembly to be held in September 1921. The Haitian financial contribution quota to the League had also been withheld by the United States. Bellegarde, for a second time, personally assumed the financial burden of Haiti's representation, paying his way out of his own pocket.[75]

A Pan-African Spirit

In a news item dated September 21, 1921, a Geneva newspaper recorded Bellegarde's animated appeal in the League's Assembly in favor of Léon Bourgeois's plan for a commission to study intellectual cooperation.[76] In four pages of his book, *Les précurseurs au Bureau International d'Education*, Pedro Rossello detailed Bellegarde's single-handed argument for the restoration in the resolution of the word *education*. Because the word *education* was too sensitive for some member states, it had been eliminated from the resolution. As Bellegarde explained:

> It is certain that educational methods can differ according to peoples, since each has at heart its development in the spectrum of its national traditions. It does not alter the fact, however, that the human soul is one,

and that these methods of education will attempt the development of all its faculties, can apply to all men, regardless of race and nation, all the while taking into account differences of time and place. Thus, there is for us a considerable interest to favor the exchange of pedagogical work accomplished in all parts of the world. Consequently, I propose that the words "and education" be restored to the text of the Resolution.[77]

Later, in 1945, William G. Carr, of the United States National Education Association, effectively summarized Bellegarde's argument in a brochure entitled *Only by Understanding:*

> There was in that Assembly one man, and apparently only one, who was willing to say a bold word in favor of restoring the word *education* to the resolution. . . . Bellegarde was a speaker of force and eloquence. From the floor of the League Assembly of Geneva on September 21, 1921, he delivered a moving plea for frank consideration of the importance of education to the endurance of the ideals which had given birth to the League of Nations.
>
> What, he asked, does the Assembly wish to accomplish by creating the Commission on Intellectual Cooperation? It is to bring together, and to make available to all nations, the fruits of the human mind and spirit. If we want to do that, how shall we, how can we, afford to ignore the very development of the human mind itself?[78]

Bellegarde's motion was withdrawn. The objections of a small state could not hope to convince the whole Assembly. But thirty-four years later, at the Eighteenth International Conference on Public Instruction held in Geneva, and sponsored jointly by UNESCO and the International Bureau of Education (BIE) in 1955, the director of the latter, Jean Piaget, rendered public homage to Dantès Bellegarde for his intervention in 1921, reminding the delegates that Bellegarde had stood alone in his effort to place education in the League's overall cultural program.[79]

The same spirit of international cooperation moved Bellegarde to intervene in the issue of colonial mandates in the League of Nations. The debate on the mandates issue presented more dangerous pitfalls than did that on education, which could be carried at a lofty theoretical level. The former involved the colonial interests of the world's major powers.

The most salient incident relating to the mandates occurred in 1922. The Union of South Africa had pursued in its mandated territory of South West Africa the oppressive policies inaugurated earlier by Germany. These policies led to an open revolt by the Hottentots. The mandated power responded harshly. A punitive expedition, which included aerial bombing raids, was launched, and more than a hundred men, women, and children were killed.[80] Dantès Bellegarde brought the tragedy to the attention of the Third Assembly and demanded, on September 8, 1922, that an investigation of the charges be made. "That women and children were massacred in the name of the League of Nations, while under its protection," he said, "is an abomination which we cannot tolerate."[81]

The motion he presented was passed unanimously.[82] Paul Scott Mowrer, a United States journalist covering the debates, forwarded a cable to the *Chicago Daily News* that captured the mood of the moment:

> Race prejudice received severe blow today when league assembly listened to brilliant speech of negro delegate of Haiti who in well-chosen moderate words addressed world on leagues duties to mankind and especially on duties of mandatory powers to native populations under their control stop referring to recent reported massacre of bondel hottentots by southafrican expeditionary force Bellegarde asked full investigation . . . it is believed here that unstates [United States] comptroller of haitian finances refused to permit league expenses be inscribed national budget more honor is paid Bellegarde who though living in modest hotel avoiding ostentation has succeeded in bringing misdeeds of conquering races before bar world public opinion stop entire assembly followed haitians well chosen splendidly delivered words with attention and many persons congratulated orator his command ideas and his courage in defending africans.[83]

Bellegarde seized the opportunity presented by the Bondelzwart massacre to renew his efforts for reforms in the Permanent Mandates Commission (PMC). On several occasions, notably on September 20, 1921, he had spoken in favor of the right of native populations to petition the PMC directly, bypassing the mandatory power.[84] On September 25, 1922, he suggested to the Assembly that the PMC add to its membership a representative of the colored races.[85] This suggestion was part of a package developed at the Second Pan African Congress the previous year. But the sympathies of the members of the League of Nations were with PMC member Sir Frederick Lugard's suggestion that a representative of the United States be added instead, although that nation was not a member of the League, because of that country's experience with Blacks in the American South.[86]

The suggestion made to the Assembly in September 1922 had had its inception early in August 1921, when Dantès Bellegarde had been visited by Methodist Bishop John Fletcher Hurst and W. E. B. Du Bois. They had requested that he participate at the Second Pan African Congress as its honorary president, together with Gratien Candace, a member of the French National Assembly from the island of Guadeloupe.

The Second Pan African Congress had convened for its Paris session, on September 4, 1921. On stage, according to Jessie Fauset, was the "efflorescence of Negro intellectuals," Blaise Diagne, Gratien Candace, Dantès Bellegarde, William Edward Burkhardt Du Bois, Edward Frazier, Walter White, and Rayford W. Logan. When it became time for Du Bois to head a delegation to Geneva, Bellegarde, according to Fauset, "gave us generously of his aid and assistance."[87] Du Bois wrote, "working with Monsieur Bellegarde of Haiti . . . we brought the status of Africa to the attention of the League. The League published our petition as an official document. . . ."[88]

The following year, Bellegarde introduced the Pan African Congress's Second Resolution, which bore the stamp of Du Bois, to the Assembly. It read as follows:

> The Second Pan African Congress wishes to suggest that the spirit of the modern world moves toward self-government as the ultimate aim of all men and nations and that consequently the mandated areas, being peopled as they are so largely by black folk have a right to ask that a man of Negro descent, properly fitted in character and training, be appointed a member of the Mandates Commission so soon as a vacancy occurs.[89]

As this statement illustrates, the participants in the Pan African Congresses held between 1919 and 1945 were in the mainstream of positivistic, Western contemporary thought, despite the fact that these individuals had suffered from racial prejudice and that racism was central to posi-tivist social thought.[90] Neither Bellegarde nor Du Bois found it difficult to accept wholeheartedly the validity of a policy of elitism, best exemplified by Du Bois's celebrated concept of the "talented tenth." This talented tenth was to be produced from within the Black population to guide it to the enjoy-ment of freedom.[91]

On the Western European reaction to the Congress, Fauset, who had been a witness to both bodies' deliberations, remarked that "the press was with us. . . . It was especially arresting to notice that the Pan African Congress and the Assembly of the League of Nations differed not a whit in essential methods. Neither attempted a hard and fast program."[92] In the meantime, Blaise Diagne and Gratien Candace told the world how fortu-nate they were to be French first, Negro second.[93] In brief, the Congress had not formulated a radical program for Black emancipation.

Nonetheless, the French government had been under great pressure from the United States to forbid the Congress's meeting on its territory. Fabian socialist and labor-movement support in Great Britain, together with French socialist support, had been interpreted by a segment of the American and the European press as part of a Bolshevik plot. Ironically, the brand of Africanism exhibited at the Congress came under attack from the more radical black organizations, such as those headed by the Jamaican-born Marcus Garvey, that stood for separatism from white society and for the development of Black pride through a cultural evolution independent of Western cultural norms.[94]

Dantès Bellegarde's prominence at the Paris Congress did not please the United States government. W. E. B. Du Bois charged that Bellegarde's efforts in Europe on behalf of his country and his race led the United States to press the Haitian government for his dismissal.[95] Later, in 1930, under similar circumstances, the chief of the American forces in Haiti, General John Russell, ordered Haitian President Louis-Eugène Roy to recall Bellegarde in Geneva, and the Ministry for External Affairs officially repri-manded him for his amicable attitude toward American Blacks.[96]

W. E. B. Du Bois wrote Bellegarde in 1925: "I am very grateful at [*sic*] your activities at the League of Nations and congratulate you upon them. I want to let the colored people of the United States know how splen-didly you have represented them as well as Haiti."[97] Echoing this sentiment, Professor Alain Locke of Howard University wrote Bellegarde in 1931:

I must put more formally my deep regret at the loss of the most representative diplomat your country and our race have furnished in the last generation. I believe your uncompromising and self-respecting statesmanship will be sorely missed. Certainly no Haitian representative has been more warmly received and admired by American Negroes, and we deeply treasure the fraternal regard in which you have held us. . . .[98]

On Several Fronts

The period from 1922 to 1930 was a lull in Dantès Bellegarde's official career. Although remaining active internationally in the hope of bringing the United States intervention in Haiti to an end, his domestic career came to a halt. These were the years of the Louis Borno presidency. As a member of a so-called *ministère de combat*, the fighting cabinet of President Dartiguenave, Borno had had ample time and occasion to irritate the United States government. But Bellegarde accused his one-time friend of having capitulated to American pressures, on all fronts, as the price for the presidency. Bellegarde labeled the Borno period of Haitian history *la dictature bicéphale*, "the two-headed dictatorship," charging that it consisted of Louis Borno and of United States General John Russell.[99]

Other scholars have been even more severe in their judgment of Borno, labeling his regime the "flourishing" of Haitian fascism.[100] Both views are basically correct. But whatever the cause of Bellegarde's disenchantment, whether it was the dismantling of Haitian resistance in the face of American pressures, an authoritarian streak in Borno's government, or the president's idiosyncrasies, the two men became enemies. Perhaps for the first time in his life, Bellegarde was a member of the opposition. During these years of "disgrace," Bellegarde, nonetheless, remained active in the private sector, particularly in the field of education and in foreign travels for the Haitian Chamber of Commerce he had meanwhile helped to reorganize.

In June, 1924, the president of the League of Nations Council, Hyalmar Branting, suggested that Bellegarde be made a member of the League's Temporary Commission on Slavery and Forced Labor, stating:

The advantage of insuring the collaboration of Mr. Dantès Bellegarde to the Commission, whose eloquent interventions in the debates of the Second and the Third Assemblies are in everyone's memories, is too evident for us to insist upon at length. Besides his personal qualities,

Mr. Bellegarde would have, in the eyes of all, the advantage of being the representative of Latin America whose collaboration in the working of the League is particularly precious.[101]

The temporary commission consisted of eight individuals who had had ties with their countries' colonial efforts; among them was Sir Frederick Lugard.

The suggestion made by the Bureau International pour la Défense des Indigènes that it be given a seat in the commission was rejected by Branting in the following words:

[It is] preferable that the Commission . . . not include as a member, the delegate of one of these numerous philanthropic organizations which dedicate themselves to the service of less-developed races [*races peu évoluées*][102]

Branting's colleagues at the League of Nations Council agreed with the wisdom of this suggestion. The Temporary Commission met in July 1924, and July 1925, in Geneva, and reported on slavery and forced labor throughout the world.[103]

Invited by the Bureau International de la Paix, whose administrative council helps in the selection of the Nobel Peace Prize, and of which he was a member, Dantès Bellegarde attended the Twenty-fourth Universal Congress for Peace held in Paris in September 1925. Under his leadership and that of Belgian Nobel Peace Prize winner Henri LaFontaine, the congress unanimously passed a resolution calling for an end to the United States occupation of Haiti.[104] Earlier, in July 1924, at the Congress of the International Union of Associations for the League of Nations, held at Lyons, a similar resolution calling for the reestablishment of full Haitian sovereignty had been adopted.[105]

In August 1927, Dantès Bellegarde attended the Fourth Pan-African Congress in New York as a special guest. He seized the opportunity to denounce the United States Haitian policy once more, and called the American attitude vis-à-vis Haiti racially motivated. While the United States had allowed Dominicans, Nicaraguans, Puerto Ricans, and Philippinos to gain a measure of political autonomy in their exercise of the right to vote, Haitians, because they were black, were being denied the same right, he said. He concluded, in a speech translated by Rayford W. Logan, that the United

States was intent on demonstrating "Haitian inferiority" so that it could be used against the demands for political equality of American Blacks. In an escalation of the rhetoric, several strongly worded resolutions demanding the end of the United States occupation of Haiti, and the annulment of measures that reinforced the economic dependence of Haiti on American finance capital were also passed by the Fourth Pan-African Congress.

Provisional President Louis-Eugène Roy of Haiti named Bellegarde as minister to Paris and Geneva for a second time, in July 1930. On September 11, at the Eleventh Assembly of the League of Nations, Dantès Bellegarde made the most celebrated speech of his career, during a discussion of the plan for European federalism presented by Aristide Briand of France.

This speech of Bellegarde, which was widely discussed in the international press, called on the United States to state its Latin American policy, and labeled the then state of affairs as one subject to "abusive interpretation."[106] The inherent fear of the United States existing in Latin America, Bellegarde argued, was detrimental to that country's efforts toward worldwide disarmament; and because no country could survive in economic and political isolation, urgent reforms were needed to meet the crisis.[107] Speaking of Bellegarde's speech, the *New York Times* summarized it and described its setting well. It wrote:

> He certainly had success for the representative of a small country, following the big leaders, keeping in their seats through a long speech devoted to the United States most of the delegates and a good share of the public who had heard Foreign Minister Henderson of Britain. The contrast was more striking because Pedro Cosio of Uruguay, who followed Mr. Bellegarde, had few listeners to hear his proposal that a new world economic conference be convoked in 1931. . . .
>
> There was no doubt in his mind, Bellegarde said, that the United States "today controls the affairs of the world" and that Europe is "especially menaced in its economic life . . . and seeks to resist domination." . . . If Europe succeeds, then let Latin Americans beware, especially because the United States is already turning in their direction and its trade with them is developing fast. He agreed that Latin America and the United States have a mutual need of each other, and though he declared the United States owed most of its prosperity to the World War . . . he said he meant it in no derogatory sense and praised the "admirable energy" of the Americans.

Mr. Bellegarde's quarrel was with the American policy, which he held was chiefly responsible for the mutual lack of confidence between the United States and Latin America, handicapping their trade and causing the latter to see "the shadow of a dreadnought behind each yankee dollar."

President Hoover, he suggested, could begin by making formal as President the policy he enunciated as Secretary of Commerce in 1927 at the Pan-American Commercial Conference that no loans would be approved for any country for military or unproductive purpose. He held that all intervention should be renounced. Until the American military occupation of Haiti has ended, he declared, fear and mistrust of the United States would continue among Latin Americans.[108]

In this speech, it will be noted, the foreign policy of the United States was seen by Bellegarde as a grave danger to world peace. Mercer Cook later wrote: "He courageously proved that American economic domination and the ruthless manner by which that domination was being achieved constituted a direct menace to European and Latin American security."[109]

The Assembly of the League of Nations was stunned; Bellegarde had dared to express thoughts that apparently were on everyone's mind, but that no one dared to state. The French newspaper *La Liberté* exclaimed:

What a spirited attack on American imperialism: What telling thrusts against the manner in which the Americans apply their Monroe Doctrine . . . But one forgot to applaud him. When he left the rostrum, all the delegates were busy tracing little figures on sheets of paper and this activity was so absorbing that it prevented them from rendering to the representative of the Haitian Republic the homage which his courage and talent deserved.[110]

It was at this point that the United States demanded the recall of the Haitian emissary.

The intensive activity of Haitian patriots domestically and abroad, and of Bellegarde's appeals to world public opinion were bearing results. The Haitian Senate and Chamber of Deputies were reconvened in October 1930. In November of that year, the Legislature elected Sténio Vincent, from a field of candidates that included Jean Price-Mars and Seymour Pradel, to the presidency.

In January 1931, Dantès Bellegarde was en route to the United States to assume his new functions as the Haitian diplomatic envoy to Washington and to the Pan-American Union. President Vincent wrote him on January 31, 1931:

> Spoiled child of success, I wish you, my dear Bellegarde, to harvest some more, because we need it in large amounts, in your new position.
>
> We see no inconvenience as to your travelling to Port-au-Prince. This sojourn would even be useful on several counts. It will allow you, notably, to be better informed of our present national action, and to imbue you with more of the details of current negotiations concerning the termination of the occupation."[111]

In his double post as Haitian envoy to Washington and the Pan-American Union, Bellegarde would attempt to seek the military and financial liberation of Haiti and to seek aid along advantageous lines.[112] At the Fourth Pan-American Commercial Conference held in October 1931, he recommended the establishment of a permanent financial and economic organism that could assist Latin American nations in the realms of public financing, currency, commerce, and international credit. To further this idea, Bellegarde took the initiative of inserting in the agenda of the Seventh Pan-American Conference held in 1933 in Montevideo, the "necessity of establishing a permanent committee for Inter-American economic and financial cooperation." Bellegarde always believed that his suggestion lay at the base of the creation of the Economic and Social Council, established fifteen years later by the Bogota Conference of 1948.[113]

During this period, in the early 1930s, Bellegarde developed a close relationship with the French ambassador to the United States, Paul Claudel (1868–1955), the mystical Roman Catholic poet of the Académie Française.[114]

Because Dantès Bellegarde opposed the new accord between Haiti and the United States (August 7, 1933), which extended United States supervision over Haitian finances, Bellegarde was recalled in November 1933. This executive accord signed by the secretary of state for external affairs, Albert Blanchet, and the United States minister to Haiti, Norman Armour, was never submitted to the Haitian parliament (as Haitian law requires), which had unanimously voted down a similar earlier accord signed on September 3, 1932.[115] At that time, several American personalities were actively supporting the Haitian cause, among them Ernest Gruening, Roger N. Baldwin, and Walter White. The latter, as the secretary of the NAACP, wrote Bellegarde at this time:

> Dr. Gruening sailed on Saturday with Secretary [Cordell] Hull.
>
> On Saturday morning I spent more than one hour with the Haitian delegation—Monsieurs [*sic*] Mangones, Barau, Moravia, Pierre-Paul, and Salgado. I told them as strongly as I could that a great responsibility rested upon them at Montevideo. I pointed out that any intimation of yielding on the part of Haiti at this critical juncture would be disastrous; that now is the most propitious moment since the Occupation to secure restoration of full sovereignty to Haiti. We talked very frankly and I pointed out the embarrassing position in which Haiti would put its friends in the United States if it did not repudiate the Accord of August 7th and demand unequivocal ending of all forms of control— financial as well as military—with the expiration of the Treaty. I further pointed out that when the Accord is repudiated we would start a movement in the United States for the scaling down of the Haitian debt since the United States was forgiving England, France, Russia and every other country which owes her money. . . .[116]

The story of Bellegarde's resignation, as it was being called, was headlined in the *Washington Daily News*, "Haitian Minister Startles Diplomats With Resignation: Dramatic Announcement Made at Pan American Governing Board Meeting; Resents U.S. Financial Administration." The article stated that in the presence of Cordell Hull, Bellegarde, his flamboyance intact, exclaimed raising both hands skyward:

> In the name of my little Haiti which has suffered so many injustices on the part of the great powers during the course of her sorrowful history—in the name of justice, peace and friendship, I beg the delegates of all our countries to remember that they have a great task to accomplish at Montevideo—that of consolidating the Pan-American Union making it repose on the unshakable base of mutual respect for the rights of our twenty-one republics.
>
> This respect can be safeguarded only thru [*sic*] repudiation of all forms of aggression. One may say that there are two forms of aggression: military aggression and what Manuel Ugarte terms financial aggression.

President Roosevelt has characterized the first with a striking
phrase: "The aggressor is he who has soldiers stationed beyond his
frontiers."

I permit myself to characterize financial aggression by borrowing
from the formula of the President [F. D. Roosevelt] of the United
States: the financial aggressor is he who administers thru his functionaries the finances of another independent state.[117]

Subtleties in the definition of *aggressor* seemed to have bothered few
American officials at that time. As was seen in Chapter 1, four successive
United States administrations, those of Wilson, Harding, Coolidge, and
Hoover, had implemented what amounted to an identical and bipartisan
policy vis-à-vis Haiti.

The struggle for the political liberation of Haiti, led by Haitian nationalists and their American liberal allies, finally culminated in the victory of
August 15, 1934, when the last remaining American soldiers embarked for
the United States. This was the end of an era, that of "active" opposition to
the United States in Haiti.

The Years of Sadness

Following the great war for independence (1791–1804), the Haitian leadership, anxious for international acceptance, had reversed the potential for
far-reaching social and economic changes implied by its revolution. It was
as if the trauma of violence and the separation that ensued were too great to
bear. As Dantès Bellegarde put it: "Haitians swore eternal separation from
France, and this eternity lasted . . . twenty years."[118] In effect, this attitude
had led to the restoration of an old ideal and patterns for social behavior
never long abandoned had been temporarily deflected by the Revolution.

Following the end of the United States occupation in 1934, a similar
albeit more complex effect than the reaction that had followed the French
defeat in Haiti may be observed. The United States occupation proved a
watershed event in Haitian historical development. In propelling Haiti into
the twentieth century, the United States helped to set in motion a violent
reaction, springing from an aroused racial and class consciousness. With it
came the realization that Haiti was being placed firmly in the economic and
political orbit of the United States. A relationship similar to, though not
identical with that previously established with France was developing with
the United States. But whereas French culture had commanded admiration,

and Haiti had sought the leadership of France in international forums, the United States benefited only grudgingly from this new situation, at the Pan-American Union, and later, at the United Nations. The almost total domination by the United States of the Haitian economy, long-standing cultural and racial antagonisms, "ideology," and the occupation itself had contributed to the malaise. The social malaise within Haiti exacerbated by the United States invasion, was soon to be reflected in the political forces at work, as these tensions culminated in the "revolutions" of 1946 and 1957, in which the Black element attempted to attain political domination over the mulatto, middle-class control over upper-class hegemony.

Those political movements also resulted in Black assertiveness in cultural matters. The symbolic beginning was the publication of 1928, of Jean Price-Mars's *Ainsi parla l'oncle*, which argued for the recognition of the African roots of Haitian society. This cultural assertiveness, which heralded the worldwide movement of Négritude, was accompanied by a simultaneous deepening of the economic and financial strictures of neo-colonialism. Some scholars have viewed Négritude as merely a diversionary tactic detracting from a class struggle over scarce economic resources;[119] Bellegarde had viewed this Black assertiveness as a leftist trend related to communism and "reverse" racism.

But it was not until political independence of Asian and African countries in the 1950s and 1960s was attained that a fuller analysis of neo-colonialism could be made. But neocolonialism was unmistakable in the tone of a confidential policy statement issued by the Haitian Ministry for External Affairs to its delegation to the Eighth Pan-American Conference of Lima (1938). The vice-chief of the delegation was Dantès Bellegarde. The interests of the Haitian bourgeoisie seemed to coincide with those of the United States, despite the long cultural and racial conflict. The document illustrating subservience to United States foreign policy objectives, stated in part:

> The Haitian delegation will, as much as possible, enter in contact with the American delegation and will not neglect anything which can, in one way or another, affirm more our complete approval of the Good Neighbor Policy of President Roosevelt, a policy which must establish, define and maintain the conditions and the spirit of the mutual aid necessary to all nations on this continent, as much from the political as from the economic and financial standpoint.[120]

Bowing to international realities, the government was a faithful reflection of the interests of the Haitian oligarchy four years after the departure of United States troops. The pretense of an "independent" foreign policy, hitherto centered on French cultural influences, had become obsolete. The United States was the victor; it had succeeded in displacing French influence in Haiti with American commercial and political interests.

Dantès Bellegarde seemed to have adjusted well to the new situation. His writing and speeches during that twenty-four-year period (1938–57), exhibited a kind of paranoia as he noted the gains of both Négritude and Marxism within the ranks of younger intellectuals. Although Bellegarde remained active throughout that period, his activities were those befitting the status of an elder and proud statesman. Most of the thought expressed in them was a mere restatement of the positions that had brought him success earlier. He had earned his laurels, and basked in his reputation as he collected honors abroad and in Haiti. Among the activities "crowning" his career were his return to education, his participation in the arbitration of border conflicts between the Dominican and Haitian Republics, and positions as a visiting professor in the United States and in Canada. He received decorations and academic honors from Cuba, the Dominican Republic, Venezuela, Mexico, the United States, Canada, Chile, Brazil, and France.

In 1940, James Brown Scott invited Bellegarde to attend the Congress of the American Institute of International Law, and there Bellegarde helped found the Inter-American Bar Association.[121] In February 1944, Bellegarde attended the meeting of the Inter-American Ministers for External Affairs in Rio de Janeiro as the delegate adjunct. In September of that year, he participated in the International Congress of Philosophy, the first of its kind held in the Americas, held at the National Palace with the president of Haiti, Elie Lescot, and the French philosopher, Jacques Maritain as conveners.[122]

When in 1946 President Lescot was overthrown by forces expressing student unrest and widespread urban dissatisfaction, Bellegarde was appointed to Washington to secure the recognition of the Military Executive Committee as Haiti's provisional government. He candidly recognized the significance of United States recognition then achieved when he wrote:

> The official recognition of the Comité Exécutif Militaire strengthened its authority domestically, and allowed it to undertake the important financial measures that would revive the country's economic activity . . .[123]

Again in 1950, when the populist regime of President Dumarsais Estimé fell from power as a result of the pressures successfully applied by commercial interests and an elite-dominated army, Bellegarde answered the call of the Junta (*Junte de Gouvernement*). After the dissolution of the legislature, he accepted appointment to the Conseil Consultatif whose functions were quasi-legislative. In October of that year, he permitted his name to be placed on the ballot as a delegate to the Assemblée Constituante that would meet at Gonaives to draft a new constitution. Bellegarde was elected (and was subsequently chosen president of the Assemblée), while General Paul-Eugène Magloire was winning the presidency in the same election.[124]

A year later (1951), appointed by President Magloire as Haiti's permanent ambassador to the United Nations, Dantès Bellegarde participated in the Sixth General Assembly, which met in Paris from November 1951 to February 1952. Strongly supporting the Israeli position against Arab and Palestinian demands, he also appealed to world opinion regarding the South African racial conflict, drawing an analogy between the two questions:

The massacre of Jews in Germany . . . has aroused the indignation and the reprobation of the entire world. Should one remain indifferent in the face of inhuman practices of similar kind for the sole reason that the victims are no longer whites, but blacks and yellows? The delegation of Haiti cannot accept such an attitude. There are no reasons of a juridical nature which can stop the United Nations General Assembly in adopting a resolution that can bring a solution, even temporarily, to a problem of alarming gravity for all the globe's peoples. . . .[125]

Later, in 1953, the General Assembly appointed a three-member commission to study the racial situation in the Union of South Africa. It was composed of Hernán Santa Cruz (Chile), Henri Laugier (France), and Dantès Bellegarde. The commission drafted three voluminous joint reports that declared the *Apartheid* policy of the South African government to be a grave danger to world peace. True to form, the South African regime was thoroughly uncooperative, refusing the commission's requests for information.[126]

Bellegarde's last diplomatic assignment was again to Washington in 1957. Now eighty years of age, he was the oldest member of the diplomatic corps. Provisional President Nemours Pierre-Louis was succeeded by provisional President Franck Sylvain, who himself was replaced by the Conseil Exécutif de Gouvernement, a collégial executive representing several presidential aspirants. At the fall of that government, Bellegarde tendered his resignation, not wanting to represent provisional President Daniel Fignolé abroad. These were years of political turmoil in Haiti, and the author's investigations show that during Bellegarde's tenure in Washington, the Haitian government seemed incapable of keeping its ambassador informed on the political situation; Bellegarde's principal sources of information seem to have been his children and the Washington press.[127]

The author remembers the rumor that swept Port-au-Prince at about this time: Dantès Bellegarde, it was said, was about to be "inaugurated" as president. It appeared that the United States embassy had been responsible for this "trial balloon," one that mercifully sank.[128] Fignolé was soon overthrown, however, but he was replaced by a Junte Militaire de Gouvernement, consisting of three high ranking officers of the armed forces. There had been five provisional governments in Haiti in six months.

The deep-seated antagonism between the oligarchy, the "new" middle-class, and the urban proletariat had produced this extraordinary situation. The peasantry (90 percent of the population) had little to do with the deteriorating political condition of the country.

In 1956 there were four principal candidates for the presidency, representing different constituencies. Professor Daniel Fignolé, a trade unionist who had emerged during the Estimé government, made a strong appeal to the urban masses, particularly those in Port-au-Prince, where he was better known. He appeared to have had some support in the armed forces' rank and file as well. He was opposed by the United States, by the army's high command, and by the oligarchy; nevertheless, he was used by the latter to forestall Duvalier. In order to more easily dispose of him, the army resorted to the trick of naming Fignolé provisionally to the presidency, a post he kept nineteen days.[129]

François Duvalier, a doctor of medicine, represented a coalition of forces that had emerged in the social revolution of 1946, and had been later stifled by the Magloirist policy of "social equilibrium" in the 1950 to 1956 period. Duvalier's support was widespread geographically, and also found in segments of all important institutions: commerce, the army's middle echelon, the Church, the Protestant sects, and the Vodou hierarchy. He also attracted to his candidacy a strong contingent of middle-class intellectuals who sincerely believed in the political potential of Négritude for national development. Furthermore, Duvalier seemed to have had decisive support from the United States government.[130]

Clément Jumelle, an economist, moderate in his developmental program, attracted both oligarchical and middle-class elements. However, his association with the Magloire regime as minister of finance seemed to have been fatal to his chances for an electoral victory.

The last major candidate, agronomist Louis Déjoie, received his support from a powerful elitist base. For the first time since the Lescot presidency (1941–46), the haute bourgeoisie dared present a candidate, eschewing the precautionary measure of an intermediary, the traditional *politique de doublure*. French-trained Déjoie elicited enthusiastic support from the aristocracy. To President Estimé's catchword *authentique*, "what was truly Haitian," which was being resurrected by the pro-Duvalier forces, Déjoie opposed his slogan, *les forces du bien*, "the rightful forces" that would sweep away the disorders created by "black" middle-class leadership in the 1946 to 1956 decade.[131]

François Duvalier was elected president for a period of six years on September 22, 1957.

Dantès Bellegarde had supported Déjoie, who represented not only the bourgeoisie's best hope of retaining power but also Haiti's best chances, he believed, for complete westernization. Bellegarde had weathered the Estimé years, traveling, teaching in Haiti and abroad, attending international conferences as a private individual, lecturing frequently.

Back in favor under the Magloire presidency, Bellegarde had realized that he had fallen into disfavor among most young intellectuals. To an extent, he had been the architect of his own downfall, since many non-bourgeois intellectuals of the sort he once was himself had benefited from the reforms in public education that he had made in the 1920s and that had borne fruit under the Estimé presidency.[132] But the young intellectuals' animosity toward Bellegarde was not usually personal particularly among those individuals who had known him personally. Dantès Bellegarde was charming, humble in his demeanor, courteous in the extreme, and his integrity had never been questioned by anyone. But the new intelligentsia saw Bellegarde as a "tragic" figure, eminently Haitian in his contradictions and destined to play out his role to the end.[133]

Bellegarde grew more irascible under criticism, choosing to see it as envy, ignorance, and sectarian hatred.[134] He was only partially right.[135] Indeed, oblivious to criticism in public, but suffering greatly in private, Bellegarde was remarkable for the continuity of his thought and his clear unity of purpose. In the final analysis, for him, Haiti was a Western nation whose formative elements were the Christian religion and the French language; no challenge to these basic assumptions seemed possible. Bellegarde's understanding of Haitian national characteristics will be discussed in Chapters 4 and 5, but it should be noted that there was a link between thought and action in his life, and that at times his thought seemed so removed from the society from which he sprung, that his life acquired an aura of unreality. The system of values he followed consistently all his life helps us to understand the title he had chosen for his planned autobiography, *La ligne droite*, "The Straight Path."[136]

Dantès Bellegarde was conscious of having become the leader of one of two divergent trends in the Haitian psyche, that of the persistence of the pro-French forces, while his close personal friend Jean Price-Mars was said, simplistically, to represent the pro-African forces.[137] Their intellectual differences did not, however, fracture an enduring friendship. At Bellegarde's death, Price-Mars, then aged ninety, was the first person to visit the family at the home in Port-au-Prince.

Bellegarde had realized the implications of the divergence of his views from those of Price-Mars, as well as the uses this divergence was put to for Haitian social and political organization and for the nation's foreign policy. Bellegarde's reality was but a wish. Despite his beliefs, scarcely 5 percent of Haiti's population spoke French, and fewer still practiced orthodox Roman Catholicism; Price-Mars's reassessment of Haitian cultural values had a stronger empirical base.

Shortly after retirement in 1957, Bellegarde signified his disapproval of contemporary thinking by becoming a recluse in his gardens, an oasis in the decay of central Port-au-Prince, usually leaving this retreat only to attend an occasional funeral.

As this author remembers him, Bellegarde was elegant, svelte, and strikingly handsome. His hands were expressively aristocratic and gestured to the cadence of his thought; his voice was clear and measured. It was relatively easy to understand why he had been considered by French critics "the most eloquent French orator after [Aristide] Briand."[138]

Dantès Bellegarde was an affectionate man who never seemed to get older; his intellectual and physical activity remained unimpaired to the time of his death in his ninetieth year. He lived and died serenely in the neighborhood that saw him come to life and that he had refused to leave despite its poverty. He died on June 14, 1966, one year and nine days after the death of his spouse of sixty-three years, Cécile, thereby barely meeting the

Haitian legal requirement that a burial vault not be reopened until a year and a week have elapsed after the last funeral. His wife's death had left him disconsolate.

On the day following Dantès Bellegarde's death, the poet Léon Laleau, who knew him well, wrote:

> He was as alert as his sentence. His speech had the calm orderliness of his life. His conscience was tall and erect, and his waist rebellious to bowing.[139]

But it was Bellegarde himself who best explained the disillusionment he must have felt at the end of his life, in a statement written on the occasion of the death of his beloved aunt, Argentine Bellegarde Foureau, in 1901, sixty-five years earlier:

> Life in Haiti is different for those who possess a beautiful internal dream. Small men and small things—this is the spectacle that is offered them. Things are sad and ugly, and one would like to gaze away, but they solicit your attention insistently. Men are odious and cowardly. They give applause to the powerful and sarcasm to the vanquished. Because yesterday's vanquished are today's victors, the sarcasm in progress [*esquissé*] ends in applause. One side of the face laughs while the other grimaces. . . . This game of physionomy would be a droll spectacle if it had not revealed the versatility of consciences. . . . Men, as if they had lost all powers for discernment once in power . . . reserving their anger for those too proud to lower themselves into these manoeuvres dare stand in the midst of general obsequiousness [*aplatissement*].
> "In a country of hunchbacks, straight men are ill-received," would say my old teacher Grospère. So let us be hunchbacked, and the more hunchbacked and misshapen our conscience, the better: Many have concluded thus, and the system—for it has been raised to the level of a system—is the best that Haitian *arrivistes* have yet enacted. Honor? One cares as much about honor as about one's first cigarette. The fatherland? Alas! Alas![140]

Early in the century, with sarcasm and in bitterness, Bellegarde had given others a glimpse of the incurable romantic he truly was inside; as the century progressed, he stifled his impulse to reveal his personal feelings.

But his internal dream remained consistent. Hence the tragic image he portrayed to his countrymen. His tragedy consisted in having had a beautiful internal dream and having mistaken it for reality. All that did not fit this ideal image became to him sordid.

The national stage on which Bellegarde acted was perhaps small for his ambitions and his dreams, although he did not think so. The League's Assembly had at least proved to be a fitting forum where Haiti, gloriously Latin—"the beacon of latinity in America" according to the French writer Henri Béranger[141]—would, Bellegarde hoped, lead a democratic and prosperous Latin America. But not only was the stage small, so were the men, and the things in it, to paraphrase Bellegarde's words.

Dantès Bellegarde was buried amid great pomp. His national obsequies gathered the Haitian cabinet, the diplomatic corps accredited at Port-au-Prince, the armed forces' general staff, delegations of school children from the capital, and a considerable crowd.[142] On the coffin of polished mahogany rested a small anonymous wreath made of tropical flowers in the national colors blue and red, on which was scrolled *"l'écolier haitien"* "the Haitian schoolchild."

As the cannon atop Fort National maintained its intermittent deathwatch and the notes of a lone trumpet died away, one could not help but think of the end of an era, of an era embodying moments of majesty, of sincerity, and of betrayal.

CHAPTER 4

SYNTHESIS OF AN APPROACH

HISTORY AND CULTURE

La sociologie, c'est l'histoire entendue d'une certaine façon.
—Emile Durkheim

From its inception, Haitian literature had been *engagée*, not being able to afford, in the words of Pétion Gérome, *"les manies de coquetterie mièvre"* found in more established literature.[1] When the Commission on Intellectual Cooperation met in Havana in November 1941 to discuss the world crisis, some warned that intellectuals should remain aloof from political activism.[2] Bellegarde differed with them. In a strong statement, he insisted that "economics, politics, the intellect are integral parts of the human reality, and it is by pure mental operation that one separates each from the other. . . ."[3] As with the human reality, as mentioned above, Bellegarde would not find it desirable to distinguish sharply between the historical past and present problems in his own work.

Three nations had occupied center stage, from the standpoint of Saint Domingue, in the late eighteenth century. France, the colonial power, received the credit for molding the minds and the institutions of its possessions. Great Britain had been called upon in 1792 by the plantocracy to "protect" Saint Domingue from French radicalism and from the rebellious slaves.[4] The industriousness of the English had impressed some Haitian leaders, particularly Toussaint and Christophe. The latter had maintained a close working relationship with abolitionist Thomas Clarkson and William Wilberforce. Last, the United States, although from a French scholar's standpoint "neither the product nor the cradle of original political doctrines,"[5] nevertheless provided Latin America with an illustration of the practical application of new revolutionary theories.

But as was seen in Chapter 2 in reference to Latin American independence movements, the United States' "Revolution" of 1776 did not signify
a true break with the past in the sense of a sociocultural reassessment.[6] A
black and mulatto Haitian contingent variously estimated between 600 and
1,400 men, the "Volunteer Chasseurs," had participated in the American
Revolution, fighting at the Battle of Savannah in 1779.[7] Many future leaders
of the Haitian independence movement had been part of this expedition,
among them Christophe, André Rigaud, Louis-Jaques Beauvais, Douyon,
Lambert, and Chavannes. In a broad sense, for Latin America as well as for
Europe, the United States' movement of 1776 was a model for a successful
revolt against a metropole rather than against colonialism.[8]

The events of the French and American revolutions had provided the
connection through which the Haitian leadership was in contact with
the intellectual ferment shaping the eighteenth century. Furthermore, the
significant economic position of Saint Domingue in world trade made it
unlikely that it could live in isolation from the Western revolutionary mood.

Strong intellectual ties existed between France, Great Britain, and the
United States.[9] Economic conditions within these societies had fostered
the growth of national bourgeoisies that superseded the old order. Jean
Touchard described the connection as follows:

> Between the works of Voltaire, Diderot, of the Encyclopedists, Adam
> Smith, Franklin and the political ideas of the bourgeoisie, as they are
> expressed in the memoirs and the correspondence of the time, the
> accord is striking. Perhaps not so much in political doctrine, the work
> of Voltaire and Franklin are fundamental if one searches for the expres-
> sion of a [bourgeois] society.[10]

In all three nations, the revolutionary leitmotiv was an expression of
national sovereignty, rationalism, utilitarianism, individualism, and legalism.[11]
All five of these impersonal forces were reactions working on behalf of an
entrenched classical definition of order; but important new alterations were
also added. Two of these forces, national sovereignty and utilitarianism,
expressed a new subordination of politics to economics. Voltaire, in his
Dictionnaire philosophique (1764) had defined *patrie* as concrete property.
And *L'Encyclopédie* had stated succinctly the duty of the state: "What the
State owes each of its members is the destruction of obstacles which would

hamper their economic effort or would upset them in the enjoyment of the products that are its reward."[12] Earlier, in his *Lettres anglaises*, Voltaire had posited in four equations the path for progress as envisioned by the bourgeoisie: "Commerce factor of wealth; wealth factor of liberty; liberty favors commerce; commerce favors the *grandeur* of the state."[13]

Economic forces, in the final analysis, transcended political and cultural differences. Jacques Droz has argued that class politics was dissimulated by the alliance that formed between the bourgeoisie and the *sans-culottes*;[14] Cesar Graña has remarked that the bourgeoisie was the first ruling class in history whose values could be acquired by other classes through a process of co-option.[15]

In Chapter 1, we established the cultural process of assimilation and its resulting effects on social and political policy. In Chapter 2 we specified further the economic basis of class formation in Haiti, as well as the intellectual rationalization taking place in the nineteenth century as the justification for bourgeois dominance. Chapter 3 presented at the microcosmic level Dantès Bellegarde's rise from the ranks of the petite bourgeoisie to the position of a respected member of the Haitian "bourgeoisie." This rise paralleled that of numerous other individuals at the century's end throughout Latin America and Europe, as ruling oligarchies incorporated them within their ranks. This chapter presents the view of Dantès Bellegarde as they apply to Haitian national development and relates them to earlier thought from which his own synthetical thought emerged.

The argument advanced earlier that neither a conservative nor a "socialist" alternative survived the Haitian war of independence may also apply to the thought of Dantès Bellegarde and to that of his contemporaries in the nineteenth and early twentieth centuries. We agree with the statement generally made that Haitian social thought exhibited mere "tendencies" rather than full-blown differences. In this respect, Dantès Bellegarde, as a synthesizer, is an incarnation of the nineteenth century, while his antagonist Jean Price-Mars, in his syncretism, gave to Haitian thought the possibility or potential for a more divergent course in the twentieth century.

The concept of synthesis, is used here in the sense of an ensemble, artificially created from diverse elements, and syncretism is understood here to mean the merging of differing elements in order to effect a compromise. These definitions must be borne in mind as explicating the difference between the two men.

History and the Development Process

The Idea, when completely incorporated to the moral being, becomes as impulsive as sentiment; it can indeed be said that it is transformed into sentiment.

—Dantès Bellegarde

The distinction between Dantès Bellegarde's historical works and his other writings is arbitrary at best, since many of his writings can be included in more than one category. But he enunciated clearly the ideas and concerns that animated him in his role of historian. He regretted that a lack of poetic talent did not allow him to recreate societies of the past adequately, that is in the sense of an impressionistic re-creation of life. His style, rather, was direct, terse, concise, and classical. In his use of language, Bellegarde was the purist in Haitian *lettres:* Léon-Gontran Damas, in an interview with the author, referred to its purity as "the classical pallor of his style."[16] The reader may judge from the following statement Bellegarde made in his *Pages d'histoire:*

> To be able to reach "total truth" through the incoherent maze of known details, to the very soul of history, to thus pass from death into life demands something better than erudition, something better than science: it asks for a divinatory talent, meaning such an extraordinary power of vision that it surpasses the shadowed reality, and sees beyond the "small certitudes of minutiae," the justness of the general sentiment, the truth in color.
>
> But the work of the historian is not limited to this. After having presented life in all its attitudes and all its manifestations, he must still give the explanation of life itself, fixing the general and specific causes that condition it, the transforming influences and the very work that society, by its internal sense of organization, accomplishes upon itself.[17]

In his historical writing, Dantès Bellegarde followed in the steps of such predecessors as Thomas Madiou, Beaubrun Ardouin, and Beauvais Lespinasse, relying largely on their facts and on their historical interpretations. He had had no ideological quarrels with these predecessors, but agreed with his French model, the conservative and positivist historian Charles Seignobos (1854–1942), arguing that since the people were the raw material of history, it behooved the historian to downplay the role of the Haitian chiefs of state tumbling on one another in barrack *pronunciamientos,* and to upgrade the evolutionary transformation that occurred in the nation over time.[18]

But Bellegarde seemed personally too far removed from the lives of the Haitian masses he tried to describe to even produce an accurate picture of them.[19] His talent for this task was sadly lacking. Furthermore, the very discipline of history was largely ineffective in effecting this kind of social history, since documentation and training for the study of nonliterate societies was problematical. But Bellegarde had anticipated, it seems, a most formidable task, that of studying intellectual history as it related to the Haitian people. However, as we shall see in subsequent chapters, his definition of the Haitian "people" was narrow indeed. Bellegarde wrote:

> To show through the moving flow of events the filiation of ideas made by the Haitian people willy-nilly the axis of its life; to seek in contemporary facts the traces of sentiments and of ancient prejudices; to establish the double-edged action of man on his material world, and of the environment upon him; to determine the economic repercussions on the moral evolution of the various classes of society; finally to fix the role of *Ideas* and of *Beliefs* in the formation of the character of the Haitian people: here is the undertaking that solicits Haitian historians. This is an undertaking of high philosophical interest that will have as a practical result, the destruction of misunderstanding that divide and weaken the Haitian nation.[20]

The task Bellegarde envisioned for historians in this statement was arduous. The promise to study the impact of ideas and beliefs proved to be one he was unable to keep, for several reasons. At the practical level, his career as a public official allowed little time to devote to such an undertaking; the immediacy of his concerns prevented his achieving a truly detached and sympathetic work. Furthermore, although a historian by temperament, Dantès Bellegarde had had no formal training in the discipline. Thus, although his talent served him well in his study of upperclass ideological culture, neither his talent nor his training enabled him to describe working-class behavior and to extrapolate social thought from the social organization and the religious beliefs of the rural masses. We are convinced that Bellegarde did not even attempt to study peasant culture, that of 97 percent of the population at the time when he elaborated much of his work. This we shall see later.

The conclusion one is forced to draw from Bellegarde's writings (and his life) is that since the Haitian peasantry was in a transitional state in its cultural evolution, it would have been a waste of effort to dwell on such a transitory present. His understanding of the concepts "nation" and "state" were such as to eliminate the majority of Haitians from their scope, placing them in a sort of cultural and social limbo. What he did not understand was that a thorough understanding of Haitian culture would have required the skills of a sympathetic anthropologist rather than that of a historian. But Bellegarde abhorred anthropology and equated the interest of anthropologists with preconceived ideas of savagery. He derided their notions of what he called "preserving the past" for purposes of scientific study.[21]

While the conservative historian Seignobos gave Bellegarde the particulars of method, specific methods that have long been obsolete according to *La Grande Encyclopédie*, Barthold Niebuhr (1776–1831) fixed for him the fundamental rules of historical research. These principles contrasted with those of the nationalist Heinrich von Treitschke (1834–1896). Niebuhr has been highly praised for his concern for minutiae and for his research, which he tried to make totally objective and divorced from prejudices of class, religion, nationality, race, ideology, and passion.[22] Bellegarde wrote that he agreed with Niebuhr when the latter said that "if we cannot accomplish this [objectivity], science and *belles-lettres* will have served only to corrupt us."[23]

To Bellegarde, both Treitschke and Johann Fichte (1762–1814), and later, Soviet historians who had pitted class against class, had all represented a danger to world peace. Treitschke had extolled the nation above all else. His militarism and preoccupation with national strength had had a large impact on the social and political atmosphere of Germany between 1880 and 1920. For Treitschke, objectivity was not only impossible, it was condemnable. Bellegarde added that Treitschke's love for Germany was but hatred for the rest of the world and contempt for those who did not partake of his militaristic and aristocratic Prussian heritage.[24] Johann Fichte elicited similar criticism for his emphasis on racial purity. But Bellegarde's assessment in this case evidently came from others and not from a personal reading. Today Fichte's ideas are said to be commonly misread and wrongly thought to be a source of Pan-Germanism, while he may have intended quite the opposite.[25]

Dantès Bellegarde agreed with Julian Huxley that it was necessary to "bowdlerize that which can harm international relations, because it is essential that history be written from an impartial and objective viewpoint."[26]

But he never realized the inherent contradiction found in Huxley's position, that truth and harmonious international relations were necessarily related. The history book, like the Bible, would serve to support what seemed noblest in humankind: worldwide solidarity, and inter-class respect and appreciation. History, from Bellegarde's vantage point, should teach concord and national unity at home, rather than hatred.[27]

The role of sociohistorical theory for Bellegarde was in fact to rationalize rather than explain and predict human behavior. At the time Bellegarde was writing, "social engineering" was an important consideration in sociological and historical theory. Thus, Bellegarde would have easily agreed with Emile Durkheim that "sociology . . . would not be worth one hour's effort if it did not hope to ease the suffering of humanity."[28]

Inherent in Dantès Bellegarde's historical conceptualizations—which did not materialize to any significant degree in his writings— were implied definitions of his concepts of people and of nation. His entire historical production and all his analyses of the past—like those of his contemporaries and his predecessors—were a pretext to expound on his favorite ideas and were often meant as contemporary social criticism. In Haiti, prudence dictated that one became a historian in order to argue the theses applicable to the present. Consequently, the events of the past have remained burning issues to date.[29]

Commenting on Bellegarde's work as a historian, the American critic Edmund Wilson has remarked that the greediness of the struggle for power in Haiti did not come through, "conscientiously though he chronicles events. His excellent classical French is too pale and too rationalistic: it seems to screen from him as well as us a good deal that is of basic importance in the Haitian situation."[30] All his life, Bellegarde remained a diplomat and Haiti's apologist abroad, and the vector of westernization at home. These characteristic traits go a long way toward explaining both the weaknesses and the strength of his literary production.

A report of a commission on education (1906) to which Bellegarde had contributed the section on the teaching of history served to clarify his thought on history's primary functions. He believed that historical facts, having had their impact on the social, political, economic, intellectual, and religious life of the nation, must now be studied to show the continuity in the human effort and to contribute to the understanding of the functions of the social organism. He also felt that through the link this history had established between past and present, it should impart civic knowledge and morality to future generations of Haitian students.[31] Recognizing Haiti's special position in the world, he wrote: "What is lacking is a little more goodwill and a greater consciousness of our special mission in humanity. The faith of men who have glimpsed the high destinies reserved for Haiti has not been powerful enough."[32]

Dantès Bellegarde expended neither time nor effort in meeting his own objectives, however. These objectives had been stated as early as 1903 and were subsequently enlarged in 1938. He was more interested in the use of the past for the present rather than writing history for its own sake. His most valuable historical works remained those dealing with contemporary history, in which he played an important role. These include *Pour une Haiti heureuse* (1927–29), a sensitive memoir in two volumes, and *La Résistance haitienne* (1937) on the military occupation of Haiti by the United States.[33]

Bellegarde's vision of the Haitian colonial past revealed his attitude toward contemporary Haitian life and the eclectic approach he would have to take in order to interpret the course of Haitian development within the patterns of Western development. He made it clear that Haiti had risen from the intermixture of races and cultures, producing a new national entity that drew its strength from the nation's turbulent history. On the European side, the various French ethnic groupings, as well as the Spanish and the English, had contributed to the formation of the country. On the African side were the various Senegalese, Guinean, Congolese, Dahomean, Yoruba, and Ibo tribal stocks that provided the second part to the complex national equation.[34]

But the essence of Haiti's originality within the American continent, Bellegarde believed, had been the French language and the Christianity it had received from the French, as filtered through history and refracted through the prism of race.[35] Because of its social and political history, Haiti could no longer claim to have an "African" culture. Together with Louis-Joseph Janvier, Bellegarde argued that "Haiti is a vast field for sociological experimentation" and that its joint European and African ethnicity (in that order) and its cultural evolution were of interest to both the ethnologist and the geneticist.[36] The "mulatto" element remains at 7 percent in Haiti.

Equally clear was Bellegarde's insistence on the economic character of racial exploitation under the colonial regime. The chronic shortage of white women in the colony, he argued, had encouraged the formation of a mulatto population that remained at first undifferentiated from the whites.

Later, when the mulatto group acquired vast land-holdings and moved into the liberal professions in numbers superior to their ratio in the free population, discriminatory measures were inscribed into law, relegating that group to the status of subelite. According to Bellegarde, the calculated results of this policy were economic exploitation, but this exploitation was not due to any philosophical or religious rationale about African inferiority. Only after the potential for wealth by mulattoes and blacks was fully realized, he wrote, were theories of racial inferiority given a scientific base.[37] He added:

> What was desired was the devising of an intermediary class between the whites and the slaves, a distinct class which could never aspire to the dignity accorded the white element, nor crash into the indignity of the slave, except in circumscribed cases. Then, who were these *affranchis* who were locked into a circle, and whose function was planned as a sort of constabulary to maintain the Negroes in servitude for the profit of the masters?[38]

In these capitalistic days of the colony, the quest for economic gain was dictating the theoretical course taken by social thought; it had affected the course of theology as well, according to Bellegarde. Already in 1732, the Comte de Boulainvilliers had posited that the ruling class's position in European society was resting on its innate racial distinctiveness and on its superiority over the European masses over which it ruled.[39] That line of argumentation was even easier to apply in Saint Domingue because of the racial differences.

Throughout the nineteenth century—and the rise of a neocolonial situation in independent Haiti was a further indication of this development—the earlier "illiberal" approach to race relations, which had been somewhat relaxed by the liberal tenets of the French Revolution of 1789, grew steadily. Positivism and the theory of evolution formulated by Charles Darwin and others and applied to society by ruling elites was the vector for new concepts in sociology whose effects are still felt today in both conservative and liberal social science. The Darwinian mood that applied the biological approach to human relations sustained the belief in the superiority of Western civilization and of the white "race."

It had not escaped Dantès Bellegarde that an economic explanation for exploitation and inequality had to be found in order to salvage the remainder of Western thought and culture. An increase in bourgeois nationalism in Western societies throughout the century had tended to foster national differences in the overall unity exhibited in Western cultures since the Renaissance. National programs of education were making great strides in Western Europe and North America in the nineteenth century, and each of these societies was hard at work pacifying its hinterland, its colonial empire, or its masses.

In accordance with the theory of evolution as expressed by Auguste Comte—so strong was its hold that black Haitians did not dare dispute it—the world was "guided far more by its dead than by its living."[40] This theoretical framework argued the continuity of the social organism, and its capacity for adaptation and progress. The spirit of the theory was success-fully encapsulated by its greatest exponent, Herbert Spencer, in the phrase "the survival of the fittest." Biological concepts were made to fit societal development and to explain and rationalize the fait accompli of power con-figurations of domination and dependence as they were found in the inter-national system and among individuals. Nineteenth-century liberalism in Western Europe and North America, including social Darwinism, were at the base of the imperialism and racism of the age.

Dantès Bellegarde's efforts to provide an economic explanation of French colonization in Haiti were aimed at defusing the racial issue domes-tically. He reminded his readers that the group of white *Saint-Dominguois* had been subdivided into three principal groupings: the high functionaries who were metropolitan whites, the *grands blancs* who formed a local aris-tocracy but were often absentee landowners, and the *petits blancs* who often lived under social and economic conditions "similar" to those of the slaves. The *affranchis* were comprised of Negro and mulatto individuals, and in the undifferentiated mass of slaves were found both Negroes and mulattoes."[41] But Bellegarde remained silent on the proportional representation of mulat-toes and Negroes among the *affranchis* and the slave populations.

According to Bellegarde, it was considered imperative that the *affranchis* and slaves be kept separated by an elaborate system of privileges accorded to the former. But it was also most important that the whites and *affranchis* be kept apart "in order to eliminate the potential of an entente between whites and people of color that could remove the colony from under royal con-trol." This fear implied a commonality of interests between the *affranchi* and the whites. The statement just quoted appeared in directions given to the governor of Saint Domingue by a preoccupied metropolitan government in 1766.[42] When it became necessary to emancipate the slaves in 1793, both whites and *affranchis* (mulatto and black) had had to be persuaded that this was the only possible course of action.[43] Bellegarde argued that only French intransigence toward the *affranchis*—it sufficed to be black or yellow to be tortured or executed, he added—was responsible for creating the grand alliance of *affranchis* and slaves that ultimately led to Haitian independence: "It was within the logic of the situation; the French having first given to the war being fought the character of a race war."[44]

Dantès Bellegarde was keenly aware that racial prejudice seemed to be particularly virulent in the Anglo-Saxon countries and, Arthur de Gobineau notwithstanding, "not much," he thought, of a factor in metropolitan France. The ideals of the French Revolution, the French colonial policy that tended toward assimilation, the constant intellectual contact between Haiti and France maintained through the travels of Haitian students that had not ceased even during the turmoil created by the Haitian war of independence, the loans financed to various Haitian governments from the French private sector without fear of French "gun-boat diplomacy," had predisposed the Haitian elite toward France. The racial animosity in Saint Domingue could then be dismissed as a factor rising out of colonial situations. To Dantès Bellegarde, however, economic factors remained dominant, eclipsing race as a factor in social relations in the colonial period.

Contrarily, in the United States, where a man's superiority became tied to the contents of his gonads, rather than to "culture," as in France, the doctrines of racial superiority erupting from the positivist theories found a special expression in the latter part of the nineteenth century and the first quarter of the twentieth. An emerging American sociology, such as that of Lester Ward, buttressed the decisions of American policymakers such as President Theodore Roosevelt and dedicated itself to the task of creating a consensus, forcing unity out of disunity in the United States through the contradictory myth of the "melting pot."

Great care, it was urged, should be taken to isolate the racial elements believed to be a hindrance to progress, such as the Negro, the Amerindian, and the Irish. At times the list was extended to include women![45] But dominance, freely translated as domination, took on both an internal and an external dimension in the United States. Domestically, it signified Anglo-Saxon hegemony cleverly labeled "melting pot" at first, but later called theories of "pluralism." Externally it meant at first territorial, then later economic, expansion in Mexico, the upper reaches of the North American continent, Central America, and the Caribbean basin. In the nineteenth and early twentieth century, "Manifest Destiny" became an American version of the English "White Man's Burden."

Rejecting racial prejudice as a digression and a serious deviation of the thrust of Western (Christian) civilization, rather than as a foreseeable outcome of class and individual greed rooted in capitalism, Dantès Bellegarde sought to place the economic dimension in its proper perspective. Economic gain, he believed, had led individuals to forgo the higher morals implicit in Western culture. At worst, whole groups had used the "racial argument" for economic gain or to undertake imperial expansion. But Bellegarde never seemed to have questioned the integrity of the institutions themselves that led to the structures found presently in the international system, nor the integrity of the Western cultures that had established them.

When politicians such as Theodore Roosevelt and social scientists such as W. J. McGee chastised those who shrank from their duty as rulers and the "self-conjured ghost of imperialism," and further "urged that statescraft and anthropology join hands in the study . . . both standing firmly 'on the rock of experimental knowledge,'"[46] Bellegarde dismissed their statements as aberrations.

Dantès Bellegarde lived through more than half of the twentieth century and must have been at least partly aware of new developments taking place in the social sciences. From the neo-positivism at the turn of the century to functionalism, sociological assumptions of a rather conservative nature had remained fairly intact. But throughout, Bellegarde remained uncritical of these assumptions.

These assumptions had given rise to doctrines and theories of social organization in which the world was orderly and in which cooperation between groups and individuals was, as it were, a natural law. This perspective eventually gave rise to various schools of pluralism in which numerous interest groups battled each other amicably within a "democratic" framework.[47] Positivism had emerged in the nineteenth century as a conservative reaction against the liberal excesses following the French Revolution; it had, at the same time, espoused science and a scientific vision of humanity. Positivism became the mainstay of Western academic sociology, creating a bulwark against Utopian socialist and, later, Marxist doctrines of social organization.

Auguste Comte had had the desire to defend the *ancien régime*— by his defense of institutions and customs, with an emphasis toward stability—against the earlier critique of the *Philosophes* and the socialism of Saint-Simon and Fourier. Later in the century, the French sociologist Emile Durkheim, and the English anthropologist A. R. Radcliffe-Brown, among others, had continued Comte's *engouement* for consensus and stability. Within this perspective, an earlier age's utilitarianism—which also was an ethical code—had had a marked impact in social science, aiding in the definition of what was "useful" to society. After Durkheim and Max Weber had developed their ideas, Spencerian evolutionism declined considerably, making room for a functional approach that ushered in a sociological classical age. Dodging the issue of economic exploitation, functionalism asserted the usefulness of institutions and structures, based, tautologically, on their very survival.[48] But the very insistence of social science that it was (or ought to be) value-free in juxtaposition to more radical analyses such as those of Marxism, was further proof that it too, was as much ideology as it was science. Alvin Gouldner had leveled a devastating critique at sociologists as members of society, and therefore subject to its pressures, whose economic and political interests in the system are transparent:

The culmination of this abiding positivist heritage is reached in Talcott Parson's Structural-Functionalism, which is quite properly celebrated by E. A. Shils as a "consensual" theory. [They championed] both order and progress within the framework of middle-class property institutions. In this continuity of essentially optimistic sentiments and domain assumptions, on the level of the infrastructure, modern Functionalism is the legitimate heir of the 19th century sociological Positivism.[49]

Dantès Bellegarde did not escape the influences of the international system; he did not wish to do so. His sincerity in espousing Western modes of thought cannot be doubted, neither can that of many of the social theorists who lived in the centers of world economic power and worked within the mainstream of the thought of their age. Their difficulty, one that persists to date, was to have not recognized sufficiently the unavoidable connection between ideology and social science theory. But perhaps because Bellegarde originated in a peripheral country whose marginality to the rest of the world has never ceased to be demonstrated, and because of Haiti's naked struggle for national survival and Bellegarde's efforts to bring about transformations he felt would allow the realization of that goal, it seems relatively easier to show connection between ideology and social thought. The Haitian critic Frederic Burr-Raynaud's statement about Bellegarde, "*il n'écrit pas pour écrire mais pour agir,*"[50] inadvertently revealed the truth of the situation. Bellegarde had not meant to refine or advance scholarship; rather, he had wanted to advance the westernization of his own marginal society.

Society and Nation

Dantès Bellegarde argued that the then convenient French colonial policy built on racial antagonism had been short-sighted. The short-term effect of that policy had been to throw the *affranchis* into the collective arms of the slaves rather than to achieve the more desirable goal of unity among all the colonial classes, as Toussaint Louverture had unsuccessfully tried to achieve. The long-term effects had been to erect a wall of political antagonism and social resentment between the two remaining classes in the colony. The French colonial policy had hoped to create a balance in favor of the status quo; but the psychological aftereffects of that policy, Bellegarde argued, had lasted into the present.[51]

Even at present, Bellegarde wrote in 1925, Haiti fights the legacy of colonial society. "How many among us think and act like colonists, and how many more are those who have kept souls of slaves!" He pursued this analysis further, citing the sum total of that colonial inheritance as military despotism, contempt for freedom and human life, aristocratic pretense, the Haitian's rebellious nature, skin-color prejudice, regionalism, the love of facile pleasures, cupidity, and servility.[52] From the listing above it would seem that the colonial heritage was overwhelmingly negative. But Bellegarde did not give equal weight to all these factors, as shall be seen, finding reasons to praise such "positive" contributions of colonization as the French language and Christianity.

The forging of a national entity and its maintenance remained one of Bellegarde's primary concerns. To a common history and common aspirations that, according to Ernest Renan are the basis for a strong national unity,[53] Bellegarde added as further proof of Haitian nationhood, language and religion.[54] In 1938 he attempted a definition of the Haitian nation based on the criteria above: "An ethnic group of African and French origin, French in its language and culture, Christian, and predominantly Catholic, forming an independent republican state."[55] This was the sort of statement that gave Bellegarde his reputation for being a dreamer. Later, in 1953, oblivious to contemporary advances in Haitian sociological research, Bellegarde reaffirmed the same definition of the nation: *"C'est la communauté de langue et de religion."*[56]

If the Haitian Revolution is seen largely as the result and the daughter of the French Revolution, and one assumes Bellegarde's definition of the constitutive elements forming the Haitian nation, race alone would seem to distinguish France from Haiti. But anchoring his response on the writings of Julian Huxley, Jacques Soustelle, Henri Neuville, and others, Dantès Bellegarde argued that the very concept of race was unscientific, racial types having been from times immemorial modified by the twin influences of milieu and intermixture. These influences had long since left only *métis* populations in their wake.[57]

Quoting Franz Boas, Bellegarde further argued that "one confuses individual heredity with racial heredity. Individual heredity is a scientific reality while to speak of racial heredity is nonsensical."[58] Because he had not spoken about race as a "social reality," he was drawn into debating the scientific validity of the concept in an attempt to convince his Euro-American interlocutors; indeed, race as a scientific concept was fast becoming indefensible in contemporary social thought, he believed. Racial intermixture being everywhere the reality and the rule, differences in the "levels of life," he said, are accounted for solely in terms of the economic base of a given society. The development of the forces of production is the fact that explains both the complexity and the rate of improvement found in each society; the lack of development would thus explain the obverse.[59]

By taking into greater account than was then customary, the impact of the social environment upon heredity, Haitian social thinkers had discovered the formula that would temper the harshness of evolutionary thought for their country, and this, from the inception of the republic in 1804: hence their emphasis on education as the surest means of transforming societal habits in Haiti. When the naturalist Jean-Baptiste Lamarck (1744–1829) posited that acquired characteristics could be inherited, little did he know that his theory had already been accepted as a matter of psychic survival by the intellectuals of a small black society in the West Indies who were convinced of their nation's relative backwardness, but not of its inherent inferiority.

Dantès Bellegarde had known of this traditional Haitian reservation to the positivist viewpoint on race and had had access to the mainstream intellectual current of his times, partly through the contacts he maintained with young friends who had studied in France.[60] So when the Lamarckian concept of environmental impact came into vogue in the United States in the period from 1890 to 1915, it was like a breath of fresh air into the staleness of Spencerian evolutionary thought, and was widely adopted as reflecting "the American emphasis upon manipulative possibilities. . . ."[61]

But Bellegarde had been well within this mainstream of current thought, as expressed both in Western Europe and North America. He retained his belief in progress that had become a "steamroller" that would overrun all countries that did not seize the opportunities given them by the modern world. And the line, thin in the best of times, between social thought, ideology, social science, and class structure vanished.

Because of Dantès Bellegarde's acceptance of Western European thought, and because of the universalistic approach he took, what was left of more nationalistic solutions to Haitian problems? Bellegarde argued:

> Our country is too small and its population not numerous enough
> to allow us to create an original civilization, by this meaning a purely
> Haitian civilization. When we declare that Haiti is an intellectual
> province of France, this does not diminish in any way our national
> personality. . . .[62]

Then, Haiti was in a position similar to that of Québec vis-à-vis France, or of Holland vis-à-vis a greater entity called Western civilization. Thus, Spanish, French, and English contributions to the Haitian bloodline should inspire the country to solve its urgent problems in an eclectic fashion, borrowing its ideals and its developmental path from all Western societies that had preceded it in civilization. Haiti, he wrote, is fortified in this undertaking by the "young and vigorous African sap" existing alongside its European blood and cultural contributions.[63] Haiti, he declared vehemently, is as Western as the other Latin American republics. But its loyalty to the French language and its adherence to the ideas of "French" humanism gives it a distinct personality among the Spanish-, English-, and Portuguese-derived nations in the Americas.[64] Without a doubt, Bellegarde felt vindicated when a visiting French dignitary declared Haiti to be a thrusting beacon of latinity in the Americas.[65] Even Price-Mars's *amour-propre* had been tickled by this accolade.[66]

Attacking those who, at home and abroad, believed that Haiti's attachment to French culture was a matter of "apish mimicry," Dantès Bellegarde criticized their lack of psychological insight. "They do not understand," he said, "that this culture is a part of the Haitian personality, and that to renounce it would be humiliating."[67] He wrote that it is from the indissoluble alloy of French and African blood, plus French spirit, that the Haitian people gathers its strength and its culture. Later in 1941, he refined his attack as follows:

> We have endeavored to search for our soul: the error of some was to believe that this soul was exclusively African. While a thinker like Monsieur Price-Mars recommended the study of folklore and of popular beliefs as a means to better understand the Haitian people, and perhaps as a source of renewal for our arts and literature as well, others, simplistically, have thought that this would suffice.[68]

Several years later Leopold Sedar Senghor was to speak of a *"civilisation métisée"* that would merge the qualities of both traditions. Jean Price-Mars—the "father" of Négritude, according to Senghor—had also confessed his attachment to French culture to a Latin American audience. He declared in a speech:

> We are . . . the heirs to the traditions and the civilization of a great country . . . great by its splendorous institutions, the glory of its ancient past and the dynamism of its resplendent culture. . . . We feel indebted to France, to you [Latin America] and to the world in our management of this spiritual patrimony.[69]

Senghor would argue:

> We will not build on a clean slate. . . . We will retain what we must of our institutions, of our techniques, of our values, of our methods even, to create from all—African acquisitions and European contributions—a dynamic symbiosis on the scale of Africa and of the 20th century, but first and foremost on the scale of Man.[70]

In these declarations of Bellegarde, Price-Mars, and Senghor, as in earlier statements by such luminaries as Blaise Diagne, Félix Eboué, and Gratien Candace, one may note a shift of emphasis rather than an essential difference in substance. This shift had led the French literary historian Auguste Viatte and others to exclaim that no substantial disagreement existed between Price-Mars and Bellegarde: "Keeping in mind reservations and nuances, perhaps one will judge that the antagonistic doctrines of Bellegarde and Price-Mars differ more by lighting [*l'éclairage*] than by their substance."[71]

As was seen earlier, Bellegarde had attended the Second Pan-African Congress in 1921 as one of its honorary presidents. At that meeting the principal demand of the assembled Negroes had been "the recognition [by the civilized world] of civilized men as civilized despite their race or color,"[72] thus recognizing a boundary between "civilized" and "primitive," and acknowledging their "inferior" status.

And indeed, at the London session of the Second Pan-African Congress, both England and Belgium had come under attack for their harmful administrative policies in Africa, which, according to the delegates, had done more to *maintain* African traditional cultures than to implement progressive change. But France was commended for having recognized a long time ago "equal right for educated Negroes."[73] The congress was far from being a coven of radical witches as had been feared by most of the American press and by the United States government. As late as the Fourth Pan-African Congress, held in New York in 1927, the *New York Times* commented on the harmony advocated in race relations by the group, and on the "absence of inflammatory racialism."[74]

But after the 1930s, such proponents of Négritude as Senghor, Damas, and Césaire had flirted with the political Left. In Haiti, the United States occupation had had the same effect on the younger generation of intellectuals. Bellegarde's fear in this respect is nowhere clearer than in the introduction to his book, *Haiti et ses problèmes* (1941), in which he gave a chronology of his efforts against such radical ideas. Since 1898, he wrote, he had urged the clergy to intensify its struggle against doctrines of "anarchic materialism."[75] This concern had grown into a veritable obsession by 1940 when he praised the Roman Catholic church for creating the daily newspaper *La Phalange*, which (based on its name) would be an organ of combat with a conservative outlook.[76]

Later, in 1959, in a letter of condolence addressed to the United States Ambassador on the death of Secretary of State John Foster Dulles, Bellegarde went further in his anti-Marxist direction commenting as follows:

> When I had given him [Dulles] the copy of my credentials in February, 1957, as Ambassador to Washington, Mr. Dulles was kind in alluding to the very clear position I had adopted in 1951 in the name of the Delegation of Haiti at the United Nations General Assembly in Paris, against the shifty and subversive politics of Soviet communism.[77]

At this point in his life, Bellegarde had joined his fear of socialism to that of Négritude; for him, they became practically interchangeable. In Bellegarde's thinking, Négritude represented a serious deviation from the Western perspective hitherto adhered to by Haiti. But even though in political terms, négritude had resulted in a widening of the circle of political participation by the inclusion of new "middle classes" and had effected a cultural revolution, it had not resulted in the revamping of economic and social structures along socialist lines as Bellegarde feared.[78] Indeed, any increase in politicization in Haiti, this author believes, will result in the "Africanization" of Haitian state structures as these become more aligned with Haitian national institutions.

But because he knew the nineteenth century so well, Négritude to Bellegarde had sounded like the old Anglo-Saxon argument that "natives" be left to their own resources rather than be pushed into participating with equality in the workings of the modern civilized world.[79] Bellegarde's viewpoint helps us to explain and understand the attitude of the *évolués* at the Pan-African Congresses early in the century.[80]

Both socialism and Négritude, moreover, represented to Bellegarde a significant danger to the status quo in Haiti, as well as to his cherished ideas about man, individualism, and the position of man in the wider context of society: *"Que deviendrait un îlot dahoméen au cœur des Amériques?"* he lamented.[81] But Négritude could as easily lead to a right-wing dictatorship. Bellegarde's anguish in this respect was transparent when he wrote:

> Those who seek to weaken the bonds of solidarity that unite the various elements of the Haitian nationality—either in exciting Blacks against mulattoes, or in pitting social classes against each other, or again in attacking the living forces of religion and culture which are the spiritual foundations of the nation—divest Haiti of all the moral prestige it has acquired from its history in the Americas, and make it lose its personality in the civilized world. They work against the Haitian fatherland.[82]

In this statement, one sees that the image Haiti had tried to project abroad had been nurtured carefully over time. That image, which in fact had carried little weight abroad, had been ultimately internalized by a portion of the Haitian oligarchy. But one also realizes how tenuous and frazzled the fabric of Haitian society had been, since all "national" institutions were now being questioned severely. This stripping of the old heritage was occurring publicly, and hence divesting Haiti of the "moral prestige" it had acquired at great cost to itself.

From within the throes of the struggle for self-realization echoed Bellegarde's definitions of *nation* and *state:* the national community that shared a common religion and language was being tested severely and only the state, "the ensemble of men submitted to the same political power,"[83] seemed to hold the country together. The North American concepts of pluralism that had been accepted implicitly by Bellegarde, and that defined the public good as arising from "conflicting" interests reaching compromise through bargaining, seemed meek indeed in explaining all political situations, the Haitian situation most of all. The concepts of economic exploitation by men and the concept of power had, for all intents and purposes, disappeared from analyses provided by mainstream (nonradical) sociological thought and from the social science of the day.

The very term *culture*, as used by the protagonists Price-Mars and Bellegarde, had different meanings. The first meaning relied upon the more modern anthropological definition, the second upon a high level of education and *savoir vivre* or *savoir faire*.[84] The former indicated a necessary condition of human existence in which each individual was the repository of societal traditions, the latter called for a degree of high individual achievement that would benefit society through the good offices of its individual members.

On *race*, however, some amount of agreement seemed to have been reached amongst Haitians. This was not true, however, in the interaction between race and culture. Anticipating the problems that lay ahead, Dessalines had declared in the 1805 Constitution that all Haitians were "Blacks." That definition had encompassed blacks, mulattoes, and a few hundred whites whose lives had been spared because of the skills they possessed. Bellegarde's white maternal great-grandfather, Ignace Fresnel, and the remnants of the Polish and German mercenary troops employed by Napoleon were among those who had benefited from the government's largesse. Dessalines himself had hoped to further his goal of national unity by marrying off his daughter Célimène to President Alexandre Pétion, but was un-successful.[85] But the vast difference in *"culture"*—in both senses of the word—between the two segments of the population persisted despite Dessalines's and later efforts to the contrary.

Dantès Bellegarde never denied his racial origins, at least publicly. In response to Price-Mars criticism about blacks who are guilty of "bovarysme,"

Bellegarde had exasperatedly scribbled in the margin next to the accusation: "Is *bovariste* the black or mulatto Haitian who believes himself to be a black African. For myself, being a mulatto and feeling no shame about it, I do not believe myself to be either white or black: I am a manmade Haitian by historical circumstances."[86]

Dantès Bellegarde had been nonetheless the first Haitian diplomat to cultivate the acquaintance of the Black American intellectual and social elite in Washington. This channel was closed at his departure because these contacts had angered the Haitian chancellery in Port-au-Prince and the United States government as well.[87] Bellegarde had been proud of his achievements and of his successes abroad, considering them further proof of racial equality. The criterion for success for him, and others in a similar colonial predicament had been established by the dominant civilization. For four centuries that civilization had been Western, that is to say, drawing its strength from Western European and North American cultures.

This desire for acceptance is a key to the understanding of the psychology of non-Western nations in a colonial situation, as well as to the understanding of the plight of minority groups operating within a Western nation. Bellegarde's acceptance of Western norms occurred partly because he had seen no alternative to Western culture taken as a model, especially an "African" alternative.

It can be argued that the psychological effects of acceptance of foreign norms that may lead to cultural assimilation are the result of Haiti's neocolonial situation, defined in terms of its economic dependence over time. Thus economic assimilation would precede cultural atrophy. That neocolonialism is usually an "absenteist" situation makes it no less powerful. It is in this sense that Albert Memmi's assertion acquires its value, that the ideology of a governing class is internalized by the governed.[88] In this case the governed were Haiti's oligarchy who thereby established a "staircase" effect in which the externally governed client-elite does a fair amount of governing internally. Memmi added that "it is the colonized who is the first to desire assimilation, and it is the colonizer who refuses it to him."[89] But since the assimilative process can only have for object the individual—as Bellegarde would have asserted himself—"it is clear . . . that a collective drama [colonialism] will never be settled through individual solutions."[90]

Ever since education had been acquired by a "challenging" [Négritude] elite, the socialization process had become further politicized and a subject of acrimonious debate, while Bellegarde's positions did not change appreciably throughout his lengthy public career. The views that he enunciated as early as 1903 or 1920, had not been altered, except for stylistic changes, in his work of the 1940s or 1950s. His consistency indicated that he belonged to the nineteenth century, and that he himself was the continuator of this thought.[91] Having survived all the members of his *génération de la Ronde*, he now felt the necessity to adhere to the values it represented. Ghislain Gouraige described succinctly the old grace and the charm that Bellegarde exuded, saying "he was an amiable man, generous toward the common people, mindful of the false values of Haitian society, who had prolonged well into the middle of the 20th century, the discreet charm of the last century."[92]

The nineteenth century, according to John S. Haller, Jr., was closer to the eighteenth century in its conception of man than it was to the twentieth,[93] despite the advances accomplished in the biological and physical sciences. Utilitarianism had merged morality with economic interests; it emerged in the eighteenth century as the dominant social and moral standard that came to define bourgeois culture and society.

Alvin W. Gouldner has written, "in a utilitarian culture knowledge and science are shaped by strongly instrumental conceptions." He adds, with Alexis de Tocqueville, "it is chiefly out of a desire for wealth . . . 'that a democratic people addicts itself to scientific pursuits'."[94] The allusion to the acquisition of wealth would have been lost on Bellegarde, who preferred to believe in the total integrity of Western ethical norms as represented by Christianity.

Auguste Comte believed that society tended to develop toward order and stability, illustrating a political need for social order and moral consensus. The moral fiber found in the "utility" of the *Philosophes* was thus broadened in Comtian positivism. For Herbert Spencer, in a sociology not unrelated to that of Comte, society was a quasi-biological organism, subjected to physical laws and evolving as it adapted. Comte, Spencer, and Jean-Baptiste Lamarck found a faithful exponent of their theories in Dantès Bellegarde, who wrote in 1927:

> The evolution of nations occurs according to immutable laws: it
> is in determining these laws that social science endeavors [to find]
> answers; I recognize its legitimacy although it is not sufficiently
> developed to allow definitive conclusions. What can be said is that

some circumstances, at times unforeseen, can accelerate or retard
the development of a given people. Haiti cannot escape the rigorous
determinism that regulates the life of societies. However, Haiti had the
liberty, without being able to subtract itself from the common law, of
modifying little by little its destiny, by the inclusion in the framework
of events that constitute its national life, new facts which, acting in
turn as causes, will change the life conditions of Haitian society.[95]

Haiti is part of an international "system," and its inhabitants are subject to the same physical and social laws as others. Never wishing to delve
into what actually constituted the system, Bellegarde reacted to the optimism achieved everywhere in the nineteenth century, an optimism that he
accepted despite the fact that it was a century that had remained pessimistic
about the potentialities of people of color for such progress.

Dantès Bellegarde saw two factors necessary to national life that were
lacking in Haiti. These were tradition and opinion. By *tradition*, he meant
the common ideals and a communality of sentiment that are transmitted,
modified, but not altered by time, to successive generations. By *opinion*
he meant the collective conscience whose principles would rule individual
behavior, principles that in turn would allow each member of society to
judge others.[96] True public opinion, Bentham had felt, was more a matter of
utility than a reflection of the general will.[97] From these factors, Bellegarde
attempted the following definition of national character:

> When one discards individual differences, and when the vision further
> penetrates in the intimity of thought and of the sensitivity, one per-
> ceives among men belonging to the same nation, living under the same
> skies, under the same physical conditions, suffering the same moral
> and intellectual influences, a community of tendencies, of sentiments,
> of ideas, of impulses which give them as it were, a family air. In uniting
> these characteristics common to an entire group, one creates a being
> which is doubtless an abstraction since he does not have an individual
> existence, but which is no less real because it lives in each individual
> and because it constitutes the very foundation of his soul.[98]

The influence of Herbert Spencer was strongly felt in Haiti, as elsewhere in Latin America. Almost equally significant was the influence of
Jeremy Bentham, Adam Smith, and John Stuart Mill, as well of what,

Bellegarde called, "these apostles of a morality so pure, so penetrated of human compassion, and whose names are Arnold, Wesley, Ruskin, Newman, Manning!"[99]

Bentham was singled out by Bellegarde for special praise as a philosopher who was willing to allow "social authority" to implement through "legal constraint" the conciliation of individual and collective happiness. But it was John Stuart Mill who had introduced a "qualitative" element into social thought, and Spencer who, with the introduction of altruism as the distinctive mark in the evolution of conscience, had, according to Bellegarde, given utilitarianism the highest nobility amongst social doctrines.[100]

When early in the century, Anglo-Saxon societies had come under attack by a number of Francophile and Anglophobe Haitian scholars on the ground that they were lacking a sense of collective conscience and were preaching egoism, Bellegarde had written in their defense, quoting Spencer:

> How can one accuse of selfishness the philosopher who, having made
> of altruism the most noble tendency of the human creature, predicted,
> by wishing it so, the "day when the altruistic inclination will be so
> well incarnated in our very organism, that men will argue occasion to
> exercize it, fulfilling the occasions for self-sacrifice and death."[101]

These thoughts were expressed in 1908 and published in 1927; but in an article published in 1959 Bellegarde still remained faithful to this opinion.[102]

For Bellegarde, utilitarianism had stood for spiritual and moral values. It had also been synonymous with the cultural values and the economic interests of the bourgeoisie. And it was after all in the name of science that Spencer had affirmed the validity of liberalism. Donald A. Zoll, on the other hand, writing on the impact of the "internationalization" of sociology— which appears to have gone hand in hand with bourgeois economic consolidation, as the rich got richer and the poor, poorer—summarized the outcome as follows:

> In more directly political terms, neopositivistic social science has,
> in very recent times, gone avowedly to the defense of democratic
> theory. . . . It has re-emphasized its long-standing preference for a
> neo-Platonic vision of a scientifically-postulated society, managed by
> the technically competent. This elitist re-enforcement of democracy,

however, leads to a profound encounter: the historical conviction of democracy that the individual alone has the final knowledge of what constitute his own best interests is ranged against the view of neo-positivism that men must be conditioned behaviorally for their own good by those who enjoy the benefit of an increased scientific and normative knowledge.[103]

As seen from the forgoing statement, developments in social science in the United States, France, Great Britain, and Germany have assumed that they had a primary task throughout, that of justifying economic and social developments and of providing rationalizations for the status quo, in accord with the economic interests of an international bourgeoisie. The political structures that the various national bourgeoisies had established in the early part of the nineteenth century had consolidated their hold, and consequently, had become more conservative. Political democracy was studied (and still is) as the epitome of "civilized" government in which individual rights are enshrined as the sine qua non of civilized existence.

At the juncture of politics and scholarship, there existed then as now a fundamental assumption and an unbroken historical spirit—that of a utilitarian vision that adapts willy-nilly to changing economic interests and that incorporates more rigorous methodologies to its social science research without changing its presumption or its focus.

That there were inherent contradictions between fact and ideal did not seem to deflect the high praise scholars lavished upon the political system that fed them. Elitism grew rather than lessened throughout the nineteenth century, freed at last from some of the radical trends expressed in the French Revolution of 1789. The tensions and inconsistencies that exist between doctrines of individualism and social conditioning did not seem to have mattered. Indeed, Gouldner is correct in seeing in consensual theory (among the contemporary variations), the champion of "both order and progress within the framework of middle-class property institutions. . . ."[104]

At an earlier period, before the birth of the theorists Robert A. Dahl and Bellegarde's friend Adolf A. Berle, Jr., Félicité Robert de Lemennais's phrase, "reestablish authority: order will be reborn," was no idle menace, despite Lemennais's reputation as a radical. He implied that a hierarchical social structure was the sine qua non to societal health and world order. These developments in ideology, social thought, and social science forced

French Professor Jacques Droz to conclude in a recent book: "Liberalism is a true class doctrine."[105]

Dantès Bellegarde could not be expected to disagree with the social necessity for a hierarchy. The tensions between the necessity for the individual to assert his or her freedom and the needs of the social order, through its constituted authorities, to foster economic development through stability were heightened in Haiti in Bellegarde's view. The social context being Haitian and underdeveloped, the nation's leadership, loosely defined, would have to carry a larger share of the burden in the achievement of progress and, at the same time, try not to be in a position to endanger personal liberties.

In reality, the political tensions between social classes and among unequal nations could not be solved by Haitian thinkers within the self-imposed confines of mainstream Western thought and political ideology without resorting to some more radical approach.[106] Bellegarde's only precedent, therefore, was the French variant of utilitarianism, within which, taking note of the specific economic difficulties France was encountering in the eighteenth century, the Physiocrates had emphasized the role of government and politics in economic development in contradistinction to the Anglo-Saxon ideal of laissez faire. The Physiocratic advocacy of "legal despotism" reminds one of Bellegarde's praise for Bentham's conciliation of individual and collective happiness, applied by "social authorities" through "legal constraints."

In conclusion, it may be said that the inherent elitism that sprang from the historic conditions of the rise of the bourgeoisie in Western cultures and that appeared in its ideology of liberal democracy, reigned supreme. Strength and power were explained in terms of survival, and survival was explained in terms of power and strength, thereby creating a tautology. In Haiti, and in Bellegarde's case, it was simply a matter of survival. The international difficulties wrought on Haiti in the nineteenth century were sufficient to explain the quest and the obsession for national survival. The revolutions of the eighteenth century that had signified the rise of bourgeois nationalism and the birth of the modern nation-state in Europe and in the Americas, were running their appointed course six generations later. Haiti, subsequent to its own victorious bourgeois counter-revolution, was not strong enough, and could not hope to compete in a world where weaker bourgeoisies were being eliminated from contention or transformed to fulfill new functions as client-elites.

But since Dantès Bellegarde had not been personally interested in the accumulation of wealth, he refused to recognize this trait in others. With Henri Bergson, Bellegarde warned that increasing material well-being, if not accompanied by commensurate efforts toward spiritual growth, would present grave dangers for humanity. These dangers Bellegarde found primarily in the "materialistic doctrines" that were sweeping the universe.[107] In the United States, these were exemplified in the writings of Sinclair Lewis where, as Bellegarde wrote, *"il s'agit de normaliser les hommes comme on standardise les briques."*[108] The question was that of standardizing men as building bricks were standardized. To these doctrines, Bellegarde opposed the ideal of God, the patriotic ideal, and the ideal of the family, as Henry David Thoreau had done.[109]

Dantès Bellegarde's sentiments about the intellect and about morality had been enriched by contact with Henri Bergson's thought and his friendship with the mystic Paul Claudel. Although Jewish, Bergson had been totally assimilated into French culture; Claudel had converted to Roman Catholicism. Bellegarde would have agreed with Bergson's biographer, Ben-Ami Scharfstein, that "man is an imitative creator. Before he can produce, he must assimilate."[110] But the danger was not so much that of assimilating as it was that of being assimilated.

Man and the family, according to Bellegarde, are the basic cells from which all progress and transformations have occurred in the social organism. Thus, the individual must remain conscious of his/her rights and his/her responsibilities in order to make practicable the ideals of order and freedom acquired. Consequently, *l'autorité sociale*, to use Bellegarde's expression, had a twofold obligation. It should give to individuals the means to acquire these ideals for themselves; it should also give them respect for all manifestations of these ideals of freedom and order, as they are expressed through each individual's personality.[111]

CHAPTER 5

SYNTHESIS OF AN APPROACH

EDUCATION AND COMMERCE

"Would you tell me, please, which way I ought to go from here?" asked Alice.
"That depends a good deal on where you want to get to," said the Cat.
—Lewis Carroll, *Alice in Wonderland*

Structures established by any elite are a means to an end that animates their existence as an elite. The end is the achievement of some societal ideal. In Haiti during the colonial era, that ideal consisted principally of ideas that arose out of the European condition, transposed and tailored to fit the historic specificity of a colonial people. After independence, and notwithstanding a warning by Montesquieu that national institutions cannot be recreated in a different environment than that for which they were intended, the psychology of colonialism had so affected the mentality of those who lived under it that the thinking of individuals confronting the realities of the world order were permanently distorted.[1] Moreover, they confronted the social fact that institutions once established tend to resist efforts to change, however unsuitable they may have become.

In Haiti (as elsewhere), within the westernized elite's quest for rapid modernization, governmental and nongovernmental structures, created in the past, and alien to national conditions, became the instruments devised for mass indoctrination. The new governing elite hoped to formulate new pervasive social institutions where previously "traditional" institutions had held the allegiance of the community.

Thus the Church, with its proselytizing spirit as the purveyor of "morality"; language, with its largely unconscious formative frame for thought; the government, with its "legal" coercive base as the overseer of

"ethical" behavior; the school as an instrument for "perpetuating while ameliorating society," as Dantès Bellegarde believed,[2] were all to be mobilized to
produce a new nation, a better nation, divorced from an old reality and in
accord with the desires of the new intelligentsia.

The expression "national education," which Bellegarde used, takes on
an ominous meaning of a polity in transformation, rather than being the
reflection of a national culture whose spirit predates the creation of the
state. But education has also traditionally implied the continuation of a
national ethos and the propagation and maintenance of values and value
systems.[3] Thus, *traditional* education and that dispensed by a state anxious
to modernize often appear as contradictory elements in an educational program. But a ministry of education can be a powerful instrument for social
control and transformation.

"Commerce," as here discussed, is most significant as an illustration of
the economic and financial interests of the oligarchy in Haiti. Commerce
is a lifeline that spreads into the smallest hamlets to important population
centers at the national level; at the international level it carries the flow of
goods and services across national boundaries.

Trade transcends domestic and national boundaries; its unique rele-
vance to both the national and international scene parallels the analogy of
individuals congregating in ever-widening social aggregates that, at their
highest, encompass humanity itself. This trend toward a "universalistic
humanism" has become particularly apparent during the last three centuries
with imperialism; it gave rise to the international system of the present.

According to Bellegarde, commerce is a unifying link between human
settlements; education allows the human spirit to transcend the idiosyncrasies
of its pedestrian existence and to soar. Both are differing facets of the same
reality, and their object is to permit human betterment. Dantès Bellegarde
summarized this point of view as follows in his *Dessalines a parlé:*

> The measures undertaken to obtain this amelioration [of material condi-
> tions] will have to have a double objective: (1) To increase the buying
> power and subsequently, the consumption level of each individual, at a
> level permitting him and his family to achieve the comfort indispensable
> to all civilized men. This establishes *social peace.* (2) To increase the pro-
> duction capacity, then the power of absorption of each country at a level
> permitting it to face its obligations to its people and vis-à-vis foreign
> countries. This establishes *international peace.*[4]

Here, Bellegarde has made the point of the interrelatedness of economics and harmonious international development as he saw it; to this
interrelationship he would have added education if he had not been writing
specifically on the amelioration of material conditions. For to him, education had the power to turn barbarians into civilized individuals, to unite
antagonistic social classes, to transcend present differences in the level of
achievement of various racial groups, and allow for international progress to
be made within a commonality of sentiments and interests.

Save for this addition of the area of education, Bellegarde's views were
not unexpectedly close to those of Voltaire who had written: "Commerce
factor of wealth; wealth factor of liberty; liberty favors commerce; commerce favors the grandeur of the state."[5] Economics and education were
symbolically joined in Bellegarde. His class status had made him vulnerable
to the vagaries of international trade, since the Haitian upper-class tended
to be commercial rather than landowning or industrial; and his "classical"
education tended to emphasize the view of such authors as Voltaire over
those of more contemporary figures.

Within the context of the life of Dantès Bellegarde, and the education
he received, it is necessary to define two terms, *patriotism* and *nationalism* in
order to understand their conceptual application to a society in transition.

The *Petit Larousse* defines *patriotism* as "love for the fatherland" and
patriot as "one who would endeavor to be 'useful' [in the utilitarian sense]
to it." *Nationalism*, on the other hand, is "a doctrine based exclusively on
national traditions, loyalties, and aspirations."[6] It is indicative of the moder-
nity of the concept "nationalism" that Voltaire's *Dictionnaire philosophique*
has no entry for *nation*; it defines *patrie* concretely as "a field, a village, a
family," rather than "an impulse." It is something that can be made prosperous by cultivation.[7]

Viewed in the context of the thought of their day, the leaders of the
United States' independence movement were labeled "patriots" rather than
"nationalists." The idea of patriotism was that of a universalistic ideological
approach that considered nations as so many tribes ultimately to be transcended for the greater good.[8]

Today in the Third World concept of nationalism, one sees a twentieth-
century phenomenon of retrenchment that arises from three centuries of
worldwide domination by Western Europeans and their cultures. Western
civilization is now thought to have made promises of worldwide brotherhood that it broke by engaging in scarcely disguised economic exploitation.

The historian, Rayford W. Logan, has labeled Dantès Bellegarde a "nationalist," basing his judgment on the latter's anti-American posture during the United States' occupation of Haiti (1915–1934).[9] But judged on the evidence provided by his writings and his actions in the diplomatic arena, Bellegarde might better be called "patriotic" than "nationalistic." His conceptions of society were closer to those of the eighteenth century than that of the twentieth.[10] This chapter, continuing the analyses of the previous one, will further elucidate this aspect of Bellegarde's thought.

Love of country, arising from the human need for self-identification, exists at all levels of society. Nationalism in its modern rendition, may be feared by the oligarchy because it would kindle the masses; these elites would prefer bourgeois patriotism instead as a safer alternative for their class interests.[11]

Both words, *nation* and *patrie*, are French and Latin in origin, and French language dictionaries establish a clear distinction between the derivative concepts of "patriotism" and "nationalism" not made by American language dictionaries. *Patrie*, originating in *pater*—which also gave us the terms *patriarch* and *patrician*, an etymology that easily led to sexism—imply a concreteness and an elitism not found in the etymology *of nation*, from *natio, natus* ("born"). Based on the meaning of the term in the French language rather than that in English, one can argue that *nationalism* concerns itself more with the material condition of a population, its traditions and collective aspirations being considered a priori sound.[12]

The *patriot*, conversely, would endeavor to *"elevate* both the moral and material level" of the masses—to employ a typical sounding Bellegardian expression—to meet an ideal residing in the mind of a gifted individual. Such a concept of responsibility relies, by definitional necessity, on an elitist foundation. And because nationalism extolled the virtues of the masses and their sound cultural values, Bellegarde equated nationalism with racism.[13]

In making this analysis of development, as we shall see, Bellegarde remained a patriot, never becoming a nationalist like Jean Price-Mars, or even in the sense expressed by Rayford Logan. Bellegarde's anti-American activities in Haiti can be summarized as an attempt to reestablish Haitian political independence in the aftermath of the United States invasion rather than a preoccupation with cultural self-assertion and economic independence. But for Bellegarde, national respect and dignity did not preclude a global and humanistic vision of the universe.[14] It is in this context that he spoke eloquently about "patriotism," the definition of which is represented in the key words of this statement of his:

> The sentiment of patriotism remains, together with religion, the source of all heroism. Can one not understand then, the pain of a sensitive man witnessing the slow but certain dissolution of this sentiment, the most profound, the noblest on the scale of passions which honor humankind, the most productive in enthusiasm and in stunning actions?[15]

Thus Bellegarde believed that the patriotic sentiment was profound and that all subsequent tasks and actions must be buttressed on it. The United States military occupation of Haiti had had a profound impact upon the entire nation. In trying to mitigate its impact, Bellegarde advanced arguments that Western powers would most readily comprehend, because these arguments were closest to their mentality and historical experience. After all, was not Haiti also Western and thus not a subject for recolonization?

Other Haitian writers opted for a no less logical reaction to the United States occupation by declaring the old elite social policies bankrupt and calling for an exposure of the exploitative hypocrisy of Western civilization and of the subservient Haitian bourgeoisie. Both reactions in this author's view, were merely the two sides of the same coin, both being an adjustment to external forces, and both, more significantly, occurring from within the bourgeoisie.

But Bellegarde's reaction reveals more clearly the idealist who believes that ideas have consequences, an idealist who hoped that his appeal to the United States would bring the latter to conclude, as he had, that Haiti was not in need of recolonization because it was Western and thus civilized. But the belief that Haiti was Western had encountered stiff resistance in many places. Thus the German Emperor, Wilhelm II, viewed Haitians as "Negroes lightly tinted by French Civilization,"[16] a veneer of culture; United States high officials had seen in westernized Haitians pretentiousness and apish mimicry.

Internationalism, Westernization, and the Rights of Small States

As understood by Dantès Bellegarde, the Haitian struggle to regain political independence in the aftermath of the United States occupation of 1915 had to be waged on two fronts: one was that against the United States; the other was against those in Haiti who, unwittingly, were giving the United States further justification for its invasion. Hence, Bellegarde argued, anything that would remind the world of Haiti's non-Western past had to be cast aside:

> Last year was published in an American publication a most detailed description of Haitian Vaudou ceremonies. This American publication is titled *The Primitive Man*. I do urge my Haitian readers to consider that the expressions "primitive religion" and "primitive man" are applied to peoples declared by sociologists to be non-civilized. I remind my compatriots who may not know it, that *peoples with the reputation of being uncivilized or simply retarded are placed under mandate or trusteeship of more civilized nations.*[17]

Paraphrasing the Haitian essayist Georges Sylvain (1866–1925), a founder of the anti-occupation organization L'Union Patriotique (1920), Bellegarde wrote that the survival of African cultural traits in Haiti was a powerful weapon placed in the hands of the enemies of the Negro race.[18] This then led to his famous cry: "What would become of a Dahomean islet in the heart of the Americas?" He answered his question, saying that the United Nations Trusteeship Council would presently be debating its fate.[19] As a consequence, Bellegarde italicized this passage in his *Dessalines a parlé:* "The only question is to know if we, Haitian Negroes, will retain the honor of imparting to our country the decisive movement, or if the impulse will be given from outside our midst and despite ourselves."[20]

Thus, if civilization is forced on the Haitians by outsiders rather than being self-generated through an acceptance of the progressive ways of the world, this would signal a form of "ethnic bankruptcy"; Haiti would have failed as the representative of a "despised race" to proudly achieve its task for "Negro rehabilitation."[21] This internal regenerative movement to implement modernization, had been an element in Haitian politics in the early years of the twentieth century, in the hope of preventing the loss of Haitian political independence. In this light, the literary renewal brought about by *La Ronde*, the new optimism occurring at the end of the nineteenth century, showed the elite's desire for a rapid modernization that would forestall Haiti's recolonization by "more civilized" nations.

Dantès Bellegarde's emphasis on French culture was linked with the concept of a modernizing society in the statement he made in 1921, when presenting his credentials as Haitian Minister to France to French President Alexandre Millerand:

> By our language, by our mores, by our institutions, by our ideals we are aligned closely with France: will I be permitted to say that France has a definite interest in maintaining the sort of moral directorate it exercises on Haiti and in preserving such a center of French culture in Hispanic and Anglo-America? The action of France will be made that much easier and efficacious now that Haitians believe it to be devoid of all hidden political motives.[22]

Karl W. Deutsch had called language a "building block of nationality."[23] Others have understood equally well the shaping of perceptions effected by language as the "picture of the universe shifts from tongue to tongue,"[24] to borrow the phrase of Benjamin L. Whorf. As seen earlier, the Haitian elite had been cognizant from the beginning of how powerful an instrument language could become in their hands, domestically and abroad. Bellegarde wrote to this effect in 1954:

> The choice of the French language was imperative, since Creole . . . would have condemned the Haitians . . . to political . . . commercial . . . intellectual . . . isolation. There was thus, a triple necessity to adopt an idiom, universal enough in character so that its possession could place them in contact with the world, rich enough in itself so that its study and the knowledge of its masterpieces would be for the Haitian people the means of access to the highest culture.[25]

The French language, he argued, would then guarantee that Haiti would not remain isolated internationally, but be a part of a universalistic whole, through some kind of a cultural compact between two juridically equal states, France and Haiti. Until Belgian independence in 1831, Haiti was the only nation other than France whose official language was French. A century and a half was to elapse before the number of French-language nations would increase dramatically to include the newly independent African states.

The influence of the French language grew by feeding upon itself. Hence, it is not surprising to hear Bellegarde state repeatedly that "No other idiom, more than the French language, has this universal character; no other possesses a literature richer in masterpieces, in no other has religious, philosophic, and scientific thought been expressed . . . with more clarity, force, and eloquence."[26] Bellegarde thus gave support to his predecessor, Anténor Firmin (1850–1911), who had affirmed the basis for Franco-Haitian commonality: "from there, an unconscious assimilation of temperaments, of inclination of the mind. . . ."[27] making of Haiti's language policy a self-fulfilling prophecy.

Dantès Bellegarde viewed United States commercial and cultural encroachments as dangerous to the Haitian nation, in terms reminiscent of Demesvar Delorme. To Bellegarde, loyalty to a politically weaker France presented a brighter alternative for continued Haitian independence. Declarations in this sense by Bellegarde answered a special ideological need of the Haitian elite and through it, the entire society it sought to shape. Militarily, France had never sought to regain a foothold in Haiti after the diplomatic attempts by emissaries of Louis XVIII in 1816,[28] while the United States had attempted to do so on repeated occasions, as was seen above. An intelligent alternative, to Bellegarde, would then be to substitute France for the United States as a benevolent paramount power as the latter nation was rapidly expanding in the Caribbean. This, he believed, could be done without any significant shift in cultural policy. For Dantès Bellegarde, the exponent of mainstream Haitian thought, the continuation of French cultural and political influence was logical. It should be added that the Third World had not achieved a collective conscience when he was writing.

Within Haiti the French language had become, as Bellegarde pointed out, "the means of acquiring science, the indispensable instrument of thought, the key that gives us access to the highest works of the human spirit."[29] The Creole language—called "Haitian" and a language "derived from Latin" by the *Webster Collegiate Dictionary*—is banished by Bellegarde as an inadequate patois.[30] Its adoption as the official tongue, he believed, would be a backward slide into savagery. In an unsound analogy, he argued in 1941 that Latin America had been conscious of that pitfall when it chose Spanish or Portuguese over autochthonous but primitive Amerindian languages.[31]

Ten years later, in 1951, addressing the question of a literacy program in Creole (which he opposed), Bellegarde quipped that Mexico had unequivocally adopted the Spanish language as its national idiom despite the fact that its Indians were even more unassimilable than "our Haitian peasants."[32] He argued, moreover, that primitive societies did not elicit respect from more civilized men. Worse, he said, such societies too easily fell prey to civilized nations. Because language had both an internal and an individual dimension, it could be a factor militating against international isolation; or, on the other hand, it could relegate Haiti to the status of an isolated tribe, without powerful friends or any hope for progress.

Similarly, wrote Dantès Bellegarde, the proper management of public affairs would enhance the moral stature of the Haitian state abroad; this enhancement could be achieved only through the development of Haitian public opinion. Violation of Haitian law, he felt, showed the nation's unwillingness to obey international norms of decency and standards of behavior. This was a fact that world public opinion would seize upon quickly to distort Haiti's reputation.[33]

As a diplomat, he reminded his superiors that Haitian foreign policy was tied to domestic conditions, writing that "our external policy narrowly depended on our domestic policy. . . ."[34] Bellegarde was constantly reminded of the colonialist argument that colonization was necessary for those peoples as yet unprepared to manage their own affairs. Thus, in a letter addressed to Secretary of State for External Affairs Abel Léger in 1931, Bellegarde wrote:

> It is said in Washington that "Haitianization" would simply mean the freedom of the government to furnish all the good jobs to its partisans and its friends, without any consideration of their merit. . . . It is assumed that the services organized by the Treaty, once turned over to the government will be shortly disorganized, that Customs more particularly, will become the prey of grafters and of smugglers, and that American creditors would thus see disappear all the guarantees established for the repayment of the Haitian debt. During the course of my sojourn in Haiti, I had entertained the President of the Republic and your predecessor, M. Pauléus-Sannon, on this important question, drawing their attention to the necessity and the urgency of legislation regarding the *Civil Service*. . . .[35]

Prudence and moderation in governmental actions and respect by individuals for the laws enacted to safeguard order would ensure a favorable climate of opinion for the maintenance of civil rights at home and peace abroad.[36] Bellegarde's "most liberal" American friends, he wrote in 1948, assured him that the overall principle they were fighting for was "the freedom of each nation to conduct its affairs, and to pursue its destinies as it saw fit, provided of course that it did not interfere [*sic*] with the interests of other nations."[37] Bellegarde, agreeing with Justin Dévot (1857–1921), added that to know how to obey the law is "one of the primary conditions around which a respectable nation is constituted."[38] Based on the criteria above, Bellegarde believed that Haiti had been most disreputable. In a confidential letter to President Vincent, he expressed clearly his belief that these Haitian faults were among the causes that had led to American control of Haiti:

> What you write me of the electorally-motivated "gimmicks" created by the discussion of the budget is saddening. How can the deputies and the senators not realize that these excesses are the most solid argument that can be provided to the American government against our financial enfranchisement? It is painful to make such an admission, but we must acknowledge that we have lived in a horrible disorder and that freedom must not consist at starting the same errors. . . . Our financial incompetence due to our extravagant spending, and our powerlessness at maintaining the peace due to our lack of discipline, are the explanation, if not the justification of the American occupation. If patriotism—of the real sort—was known and practiced, each would endeavor to show that we are capable of maintaining both financial and public order.[39]

The strength of individual nations, members of the world community, he believed, would decide the efficacy of the international system at large. States suffering from congenital weaknesses, he wrote in *Dessalines a parlé*, could to a degree rely on the powerful instrument of international law as the guarantor of human civil rights, a concept that had exploded the confines of any nation to become international. National law therefore, should defer to the "superior authority" of international law.[40] Human economic and scientific progress made this international development inevitable, and Haiti, with all other nations, should stand willing to accept the limitations imposed on its sovereignty by international law. "Haiti cannot refuse to associate itself with this [position], lest it renounce its status of [a] civilized nation."[41]

Although he argued that economic expansion and trade would benefit all individuals in the nations concerned and would bring advantages in the form of political stability and worldwide social progress, Bellegarde never condoned economic or territorial imperialism. He may have been more Spencerian in his attachment to "evolutionary pacifism" than the American synthesizer of social Darwinism, the philosopher John Fiske, who had difficulty reconciling the Spencerian ideal with the expansionism that he approved. In his *Outline of Cosmic Philosophy*, Fiske had endeavored to demonstrate that conflict was a fact of savage society, a form of society to be replaced by a kind of federalism firmly controlled by the "superior, more differentiated, and integrated societies."[42] For Bellegarde, however, international cooperation in trade and finance should not and need not become the pretext for Fiske's kind of economic exploitation and the racism that prevailed in the generally positivist thought of the time.

Bellegarde made a conceptual distinction between United States' imperialism and Pan-Americanism. For him, the first signified that the continent was at the service of its most powerful nation. The second meant the unity of the American republics to ensure the security and the well-being of all. Proceeding from this distinction, he argued that great care should be taken to see that a "political takeover" did not follow an "economic takeover." Pan-Americanism, he wrote in 1941, pioneered by Haiti in its military assistance to South American independence in the nineteenth century, should be based on common interests and the common principles springing from a free association of democratic states, juridically equal.[43] He felt that the historical solidarity seen in the Americas was based on the republican institutions the continent had developed and on the "moral unity" achieved through the democratic process.

Unfortunately, because of its power, the United States was in a position to undo what was noblest in the heritage of the Western hemisphere in its effort to acquire wealth.[44] But ten years later, in 1951, in deference to the "cold war," whose goals he espoused wholeheartedly, Bellegarde argued that because inter-American solidarity was based on the "spiritual unity" of these nations, it was comparatively easier to undertake the military defense of the hemisphere against communist imperialism. This spiritual unity, he argued, would be the basis for an effective collective security.[45]

Collective security, Bellegarde said, encompassed economic collaboration and intellectual cooperation as much as military defense. Because all nations are interdependent and none can remain wealthy in the midst of others' misery, they are compelled to seek collective measures for economic reconstruction, with justice for the poorer nations amongst them.[46] Because Bellegarde had placed on the agenda of the Seventh Inter-American

Conference to be held in Montevideo in 1933, an item on the necessity of establishing a permanent inter-American economic and financial committee, he later, as mentioned above, gave himself credit for the creation in 1948 of the Economic and Social Council of the OAS.[47]

In a speech presenting his credentials as minister of Haiti to President Herbert Hoover in 1931, Bellegarde summarized his ideals in this respect: "What we desire in fact, is peace, justice, and prosperity for all, assured by the cooperation of all: cooperation among the citizens of a same nation, cooperation between social classes, cooperation between peoples, cooperation between races."[48] The harmonious consensus Bellegarde sought is scarcely distinguishable from the ideal Voltaire espoused in 1766, according to Touchard, when he defended the hierarchization of social classes as useful to the state.[49]

Bellegarde argued further that the American republics, daughters of the Anglo-Saxon, Luso-Hispanic, and French currents of Western civilization, did not wish to create a cultural autarchy, but rather to associate their cultural inheritances in the common task of mutual understanding.[50] This was the task Bellegarde has assumed for himself as the vice-president of the Pan-American Union Commission on Intellectual Cooperation and Moral Disarmament, meeting in Lima in 1938. At this conference, he found yet another moral lesson to be derived from the Pan-American Association for Haitians. "Haiti," he said, "would cut a poor figure if she, alone in the Pan-American community, divested herself of her French culture and presented herself naked as a little savage in the midst of her twenty sisters who themselves have never thought of renouncing the magnificent finery of their Western Civilization."[51] Basing his arguments on the same cultural and economic considerations, he also advocated the admission of the Dominion of Canada into the Pan-American system.[52]

Years before, in a lecture given before the Société d'Etudes Juridiques (Society for Juridical Studies) at Port-au-Prince in 1928, Bellegarde, fearing an escalation of the arms race, had expressed his regret for the failure of the 1924 Protocol to achieve the goal of establishing a system of compulsory arbitration that he had called for at the League of Nations Assembly in 1922. Only compulsory arbitration of all matters, he argued, buttressed by the threat of varied sanctions within the twin concepts of collective security and disarmament, would by itself be effective.[53] Such stopgap measures as the Locarno Pact (1925), he said, measures that attempted to guarantee stable borders and nonaggression, and the Paris Pact (Kellogg-Briand, 1928) in which sixty-two nations renounced "war as an instrument of national policy," were merely pious gestures that could not be effective without sanctions against the aggressor.

But since his immediate concern was the role and the position of small powers in the international structure, Bellegarde added thoughtfully:

> Must armed intervention of a powerful state in the affairs of a smaller power, or the seizure by one of the finances of another in order to recover money owed or to protect private interests, be included among the pacific means demanded by the authors of the Pact? If the small nation rises and resorts to arms to push back the military aggression or this financial seizure imposed by force, will this reaction be labelled war or insurrection? Will the stronger state be allowed to say that its violent repression of the revolt is a simple police operation which only concerns itself?[54]

On the basis of this statement, Dantès Bellegarde appears to be fully cognizant of the difficulties encountered by all small states. The problem of colonialism and neocolonialism, of strong versus weak states, a problem that Haiti should attempt to sidestep by its adherence to Western precepts, remained unresolved in Bellegarde's thought. In considering problems closer to home, Bellegarde saw that the United States was accepting no diminution of its power to influence or to control politics in Latin America. He saw this power expressed as early as the Monroe Doctrine of 1823. This doctrine, he believed, originally meant to protect the United States itself by preventing or restricting European intervention in the hemisphere, had been extended in the late nineteenth and early twentieth centuries to justify unbridled United States intervention in the nations of Latin America. The Doctrine "had become for the Latin American republics a perpetual threat and the very basis for North American imperialism,"[55] he declared.

Pursuing his criticism of United States policy, Bellegarde decried United States' intervention in Panama (in order to secure rights to a transoceanic canal) and the Platt Amendment imposed on the Republic of Cuba, writing, "Imperialism can vary its language, but it always remains true to itself."[56] Upon this premise he developed his most important principle in international relations: "International life is based on the respect of conventions, on [the] condition that these conventions were agreed upon freely by each side."[57]

The paramountcy of French culture and *humanisme* in the formulation of Haitian foreign policy, the possible inclusion of Canada in the Organization of American States as a further counterweight to United States' economic, cultural, and military dominance, the insistence upon the value of the Pan-American system as a moral force, the defense of the League of Nations and, later, of the United Nations as the guarantor of small-state security, the emphasis upon the primacy of international law over national law and, no less importantly, the juridical equality of states—all of these became significant elements in the thought of Dantès Bellegarde and in his action in successive Haitian governments from 1907 until 1957. Together, they form the basis of a conception of small-state foreign policy, of states whose major anxiety and major concern for achievement depended upon their survival.

Unilateral action on the part of any major state would tend to destroy the fragile balance of harmony that international law attempted to achieve. Opinions such as these tend to be held in small states, irrespective of their system of government or of any individual's political ideology. In more powerful states, on the other hand, they are found amongst the "most liberal" group of the citizenry, to use an expression Bellegarde might have used himself. This emphasis on legalism in Bellegarde's thought, logically led him to call for the creation of an Inter-American Court of Justice.

To Dantès Bellegarde, the fact that the Organization of American States did not institutionalize the veto as the United Nations Security Council did for the major powers, made the OAS basically more democratic: *"force morale,"* he believed, could vanquish brute force. In 1946 he wrote:

> Haiti's voice has the right to be heard within it [Pan-American Union] in
> all independence; and the value of its vote depends, not on the expanse
> of its territory, of the size of its population or its physical riches, but on
> the technical competence, the moral authority, the force of character,
> the tactfulness and the qualities of moderation of those honored to be its
> representatives.[58]

The internationalism Bellegarde professed and justified in the realm of law, and in economic cooperation for development, existed as well in the areas of commerce and finance. Writing in 1930, he had agreed with Elemer Hantos, professor at the University of Budapest, that the term *world economy* described the sum of all national economic activities, their dependence on each other, and the relationship that directed such activities. Because the peace of the world depends heavily upon the principles from which economic policies are derived, he believed that it becomes "necessary to attempt its organization according to natural laws which have governed within each state the organization of national economies through the collaboration of the citizens in private enterprises and in public services."[59]

These principles of economic organization had been criticized, especially for their reliance for development on artificially high tariffs. Hence in a paper for the American Academy of Political and Social Sciences (AAPSS) Bellegarde wrote in 1930:

> The very great differences in the conditions of labor and of production in the different countries, serving as pretext for protectionist tendencies, have created and maintained a system of competition which placed an obstacle in the way of the free circulation of goods and hinders the realization of a perfect equilibrium between production and consumption.
>
> For this system of competition, which has given birth to a race for high tariffs just as dangerous as the race for armaments, it is necessary to substitute a system of cooperation which permits, in the first instance, giving to the circulation of merchandise in the world the most rational and just foundations.[60]

Dantès Bellegarde's ideas on economic policy did not appreciably differ from the classical concepts of free trade. They were elaborated from the principles of the forgoing quotation, internationally and domestically. He took great care, nonetheless, to differentiate what he defined as conditions of economic imperialism from those conditions that would allow for prosperity for both partners. In 1930 he attributed economic imperialism solely to the United States, which, because of the weakened position of other Western powers following World War I, had become the principal beneficiary of that war.[61] The United States, he argued, had already imposed its will on Latin America and subjugated European economic life. But Bellegarde warned that prosperity also had its costs. The stock market crash of 1929, he said was a consequence of credit inflation and overproduction in the presence of saturated domestic consumption. He explained the United States' situation as follows:

> The economic and financial policies applied in the United States have led to an accumulation of enormous capital, the total of which cannot be used in the country itself, and to a massive production, superior to

the needs of national consumption, which, due to the fear of unemployment, is not permitted to slow down. *From this comes the absolute necessity for the United States to find outlets for her surplus capital and production.*[62]

Because of this American necessity to find outlets for its economic production, weaker states, he wrote, must constantly stand watch to see that economic expansion by creditor nations does not degenerate into territorial expansion at their expense. Since credit and confidence are etymologically synonymous, he said, the latter must be cultivated assiduously to see that the former is made effective as an instrument for economic development. There are no alteratives.[63] Thus, in the same paper for the AAPSS, he wrote:

But the borrower should also have confidence in his creditor; confidence that his creditor has no concealed thought of conquest, of violent seizure of his goods, his liberty, or his rights; confidence that the money offered him is not a limed trap where he risks losing all his feathers and even his life.[64]

For Bellegarde, it was a forgone conclusion that the trust he described had not been established between creditor and debtor in international relations. It could not be otherwise, for President Calvin Coolidge had declared in 1928 that "the person and the property of an American citizen being a part of the general domain of the nation even if abroad, the duty of the government is to insure his safety and to follow him wherever he is."[65]

Shortly before, in 1927, as a means to create goodwill, Commerce Secretary Herbert Hoover had suggested at the Third Pan-American Commercial Conference that no loans be made for unproductive or military reasons. The Department of State disavowed Hoover's opinion, however, saying that it was not in accord with United States Latin American policy as stated by Secretary of State Frank B. Kellogg.[66]

The Coolidge and Kellogg statements left Latin Americans continuing to fear "the shadow of a dreadnought behind each Yankee dollar," said Bellegarde.[67] Fear was indeed a most dangerous national emotion, he wrote, paraphrasing a statement made by President Hoover. But, he added, "this uncertainty cannot be cut short . . . unless a formula of non-intervention is adopted which leaves no place for any misunderstanding and becomes a positive rule of [inter] American international law."[68]

Trade with France and French commercial activity in Haiti, Bellegarde thought, had never produced as stormy a relationship as that which had existed over time between the United States and Haiti. For this reason, despite some American pressures against them, Haitian loans had been made in France in 1870, 1896, and 1910 through the French private sector.[69] In his *Dessalines a parlé*, Bellegarde expressed his feelings on the amicable relations that had always existed between France and Haiti:

> Our economic relations with France, as much as our intellectual intercourse, have contributed to make more intimate the *rapprochement* that exists between the Haitian and the French peoples. If— abstraction made of the bonds created by common blood, language, religion and mores—a brutal utilitarianism established a scale of sympathies based on commercial statistics, it is to France, again, that our affection would go. . . . it is roughly sixty-six percent of love that we would owe France.[70]

Bellegarde was persuaded that "true" businessmen in the United States and Western Europe were opposed to military interventions in Haiti as elsewhere, and believed that a strong economic production would give the Haitians their previously elusive place in the world.[71] The foreign businessmen residing in Haiti, he further contended, should be incorporated as full participants into the administration of the smallest unit of rural government in order to pursue actions leading to progress and civilization.[72] This latter statement was a commentary on the organizational skills of the foreigners as much as a recognition of their nations' advanced status. Thus, he wrote:

> What we lack, what we have always lacked, is organization. Progressive forces exist in Haiti, but they tend to be lost and go wasted because of the lack of coordination. The elements of civilized life are scattered; a powerful will must bring them to be harnessed and welded into an indissoluble association. Efforts have been made in the past and are being undertaken every day to adapt our national life to the requirements of a civilized existence; they remain ineffective because the efforts are intermittent and dispersed.[73]

To attempt such a basic organization, Bellegarde pondered topics as varied as a rural code, import-export policies, customs policies, agricultural diversification and self-sufficiency, fisheries, rural cooperatives, financing and credit, nutrition, housing, rural and vocational education.[74] In his mind, all these questions were interrelated and he emphasized this interrelationship when he presented his perspectives and solutions in speeches and lectures to governmental bodies or to private associations. He made proposals and argued with the chief executive, with his peers at cabinet meetings, and at sessions of the Council of State, never losing sight of his goals and of the realizable.

He deliberately chose an incremental, reformist policy that he justified by saying "let us beware of too ambitious undertakings. Let us go to the most urgent and the most realizable. . . . Before undertaking a project, let us ask ourselves what it will give in social results."[75]

Bellegarde proposed to go beyond providing housing for the poor; to further the process of civilization, he suggested instead that villages be established around a nucleus formed by the church, the school, and the clinic. In so proposing he was deliberately moving away from the existing patterns of Haitian rural settlements. The funding for such development would be furnished, he suggested, by a consortium of local communal sources, the central administration, and, particularly, by private industry.[76]

As early as 1907 Bellegarde had enunciated the tenets that would later link the various facets of his thought. "I believe," he wrote, "in the possibility of reform, outside politics, through private initiative."[77] This belief in reform by private enterprise was for him an article of faith. But this belief, as he realized, incurred twin difficulties, those of increasing, and at the same time of providing, an equitable distribution of wealth between the two forces of production, labor and capital.[78] On this point, he concluded: "Poverty is an economic phenomenon. It must be combated by economic measures. But these measures to be efficacious will require first the realization of moral and political improvements."[79] By this statement he meant governmental reform rather than structural change of a revolutionary nature.

Government and Education in Society

The government of any country amasses strong powers, and these powers seem to increase over time. Within the area of commerce and trade, the function of government, according to Bellegarde, was to disseminate information.[80] He added that "the government must become the coordinator of these [progressive] efforts, the powerful will that connects the scattered elements and directs the national forces that struggle against one another and otherwise are wasted, toward a precise ideal of civilization."[81]

Governmental economic policies, by their very nature, become social policy, he argued, not so much in their results as in the ideal that fostered them in the first place.[82]

In 1928, Bellegarde thought that while diplomatic representation answered a need for moral profit internationally and that Haiti had benefited by sending abroad brilliant envoys, economic considerations had made this function a thing of the past. Diplomacy, he argued, could not be at the service of industry and of commercial expansion. Commercial accords abroad and adequate domestic legislation could well replace the old emphasis on treaties of yesteryear.[83] The government, he wrote, must presently establish an export policy, more rational than what exists.

Pursuing his thought on the matter, Bellegarde had written in 1925 that the primary task of government is technical in nature and could be summarized within two broad categories. First, it must seek to elevate the moral and material standard of the nation through education and by sensible policies in the areas of nutrition, housing, and hygiene. Second, it must seek to create the proper climate for economic development through an increase in productivity, must search for advantageous markets abroad, and must insure an "exact distribution of profit" in accordance with the relative contributions of those in the ranks of capital and labor who have brought increased wealth to the nation.[84] In conclusion, he had added, "the government must assume the direction of the social evolution of the Haitian people, taking the necessary initiative to hasten that evolution, encouraging the private efforts which also tend toward that direction."[85]

The system of government he extolled was based on the principles of liberalism. This liberal concept was defined by Bellegarde as "a government within the law, and freedom, and honest management of public affairs, controlled by the organs to which the Constitution has assigned this necessary function."[86] The government must be a collaboration, first of the people who have ultimate control through its elected representatives, second, of the cabinet officers who must have primary responsibility in their departments in contrast to the customary practice of presidential responsibility.[87]

This proposed power and responsibility delegation to be entrusted to cabinet members (reminiscent of the French parliamentary system), accompanied by a parallel decrease of presidential power and prerogative, fitted two of Bellegarde's basic political concepts for government reform: decentralization of power and geographic decentralization, based on individual responsibility.

The first of these, decentralization of power, must be accomplished at all levels of the administration. Within the executive branch, it meant a sharing of the task in a mood of collaboration rather than one of collective leadership. Decentralization of power, he believed, was also needed among the three branches of government: legislative, executive, and judicial. As a member of one of the branches, an individual would relinquish all rights and functions he or she might have in the two other branches.[88] This decentralization, which Bellegarde considered essential to a democratic system, should also occur in provincial administration, allowing a greater role to locally elected officeholders.[89]

Secondly, in accordance with the concept of individual responsibility, the presidency not only required that an occupant should be humble enough to realize his own human frailty, but also that he would accept advice, delegate power, and obey the laws even more strenuously than any other citizen in his role as an exemplar.[90] Similarly, individual responsibility should be acknowledged in international situations, and the perpetrators of crimes against humanity, as Bellegarde was later to argue (1951), should be brought to trial.

At the Fourth Consultative Reunion of Foreign Ministers of the Americas, held in March and April 1951, in Washington, Bellegarde submitted a resolution expressing this concept of individual responsibility. Near the end of his life (1962) he wrote about it as follows:

> The project of Resolution presented by Haiti had to our eyes an exceptional significance, because it posited, simultaneously to the responsibility of states, the principles of the individual responsibility of government leaders and other public officials in the launching of war on the conduct of hostilities. This project demanded the application of penal sanctions by specialized institutions against persons that would be war criminals and had inflicted violence or torture upon defenseless populations.[91]

Dantès Bellegarde asserted that Communist Chinese and North Korean crimes made the adoption of his resolution imperative; he argued that if the sanctions he advocated had existed before Hitler's rise to power, the world's civilized powers would have had a mandate to intervene collectively in Germany. But he failed to persuade other delegations when objections were raised regarding the appropriateness of the resolution, although the meeting had been called to deal with the emergency created by the Korean conflict.[92]

Still, within the framework of his thought on individual action and responsibility, Bellegarde had an overall vision of a society in which Haitians had the duty to become individually wealthy. The government was an associate rather than an "adjunct" of private enterprise, having as its main function that of defining social goals. This vision left no room for a dictatorship of either the Left or the Right.

Personal dictatorships, he believed, had been prevalent throughout the course of Haitian history and had resulted in little actual economic and political progress. On the other hand, a proletarian dictatorship—organized by which individual, Bellegarde asked theoretically—would simply ignore the peasantry's strong individualism that had fortunately developed in Haiti, despite ancestral African attitudes.[93]

The concept of a true collective leadership had no meaning to Bellegarde. No, he had said in 1926, communism can only be a game devised by pure intellectuals divorced from Haitian realities. Academic discussions about governmental systems must not ignore Haiti's social, political, economic, and ethnic realities.[94] Interestingly enough, the position in this statement was a reproach made against Bellegarde; the realities of Haitian life were seen very differently by the younger intellectuals than they were by Bellegarde.

For Bellegarde, the Haitian social reality had been inherently democratic. "Slavery," he wrote, "in passing its level on all foreheads had achieved equality in stupor."[95] Abstraction had been made of the *affranchis'* privileged social and economic position. While this was a democracy of sorts, it had had nonetheless a negative base. The needed innovation, according to Bellegarde, was to introduce liberalism into this preexisting social democracy, making it second nature in the leadership, in the governmental apparatus, and finally in the populace, through an education carried on by the appropriate institutions.

For Bellegarde, the Haitian problem could be analyzed as one resulting from superimposing modern structures and concepts upon a community whose institutions and whose very foundations impeded their workability.[96] This was an open admission of the force of African tradition in Haitian life. It was an admission that seemed to contradict Bellegarde's vision of Haitian social democracy established through slavery, a process that would have had the effect of making Haitians "more malleable." But Bellegarde had seemed aware of the reality hidden behind Haiti's modern political structures when he wrote in 1948:

The organization created by the Constitution does not correspond entirely to reality, public mores do not entertain around constitutional principles a sufficient atmosphere of reverence. The interplay of institutions is not . . .as perfect as one would have desired. The machinery creaks, its springs screech, and the principles . . . emerge badly cracked.[97]

Even earlier, in 1906, Bellegarde had outlined his thinking about the discrepancy between objective reality and structures in Haitian society. Reality, transitory in any case, should be transcended, he urged, by the "suggestion of an ideal." This ideal, though perhaps unattainable, he thought, was nonetheless valid. This ideal was liberal democracy.[98]

The factors limiting the application of the democratic ideal to Haiti were rooted in colonial history. They also arose from the thirst for power of political opportunists who were interested in wealth acquired at public expense in the bureaucracy. From these factors came the chaotic struggle for power, countless revolutions, the endless strife to which the government should apply a remedy. As Bellegarde wrote, "the government will have to undertake a systematic policy of domestic peace based, not on the brutal force of bayonets, but on the consent of hearts and on willful adherence."[99] This analysis led him to consider the realm of education as being best equipped to transform society.

Education, Bellegarde believed, had a double purpose. It is the purveyor of essential industrial skills and helped one to transcend his or her origins. In a worldwide intellectual atmosphere that was optimistic about the powers of human transcendence, and in a Latin America anxious to seize any opportunity to prove and to improve itself, it was not surprising to see Bellegarde adopt such a neo-Lamarckian attitude, basing both the social problem and its solution upon the effects of an environment defined historically within an evolutionary framework.

In a modern world that celebrated material progress as an indication of social advance and the basis of spiritual progress, American pragmatism held some attraction for Bellegarde. He seemed to have accepted John Dewey's educational philosophy in its broad lines. Pragmatism could not, however, completely replace the precious inherited French rational tradition that culminated in Henri Bergson's revised evolutionary thought. It is this pattern of thought that led Dantès Bellegarde to an *"éclectisme éducationel."*[100]

The choice for him was clear. Material and spiritual progress must go hand in hand to be valid and lasting, even at the risk of displeasing aristocratic feelings in Haiti, he said, in obvious reference to the "anti-vocational" education bias of the Haitian upper class. Baudelaire had celebrated putrefaction in his poem "Une charogne." At the risk of being proclaimed a *"sale bourgeois"* who opposed literature, Bellegarde exclaimed: "Pity we do not have a Baudelaire or a Goya to sing and to paint these carrions! But they must disappear from Haitian life,"[101] even if literature suffers from it.

In the same breath, however, he defended his conception of a *"haute culture"* that does not merely coexist with material progress, but reaches ever-increasing heights from the symbiosis of the two realities. A synthesis occurs, and from it emerges a condition that Bellegarde defined as moral and spiritual growth. He summarized his point of view as follows:

> One sees war declared upon *haute culture.* . . . Will Haiti truly enter the path of progress when one will have renounced all altruistic occupations, and when poetry, music, and all the arts will have been banished? This proscription, [were it to occur] is it really the necessary precondition to our evolution; and art, would it not know how to co-exist here with manual labor?[102]

Dantès Bellegarde found numerous occasions to laud North American pragmatism and British utilitarianism, which, he said, molded strong societies upon the basis of a strong individualism, thus leading to collective action imbued with purpose and organization. English socialism, he said, had not needed such brilliant theoreticians as Karl Marx, Jean Jaurès, and Jules Guesde, but yet had been capable of great practical social achievements: "This practical aspect of socialism in Australia is also the distinctive characteristic of English socialism which tends to be more and more some kind of utilitarianism or even an opportunistic collectivism."[103]

Bellegarde's assessment of the bourgeois origin and "individualistic" emphasis in the development of English socialism, as distinguished from French and German socialism, which was both more collective and more radical, was in basic agreement with such analyses in the field of sociology as that of Alvin W. Gouldner in his *The Coming Crisis in Western Sociology.*[104]

But it was primarily the British sense of national unity and purpose, of a social solidarity "that moves mountains," rather than any socialistic scheme, that Bellegarde hoped to impart to Haitians. The achievement of this purpose, he argued, entailed a fundamental mental transformation to be accomplished through the educational process. This position led him to differentiate between *"instruction"* and *education* as follows:

> Each time one looks to means of uplifting the rural masses in Haiti, one considers the question from the angle of *instruction*. The problem goes deeper; it is a veritable social transformation that must be effected through the moral and economic reeducation of our countryside populations.[105]

Indeed, if "the fatherland is a continuous creation,"[106] as Bellegarde asserted, each generation adding its creative effort to the *grandeur* of the nation, such progress is achieved only through the individual. Thus, education in its broadest sense, rather than *instruction*, must prevail. Based on the historic formation of society, education must be tailored specifically to meet the challenge of upgrading that society, without falling into an excessive educational nationalism that might tend to subjugate the individual to his or her society, or to erect a spiritual autarchy.

Still, according to Bellegarde, the end result of all education is to instill the realization of one's place in creation, a realization of the solidarity that must unite the individual to others and to all things, to prepare man for the superior concerns postulated by civilization, and to prepare him to meet his obligations to himself, his family, his fatherland, humanity, and God.[107] Pursuing this idea he further specified:

> The problem of education . . . is all at once a moral, social, and economic problem. Its social and economic character does not overshadow the fact that it exercises its beneficial action upon society only indirectly, since it has as its subject the individual. To educate the individual is to act on his body, his soul, his mind, his will by the methods pedagogy, in perpetual progress, has demonstrated to be the best in the present state of the biological and psychological sciences that serve as auxiliaries to the science of education. The objective of the educational system of a given country must be the formation of an individual, man or woman, physically vigorous, with a clear intelligence, a limpid heart and of energetic will, adapted to his milieu, but capable when need be to dominate it in order to modify it. The role of education will be then, to place the child, whatever his origins, his race, or his religion, in a position to utilize his aptitudes for himself and for the betterment of the group to which he

belongs, making of him an instrument of individual progress and of collective improvement.[108]

This educational formula called for the educational system to allow a society to "perpetuate itself while ameliorating itself."[109] These goals may be interpreted variously. On the one hand, they show explicitly, the idea of a continuation of historic realities, that of a national entity deserving and struggling to survive. On the other hand, they express the belief that progress occurs at an accelerating rate and that a society that remained stationary would surely invite destruction by stronger and more energetic states.

Both these viewpoints are united in the concept of the quest for national survival. The belief also remains that although might does not make right, might is likely to be an expression of right, springing as it were from the moral and spiritual forces of individuals living in an energetic national community. Conversely, any congenital weakness shown by a nation may well arise from the deficiencies and weaknesses of the individuals that constitute it. Lethargic nations are inviting disaster (wrought by powerful states) in Bellegarde's formulation of Spencer's "survival of the fittest."[110] Individualizing guilt and responsibility at the individual's or the nation's level absolved the system itself of any wrongdoing or exploitation in this classic formulation of (consensus) mainstream Euro-American social philosophy.

Bellegarde believed that the Western world, with the superior power it had acquired through relinquishing the individual to his or her own custody, its superior organization, its skills, and its spirit, was destined to rule the world. Thus, the Republic of Haiti was fortunate to have had in its colonial heritage the instruments of the French language and Christianity. Haiti, he believed, must follow the lead these instruments provided. Humankind, in his view, formed a syncretic whole whose parts contributed to the general health. As late as 1959 according to Bellegarde, who had not abandoned the organic analogies of the past century, social progress was the result of individual progress. He went on to say:

In a specific community, general progress will result from the progress accomplished by individuals that form it. In the international society, progress will be the results accomplished by the ensemble of nations that constitute it. To develop maximally all the forces of one's nation— moral, intellectual, economic forces—is to work for the progress and the welfare of humanity in its entirety."[111]

Never should the state substitute its efforts for those that should be forthcoming from individual citizens. The state itself should not become wealthy at the expense of its citizenry, but should draw its strength from the specific realizations and the achievements that its citizens produce. The interests of the community must harmonize with those of the individuals comprising it.[112]

Bellegarde pursued this thought further, stating that "in a country where the individual refuses to become the artisan of his own happiness, and appeals to the State for all decisions, no progress is possible."[113] Similarly, the state must not interfere with the economic and financial endeavors of its most energetic citizens, who provide a gauge of general societal health. In these views Bellegarde was well within the orthodoxy of neo-positivistic thought.

But in recognition of the special factors, discussed earlier, that had negatively influenced Haitian social evolution, Bellegarde admitted that the government was in a special position that enabled it to create a favorable environment, a *cadre*, a framework, or a stage upon which the action takes place.[114] The modern state, he declared, has an essential duty to work for the complete development of the individual within society.

In its search for democracy, in which the individual truly flourishes, the state must work to favor public health. It must also organize an educational system based on the principles of worldwide solidarity, morality, and freedom—a system in which all will benefit according to their merits and their gifts, drawing upon the vast reservoir of literary, artistic, scientific, and technological progress realized everywhere in the world, and to which all humans are heirs.[115]

The tasks Bellegarde thus established for the state, those of modernizing a backward society, are also those of such other institutions as the Church. The latter must not be hampered by the state, "since the Church, holder of Christian truth, is the most complete illustration of a democratic society founded on order, hierarchy, virtue, and merit." Furthermore, the universality of the Church has assured humankind that morality would not be submitted to man's caprice, and Church rule expresses "an ideal universal form for human behavior, expressed in valid principles for all normal and healthy thought."[116]

Paraphrasing the French sociologist and neo-positivist Emile Durkheim, Bellegarde wrote that the high human values that create civilization are incarnated in Christianity.[117] Religion and education are said to have the same goal: "The formation of individual conscience."[118] Whether or not this goal could be achieved through Christianity's worldwide standardization of morality, Bellegarde did not say. But what he did say is that not even a scholar like Price-Mars had preconized Vodou over Christianity, since the latter represented a superior stage in the evolution of religious thought and practices.[119]

Yet, Bellegarde recognized a certain amount of contradiction in his position. He admitted some difficulties concerning the full acceptance of the Christian ideal in Haiti—without giving any further details—agreeing with George Galloway, that "the ethnic element is of fundamental importance in determining the quality of a religion."[120] Europe itself, Bellegarde indicated, had often fallen prey to waves of mysticism without incurring the charge of barbarism. But Haiti often met with such criticism, unjustly he felt, from European and North American writers.[121]

Under pressure from recent ethnological studies that started in the 1930s under the inspiration of Price-Mars, Bellegarde wrote that Vodou had the making of an embryonic religion, since it had a belief system and priestly functions carried out by men and women alike, both sexes being equal. Yet, he concluded, Vodou is hopelessly primitive. It consists mostly of entertainment and drunken orgies for its adherents.[122]

Dantès Bellegarde, it must be noted, seems never to have acquired a firsthand knowledge of the cult—strange as it may seem in the Haitian milieu—but relied heavily on other Vodouphobes such as Dr. Léon Audain and Georges Sylvain for his assessments. And while Bellegarde declared that Vodou had been a significant force in the struggle for independence because its services had been a pretext for political gatherings, he never explained why it had degenerated into drunken orgies after independence was won, or why the Haitian intelligentsia and ruling class had feared its political significance over the masses for over two centuries.

The phobia against Vodou had culminated in nationwide persecutions. These were led by the Haitian bourgeoisie, the Roman Catholic establishment, and the United States military authorities in the 1920s, 1930s, and 1940s. Yet Vodou had helped maintain the antislavery fervor in 1804 and, under the United States occupation of the country, it may have symbolized further resistance to American cultural and political intrusion. Incorporating in its pantheon the leaders of national independence, the cult has remained a cultural force, nationalistic in its outlook, during the entire span of Haitian national existence.[123]

Of Roman Catholicism's role, Dantès Bellegarde had no doubts. Politics and religion were to reinforce each other positively; this aim could be accomplished through policy decisions, policy being the tangible arm of ideology. In this connection he complained in 1948:

What would have become of the Haitian community—born from the clash of weaponry and the incendiary torch of stupefying slavery—if it had not immediately adopted the norms of Christian civilization? It is to this Christian civilization that Haiti owes, without any possible doubts, the progress it has made in the midst of the tumultuous vicissitudes of its national existence and [it is this] which has allowed Haiti to maintain its rank with dignity and oftentime brilliance, in the concert of civilized nations.[124]

The fact that at least 90 percent of the Haitian population probably practice Vodou, or that up to the very year of Bellegarde's death in 1966 the Roman Catholic hierarchy consisted largely of French and North American bishops, and that the lower echelon of the priesthood was mostly French, Canadian, Belgian, and North American, never seemed to have impressed Bellegarde negatively. He believed that these priests and nuns, who had assumed a major role in "national" education since 1862, had selflessly accepted the *sacrifice* of incorporating themselves into Haitian life. Their love for humanity, he believed, and their devotion alone had made them *persist* in their civilizing mission.[125]

Haiti had had its anticlericalism, but it did not hold a monopoly on it, Bellegarde wrote apologetically. France had suffered from it as well. The French Revolution of 1789 and its Haitian "daughter" had been strongly anticlerical. But the dangers of that doctrine were relatively higher in Haiti because of the country's large mass of unassimilated Negroes scarcely a few generations removed from the African continent. "Will there be Haitians despising their race sufficiently to believe themselves incapable of elevation to these lofty [Christian] heights?"[126] He had turned the argument on its head, not comprehending that to "despise the race" could have also meant wanting its wholesale conversion to Christianity in order for it to join the world. Bellegarde then added: "Religion has an extremely dangerous category of adversaries. . . . They have read Freud! They sneer with an air of grotesque superiority at the piety of a Pasteur, or at the conversion [*sic*] of a Henri Bergson."[127]

Dantès Bellegarde never "practiced" his Catholic faith. In view of what he said about it, therefore, it becomes increasingly clear that Bellegarde's defense of Christianity was not based simply on religious criteria, but was motivated by the "universal humanism" it seemed to provide, which, he believed, transcended national and racial boundaries.

Individualism and the Family

Any progress, Bellegarde wrote in his *Haiti et ses problèmes*, is spearheaded by the priest, the teacher, the agronomist, the doctor.[128] These individuals, he wrote in *Histoire du peuple haitien*, are the symbols of society's final form; they represent an elite. Freedom, having liberated individual energies and allowed them to flourish, has evolved the constitutive elements from which to base an elite.[129] Based solely on merit and on achievement, this elite is the guarantor of democracy. In his *Pour une Haiti heureuse*, Dantès Bellegarde explained his concept of the elite in a democracy:

> There is no elite whose recruiting docs not go through a rigorous law of selection. If this recruitment is made according to conventions or arbitrary prejudices, one finds oneself in the presence of an artificial grouping—a caste or a mandarinate—that exists without contact with the populace, living a fictitious life. Such a group, instead of being the blossom of society, nourished by its healthy sap, becomes a parasitic growth that weakens the body on which it lives. In a democracy, the elite must rise from all ranks of society and be born from the deepest roots of the nation, since it is in the vast reservoir of strength and of energy that it will seek the renewal that assures it eternal youth.[130]

This seemed a perfect defense for the renewal and the self-perpetuation of the bourgeoisie, in line with Graña's assertion that the bourgeoisie was the first ruling class in history whose values and status could be acquired through co-option.[131]

The powers of transcendence that would lead the individual out of bestiality were found, according to Dantès Bellegarde, in patriotism and in religion. In this connection, he stated that "the sentiment for the fatherland remains, with religion, the source of all heroisms" (*le sentiment de la patrie demeure, avec la religion, la source de tous les héroismes*).[132] For Bellegarde and liberal thought in general both the paradox between nationalism and universalism and the contradiction between democracy and elitism remained intact. Bourgeois liberalism had fostered pride in national institutions, even among the lower classes, but it was also the proponent of universal values[133] and ever-widening economic interests on a worldwide scale.

At the Congrès de Philosophie held in Port-au-Prince in 1944, under the joint leadership of Jacques Maritain and President Elie Lescot,

Bellegarde had candidly alluded in a simulated conversation, to the frustrations faced by educated Haitians abroad, due to the backwardness of their countrymen:

You are not Haitian yourself? You possess a superior culture.
Yes, we are pure Haitians, and it is through education [*culture*] alone that we differ from our country brothers. . . . We have succeeded in elevating ourselves to the loftiest peaks of human culture. . . . This is why we must seek to spread learning and a *humanistic* education to the entire Haitian people in order to elevate it to the level we have ourselves reached.[134]

As time went by, Bellegarde's ideological definition of what constituted Christian civilization, a term which he used interchangeably with Western culture, became narrower and seemingly more intolerant. Worldwide political upheavals in the wake of the Great Depression (1930) and following two world wars, and Haitian social upheavals brought on in part by the racialist policies under United States occupation (1915–34), seemed to be taking the nation toward the left, away from the course Bellegarde had envisioned.

In an article entitled "Harbingers of Communism," printed in the conservative Roman Catholic daily *La Phalange* in 1939, Dantès Bellegarde launched an attack against communism, charging that it was against the best interests of Christian civilization and scarcely a Western ideology, "being Russian [*sic*]." He accepted Wladimir Weidle's assessment of the Revolution of 1917, that revolutionaries were inviting soldiers to desert at the height of the war, that peasants were being advised to seize property without awaiting government permission to do so, and that workers and "semi-intellectuals" were being called upon to massacre and, (still citing Weidle) to

burn lordly mansions together with their owners, their antique furniture and their libraries, to manifest a ferocious hatred against all which was not "of the masses" . . . The revolution was accomplished, not solely against capital and the bourgeoisie, but *against elites in general.* . . . The natural ally of the people in this revolution was the semi-elite to which was attached a significant number of workers, more alert and educated than most of their peers.[135]

At the time when Church, clerics, and elites in general, as well as the economic supremacy of the bourgeoisie, were being questioned in Haiti, Bellegarde's position became more entrenched, unbending, and his expression more strident. In two articles published in 1947, he opposed to the "dark harbingers" of discord the pristine thought of Henry David Thoreau, who had admonished leaders to "love virtue, and the people will be virtuous. The virtues of a common man are like the blades of grass. When wind blows, the grass bends."[136] It is the same Thoreau, he said, who had also written, "the ideal of God, the ideal of the Fatherland, the ideal of the Family are the three cornerstones of the collective conscience."[137] Dantès Bellegarde fully endorsed these concepts of Thoreau.

Of the symmetrical trinity to which Bellegarde referred, religion and patriotism and the point at which they intersect in providing society a moral armature have been discussed.[138] The third facet is that of the family and its role as the organic cell of Bellegarde's (and Thoreau's) three-tiered analysis.

In a lecture presented early in this century, probably in the year 1906, Dantès Bellegarde expressed the desire to "exalt the Haitian woman." It was his duty, he said, because the woman was the nation incarnate. Her fate was tied to the future of society, of which "her husband and children" were the nucleus. In her task as mother and spouse, the Haitian woman formed the citizens of future generations. She was responsible for the development of that "internal music" that springs from the harmonization of the needs of the body, the soul, and the heart. As the "queen of the hearth," she oversaw the apprenticeship required of individuals for good citizenship. She had also been the creator of societal mores and values, probably as much as men Bellegarde quickly added, and this creative function imposed upon her certain duties. He concluded that one easily judged the level of a civilization by the place a woman occupied in the family. Auguste Comte would have approved.

Love is the cornerstone of civilized existence, wrote Bellegarde. It has its foundation in the family structure, from whence it grows, ultimately encompassing the entire society. Bellegarde added: "Love is really possible only among equals. Two creatures that so melt in each other until they form only one, can only be associates to a common enterprise. Equality and collaboration, such are the traits of conjugal union in Haiti."[139] At that time, there were no public secondary schools open to women in Haiti, they were disenfranchised politically, and suffered various kinds of discrimination under the [Napoleonic] Haitian legal code.

On later occasions, Dantès Bellegarde had the opportunity to amend and expand his thoughts on the role of women as he himself progressed from the view of women as so many Clothilde de Vaux on pedestals,[140] to a concept of woman's role in urgent schemes for national development.

Influenced by his five daughters perhaps as much as they were influenced by him—two were founding members of an embryonic Haitian woman's movement in the 1930s—Bellegarde came to argue for an equal position for men and women, taking note of physiological differences. Perhaps also because of personal circumstances, as we have seen in Chapter 3,[141] he had never doubted that women could rival men in all fields.[142] But only through comprehensive education could women come to understand and exercise their *proper* role in the family and in the nation. Bellegarde refined his position in 1938 in *La Nation haitienne:*

> There are strong women, of energetic will, clear intelligence, capable of beneficent action. Why should legal constraints hamper their activity? Of course, these women are not numerous, but how many men of this caliber exist? While men, even when immoral, weak, and incompetent, find open to them all doors, women, even when competent, find these doors tightly shut. Herein lies the injustice. Is it not absurd that the most honored mother, the shrewdest businesswomen, the most brilliant lawyer, the most expert pharmacist, the most competent teacher are judged unworthy of the vote, when the most stupid ostler . . . has the power . . . to decide . . . on the highest constitutional and economic questions?[143]

These lines were written in 1936. A constitutional assembly meeting in 1946 failed, however, to grant equal rights to women. Then in 1950, Dantès Bellegarde, president of a new constitutional assembly, made women's rights one of his primary concerns, basing his argument partly on the international agreements Haiti had signed. The nation had to legislate equal rights for women, he argued, lest it abdicate its status as a civilized nation.[144]

Throughout the debates, Dantès Bellegarde could hardly resist indulging in sarcasm against those younger delegates who opposed suffrage for women but in the end voted for a compromise resolution that withheld such suffrage until the presidential election of 1956. Bellegarde lectured his colleagues in these words:

Be serious gentlemen, be sincere, be frank. Will you dare admit that
you refuse to grant women their voting rights because you think them
inferior to yourselves? . . . Well let us see what these superior men have
done to our country. The United States occupation . . . are women
responsible for its occurrence? All the thievery, all the assassinations,
all the crimes which have been committed throughout our history and
which have unfortunately hindered the moral and economic progress
of our people, were they perpetrated by women? No, it is men, these
men whose names are in all memories. And it is men you want to give
to our women as civics teachers! . . . What a mockery! What is needed,
on the contrary, is the introduction to the direction and the management of public affairs of this feminine element which has remained
healthy in its ensemble, and which represents in the family and in the
work fields a primordial factor in the social evolution of our people.[145]

Bellegarde had never deviated from his political and social objectives.
Politics, as he understood it, had been the reason for the nation's ills. Politics
meant intrigue, gossip, informing on each other, flattery, spoils of public
positions, duplicity, insincerity. Whereas it should have been education,
health care, housing, hygiene, nutrition, the struggle against superstition,
and, he believed, "in this domain, the action of woman is sovereign."[146]

His individualism was rooted in his own experience. How else could
he explain his achievements and his successes, contrasting so sharply with
his "humble" origins? The reputation he acquired in Haiti for vanity is partially explained by the pride he felt in being an inspiration for others.[147]
Faced with racial theories that would deny the possibility of progress for
Haiti, nineteenth-century Haitians had to prove themselves individually in
order to transcend the limits of their society and the limits imposed upon
that society by international conditions. Thus, Bellegarde wrote in *Pour une
Haiti heureuse* in 1927:

The uncultivated man has nothing to communicate to others. His
mind remains closed like a cold prison. Intelligence is a flame. The
more vivacious it is, the better it shines. The man who carries within
himself a beautiful dream does not feel satisfied until he has commu-
nicated it through speech or in a book. The insensitive is condemned
to live alone, without impulse, without enthusiasm. He can neither
enjoy with another, nor suffer with another. The man who has made

his heart loving and helping all, multiplies his soul. . . . His conscience is the vibrant and sonorous chamber where all suffering and joys echo. The human being without will is perhaps incapable of wrongdoing, but he is even more incapable of right. Only the energetic man works for societal well-being: useful to himself, he can be useful to others.[148]

The quotation above reveals much of Bellegarde's frame of mind through the juxtaposition of ideas he makes, and through the terms he made equivalent in meaning; it explains him even more as a social thinker, not in terms of a disciplined social scientist searching out truths methodically, but as a sensitive soul whose words, were at times more poetic than accurate. In the first place, the cultivated person develops beautiful dreams that he/she yearns to transmit to others. The uncultivated person lacks intelligence and is insensitive to the plight of others. He or she is without a conscience and without a will. In the second place, the man or woman of action is the logical extension of the woman or man of thought who creates the conditions for societal transformation through his/her own transformation in a constant deployment of energy and exercise of will.

All social endeavor, for Bellegarde, had as its object, not the transformation of humankind, but the transformation of the individual. The person, thus, became both the means and the goal of social evolution. That person, then, had to be reformed so that the result of a proud science, which had increased its power over the universe, did not lead to a catastrophe. Like Bergson, whom he quoted to that effect, Bellegarde believed that an effort for spiritual progress and toward the brotherhood of souls must parallel that toward technological progress. The absence of such spiritual progress must lead ultimately to human destruction.[149] That destruction can be physical, as in the case of warfare, or moral, as in the collectivization of humanity.[150] In this latter vein, Bellegarde wrote in 1907:

> To await one's salvation from another but oneself, or to consume oneself in the apprehension of a catastrophe— which only our inaction can make inevitable—is the policy of a people that will die, more speedily perhaps because it will have pronounced its own death sentence.[151]

Within Christianity and the moral principles it proposes, Bellegarde had found the link he sought between the individual and the community. The ideal of love has within its component parts, he wrote, the ideas of respect and admiration, as well as the notions of self-respect, the quest for approval, the love of freedom, possessive love, and the capacity for empathy. All these dimensions, in all their complexities and when excited to the highest pitch, reflecting this "excitement" upon one another as would the facets of a prism, formed the psychic state of love. As described by Herbert Spencer, Bellegarde wrote, love realizes itself in the perfection of sentiment. But there remains something in personality impossible to analyze, said Bellegarde. This is "an individuality in which no one penetrates. But in love, as is presently the case, the barriers are overturned, the free use of someone's individuality is accorded us, and thus, love is satisfied in boundless activity."[152]

Rising from pure instinct, Bellegarde continued, human love travels an evolutionary path to mystical love. Between the two extremes lies the element of choice. In ordinary cases, love develops slowly, surreptitiously, as stalagmites are formed into solid masses from the quiet condensation of countless droplets.[153] The instinct that Schopenhauer and Hartmann have described as the "genius of the race," he noted, ensures an equilibrium to the child born from the fusion of two distinct individualities, "but how will the survival of the race be assured? By the production of persons capable of giving birth in turn to vigorous descendants [*rejetons*], in conformity with a perfect type of humanity," wrote Bellegarde.[154]

All attempts by philosophers to explain this subject of love are destined in advance to fail, wrote Bellegarde. Physiology grants us a partial key to understanding the phenomenon, but the complexities are too vast to unravel completely. Allowance must be made for passion, which is the rupture of equilibrium with its retinue of conflicting and violent sentiments. Bellegarde was led to add that "when love thus having become passion, finds satisfaction, it can either be quenched by satiety or fortify itself more and more. Imagination, from this standpoint exercises a most powerful action on the development of passion."[155]

Choice itself, limited by numerous circumstances and by influences stemming from the character, the imagination, and the vanity of the individuals, as well as from factors of imitation and fashion, is further attenuated by time and space, by temperaments reacting to societal mores, and by personal education achievement. Bellegarde went on to comment further on the social role of sentiment:

> You know what considerable place sentiment occupies in the human existence. One can say that it is that which gives its rhythm to life. The

idea, of itself, is inert. It becomes the motive for action only when it determines an effective state; it must become "sensitized" . . . to startle the human machine into movement. It is only at this moment that one can say truthfully that the idea becomes a force. Intelligence, in its totality—and to which I should add will power—does not express itself without sensitivity. Suppress sensation and sensitivity, and you will have rendered all intellectual operation impossible. . . .[156]

These ideas were expressed by Dantès Bellegarde in 1906. Over the span of six decades following their expression, he tried to incorporate them into his action and his life. He concluded the philosophical statement in his unpublished "Souvenirs de 1906," the most complete record he made of personal feelings, adding what he considered to be an axiomatic truth: "The more civilized the man, the more numerous are his sentiments of tenderness."[157] Unwittingly, Bellegarde then provided what must have been his image of himself:

Have you ever contemplated a sugarcane field? One would say an immense green sea, immobile. But the wind blows . . . the green mass undulates, the long stems bend . . . the movement of each is lost in the mass. But a few are higher: they strut proudly above rest. It is justly those stems that bend the lowest under the action of the gentle yet invisible winds.

In the human mass we are, those of us with a medium sensitivity, the stems that do get lost in the whole. Those who have elevated themselves highest have felt the brisk strength of the winds that pass over their souls: they have known the plenitude of life. They have cried, they have suffered, they have lived. Of those great impassioned ones of all times and from all nations much will be forgiven because they will have loved much.[158]

CHAPTER 6

PERSPECTIVES ON SOCIAL CONFLICT AND CULTURE

Uh homme sans espoir el conscient de l'être n'appartient plus à l'avenir.
—Albert Camus, *Le Mythe de sysyphe*

Dantès Bellegarde was a product of the nineteenth century. By birth he was a member of the petite bourgeoisie. At the time of his adolescence, twenty-six Haitian seaports, serviced by nine steamship companies, were open to foreign and domestic commerce; only one of these was under Haitian control. Ships from these ports linked Haiti to ports in the Caribbean, in Central and South America, in the United States, and in Western Europe, traveling on a regular basis.[1] Earlier, Haiti had signed the Universal Postal Convention (1880). A submarine telegraphic cable allowed for rapid international communication, but inland communications were not as well established. No domestic telegraph existed in the late 1800s, roads were nonexistent, except as horse trails and footpaths, and it was easier for wealthy inhabitants of Jéremie or Jacmel to sojourn to Paris than to reach Port-au-Prince. Provincial capitals were often on the same level as Port-au-Prince in their ease of contacts with Europe.[2]

During Dantès Bellegarde's youth, Haiti maintained more than fifty legations and consulates throughout the world. The Bureau of American Republics *Bulletin* states that all the Haitian diplomats spoke the language of the country to which they were accredited.[3] Significant Haitian foreign relations questions of the time included negotiations with the United States for an American naval station to be established at Môle Saint-Nicolas. There were also constant questions relating to the as yet unsettled land boundaries with the Dominican Republic, and claims by the United States, Germany, and the United Kingdom on behalf of their citizens concerning alleged losses during Haitian domestic turmoil. Internationally, Haitian policy was most cautious, as illustrated by this passage from an 1893 *Bulletin* of the Bureau of American Republics:

> It may be stated that, in the long run and in her own way, Haiti always met every financial obligation, and it is confessedly a fact that she has sometimes consented to pay and has paid claims which no great powers like France or Great Britain would have been expected to recognize. It is believed that she has taken this course in order to avoid what seemed at the moment like possible complications with foreign powers which, at times, as she has thought, have appeared to be only too ready to take advantage of her comparative isolation and weakness.[4]

In this connection, Dantès Bellegarde related with bitterness the story of the 1897 crisis between Haiti and Germany. In this case, two German gunboats, acting in support of the claim of a Germano-Haitian,[5] named Emile Luders, presented the Haitian government with an ultimatum. Within four hours, Haiti was to pay the sum of $20,000 (in U.S. dollars) to the businessman, was to promise that the latter could return freely to Haiti from where he had been deported, was to address a letter of apology to the Berlin government, and was to salute the German flag with a twenty-one-gun salute. These were Germany's nonnegotiable demands. Failure to meet these demands, according to the ultimatum, would result in the shelling of Port-au-Prince by German warships.[6]

After consultations with the diplomats accredited to Port-au-Prince, who refused to intervene on Haiti's behalf, the white flag of surrender was hoisted at the presidential palace. Bellegarde, then twenty, said that he hoped for death, unable to face this humiliation.[7]

German business interests in Haiti were on the ascendency throughout the latter years of the nineteenth century. They were prominent in whole-sale trade, in the service sector, in utilities, and in finance. By 1900, these German interests in Haiti surpassed those of the French who had had less home government support than had the Germans. German success was accounted for, to some extent, by the intermarriage of young German men with women of the Haitian aristocracy, thus adroitly circumventing Haitian laws against foreign ownership of real estate. They mingled freely with the country's elite with, surprisingly, few racial reservations.[8] But despite this flurry of activity, German investments in Haiti, Cuba, and the Dominican Republic as late as 1918 were only estimated at $1 million in U.S. dollars.

The period 1890 to 1915 was also pivotal for the expansion of financial activities by the United States in Haiti. United States colonial expansion was in full swing at that time in the Caribbean, Central America, and the Pacific. Except for Jamaica, which was under British control, American military control extended to all the Greater Antilles by 1916, ostensibly for the defense of the Panama Canal. By 1910, the United States controlled 60 percent of Haiti's import market, and by the end of the First World War, it was the dominant power in the Caribbean. Between 1857 and 1915, it would intervene twenty times in Haiti.[9] But while the Germans had intermarried with Haitians, the North Americans displayed an attitude of racial superiority and separation in Haiti.

In 1907 Dantès Bellegarde, had uttered this warning: "God is too far and the United States is too close."[10] The combination of United States military power and private American investments created an American economic hegemony in Haiti. In contradistinction, Levantine and Italian merchants, who as a group became important in commerce at the same period, because they did not benefit from "home government" support, did not present a direct threat to state security, although they weakened the national bourgeoisie. Small nation's capitalists never need be feared as much as those from more powerful nations.[11]

It was under these conditions that Dantès Bellegarde played out his role.

Nationality and Liberalism

Dantès Bellegarde's ideological positions were those of the Haitian bourgeoisie in general, so much so that he appears chiefly as a synthesizer of their views par excellence rather than as an original thinker. He faithfully reflected trends and attitudes already present, at least incipiently, in the ruling group. Aware of international reality, and of the dangers it reserved for small powers that would attempt an independent political course differing from that tolerated by world powers at the time, Bellegarde had concluded that Haiti's salvation lay in subordination to Western culture and to the economic interests of Western powers. Otherwise, he believed, Haiti ran the risk of being recolonized. With Haiti caught between the power play of adversary Western states that were moving to strengthen their hold on the world economy, Bellegarde was concerned about the implications of the concept of the center and the periphery in international relations. He was convinced that a truly independent course of development for Haiti was futile. To such development, he opposed his concept of "provinciality": Haiti's adherence to Christianity and to the "high" ideals of Western civilization would disarm Haiti's adversaries. Haiti's claim to Western culture was a moral imperative for him personally as much as it was an essential for national survival; it never was a matter of cold calculation. It was in this spirit that Bellegarde declared Haiti to be "a French cultural province," without attaching to this declaration any pejorative meaning. Haitian subordination to Western cultural norms did not, for him, imply Haiti's inferiority; rather, it was a highly moral decision, signifying the country's acceptance of its responsibilities and its desire to join the civilized world.

That Bellegarde's rationalizations were couched in cultural terms was symptomatic of the group he represented, an elite in which cultural considerations had come to predominate over purely economic interests. These rationalizations were also an attempt to transcend economics and the interests of the moment in order to deal with the "higher" questions of the individual and civilization, as well as with the question of how social perceptions, attitudes, and behavior would affect individuals and through them, the entire society. These concerns were formulated by Bellegarde and other Haitian thinkers of the nineteenth century in their acceptance of proven ways, that is, by accepting the safety of international mainstream thinking of the age.

Throughout, a not so subtle racism seemed at work[12] in Beaubrun Ardouin's approval of "superior classes" and in Bellegarde's belief in a "superior culture." The Haitian elite, as well as all others, was inherently elitist and craved recognition from the more established European elites. The Haitians sensed that on account of race, foreign rejection of their nation had been more social than economic. Because of this belief, and because of cultural and historical affinities, the French nation had been favored as a model by Haitians.

Speaking in 1975, Professor Jacques C. Antoine, a member of the reformist *génération de l'Occupation* and a former diplomat, declared to this author: "Only in France [in the nineteenth century] were Haitians accepted in human terms *(qualité d'hommes)*.[13] Much earlier, in 1919,

Alfred Nemours, a member of the earlier *génération de la Ronde* and a vice president of the League of Nations Assembly in 1927, had expressed sentiments similar to those of Antoine when he wrote:

> The first time that a man of the black race was ever a citizen, he was a French citizen; the first time that a man of our race was ever an army officer, he was a French officer. And our birth certificate, where it is found? Was it not in France, in the Declaration of the Rights of Man?[14]

The record of France in dealing with blacks had been more "enviable" than that of any other European power at that time.

Faced with racial prejudice from abroad and with a ruinous class conflict at home, and burdened, moreover, with the responsibility of public office, Dantès Bellegarde accepted a Western-oriented ideological framework within which to operate and by which to justify his action. One difficulty, he saw, was to convince the United States to accept the possibility of black achievement in order to forestall recolonization.

After the occupation had occurred, Bellegarde's objective became to soften North American racial and cultural antagonism. His reading of the evolutionary biological thought of John Fiske and others had revealed to him a North American obsession with heredity, a pervasive concern for racial purity, and, shocking to the Haitian bourgeoisie, very little understanding of the concept as well as the reality of "social class" and its intricacies, particularly since the United States assumed that it was rather classless itself. It is not surprising, then, that to the Latin's assimilation and to the *évolué*'s emulation, the Anglo-Saxon opposed his concept of "mimicry."[15] He had little sympathy for blacks acting like Europeans, even when these were mulattoes scarcely distinguishable from whites in skin tone.[16]

Because of racial antagonism abroad, because of the Haitian historical evolution that had hindered the development of a conservative political faction, and because of the seemingly urgent necessity for reforms, Dantès Bellegarde was a liberal. Haiti's liberalism was dictated by international circumstances. The country had never been isolated economically and intellectually from the rest of the world, and conditions of the international system had shaped it as much as any other nation.

Haiti's ostracism by Western powers during the first quarter of the nineteenth century was not a self-imposed isolation as was widely claimed by some writers. On the contrary, it indicated a distinctly negative factor operating against Haiti's development from *within* a pervasive international system. Self-isolation, being self-generated, would have had a more positive character, since it would have indicated Haitian internal psychological strength in its ability to withstand pressure, a strength that was sadly lacking.

Intellectual history has always been the preserve of a few individuals in every society who provide to the human group they serve a sense of intellectual continuity. Ali Mazrui, who believed that Western intellectual development demonstrated the adage that *plus ça change, plus c'est la même chose*, expressed the ebb and flow of human intellectual achievement, lyrically, as "a succession of waves, or alternatively a long chain of moments of inspiration linked together into a tradition of thought."[17] And because Bellegarde understood, as a historian, that "reciprocal relationships between ideas and events, men and events,"[18] are crucial in the development of nations, he too seemed to have deliberately opted for an alliance with groups and individuals in the international arena that would best favor what he called Haiti's equality.

Characteristically, a liberal faction existed within the elite of the nineteenth- and twentieth-century colonizing powers.[19] Bellegarde's acquaintances and friends abroad were that "enlightened" (his expression) portion of the Western European and North American bourgeoisies that saw both justice and their national interests as being best served by an alliance between themselves and the "enlightened" colonial elites.[20] In contrast to the regressive conservatism and crude racism of North American military officers and civilians stationed in Port-au-Prince, Bellegarde's staunchest allies and personal friends in the United States were such liberals as Ernest Gruening, Adolf A. Berle, Jr., various other members of President Franklin D. Roosevelt's "Brain Trust," and the Black American "bourgeoisie," all of whom believed that United States influence upon Haiti, for them an a priori "good," would be better served by trade and friendly relations than by military occupation.

In Western Europe, those who had showed sympathy for Bellegarde's causes were, among others, the president of the League of Nations Council, Hyalmar Branting of Sweden, and Lord Robert Cecil of the United Kingdom, who, according to a student of the League, Francis P. Walters, "formed what might be called a left-wing group, their general thesis being that the Council [League of Nations] should show a higher degree of initiative, should be less dominated by the great powers, and should pay more attention to public opinion. . . ."

The opposite position was maintained, as before, by [Lord] Balfour and [Léon] Bourgeois."[21]

Dantès Bellegarde's liberalism had three interacting components: (1) international, (2) domestic, and (3) individual. Internationally, he defended small states against political and military encroachment by larger powers. Like the Spanish-American student of international law, he had proclaimed the juridical equality of all states in a parallel to the traditional liberal belief of the juridical equality of individuals, and made this declaration the cornerstone of his international thought. In doing this, Bellegarde perceived his position as furthering the social goals he had sought. He had observed among scholars and diplomats a commonality of "culture" that transmogrified them into a worldwide intellectual elite that served as a prototype for the whole of humanity to follow. This type of international result, he believed, had effectively transcended such divisive factors as race.

In the domestic scene, Dantès Bellegarde's liberalism was expressed in his belief in the individual's worth and in the importance of citizens' independent action to insure their well-being; all, he thought, should be given this opportunity. Governmental action in accordance with reformist policies would provide the impetus and the framework for accelerated social change. But governmental action, he believed, must occur within an ideological context that allowed the creation of rules of moral behavior and that sought to perpetuate society through judicious and timely transformations; it must never challenge the individual's freedom of action and his or her responsibilities to him or herself and to the polity.

Finally, in Bellegarde, the role of the individual in achieving civilized status was elaborated further from an adaptation of prevailing Spencerian positivist and social Darwinian formulations of the primacy of the elements of heredity and evolution in the social process. For Bellegarde, as for other earlier Haitian social thinkers, the concept of heredity was liberalized by the injection of a Lamarckian emphasis on the possibility of inheritance of acquired characteristics. At a later time, Bergson's concept of a "leap in evolution" seemed to have been similarly influential, especially in the writings of social philosophers such as Justin-Chrysostome Dorsainvil and Camille Lhérisson.[22]

To Bellegarde, as he translated them into human terms, these concepts of "subdued" heredity included knowledge acquired through education. Hence, the Bellegardian emphasis on both education and evolution that, far from being original and, on the whole, positivist, nonetheless placed

Bellegarde in the ranks of optimistic reformers. In a word, he bespoke a liberalism in the broad, late nineteenth century sense of the term and not the Romantic Liberalism of an earlier age.

But Dantès Bellegarde's liberalism must be placed within the context of his lengthy lifespan. The literary critic John Ciardi's pithy description of Robert Frost might well be applied to Bellegarde: "Frost was a great nineteenth century poet who confused everyone by living through more than half of the twentieth century."[23] This parallels Professor Gouraige's assessment that Bellegarde had carried into the twentieth century the niceties of the nineteenth.[24]

Bellegarde's long life also illustrated well how the present and relatively recent past are often fused in one's understanding of history. Thus, the early nineteenth-century romantic liberal leader and writer Victor Hugo lived until 1885. The Haitian and the French Revolutions in the eighteenth century were a scant four generations away from Bellegarde's era, a negligible time in history, but their influence was continuing long after they had occurred, down to the present.

Dantès Bellegarde, like many members of the petite bourgeoisie elsewhere in Latin America (as well as in Western Europe and in the United States), could not help but be optimistic about the potential for reform in a system that, after all, had recognized his worth and permitted him personally to rise. Cesar Graña's assertion that the bourgeoisie was the first ruling class whose values could be acquired,[25] places Bellegarde in the proper frame of reference. He became the defender of the basic goodness of society, and of the international status quo, qualifying his concept of this status with the ardor of a neophyte by adding a modicum of respect for all states, regardless of size, and for all individuals regardless of race.

But Bellegarde's rapport with the lower classes was predictably paternalistic, ascribing to them an inferior status in his scale of values. In this attitude this author sees an element of determinism or even fatalism, as well as a great deal of blindness as to what may be the requirements of a capitalist economy, such as the requirement that some level of poverty would be a permanent fixture of a harmonious *tableau d'ensemble*.[26]

Bellegarde's rapid ascent to power in the Haitian republic cannot be dismissed as an accident, since the petite bourgeoisie as a group were acquiring a share of the power in the nation at this time, both politically and economically.[27] Similarly, in the remainder of Latin America, the latter part of the nineteenth century had brought a rapid economic expansion; as a corollary, "the small *criollo* oligarchy that ruled in all the nations at the time of independence had extended its ranks," according to Davis.[28]

A conservative trend, illustrated in the emergence of strong conservative political parties, co-opting many liberals, throughout Latin America at the end of the last century, expressed the union of the old landowning elite with newer power groups whose interests lay in industry, commerce, banking, and railroads. A similar development is noted in Western Europe during this era.[29] Consequently, the Latin American petite bourgeoisie's former reformism, born out of its lack of political power, was on the wane. The inclusion of the petite bourgeoisie into the oligarchy had also strengthened and rejuvenated the latter.

Thus, liberalism, as it developed in the nineteenth and into the twentieth century in Western Europe and the Americas, may be defined essentially as an extension of a social and political system found by an ever-increasing number of individuals to be good in essence and motivation. But, as Karl Marx noted, that doctrine had never divested itself of its belief in the validity of private ownership of the means of production, a belief it still shares with conservatism. In fact, as the various national bourgeoisies consolidated their power, liberalism tended to become more and more an expression of conservative forces and trends. Thus bourgeois revolutions at the end of the eighteenth century did little but transfer power to owners of industrial property from a class whose concept of wealth lay in land owner-ship.[30] By extension, liberals then, were the individuals who, by conviction or calculation, attempted to implement a policy of greater public participation within a preexisting social framework; they were averse to considering that the system may be exploitative. But the political success of liberalism, as noted by Harold J. Laski, was contingent on two conditions:

> It required, first, the sense of security that came from the ability to go on making profit that enabled it, from its surplus wealth, to continue the distribution of amenities to the masses. It required in the second place, an agreement among parties in politics to all matters of funda-mental social constitution. . . .[31]

A basis for consensus, order, and stability was thus established. The state was assumed to be neutral, seeking everyone's well-being: it was not consid-ered to be the repository of legal coercion that it is. The law was enshrined as blind and fair. Saint-Simon, as Laski pointed out, had had a different view of the law when he wrote in 1832: "The law which constitutes the powers and the form of government is less important and has less influence on the happiness of nations than that which constitutes property and decides its use."[32] In a similar vein Laski concludes:

> That was the seminal truth that liberalism was never able to see. It did not realize that the political democracy it brought into being was established on the unstated assumption that it would leave untouched the private ownership of the means of production. . . . Political democracy, and the liberal ideology which expressed its inner purposes, could no more pass beyond the framework within which it was confined than feudal society could pass beyond its own constitutive principle. A fundamental change in class relations requires now, as it required at the end of the fifteenth century, a revolution in the idea of property, of, therefore, the state that is its guardian, if it is to be effective in altering the character of the forces of production.[33]

Governmental structures were assumed to be value-free. Social institutions did not need to be changed; they merely needed reforms. They needed to accommodate those individuals who had recently acquired upward mobility (as individuals, and not as a group) and a measure of respectability.[34] This doctrine allows "society to perpetuate itself while ameliorating itself," to use Bellegarde's often-repeated statement.[35] It allows society to perpetuate itself, improving through reform, while remaining "basically" unchanged.

In the perspective of the evolution of ideas, taking into account shifting contemporary definitions, liberalism and conservatism developed doctrinally from similar ontological assumptions found within an orderly conception of the universe. They are doctrines of social organization in which the world is orderly and predictable and allows for the growth of cooperation between groups and individuals. Their sociopolitical assumptions, rooted in the rule of law, emphasize legalism and predictability; they posit that all problems can be solved rationally within the existing social system. Obviously, these are not doctrines of "revolution."

The liberal doctrines that erupted in the late eighteenth century in Europe and North America, and that, with some changes, became the official doctrines of the bourgeoisie in the nineteenth, expressed the frustrated efforts of European bourgeoisies, from the time of their rise in the sixteenth century, to partake of political power. Challenges to bourgeois hegemony were to appear simultaneously with the achievement of bourgeois power in the nineteenth century for it was then realized that once the privileges of the bourgeoisie were secured, these forces were meant to keep others in chains. As the French intellectual historian Jean Touchard wrote a few years ago: "Insofar as liberalism appears as the philosophy of the bourgeois class, it only assures freedom for the bourgeoisie, and it is against liberalism that non-bourgeois, such as Proudhon, attempt to create liberty."[36]

Within these definitions, Dantès Bellegarde was well within the mainstream of liberalism as it had developed historically. That liberal tradition had spread worldwide through Western commercial expansion and colonization. As it spread, it created an inequality in the terms of trade, and other more subtle inequalities in the cultural realm in colonized areas in which the rising local bourgeoisies could not compete with metropolitan bourgeoisies successfully.

European and North American expansion in the nineteenth century was the origin of a process that rendered these colonial areas "peripheral," making them the purveyors of raw materials and the cultural backwaters of empires at the same time. Dantès Bellegarde, a mainstream thinker, was geographically in the periphery. On one hand, he had acquired his Western values through osmosis, that is, in the interaction of family and school and through the friendly intellectual competition between students at the *Lycée* and those Haitians who had studied in France.[37] These conditions had given rise to Bellegarde's eclectic and intuitive social thought.

On the other hand, "universalistic" Western thought, although more nationalistic than internationalist (the emergence of the "modern" nation-state in the eighteenth century, the development of national sociology in the nineteenth), was in continuous conflict with the diplomatic requirements that a small state, such as Haiti, be defended against all encroachments to its sovereignty. These contradictions created for Bellegarde a dilemma that he never resolved nor understood.

Haiti had much to gain from its Westernized approach to problems of foreign and social policy as understood by Bellegarde. This approach was logical in the sense that an alternative to rapid modernization was not seen to exist. To counteract such writers as Spencer St. John, who favored mandating Haiti to a "civilized" power, Haiti felt itself to be Latin American and joined in the founding of the Pan-American Union in 1890.

Because of the preeminent position of the French language within Haiti's tiny elite, the continuing growth of French cultural influence throughout Latin America,[38] as well as the dominance of that language in the field of diplomacy, Haiti felt itself to be French. Professor Antoine summarized *La Ronde*'s rationale in 1898 thus: "Thanks to the French language, the Haitian elite and literature could join hands with the world's intellectual elite."[39] Parenthetically, it was characteristic of Bellegarde that he lectured and addressed Spanish-American, Brazilian, and North American audiences in French, expecting them to understand him as a matter of course, and apparently caring little if they did not.[40] He could have spoken in English or Spanish had he chosen to do so.

Antoine said that Bellegarde had made a "cerebral synthesis" that in the philosophical sense, was a deductive reasoning from cause to effect, from a principle to its application, and that Bellegarde had accordingly concluded that the advantages of French culture over others were overwhelming.[41] Having thought as much, Dantès Bellegarde further justified Haiti's rights to such a course of action on the basis of the country's mixed European and African, biological heritage. The latter element in the national equation, the African, only added "vigor" and were the "humus from which the *semences latines* would grow strong."

Bellegarde was paraphrasing Constantin Mayard (1882–1940), who wrote in a poem at the turn of the century:

Tant que sous notre ciel plein de fleurs adamantines
Notre Ile, comme un corps de femme, frémira,
Soyez sur que ce sol seulement nourrira
Dans l'humus africain des semences latines.
(Constantin Mayard, 1882–1940)
As long as in our heaven diamond-hard glittering flowers bloom full
our spasming isle, as women fool, will quake
be sure, our soil will only feed
in the African mould, a Latin seed.
(trans. P. Bellegarde-Smith, 1984)

In Latin America thought often preceded action, and this heightened the preeminence of intellectuals in Latin American public life. That interest of the *pensadores* was symbolized in Domingo Sarmiento's injunction, "governar es educar." These thinkers usually were honest enough, however, to realize at what point their imperfect system differed from the European model they were trying to surpass through emulation.

Because European doctrines adopted by Latin America answered the needs of its elites more than they reflected the continent's social realities,[42] liberalism, as it adapted positivism, fostered hope for Latin American progress. Positivist social thought became ideology to be translated into policies. In this sense, social thought was rationalization, hope, and adjustment to changes occurring in the trend-setting nations more than response to local conditions.

Within this framework, Haitian social thinkers in general may be considered ideologues rather than philosophers. Based on the contents of his library, Dantès Bellegarde did not seem to have had great contact with the original works of the philosophers he incorporated in his thought.[43] This fact strengthens this author's view that osmosis had taken place. It would appear that the student of Haitian intellectual history must deal more with perception, *mentalité*, and attitude than with substance, defined in terms of well-digested philosophical systems.

Négritude as Cultural Politics

A problem that presented itself in the elaboration of this work was the definition of right, left, and center in the political spectrum. Such a definition acquires, in all societies, an internal dimension—to which one must remain constantly alert—to distinguish it from its international definition and its changes over time.[44] Because of the scope and the time frame of this book, the challenge here was particularly strong. But extenuating circumstances eased these difficulties: Dantès Bellegarde, perhaps tragically for himself, as this explains his lack of influence in present-day Haiti even under a right-wing regime, remained amazingly consistent throughout his life.[45]

Bellegarde never outgrew his Spencerian and generally positivist frame of reference. He kept his distance from "political extremes," staying out of the governments of Louis Borno (1922–30), and Dumarsais Estimé (1946–50). This abstention enabled him, he seemed to have felt, to maintain his position as a centrist in the mainstream. But domestic conditions and a rapidly changing world situation forced him, without his realizing it, into the Right of the domestic political spectrum.[46]

As time went by, Bellegarde tended to withdraw within himself. His thought became increasingly static, and in his literary production in the

1940s and 1950s he merely restated earlier positions. While his friend and antagonist, Jean Price-Mars, befriended the younger generation of Haitian intellectuals, Bellegarde shunned them and preferred *"les beaux vieillards de La Ronde"* to use his own expression. He considered all literature written after 1930 essentially sterile.[47]

On the whole, however, Bellegarde's thought and action was somewhat less contradictory than that of Price-Mars. The latter came to symbolize *cette autre tendance* of the Haitian psyche, the nationalist and Africanist, in juxtaposition to the pro-Western position represented by Bellegarde.[48] But this assessment of the Bellegarde/Price-Mars "conflict" would be an oversimplification of the struggle for control of the nation that had continued since its beginning. Because that struggle had cultural or "ethnic" overtones, it is difficult to define, but the elements that comprise it have remained fairly unchanged throughout more than a century and a half of independent life.

Thus, the Western tradition continued in Bellegarde was locked into battle with an ill-defined Négritude embodied in Price-Mars, who affirmed the nation's right to a cultural evolution freed from the slavish imitation of European norms. Bellegarde had affirmed that Haiti was too weak to undertake an independent cultural evolution. Professor Ghislain Gouraige summarized this Haitian cultural ambivalence, represented in the diverse ideas of Bellegarde and Price-Mars, by placing it in the context of men, events, and politics, as follows:

> But Price-Mars was proclaiming in the name of Africa and the same national ambitions Bellegarde had claimed in the name of France. It was, on one side as on the other, a cultural choice. But no one has chosen to thus observe these things: one prefers to erect a mulatto champion against a black champion, bringing both [men] to the milieu's level of mediocrity [which consists] of cruel and uncultured ninnies.[49]

Haitian Négritude, as well as Black consciousness in general, had been called leftist because it challenged the dominant culture and because in its early period it had flirted with the European Left. But although Négritude, starting in the 1930s, had argued a radical cultural realignment and proclaimed Black independence, it did not make any subsequent effort to translate this cultural radicalism into a parallel economic and political radicalism. Perhaps because of this deficiency, Négritude appeared to Bellegarde to be a movement serving well certain malevolent conservative forces in

North America and in Europe and causing the political struggle, once more, to be fought along racial lines reminiscent of social Darwinist argumentation of the late nineteenth century.

It would be said that United States policy would favor Black assertiveness over a class struggle. The perspective of an economic struggle was being jettisoned in the interest of racial self-assertion. Older Haitian thinkers had fought hard to cause the issue of race to be forgotten.[50] The younger Haitian intellectual, defiantly, was fighting after the 1930s to sing the praise of Blackness. Taking a leaf from the Western culture they were combating, this younger generation of Haitians sought to internationalize their struggle. Rayford W. Logan's statement in regard to Bellegarde's political aims applies here as well: "A nationalist understands . . . that his aims cannot be achieved solely within his country."[51]

This Logan sentiment was echoed by Jacques C. Antoine, the former editor of *La Relève*, an organ of Haitian *indigénisme* as he delineated the immediate causes and the impact of the movement. Afro-American sympathies, he said, were sought by Haitians. This Black American and Haitian cultural and political rapprochement was one element in the struggle against the United States military invasion of Haiti. Négritude and nationalism, he added, had merged.[52] Thus, Dantès Bellegarde's previously dim view of nationalism, as he found it expressed in Europe in the ideas of Treitschke, was being reinforced by his hatred of "africanisms" glorified in Négritude.

Because Haitian nationalists felt it necessary to seek new allies, the Haitian political spectrum was enlarged in the 1940s and acquired for the first time a true left wing, to the desolation of Dantès Bellegarde. He had not changed his political position appreciably, his thought remaining remarkably consistent throughout his life span in the form in which it had developed between 1898 and 1935. But political events in Haiti after that period had resulted in his "kind of "thought being moved by these events, from the "progressive" center to the "extreme-right."[53]

Since the state apparatus found it difficult to accommodate newcomers rapidly, the political center moved inexorably to the left in a parallel observed in many neocolonial societies, in Latin America and elsewhere. Gradualness, as advanced by such liberal reformers as Bellegarde, could not meet the increased demands placed on the system. As Harold E. Davis noted, positivism of the kind Bellegarde held to and that had earlier been a philosophy of reform throughout Latin America,[54] later, "proved useful to the ruling class in its defense of the status quo. . . . [It] provided a scientific answer—the inevitability of gradualness—with which to meet the impatient demands of radical reformers."[55]

Viewed within this intellectual historical context, Dantès Bellegarde was neither a radical nor a reactionary. But events had passed him by and he had been unable or unwilling to revise his positions, to accommodate new trends, or to "compromise his rectitude," as he would have it. "Semper fidelis" could have been his motto, for he remained faithful as much to an ideal as to the supportive cast of literati who had lived intense lives like his in the closing years of the nineteenth century. Banded together in the *génération de La Ronde*, they formed a circle from which he was reluctant or unable to escape.[56] The diplomacy he practiced was civil; agreement could be found among reasonable men of like sentiments. In contrast, the *génération de l'Occupation* seemed brash, hateful, and strident, and its politics seemingly accepted no compromise at home or abroad.

Dantès Bellegarde's friend in Washington in 1931 was Paul Claudel, whose "need for universality . . . was satisfied within Catholicism,"[57] but not in the ideas of Sartre. Bellegarde likewise felt that Jean-Paul Sartre, in his espousal of radical causes—he had written the preface to Senghor's *Anthologie nègre*—and in his liaison with the French philosopher Simone de Beauvoir, was criticizing bourgeois morality. Sartre's ideas left Bellegarde with the feeling that treason against Western civilization was being committed. Moreover, he considered that "atheistic materialism" was scarcely European, being, as he put it, "Russian."[58]

The acute cultural crisis that Europe suffered, partially as a result of two world wars, and that was reflected in the visual and literary arts, was never fully understood by Bellegarde. Surrealism left him cold, as did the *renouvellement* in art that incorporated important elements of African artistic expression in European art. For him, this degeneracy of European culture, fostered by Europeans themselves, was almost too great to bear. Characteristically, Dantès Bellegarde continued to read the conservative *Le Figaro* and *Paris-Match* until the very end of his life.

But André Breton, and the Négritude poets Senghor, Césaire, Damas, and Jacques Roumain had joined the Left only in a cerebral sense; their elitism was seemingly unshaken.[59] As one examines the movement of Négritude from the cultural angle alone, as it strove to effect a strong personal and collective identity that would owe little to European perceptions of self, the movement was indeed radical in the sense of a serious deviation from the mainstream of social and political thinking that had held sway up to that time in Haiti. While emulation of Western culture had been a matter of critical adjustment to the world and had been accepted almost uncritically, Négritude became an ideology of "reaction" against the dominant value system.

Négritude was not new in any real sense of the term, however. It was the product of a long, though politically dormant, tradition of cultural assertion dating from Haiti's preindependence—an ideology that had waited for a change in domestic and international conditions to become viable. In Aimé Césaire's famous formula, it is in Haiti that "Négritude has stood on its feet for the first time and said that she [Haiti] believed in her humanity."[60]

In Haiti, this dormant Negro-African ideology had awakened at such key points in the nation's history as the Dessalines Empire (1804–06), which symbolically had its capital inland; the Piquets rebellion of 1844; and the Soulouque Empire (1848–59), to mention some watershed events of the nineteenth century. All these developments, of course, had been denigrated in the international press of the time and had been crushed by the bourgeoisie. Dantès Bellegarde, the historian, saw little merit in these sanguinary historical episodes to which Black aspirations led. To him, these were the work of bands of bandits who had descended periodically upon mulatto neighborhoods of Port-au-Prince to plunder and set the city afire.[61] Bellegarde went further, stating that after the fall of Soulouque in 1859, when elite President Fabre-Nicolas Geffrard took office, "it was one long Caco war" lasting until the 1920s.[62]

In a larger sense, Négritude, as a cultural phenomenon, was also part of the greater Latin American sociopolitical development that found major expression in the Mexican Revolution of 1910, a political movement that made *indigenismo* one of its bases.[63] A century earlier, Miguel Hidalgo and José Maria Morelos in Mexico, like Tupac Amaru in Peru, had attempted to change the social condition of the *Indio* but to no avail. The Haitian *indigénistes* (circa 1930) had done as much as the Ateneo de la Juventud and other Mexican leaders in rebelling against positivist social theories. The former, however, had more clearly made an issue of race in launching a reassessment of the national heritage, not only vis-à-vis Western culture, but also as against the dominant native elite that was its extension.[64]

Dantès Bellegarde assumed that Négritude was leftist; he may have merely sensed intuitively its propensity to totalitarianism. For this author, Négritude was, in political terms, the historical continuation of a certain Haitian "traditional" thought that had led to numerous slave insurrections in the colonial period. The experience of slavery seemed, according to this writer, to have been partly responsible for dictating to Négritude an authoritarian outlook.[65] If successful, these slave insurrections could have led to proto-African societies.

Bellegarde did not realize that Négritude was not leftist in the modern sense of the word, but had simply identified with the populace. In this context Bellegarde's confusion of the concepts of nation and state become clear. It is apparent to the reader of his works that to Bellegarde the nation was, in fact, only 1 or 2 percent of Haiti's population: the remainder, for him, existed in a sort of limbo. How else could one interpret his definition of *nation*?

According to Bellegarde, a *nation* is a community that shares a common language and a common religion, these being the two pillars of national culture and unity. The Haitian nation for him was French-speaking and Roman Catholic. When James G. Leyburn wrote his sociological treatise *The Haitian People* in 1941, he argued that the Haitian elite and the peasantry formed social castes living distinct cultural lives. Bellegarde was then left with the need for calling Creole "bad" French and Vodou "bad" Roman Catholicism; this he did. He further revealed the extent of his confusion by assuming that he had risen from the masses merely because he was born in poverty; the masses to him, in this context, seemed to have signified the petite bourgeoisie.

In his *défense et illustration* of Haiti at Molière's tricentenary in 1922, Dantès Bellegarde had answered with a straight face the questions put to him by French intellectuals in the following exchange:

(Q) What is the language spoken in Haiti?
(A) French.
(Q) What do Haitians read?
(A) A bit of everything: from Pierre Benoit to Marcel Proust. We receive the *Revue des Deux-Mondes*, and *La Vie Parisienne*.

What an astonishing little people, someone said, buttoning his coat; I had never thought it possible that La Bruyère was commented upon in Port-au-Prince.[66]

In this respect, Jean Touchard's comment about French liberalism in the nineteenth century fitted Bellegarde particularly well: "Liberal ideology is essentially confused: confusion between bourgeoisie and mass, between the Revolution and the Empire, between liberties and freedom, between policy and good sentiments."[67]

Charles A. Hale has said, in a more general sense, "when Abbé Sieyes said that the third estate was the nation, he meant the French bourgeoisie, the class that became the beneficiary to the distribution of aristocratic and clerical property."[68] Bellegarde similarly used the terms international *system* and international *community* interchangeably.

The Haitian bourgeoisie expressed in human terms what was already expressed in Haiti's economic geography: all significant cities are coastal, turned toward a metropolis from which they receive sustenance. The elite, relying on trade for its livelihood, turned toward Europe for cultural and intellectual sustenance. Some members of that class had dual citizenship (and sometimes, more) as insurance for their economic and financial security.[69]

After the 1930s, the educated challengers to Western cultural hegemony in Haiti ardently desired to identify with the masses. The Haitian Marxist thinker René Depestre gave a succinct account of this process, writing in 1968:

This concept of négritude [that of François Duvalier and Lorimer Denis] had been, at a specified moment of the history of decolonization, the effective ripost of the exploited and humiliated black man, facing the global scorn of the white colonist. As the latter, from his privileged situation in colonial society had epidermized his alleged biological superiority, the black man similarly, in function of his oppressed condition of a pariah, of his condition as a man alienated in his very own skin, was carried . . . to epider-mize his lamentable historical situation. Thus, négritude, in its best sense was the cultural operation from which black intellectuals from Africa and the Americas were made conscious of the validity of Negro-African cultures, of the esthetic value of the black race, and of the capacity of their respective peoples to exercise their right to historical initiative colonialism had completely suppressed. . . .[70]

But it would be some time before the black man would realize his double alienation; his racial alienation had blurred his belonging to the proletariat.[71] This revolutionary realization could not have occurred at the outset of Black cultural consciousness when the protagonists were either upper class or nearly so, and when such African leaders as Senghor had refused to admit the existence of social and economic classes in Africa, let alone the existence of a class struggle.[72] It would have been too clear an admission of their status as an elite.

Because Négritude's exponents were members of the intelligentsia and emphasized the cultural factor in social relations, minimizing other factors, Haitian economic conditions were left nearly unchallenged. This lack of concern for the economy was illustrated in President Estimé's regime, which, despite such innovations in politics as the emergence of political parties and labor unionism, and despite an enlightened cultural policy, left untouched the economic and financial structures.

Subservience to United States commercial interests and investments in Haiti are not a sufficient explanation of Estimé's lack of interest in more fundamental changes. Rather, we must see that despite its cultural radicalism, Négritude did not offer a comprehensive economic policy. Its political program seems to have been limited to *"ôtes-toi que je m'y mette"* ("move over"). It did not readily perceive the link between international conditions furthering the inequality of nation-states and the conditions of domestic misery. The absence of this perspective by the leaders of Négritude has been illustrated by the conservative economic and foreign policies of President Senghor in Senegal and those of the François Duvalier government in Haiti.

The concepts of cultural and economic independence, as they express the collective soul of a nation and favor communal or state ownership of economic resources, as distinct from political independence, may prove to become the Third World's major contribution to the international community. In many respects, these concepts have suggested a new direction in international law.

Dantès Bellegarde lived far enough into the twentieth century to sense, although he never seemed to have understood completely, the rejection of his social and cultural ideas. When he began his career in the early part of the century, three black states existed in the modern world: Haiti, Liberia, and Ethiopia. All three were ruled by socially conservative or traditional elites. The only serious attempt to express a separate black cultural evolution had been that of the Jamaican populist Marcus Garvey and his effect had been felt primarily in the United States, Cuba and, the British West Indies. His populism had been repugnant to black intellectuals everywhere, largely one suspects, because of "class" differentiation between the groups involved.

By the end of Bellegarde's life, however, a great number of African and black Caribbean states had achieved political independence and were beginning to realize that their freedom of action was limited. Understandably, Bellegarde's legalistic approach, that of the juridical equality of states within the context of a Western universalistic culture did not prove appealing to much of the intellectuals of these nations. In this respect, much of the new leadership had no illusions about the intentions of larger powers; human brotherhood, these new leaders believed, would come with economic equality, not through the adoption of an abstract principle and a promise.

How liberal/conservative ideologies are able to differentiate between liberty and equality are the mystery (and hoax) of the past two centuries. Thus, what then seems to differentiate the new radicalism in some Third World leaders and the liberal democratic ideal of some Western leaders is the source of ultimate control of the means of production and the direction to be given to each national economy. This Bellegarde never understood. The illusion of power under obvious international constraints would tend to circumscribe the arena for independent action.

During his last years, almost thirty years of his life, Dantès Bellegarde became an anachronistic figure; yet he was a figure intensely Haitian. His alienation, his despair, and his frustrations were those of his country. The contradictions within himself that he never mastered were also those of the nation. One might well say that Alphonse de Lamartine's assessment of Toussaint Louverture, "*cet homme, c'est une nation*," applied to Bellegarde as well. His "*parler, écrire, c'est encore agir*,"[73] explain his constant role as his country's educator par excellence. As a historian, he remembered that the dilemma facing Placide and Isaac Louverture had remained largely unresolved in many Haitians, and that the last French general to leave an independent Saint Domingue was the black General LaPlume.[74]

But despite his intellectual preeminence, (he "embodied" official Haiti in the 1920s against the new "Marsian" order), Bellegarde never rose to meet the need of providing a viable sociopolitical theory or ideology for twentieth-century Haiti. As an act of faith in the Haitian people, whom he assumed would rise to the challenge, Dantès Bellegarde accepted the validity for Haiti of the mainstream Western European ideology, including capitalism and liberalism. He thought it sufficient in terms of universality to bring forth what was best in the human person.

Price-Mars, Césaire, and Senghor spoke in terms of a "dynamic symbiosis" that would harmonize African and European cultural contributions, eventually leading to a *civilisation de l'universel.* Bellegarde, however, rejected the African contribution, seeing in it no future. Partly because of this rejection, he joined the ranks of eighteenth- and nineteenth-century Negro thinkers and this represents what is clearly an older strain in black thinking internationally. It had escaped this unusually gifted diplomat and ideologue that any real synthesis necessitated, as a precondition, to paraphrase the language of Aimé Césaire, the freedom of those who are to be its bearers.[75]

Dantès Bellegarde never sought the presidency of Haiti. He despised politics and politicians.[76] When the French literary historian Auguste Viatte asked him why he had not wanted to become president, he replied: "I have remained poor, and such an election costs money. I have not reached a respectable age to now place myself into the hands of money-lenders."[77] The compromises that a presidential aspirant would be expected to make in a political situation were also alien to Bellegarde's nature. The bluntness that characterized him as diplomat may not have been appreciated in his country.

Furthermore, Bellegarde had remained "suspiciously" poor despite a lengthy public career, a fact that could unsettle potential backers. His temperament would have made him amenable to being drafted as chief of state; seeking support actively was, on the other hand, out of character. But most significantly, his ideas were fast becoming unacceptable during his late years. Probably his strongest personal achievement, as well as his chief asset, was to have remained totally incorruptible in a milieu in which corruption in government was often seen as a matter of mere survival.

Bellegarde symbolized an entire era in the history of Haiti. His life spanned what was a period of transition in its national development. The struggle, however, was not between two literary men, Bellegarde and Price-Mars, for they remained personal friends and political moderates during their entire lives, despite their intellectual differences.[78] The real struggle was between two conceptions of the Haitian nation, between two centuries, the nineteenth and the twentieth, between differing sociological and anthropological definitions of culture. Bellegarde, the synthesizer, was the culmination of nineteenth-century thought in Haiti. Price-Mars, the innovator was the originator of twentieth-century Haitian social thought. Price-Mars, incidentally, was a year older than Bellegarde.

Dantès Bellegarde's most important work, *Pour une Haiti heureuse*, in two volumes, appeared in 1927 and 1929; but it consisted in part of articles written a decade earlier. Although it made a sensation at publication and sold rapidly, it never achieved the significance of Jean Price-Mars's *Ainsi parla l'oncle*, published in 1928. Yet Bellegarde's works remain basic to the understanding of Haitian intellectual development and psyche because, as Gouraige stated:

> They reveal an era and the conscience of a people in its moments of despair. One cannot partake of all his convictions, but one can ignore neither their force, nor the imperious necessities that created them. Facing a Protestant and Anglo-Saxon America which constituted a menace to national integrity, it is not surprising that Bellegarde had chosen to grant a chance to French culture, [which is] Latin and Christian.[79]

Jean-Jacques Dessalines' imperial flag, black and red, had replaced the republican blue and red standard of 1804. Christophe had maintained the Dessalinian flag for his kingdom. The republican emblem had been created on Bellegarde's birth date, May 18, 1803, seventy-four years before his birth. The black and red banner was again resurrected in 1964, symbolizing the "Life Presidency." Two years later it draped Bellegarde's coffin. The change in the national flag reflected a shift of elites in power. But of elitism, it can be said, paraphrasing Bellegarde on imperialism, "it can vary its language, but it remains true to itself always."[80]

Yet whether it is of the Western European or American liberal sort or that of Négritude, elitism, whose ultimate foundation is individualism unfettered, accepts in general the inequality of individuals and the class structure of society. Price-Mars, early in his career, intimated this danger, saying that to grant Haiti a culture based on Greco-Latin civilization was to condone the existence of social classes. This concept was to furnish the beginning of a more radical Haitian ideology and social thought.

EPILOGUE

THE TRAUMA OF INSIGNIFICANCE

"Sentinelle, que dis-tu de la nuit?"
—*"La nuit est longue, mais le jour vient," répond la sentinelle.*
—French traditional formula of hope

This study of the ideas of Dantès Bellegarde in relation to the social realities of Haiti, suggests certain further observations on the impact of the international system upon small underdeveloped states in general.

Vulnerant omnes, ultima necat ("All wound, the last kills"). This epigraph/epigram originally meant to explain the passing hours and human ability to withstand them, pessimistically encapsulates the difficulties that must be surmounted by small states in an inclement environment and the usual outcome. Survival, identity, and self-assertion are but different facets of the same reality. Under prevailing conditions, the policies of small states become defensive measures even, in a certain sense, when they pass to the offensive. The politics of small states are thus often a reflection of international conditions acting as vectors for domestic political situations. This relationship advances the feeling of powerlessness of the small state, since the crucial economic and financial decisions affecting it are made abroad in a decreasing number of loci of power.

These traumata of insignificance affect individuals and states alike. The former are affected in direct proportion to the size of the state's economic and cultural wealth and its past glory, it would seem, even though small individuals are not all born in small nations. It becomes simpler, therefore, to understand why such a problem arises in the countries of the West Indies, which owed the formation of their common culture largely to the inheritance of exploitation and slavery.

The latter factor, slavery, had implied a break with the "distant" African past; West Indians were to develop self-identities partly based on the negative social conditions slavery had brought about. The former condition, economic exploitation, persists to the present day, benefiting much of the same kinds of individuals and groups throughout five centuries.

The saying that "nothing succeeds like success" is illustrated in the history of Western civilization during the past five centuries. Broad optimism and ethnocentrism were elements in this Western development, and the achievements of populations included in what is called Western civilization contrast sharply with what is considered the "meager realizations" of younger hybrid cultures such as that of the West Indies.[1]

The Caribbean area had been integrated fully into world economic activity shortly after its discovery in the sixteenth century, the period that saw the rise of mercantile capitalism in Europe. West Indian plantations and trade rapidly showed enormous profit, producing capital (and raw materials) that promoted the industrialization of Western Europe. The economy of Saint Domingue had been incorporated into French economic life. Robert L. Rotberg has shown that nearly 19 percent of the French population depended upon this trade in some way at the end of the eighteenth century.[2]

But this economic integration achieved in the seventeenth and eighteenth centuries, which persisted with varying partners in the nineteenth and twentieth centuries, was characterized by the gross inequality of the trading relationship. This inequality could be perceived in the human element as well, for increased economic integration of the colony into the mother country's economy was accompanied by the cultural assimilation of European cultural norms by the Africans. As a consequence, institutional and structural development, being patterned after those of Western Europe and North America, lagged considerably behind the prototype. Institutions and structures in the West Indies, lacking a self-propelled popular base, were tributary to world events in the sense that outside occurrences had a relatively larger impact upon colonial life than they did in the metropolis.

One must not assume an automatic reluctance of the colonized, however, to emulate the colonizer. Nothing in the colonial relationship subtracted from the intensity with which cultural adoptions were often made by the colonized. That intensity was reflected oftentimes in an exaggeration or caricature of European norms; it became ever more apparent in the crises that beset the colonial system.

In economic terms, while the rates of inflation and unemployment might be higher in the colonies than in the metropolis, governmental repression—a sign of structural weakness and a reflection of the international status of the local bourgeoisie—might tend to be more brutal, because the hold of the client-elite is tenuous, and foreign domination of the economy obvious.

This dislocation or malaise was normal; it was a sign of the neocolonial society's integration into a world order. Today, the symptoms of this malaise are often studied by American social scientists under the assumption that they are the growing pains of "modernization." Such an assumption, however, is too self-serving to be valid in its totality. Only recently some United States scholars have followed the lead of Latin American and European social scientists in studying underdevelopment as the end-product of an economic world order, rather than viewing it in the microcosmic sense to which they formerly adhered.[3] The late President Sténio Vincent of Haiti summed up the colonial dilemma in a famous phrase: "When France sneezes, Haiti has the whooping cough." Indeed, the center seems better equipped to deal with emergencies and challenges to the status quo than the periphery.

In the domain of literature, reserved for the Haitian *hommes de lettres* who found moments of leisure to cultivate haute culture, the effort at the discovery of self was poignant. The literary critic Emile Nau expressed it as early as 1836 in these words:

> Upon the ruins of a colonial society, a new people has taken its place and, previously enslaved and a true pariah of civilization, has conquered them through the force of arms. . . . Certainly, we cannot deny that we are under the influence of European civilization . . . we are, like the United States citizen, transplants lacking a tradition, but there exists in the fusion of the European and African genius which characterizes our people, something that makes us less French than the American is English. This is truly an advantage; indeed, it is already much evident, and the artist can devise the rest.
>
> We have thus clarified the presentiment we have of the distinguishing marks to be acquired by our literature. But we do not have a literature as yet; the time has not yet arrived, and the essays we will write under that title will be but modest anticipations. But we are convinced that someday we shall have a literature, more national it is certain than is American literature.[4]

The *cri du coeur* of Emile Nau, who believed that the time would come when a markedly Haitian literary expression would emerge, went to the heart of the matter. It did not, however, represent a simple concern for artistic creativity: rather, it expressed the total dilemma that results from the interaction between a nation and its physical expression, the state. Was Nau anticipating Jacques Maritain's "the State causes the Nation to be,"[5] from the exigencies of the moment that saw Haiti come into existence?

The compound "nation-state" is a Western concept that arose from European political and economic conditions of the seventeenth and eighteenth centuries. This juxtaposition of the two earlier concepts of nation and state gave expression to the idea of national sovereignty, divorced from the divine right that had previously been invested in the ruler; it legitimized nationalism. But taken separately, the components nation and state will retain their individual characteristics in the twentieth century, and are often in conflict conceptually.

While the state creates a leadership and a "commonality" of interests defined by its ruling class, the nation, as a community of sentiment, is acephalous; it requires no elite for its survival. In neocolonial societies, to paraphrase Maritain's intent, the elites that form subsequent to colonization, and that are the direct result of colonialism, because of their preeminence as a ruling class, would seem to have a determining influence on the development of norms and values of the nation.

Thus, the tensions between state structures, an expression of the concerns of the ruling class, and developing national institutions, which result from an inherently more democratic process, would seem to increase the importance of the elite that becomes, all at once, both the ruling authority and the center of social and cultural influence. This development appears clearly in the nations of the Caribbean, whose collective memories extend back to include the demographic void created by the European massacres of indigenous populations in the sixteenth century. As a consequence, social policy cannot be studied outside the political system from which it arose or, as Gordon K. Lewis has phrased it, "social policy . . . is a function of social and political structure,"[6] as it reflects the economy.

But an examination of "social reality" in the early history of a society— to use Karl Marx's expression—demonstrates that the animosity among classes and individuals as they seek to advance their interest in the rapidly forming social context is real. Moreover, as Dilia Vieux has summarized the struggle for power, "there is scarcely anything uglier than a social class in the process of formation."[7]

It is not an exaggeration to write that, within the confines of nation-states created out of colonialism, a principal preoccupation of elites has necessarily been that of societal integration.[8] This integration process has three fundamental dimensions: (1) an individual dimension, that of individuals attempting to fit into evolving national institutions and state structures; (2) a national dimension, that of states creating nations out of essentially "tribal" associations and the parallel societies that may have existed during the colonial period; (3) an international dimension, that of nation-states falling into place within a preexisting international system. These dimensions of integration are but aspects of a total reality, in the same sense as in Dantès Bellegarde's assertion that economics, politics, and intellectual history were arbitrary divisions of human reality that should not be separated. The integrative process carried out by the elites can be visualized as a box within a box within a box. The borders of the box represent the borders of the international system, while the innermost box represents the individual.

While these integrative dimensions may also be "adjustments" to conditions largely beyond anyone's control, class and individual resentment leading to concerted efforts to change these conditions can be exerted. Three states in this historical development of the nation-state can be seen emerging from these "reactions": (1) a period of concern strictly for political independence (in Haiti this extended from 1790 to 1920); (2) a period of perceived necessity for cultural independence (in Haiti, from the 1920s to the 1960s); and finally, (3) an era of growing awareness that the achievement of self-determination must include a modicum of economic independence as well. This era may be observed in the Caribbean as a period in which measures adopted in Cuba, Nicaragua, and Grenada (before the United States invasion in 1983, that shows that a leopard does not lose his spots) have been steps toward a socialist economy and national solutions to international problems.

These forces toward societal and international integration, independence and self-respect have been expressed within Haiti. The fact that the loci of economic decisions affecting Haiti lay outside the country in world financial centers, explains the existence in Haiti today of a healthy amount of realistic pessimism, not unrelated to a tendency in early

Haitian thought to favor policies that would humor the powers that be and to adopt ideologies of "adjustment" rather than more creative and also more dangerous solutions.

Dantès Bellegarde's expression, *"Haiti est née sans tête,"* expressed the view of a truncated society in the sense of the "unfortunate" departure of the upper stratum.[9] The decisions affecting Saint Domingue had been made in metropolitan France, and the large landowners were often absentees.[10] Achieving independence through revolution had led to the departure of a portion of the upper stratum, white, mulatto, and black, thus leaving the bourgeoisie fragmented, its more conservative elements in permanent exile in Louisiana, Maryland, Cuba, France, Trinidad, or Puerto Rico, and its liberal wing in newly founded Haiti. Haitian political independence came partly as a result of bourgeois liberalism against a colonial *"ancien régime"* that appeared grossly inefficient in economic terms and whose grip upon the economy had become too heavy.

Throughout the nineteenth century, as the bourgeoisie entrenched itself in each nation, nationalism and social conservatism grew rather than diminished. During this period of consolidation of power, the bourgeoisies of Latin America, with work to do and room in which to expand, seemed to have cared less about other dimensions of independence than about the political. This disregard for cultural and economic independence was particularly tragic in Latin America, where national integration should have required theoretically the conscious development of "independent" cultures. In Latin America and the United States, the vision emerged of a new world with new opportunities for a new individual, in contradistinction to old European practices, rather than to the old European spirit. The Americas, it was believed, were to improve upon Europe, with which it shared a "common culture." It was, therefore, not surprising to hear the Brazilian poet, Olavo Bilac, exclaim as late as 1907: "Our soul is still, and I believe always will be, an extension of the French soul."[11]

National integration is the sine qua non of national existence; it also ensures the national state of continued existence. A society living within the confines of an established state, subject to the same ruling authority, will usually tend toward greater homogeneity and an *intégration de base*. Social stratification adds a further element to the equation. Thus, in France, the bourgeoisie had originally sought incorporation into the ruling aristocracy, but had failed.[12] The Haitian *affranchis* had likewise attempted repeatedly throughout the seventeenth and eighteenth century to become accepted socially by the white bourgeoisie but they had failed because the colonial policy of racial exclusivism proved too strong.[13] Only in England, where the aristocracy had joined with the bourgeoisie, did a composite ruling class emerge.[14]

Cultural independence, at the time of Latin American independence in the early nineteenth century, would have signified a break with European cultural tradition. Because of their economic interests and cultural heritage, the *criollo* and *affranchi* elites of Latin America were unlikely to produce such a break. And although these elites recognized that their middle-ground position in the colonial social hierarchy had implications for later political and cultural developments in the new states (as exemplified by Emile Nau's statement mentioned earlier), the independence leaders of Spanish America clearly indicated where their allegiance lay. Many of them had feared Bourbon reforms and liberal dominance of the Iberian peninsula. Although liberals led some of the independence movements, conservative interests in the economy continued to predominate in the state and in Church circles.[15]

Emile Nau's declaration was echoed by Simón Bolívar, who had written in his Jamaica Letter in 1814 in a form reminiscent of Beaubrun Ardouin:

We are . . . neither Indian nor European, but a species midway between the legitimate proprietors of this country and the Spanish usurpers. In short, though American by birth we derive our rights from Europe, and we have to assert these rights against the rights of the natives, and at the same time we must defend ourselves against the invaders.[16]

The situation seemed simplified of course in Haiti and North America, where the toll of genocide had been particularly heavy.

During the nineteenth century, "native" thought, to use Bolívar's expression, would have meant the extrapolation of thought from social organization as understood by the Indio in Central and South America and by the African former slave in Haiti. That aboriginal thought, which was traditional in a general sense, had but a veneer of European thinking and would have signified by its acceptance by the ruling groups a profound change in politics and a real cultural independence from Europe.

At the time of independence, though, there was seemingly no alternative to modernization seen as westernization. Even if some ex-slaves in Haiti had wished that country's political and cultural isolation, that goal would not have been possible: Maroon societies (West Indies), Bush Negroes (Suriname), or a Palmares undertaking (Brazil) could not have resisted eventual recolonization. In this sense, Dantès Bellegarde may have been right. As the century advanced, later attempts at cultural independence came, not from nonassimilated "natives," but from an intellectual elite that had grown geographically away from the European parent culture. This evolutionary process was illustrated by the declarations of Francisco Bilbao in Chile, by the Asociación de Mayo in mid-nineteenth-century Argentina, much later by the Ateneo de la Juventud (Mexico), and in the mid-twentieth century by the members of the *génération de l'Occupation* (Haiti).

The concept of cultural independence came relatively late in all parts of the colonial world. It became significant as a concept only when the structures of economic neocolonialism were being elaborated in the late nineteenth century. In Haiti, the formation of the movement known as the *génération de la Ronde* (1898) was observed at a time when American, German, and French business pressures were increasing in the country. But the spirit of Haitian cultural independence would not reach its full potential until the 1930s, when the United States occupation of Haiti raised the specter of "Americanization," when racial prejudice from North Americans reached its zenith, and when Haitian peasants asserted themselves against the United States Marine Corps.

As late as the 1950s Leopold S. Senghor of Senegal felt the necessity for cultural independence in the subjugated nations more keenly than the need for political independence. He deemed necessary a healthy national self-image, self-esteem, and a measure of ethnocentrism. These qualities were indeed essential if colonial societies were to transcend the definition imposed upon them by colonialism. In this sense, Négritude became a necessary phase, leading to more radical thought, such as that of Frantz Fanon.

In the twentieth century, Third World social thinkers and the groups that give them sustenance have owed their influential position to the existence of a lasting colonial system that itself reflects the prevalent conditions of worldwide inequalities between classes, states, and individuals. The individual's recognition by intellectual elites at the center would justify his or her preeminent position at home as that person best suited to meet the challenges of "modernization. . . ." Because the local bourgeoisie derives its power mainly from contacts between itself and the representatives of the powerful Western presence, the theories it was most tempted to adopt were adaptations of Western theories of social organization. The Western economic doctrines were those by which they rationalized their own domination.

In Haiti, as may be expected in most small states, the elite's justification of its dominance gave rise to the most enlightening rationalizations. Because great economic concentration of power occurred increasingly in fewer nations in the twentieth century and was accompanied by a decrease in the international standing of small states whose bourgeoisies could not hope to compete economically in the international system, cultural matters acquired a proportionately greater significance in the definition of social class in these small states, than otherwise might be the case. And because the power for making decisions was located abroad and because the capital required for the exploitation of Haitian economic resources was foreign, "social" considerations expanded, while a strictly economic definition lessened somewhat in social class ascription.

From its lack of expertise and capital, Haiti's marginality to the world economy was fixed.[17] But the Haitian elite, although the possibility for capital formation was meager, remained capitalistic in sentiment and developed the aristocratic demeanor for which it became known abroad. That the content of the class struggle in Haiti had shifted somewhat from a strict economic basis to that of other factors such as "culture," changing, as it were, from substance to form, is most clearly seen in the writings of the country's ideologues in the nineteenth century. Their arguments tended to move away from the economic considerations characteristic of the pre-independence period, toward establishing Haiti as a civilized nation under the directorship of those *who knew best,* "as these citizens formed the most enlightened class in the nation. . . ." according to Beaubrun Ardouin.[18] The elite's ideology was an elaborate rationalization for its sociopolitical and economic dominance.

As statements of ideals, ideologies explain elite actions in light of both motivations and rationalizations. One understands, then, the importance of ideological formulation in the development of policy. The making of governmental policy is the prerogative of elites, and ideologies help determine the kind, the rate, and the limits of change that can be expected in a given society.

In this connection, Walter Rodney's words acquire their full meaning: "So long as there is political power, so long as a society has the opportunity to define its own ideology and culture, then the peoples of that society have some control over their own destinies. . . . [and] to greater or lesser extent, the ruling class in any given society is always engaged in the developmental process as conscious instruments of change or conservation.[19]

The cultured leaders did not realize that the revolution had triumphed because their words had unshackled the soul of the nation and that they had to govern with that soul and not against it or without it.

Jose Marti, *Our America*

APPENDIX

HAITI AND HER PROBLEMS

A LECTURE

by *Dantès Bellegarde*
former delegate of Haiti at the League of Nations
Delivered in the University of Puerto Rico under the auspices of the
Ibero American Institute of the University,
April 1936

Originally published in the *University of Puerto Rico Bulletin* (Rio Piedras, P. R., Series VII, No. 1 [September 1936]).

Haiti and International Cooperation

The day after the surrender of Yorktown, in a letter of October 20, 1781, General George Washington wrote to the French Admiral, Count de Grasse: "The surrender of Yorktown, which has brought such glory and success to the Allies and of which the honor belongs to Your Excellency, has greatly surpassed my hopes." You know what decisive assistance Admiral de Grasse rendered to the cause of American independence. I wish simply to remind you here that the 3,400 troops of line that he disembarked on August 31, 1781, in Chesapeake Bay, under the orders of the Marquis de Saint-Simon, came directly from Haiti, then a French colony, and that these men contributed to the taking of Yorktown as they had previously participated, under Count d'Estaing, in the battle of Savannah on October 9, 1779.

It has been the singular good fortune of my little country to have had a part in the greatest events in the history of America. Assuredly, it cannot be necessary to remind you of the aid given by our Alexandre Pétion to

Simón Bolívar in the emancipation of the Spanish colonies of this continent. The examples of Pan American solidarity that Haiti has given in the
past, her economic bonds with Europe, her spiritual and commercial ties
with France, permit her, in all inter-American discussions, to take her part
on a broad international plane. This explains the character of the observations to follow.

Some idealists have long dreamed of creating a world which should be
the harmonious union of all the continents. It was their generous ambition to found, on a plane higher than that of the individual nations, a universal fatherland where men of all nationalities, all religions, all races, could
work together in a spirit of brotherhood for the common good of humanity.
These people knew men. They loved them. They had faith in the destinies of
the human race. Their own acute thinking led them to the conviction that
peace between the classes of society and between nations was a fundamental
condition for assuring the well-being of mankind. Their personal knowledge
of great affairs made tangible to them the economic and political interdependence of the nations.

The interdependence of nations implies that each one shall profit with
the success of the others and suffer with their sufferings. Hence the necessity for all to work together in close cooperation for the welfare of all.
Cooperation is the firm foundation for universal peace.

But the great discovery of our times was to understand that there is a
"technique of peace"—as there is of war—and that this technique should be
elaborated and constantly improved to adapt it to the necessities of a world
in perpetual motion, through permanent institutions whose activity would
be mainly directed to the pacific organization of humanity.

The work for peace must be staged, I might say, on three planes: internal
peace of each nation; internal peace of each continent; inter-continental or
universal peace. What we have first to seek is the best way to establish peace
within each of our countries—on the firm foundation of national prosperity
and social justice. But we know only too well that the prosperity of each
nation is closely bound up with that of others, and that we can only escape
from our common distress by means of collective measures resulting from
the conciliation of our respective interests.

Charles Lamb has expressed the truth that "To know one another
is to love one another." Hence the necessity for people to become better
acquainted with one another and, in consequence, to love each other more.
But love reposes essentially on confidence. It is confidence that the world

needs above all at this very moment. A wind of pessimism is blowing over all the earth. Internal discords, economic crises, commercial unrest, paralyzation of industry, signs of war, cries for vengeance: all these create a heavy atmosphere which seems scarcely favorable to universal peace. But these anxieties make the necessity for "peace organizations" more evident and must make their existence more desirable to us.

The most complete of all peace organizations is without doubt the League of Nations. One is struck with astonishment to see with what distrust its birth was welcomed and how savagely it has been attacked in certain centers. And, nevertheless, an institution like the League, founded to ensure the peace of the world, should have the confidence and the support of everyone desirous of seeing amity and concord established. Enveloped in an atmosphere of distrust, obliged to conduct itself so as not to imperil its still fragile existence, fearing to take energetic decisions which it knows it has not the means to impose on recalcitrants, it appears fearful and hesitant. And complaint is made of this very thing. Each decision is criticized with evident desire to diminish the League's authority and its prestige. It is said with a sneer that the League has been in existence for sixteen years. "What has it done actually to prevent war and its monstrous consequences?" Sixteen years! That is indeed little enough time in the life of a great institution like the League of Nations. In those sixteen years it has nevertheless done a great deal for the technical organization of peace. Much more remains to be done. But can we reproach the League for not having yet succeeded in establishing universal peace and internal justice on a definite basis? Can we reproach it with not having in sixteen years overcome the misunderstandings, conflicts, rancors, antagonism and hate created through centuries of open or concealed rivalry?

To paraphrase the words of a great French statesman, Raymond Poincaré, the League of Nations is "a continual creation." Yes, it is being created continually. But let us not forget that it is the nations which create it by giving their confidence and their good will. It is a statue that the chisel of the sculptor is fashioning slowly from the marble. The people, they are the sculptor. The more they come crowding and enthusiastic to Geneva, the more they bring to Geneva their spirit of peace, their sincere desire to collaborate in the great labor of friendship and justice which is being realized there, the stronger the League of Nations will be, the greater its authority, the more easily can its decisions be imposed on the conscience of nations—on the weakest and the most powerful alike.

That is what our Latin American nations have understood, when from the very beginning the great majority of them. gave their enthusiastic support to Geneva. With great joy we saw in 1931 Mexico come to take her place in the League. And what of the United States?

On September 9, 1922, speaking as the delegate of Haiti at the Third Assembly of the League of Nations, I said to the meeting at Geneva: "Even now when the League of Nations feels sure of living, a secret anxiety troubles it because it is not yet the world association that it wishes to be and should be. Three great nations—Germany, Russia, and the United States—are still absent. But surely they will come when the difficulties of internal policy or foreign policy which now prevent them from taking their places among us shall have ceased to exist." And I appealed hopefully to that happy day when the United States, which has become the most ardent propagator in the world of the gospel of peace, should come to take its place in the temple that its strong hands have contributed to build, and where today the dearest hopes of mankind are fostered.

Since I expressed this hope, Germany has come and departed. Japan has departed. Russia has come and remains. But Germany and Japan must return. They will return. Will the United States come?

It would be indiscreet on my part to discuss here the reasons which explain or justify the absence of the United States from the League of Nations. The matter is one of domestic order which only concerns the citizens of North America. But nobody can forget that Wilson is the father of the League. Nobody can pretend that the collaboration of the United States with this institution is not indispensable to the peace of the world.

For instance, the question of disarmament is one of the most important that the League has to settle. Who would dare to say that Geneva can solve this difficult problem without the help and the direct participation of the United States? What a relief for the people if the billions deducted from world resources and devoted to dangerous armaments were employed in productive enterprises which would add to human welfare! But the problem is not simple; and I dare say that disarmament, however desirable it may be, would not alone suffice to settle the question of world peace. Bring two nations, unarmed in the material sense of the word, face to face: they would make war on each other if the spirit of war existed between them, and it is the stronger by reason of population, industrial organization, and the discipline of the masses, that would emerge victorious from the fight. The former Prime Minister of Great Britain, Mr. J.

Ramsay MacDonald, said in an address on July 11, 1931: "History is the uninterrupted recital of armed peoples attacking armed peoples." Yes, but also of armed peoples attacking *unarmed* peoples. A great nation, however reduced its armaments may be, will always remain formidably armed for a small and weak nation. With ten gunboats and two bombers the United States can dispose of Haiti.

So, it is in the reduction of armaments that little nations will find the guarantees of peace necessary to their security. While hoping most earnestly for the complete and so difficult success of the Disarmament Conference, they would like to see collective measures adopted, measures that would be strong enough and conclusive enough to prevent any outbreak of aggressive war. What would these measures be? It is for the Governments to decide. We can understand their reluctance to commit themselves, fearing that they will not have public opinion in their countries behind them. International evolution renders the adoption of such measures indispensable. Unfortunately, public opinion in many countries is not yet on a plane with international evolution: this is what hinders the establishment of the "mutual guaranties" which would be the bulwark to withstand any warlike aggression. However, we must recognize the fact that in the anarchic conditions we see in the world today, no nation will accept a reduction in its means of defense and personal protection unless it finds, in a firm international accord—the most extensive possible—a set of guarantees to assure it peace in the present and confidence for the future. When the former Belgian Minister for Foreign Affairs, M. Hymans, using a very apt figure of speech, advised "putting teeth" in the Kellogg-Briand Pact, he did not mean to recommend that it should actually "bite": he was thinking that "to show the teeth" would suffice in the majority of cases to bring the most angry to reason. It is necessary that right be endowed with the strength to enforce itself.

But our ideal is not limited to this. If the present state of international society obliges us to use violent procedure—economic pressure or military measures—to impose peace, we cannot resign ourselves to such an extremity without repugnance. It is on a more human basis that peace must be established: the consent of the hearts and the adherence of the wills of all the people on earth. It is a great source of pride to Haiti that its delegate to the first Assembly of the League of Nations in 1920, M. Frederic Doret, was the first at Geneva to use the expression "moral disarmament." Let us remember that, while seeking to achieve political disarmament by the reduction of military forces and economic disarmament by the reduction of tariffs, we have a higher work to accomplish: spiritual disarmament by the suppression of that hate and distrust that poison the life of nations.

We invite everyone who is loyal and faithful to take part in this work; but our appeal is directed particularly to women, because it is they who can prepare a peaceful future for humanity by forging the man of tomorrow from the pure metal of infancy. My dear friend, Salvador de Madariaga, former Ambassador of Spain in Washington and in Paris, by an equivocal vote of the Twelfth Assembly of the League of Nations in 1931, ensured effective feminine collaboration in the great task of disarmament.

To attain the desired end we must develop that "international spirit" in the world which the President of Columbia University, Nicholas Murray Butler, has so well defined in the following terms: "The international spirit is only the habit of thinking of foreign relations and foreign affairs and the habit of treating them as if all the nations of the civilized world were *equals* and *friends* cooperating in the progress of civilization, in the development of commerce and industry, in the diffusion of light and education throughout the world."

Equality and friendship: here is the firm foundation of the Pan American Union. Opposite the Union of our 21 Republics of America we should like to see a united Europe arise, a united Asia, a united Africa, not to combat one another but to form, in liberty, labor and light, the great human Federation that is the ideal in our hearts and our minds.

At the meeting on May 4, 1927, of the Third Pan American Commercial Conference at Washington, I had the honor, as the delegate of the Chamber of Commerce of Haiti, to propose the following resolution:

> Recognizing the economic solidarity of all the nations of the world, the Third Pan American Commercial Conference begs to present to the International Economic Conference, which has assembled at Geneva under the auspices of the League of Nations, its warmest wishes and to express the hope that the labors of the Conference will bring about happy results for the reconstruction of Europe and for the amelioration of conditions of living in all the nations of the world.

I have recalled this resolution, which was unanimously passed by the 1927 Conference, just to show that no Pan American Conference or organization can, from an economic point of view, confine its activity to the study of purely American questions; that is to say, questions affecting only the countries of America represented therein. There is no economic problem that is purely American. America, as a whole, does not and cannot constitute a closed economy. To be fully convinced of the truth of this statement, one need only read the statistics of the foreign trade of our twenty-one Republics. I recall that Haiti sells 90 percent of her exports to Europe, France receiving 60 or 75 percent.

The principle of international economic solidarity has long served as a topic for discussions of a rather academic character. Today this principle is evident as a fact even to the man in the street. The present crisis, which affects the small nations as well as the great ones, the rich as well as the poor, bankers as well as manual laborers, great industrialists as well as the most humble tiller of the soil in every country, in a way makes tangible the interdependence of nations. Among its repercussions in the internal affairs of each country, it shows in a surprising manner how the different elements of the national activity—agriculture, industry, commerce, credit, labor—are all indissolubly linked together, like the organs of a single body: one cannot perish without dragging the others with it to extinction.

There is a "world economy." Prof. Elemer Hantos, of the University of Budapest, defines it as follows: "The sum total of national economic activities, each depending upon the others and each having need of the others." That this world economy is a reality, founded upon interdependence of peoples and economic solidarity, no one can doubt. The simultaneous appearance of crises in the economic life of different nations testifies to it in a clear manner. The present world crisis is manifest proof that no country, no matter how vast and rich, can shut itself inside its four walls and isolate itself from other parts of the globe.

But it does not suffice to point out the existence of this world economy. It is necessary to attempt its organization according to natural laws which have governed within each state the organization of national economies through the collaboration of the citizens of the nation in private enterprises and public services. This organization of the international economy is necessary, for it is certainly the essential basis of world peace. This has been clearly noted by the World Economic Conference meeting at Geneva in 1927, when it wrote in the preamble to its General Resolutions that: "The maintenance of the peace of the world depends in large part on the principles according to which the economic policies of nations are conceived and applied."

According to what principles have the policies of the various states of the world been conceived and applied? An important publication of the League of Nations, *The Memorandum of International Commerce and Balancing of Payments*, permits us to secure an approximate idea by noting the statistical effects of the foreign commerce of the sixty-four countries. It is not possible to analyze this work here. It is important however, to note the lesson which can be drawn from it; namely, that the very great differences in the conditions of labor and of production in the different countries, serving as pretext for protectionist tendencies, have created and maintained a system of competition and economic nationalism which places an obstacle in the way of the free circulation of goods and hinders the realization of a perfect equilibrium between production and consumption.

For this system of competition, which has given birth to a race for high tariffs just as dangerous as the race for armaments, it is necessary to substitute a system of cooperation which permits in the first place, the most rational and just foundations.

The United States, in the legitimate desire not to entangle herself in the quarrels or political rivalries of a turbulent Europe, has long believed and still believes in the wisdom of an attitude of isolation. The United States constitutes too great a force in the world, and her interests are too intimately bound up with those of other nations, for her to be able to hold aside from European affairs or the affairs of any other continent. But the difficulty is to know how far one can separate financial and economic problems that have not a political aspect. The absolute distinction that we make between economics and politics is the result of a simple operation of our minds. We must take care not to reason only on the basis of abstractions instead of considering the reality in its complexity and its indivisibility.

Recognizing that the economic reconstruction of Europe is indispensable to the reestablishment of our own affairs in America, we should not hesitate to look reality in the face and seek the real causes for the present sorry state of affairs, and the means for its amelioration.

On the advice of those who studied the world depression in all good faith, seven Powers, the United States, France, Great Britain, Italy, Germany, Russia and Japan, have in their hands the solution of the problem—and this solution is to be found only in their active and loyal cooperation in the task of reestablishing the economic health of the world. But we all agree in recognizing that this cooperation is not possible unless, first of all, close collaboration is established between France and Germany. And here the political point of view makes its appearance.

Any collaboration implies confidence. Does confidence exist between France and German? No. What measures are, then, necessary to create it and maintain it, complete and permanent? . . . We run the risk of being unjust toward nations when we do not make the necessary effort to understand their state of mind, their feelings, their sufferings, their fears, and aspirations.

We have sympathized with Germany in her distress. We have understood the sufferings of this great nation humiliated in its pride by an unsuccessful war. We have all desired that she should be saved from the financial catastrophe with which she was menaced. We all desire that she shall live, work, be prosperous, taste the joys of fruitful peace; because German culture is necessary to the intellectual life of humanity and because the ruin of Germany would spell the ruin of world economy. On the other hand, it does not seem to me that in the course of the present discussion about European affairs many are entirely just to France. They have forgotten her past misfortunes, forgotten the admirable efforts she made to bind up the wounds of war, to reconstruct her savagely devastated regions—I saw them two years after the war—, to build up her economic life, restore her finances, stabilize her currency . . . Because she demands security when sacrifice is asked of her, she is accused of being a nation without heart and without pity. Such injustice does not advance the work of peace, but, on the contrary, retards it, hardening hearts and arousing passions.

I do not profess to be the advocate of France. That would indeed be too great a presumption on my part. But I belong to the only independent state of French speech in America. The official position that I occupied at Paris and the personal knowledge that I have of the French people permit me to affirm that France would gladly renounce the enormous burden of alone ensuring her own security, if collective measures were sufficiently efficacious and sure to establish confidence on a solid and permanent basis.

The restoration of confidence is the first condition for economic rehabilitation. It is indeed lack of confidence that is at the bottom of the present crisis. We are debating in the midst of confusion. As we see so many different opinions, so many different remedies, one cannot help thinking of the madman whose mania it was to collect timepieces and who had a strange eagerness to try to make the innumerable clocks that cumbered up his room all keep the same time. It seems difficult to conciliate the many opinions and to make all the doctors agree . . . except to disagree. However, we have some definite data, both on the causes of the depression and on means for remedying it. It is now a question of applying the best solutions proposed, and of applying them quickly, for time presses.

The people of the United States have to restore confidence in themselves, that is to say, in the marvelous resources of their labor, and, above all, in their admirable qualities of energy which have permitted them to emerge victorious from all previous crises and which have made of their great country the most powerful in the world.

We also, in the Latin countries of America, have need of renewing confidence in ourselves and inspiring confidence in others. Nature has endowed us with too much in the way of resources, our peoples are too eager for work, too anxious for progress, too devoted to their ideals, for us to have any reason to doubt ourselves and to abandon ourselves to despair. Because others do not know us well enough, they have attributed to us a reputation for revolutionary turbulence which is extremely prejudicial to our credit. In reality, our revolutionary troubles find their explanation, if not their justification, in the economic crises from which all our countries suffer so keenly. The immediate cause of our present depression is the fall in price of our principal export products. One might even say that the scale of prices of these products is the political barometer of the majority of the countries of Latin America. When prices are high, prosperity reigns and everyone is content. When prices fall, governments are in danger of falling too, because poverty rules and discontent becomes general. Recent events in the political history of some of our nations show to what extent revolutionary movements are bound up with fluctuations in the prices of certain products, such as coffee, wheat, cotton, sugar, nitrates, cocoa, etc. But it is also right to say that the great majority of our countries of America—even if they have not yet arrived at a state of complete political stability—possess, what is more precious, social stability; that is to say, they do not know class conflict. Nevertheless, *it is to be feared that a continued state of poverty and the dread of not being able to emerge from it by means of work, may lead the people to too great discouragement; and subversive doctrines may find them an easy prey.*

It has been estimated that, in the past ten years, the population of the world has increased 10 percent, the production of raw materials 40 percent, and food supplies 16 percent. Humanity as a whole has not derived from this progress a proportionate profit, because of an imperfect distribution of wealth and the lack of between production and consumption. And this brings us to the most serious problem that the conscience of nations has to face today: the constantly increasing number of unemployed. Farmers are ruined because they produce too much wheat and this wheat sells at too low a price: but at the same time millions of men, women, and children are threatened with starvation, because either they are without work or they receive too low a wage. It is a tragic situation. A French writer, M. Constantin-Weyer, has said: "Civilization is a collective defense against death, disease and poverty. Civilized nations are those which have best been able to organize this collective defense." Civilization no longer merits its name if we permit the tragic situation I have just described to continue.

I remember that at the Third Pan American Commercial Conference in 1927, a resolution inspired in the highest spirit of social solidarity was presented by Mr. Abbot Goodhue, of the United States Delegation. This resolution, which was passed by a unanimous vote, was to the effect that commerce and finance are intended to serve human needs and lessen the burdens of life and labor, and it recommended expressly to the attention of future conferences a study of the best ways of "improving the material standards of life and labor of the masses of the people of the respective American countries." The measures to be taken—I think—to obtain this improvement should have a double objective: (1) to raise the purchasing power and, in consequence, the power of consumption of each individual, to a level permitting him to achieve for himself and his family the comfort indispensable to every civilized creature—and this is social peace; and (2) to increase the capacity of production and, in consequence, the power of absorption of each country to a level which permits it to meet its obligations toward its people and toward other nations—and here you have international peace.

The economic and financial depression in which all of our countries find themselves submerged shows clearly that Latin America needs the United States as the United States needs Latin America. In these hours of common difficulties, they have to search for and take those common measures which are demanded by the situation. Not one of our nations can alone and unaided resolve its economic and financial crisis. The improvement and final restoration of affairs in America can result only through collective efforts, adopted through an intensive collaboration among our various countries, between the producers of raw materials and those who sell manufactured products, between creditors and debtors, between capital and labor, in order to reach exact equilibrium between production and consumption. To a bad economic condition, only economic remedies can be applied effectively. And these remedies can be found only within collective action, that is, through cooperation.

Inter-American solidarity is not simply a verbal expression, but a concrete reality made up of a colossal mass of raw materials and resources of all sorts. As a matter of fact, the United States takes from Latin America a large share of the raw materials and agricultural products necessary for her industries. On the other hand, her industrial production, stimulated by the World War, has surpassed and tends to surpass in increasing proportions the need of her internal consumption. The sole remedy for this dangerous overproduction is the extension of the American market. But the word extension should not be taken in the sense of territorial expansion. To extend the market is to secure a clientele of great purchasing power, the absorptive power of which will increase in proportion to industrial production. It is clearly to the interest of the United States, then, to increase the purchasing power of her Latin American clientele, provider of her raw materials and consumer of her manufactured products.

How can the purchasing power of Latin America be increased? By developing her productive power and finding outlets for her products. From what source can she get the necessary capital for this development of production; that is, the exploitation of her enormous natural resources? From the United States, which, from having been a debtor nation before the War, has today become a creditor and the biggest lender in the world.

Here arises a most delicate question—one which affects the whole future of inter-American relations.

Credit, in the etymological sense of the word, is synonymous with confidence. To lend money to someone is to have faith in his honesty, in his solvency, or in the value of the real guarantees which he can offer. But the borrower should also have confidence in his creditor; confidence that his creditor has no concealed thought of conquest, of violent seizure of his goods, his liberty, or his rights; confidence that the money offered to him is not a limed trap wherein he risks losing all his feathers and even his life.

We must admit that this confidence is lacking on both sides. The North American lenders—those who do not look for other than economic advantages—are afraid to place their money in uncertain enterprises or in undertakings which do not have for their aim a substantial increase of profits for themselves and, at the same time, definite increase in the standard of living and the comfort and prosperity of the borrower. The Latin American borrowers on their side, in a sort of fugitive vision, see behind each Yankee capitalist regiments of marching marines or the formidable silhouettes of American superdreadnoughts.

It is this reciprocal fear which it is necessary to dissipate by political action composed of frankness and loyalty, as well as by close cooperation between business men and the *élites* of all our American countries. They can suggest the best measures for giving to American continental economic policy a solid moral, cultural and political foundation, which will rest firmly on the organization of international justice, on the principle of the legal equality of States and on an absolute respect for the independence and the territorial and administrative integrity of our twenty-one American Republics.

This policy of unity and friendship has had no more eloquent interpreter than Mr. Franklin Delano Roosevelt, who has named it the "policy of the good neighbor." Nor has the President of the United States limited himself to the enunciation of a formula. He has expressed the substance of this policy in two declarations which of themselves would suffice to crown his career as a statesman: first, his declaration of April 12, 1933, in which he transforms the Monroe doctrine into a Pan American doctrine; that is to say, he gives Pan America the character of a collective guarantee of the 21 Republics against extra-continental aggression, the adoption of which by the states of America would guarantee each American state against aggressions by another.

In this capital enterprise the role of leader has been proposed to the United States by the recent eloquent appeal of President Roosevelt for an Inter-American Peace Conference at Buenos Aires. The meeting of this Conference, at a moment so critical in the life of our nations, will be certainly beneficial. We hope that from its labors concrete and practical solutions will result to put an end to the present economic disorganization of our countries of America and to establish inter-American peace on a sound and permanent basis.

What I have wanted above all to bring out in my lecture is that Pan Americanism must not have any selfish thought and that its life principle should be "cooperation"; cooperation among the American nations; cooperation with all the groups of legitimate interests which have been or may be constituted in the world. Let us hope—when good times have come again, for they will return—that the peoples will not retire each into its own prosperity as into an impregnable fortress; that they will recall that a common distress made them all work together for the welfare of all, and that the solidarity thus achieved should stand as a permanent lesson for all future cooperation.

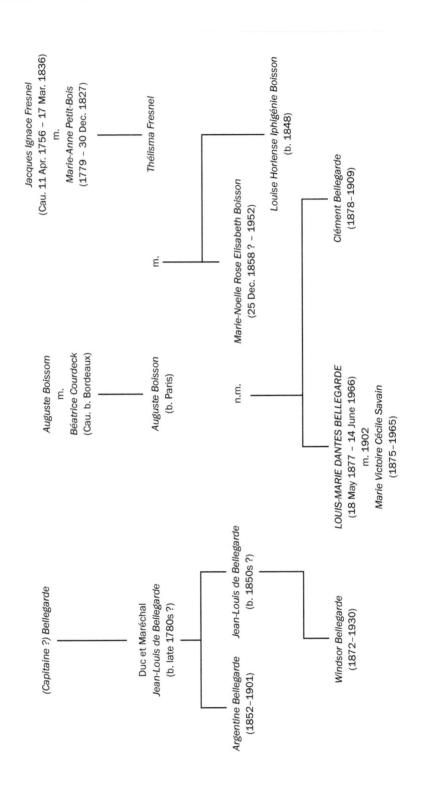

NOTES

NOTES TO PREFACE

1. Jeffrey Rothfelder, *McIlhenney's Gold: How a Louisiana Family Built the Tabasco Empire* (New York: HarperCollins, 2007).

2. The National Association for the Advancement of Colored People's James Weldon Johnson pointed out McIlhenny's clear lack of qualifications for that position in his exposé of the occupation. See James Weldon Johnson, "Self-Determining Haiti, III. Government Of, By, and For the National City Bank," *The Nation* 111, no. 2880 (September 11, 1920): 295–97.

3. Hans Schmidt, *The United States Occupation of Haiti, 1915–1934* 2nd Edition (New Brunswick: Rutgers University Press, 1995), 111.

4. Along with *In the Shadow of Powers,* other foundational works on Bellegarde include Mercer Cook, "Dantes Bellegarde," *Phylon* 1, no. 2 (2nd Qtr., 1940): 125–35 and Hénock Trouillot, *Dantès Bellegarde, de écrivain d'autrefois* (Port-au-Prince, Haiti: N. A. Théodore, 1957).

5. Why the United States occupied Haiti is a question beyond the scope of this foreword but for additional reading see Jeffrey Sommers with contributions from Patrick Delices, *Race, Reality, and Realpolitik: U.S.-Haiti Relations in the Lead Up to the 1915 Occupation* (Lanham, MD: Lexington Books, 2016).

6. Michel-Rolph Trouillot, *Silencing the Past: Power and the Production of History* 2nd Edition (Boston: Beacon Press, 2015), 73.

7. On Trouillot's writings on the Haitian Revolution and historiography, see especially Alyssa Goldstein Sepinwall, "Still Unthinkable? The Haitian Revolution and the Reception of Michel-Rolph Trouillot's 'Silencing the Past,'" *Journal of Haitian Studies* 19, no. 2 Special Issue on Michel-Rolph Trouillot (Fall 2013): 75–103.

8. David Patrick Geggus, *Haitian Revolutionary Studies* (Bloomington: Indiana University Press, 2002) and Laurent Dubois, *Avengers of the New World: The Story of the Haitian Revolution* (Cambridge: Belknap Press of Harvard University Press, 2005).

9. George Frederickson, *Racism: A Short History* (Princeton, NJ: Princeton University Press, 2002).

10. Speech of Mr. Benton, of Missouri, Delivered to the Senate of the United States, (In Secret Session), on the Mission to Panama, March 13, 1826 (Washington: Columbian State Office, 1826), 35.

11. Recent and foundational works on U.S. anxieties about Haiti and Haitians include Alfred N. Hunt, *Haiti's Influence on Antebellum America: Slumbering Volcano in the Caribbean* (Baton Rouge: Louisiana State University Press, 1988); Ashli White, *Encountering Revolution: Haiti and the Making of the Early Republic* (Baltimore: Johns Hopkins University Press, 2010); Matthew Clavin, *Toussaint Louverture and the American Civil War: The Promise and Peril of a Second Haitian Revolution* (Philadelphia: University of Pennsylvania Press, 2011); and Gerald Horne, *Confronting Black Jacobins: The United States, the Haitian Revolution, and the Origins of the Dominican Republic* (New York: Monthly Review Press, 2015).

12. Sommers, Ermitte St. Jacques, and Patrick Bellegarde-Smith, eds., *Journal of Haitian Studies* 21, no. 2 Special Issue on the US Occupation of Haiti, 1915–1934 (Fall 2015).

13. Mary A. Renda, *Taking Haiti: Military Occupation and the Culture of U.S. Imperialism, 1915–1940* (Chapel Hill: The University of North Carolina Press, 2001).

14. Michel-Rolph Trouillot, 73.

15. Dash, *Haiti and the United States: National Stereotypes and the Literary Imagination* 2nd Edition (London: Palgrave Macmillan, 1997).

16. On post-occupation Haiti, see especially Matthew J. Smith, *Red and Black in Haiti: Radicalism, Conflict, and Political Change, 1934–1957* (Chapel Hill: The University of North Carolina Press, 2009) and Chantalle F. Verna, *Haiti and the Uses of America: Post-U.S. Occupation Promises* (New Brunswick, NJ: Rutgers University Press, 2017). Foundational works on the Duvalier dictatorship include Bernard Diederich, *L'Héritier* (Port-au-Prince: Henri Deschamps, 2011); James Ferguson, *Papa Doc, Baby Doc: Haiti and the Duvaliers* (Oxford: B. Blackwell, 1988); Trouillot, *Les racines historiques de l'État Duvalierien* (Port-au-Prince: Henri Deschamps, 1987); and Trouillot, *Haiti, State Against Nation: The Origins and Legacy of Duvalierism* (New York: Monthly Review Press, 1990).

17. Elizabeth Abbott, *Haiti: The Duvaliers and Their Legacy* (New York: McGraw-Hill, 1988).

18. Paul Farmer, *AIDS and Accusation: Haiti and the Geography of Blame*, Updated Edition (Berkeley: University of California Press, 2006).

19. C. L. R. James, *The Black Jacobins: Toussaint L'Ouverture and the San Domingo Revolution* (London: Secker and Warburg, 1938); David Nicholls, *From Dessalines to Duvalier: Race, Colour, and National Independence in Haiti* (Cambridge: Cambridge University Press, 1979); J. Michael Dash, *Literature and Ideology in Haiti, 1915–1961* (London: Macmillan Press, 1981). Gordon K. Lewis, *Main Currents in Caribbean Thought: The Historical Evolution of Caribbean Society in its Ideological Aspects, 1492–1900* (Baltimore: The Johns Hopkins University Press, 1983) might be included, too.

20. Bellegarde-Smith, *In the Shadow of Powers: Dantès Bellegarde in Haitian Social Thought* (Atlantic Highlands, NJ: Humanities Press International, 1985), xi.

21. Rayford Logan, *The Diplomatic Relations of the United States with Haiti, 1776–1891* (Chapel Hill: The University of North Carolina Press, 1941). On Haitian diplomatic history, see also Ronald Angelo Johnson, *Diplomacy in Black and White: John Adams, Toussaint Louverture, and Their Atlantic World Alliance* (Athens: The University of Georgia Press, 2014); Brenda Gayle Plummer, *Haiti and the Great Powers, 1902–1915* (Baton Rouge: Louisiana State University Press, 1988); and Plummer, *Haiti and the United States: The Psychological Moment* (Athens: University of Georgia Press, 1992).

22. Magdaline W. Shannon, *Jean Price-Mars, the Haitian Elite and the American Occupation, 1915–1935* (New York: St. Martin's Press, 1996).

23. Patrick Bellegarde-Smith, "Haitian Studies Association Plenary Address: 22nd Annual Conference, Brown University, November 13, 2010," *Journal of Haitian Studies* 17, no.1 (Spring 2011): 230–44.

24. Liz Fekete, *Europe's Fault Lines: Racism and the Rise of the Right* (New York: Verso Books, 2018)

25. Thomas Piketty, *Capital in the Twenty-First Century* (Cambridge: Belknap Press of Harvard University Press, 2014).

26. Keeanga-Yamahtta Taylor, *From #BlackLivesMatter to Black Liberation* (New York: Haymarket Books, 2016).

27. Millery Polyné, ed., *The Idea of Haiti: Rethinking Crisis and Development* (Minneapolis: University of Minnesota Press, 2013) and Gina Athena Ulysse, *Why Haiti Needs New Narratives: A Post-Quake Chronicle*, trans., Nadève Ménard and Évelyne Trouillot (Middletown, CT: Wesleyan University Press, 2015).

28. Celucien L. Joseph, "'The Haitian Turn': An Appraisal of Recent Literary and Historiographical Works on the Haitian Revolution," *Journal of Pan African Studies* 5, no. 6 (September 2012): 37–55.

29. "Dantes Bellegarde: International Spokesman of Black Folk," *Crisis* 31 (April 1926): 295–96.

INTRODUCTION

1. Dantès Bellegarde, *Au service d'Haiti: Appréciations sur un haïtien et son œuvre* (Port-au-Prince: Imprimerie Theodore, 1962), p. 222.

2. P. W. Buck and M. B. Travis, Jr., eds. *Control of Foreign Relations in Modern Nations* (New York: W. W. Norton, 1957), p. 223.

3. Paul Blanchet, "Sur la tombe de Dantès Bellegarde," *Le nouvelliste* (Port-au-Prince), 17 June, 1966.

4. Ibid.

5. The various Pan-African Congresses, the Marcus Garvey movement, the impact of African art upon Western European art forms and literature, and the Harlem Renaissance are all illustrations of this Black awareness.

6. Dantès Bellegarde, *Pour une Haiti heureuse, par l'éducation et le travail,* 2 vols. (Port-au-Prince: Cheraquit, Imprimeur-Editeur, 1927–1929), 2: 3 (uttered on February 1907).

7. Paul Berthelet, "Une etrange histoire," *Le salut public* (Lyon), 19 September, 1922. This "declaration permits the conciliation of the two tendencies that manifest themselves in Geneva."

8. Harold E. Davis, *Latin American Social Thought: A Historical Introduction* (Baton Rouge: Louisiana University Press, 1972), and *Latin American Social Thought: The History of its Development since Independence, with Selected Readings* (Washington, DC: The University Press of Washington, 1961). See also, Pedro Henriquez Urena, *A Concise History of Latin American Culture*, trans. Gilbert Chase (New York: Praeger, 1966); W. Rex Crawford, *A Century of Latin American Thought* (New York: Praeger, 1961); Miguel Jorrin, and John D. Martz, *Latin American Political Thought and Ideology* (Chapel Hill: University of North Carolina Press, 1970); Edward J. Williams, "Secularization, Integration, and Rationalization: Some Perspectives from Latin American Thought," *Journal of Latin American Studies* 5, part 2 (November 1973): 199–216; and the classic by Leopoldo Zea, *The Latin American Mind* (Norman: University of Oklahoma Press, 1963), as works that never mentioned Haiti. For those that do mention Haiti, see David Nicholls, *From Dessalines to Duvalier: Race, Colour, and National Independence in Haiti* (Cambridge: Cambridge University Press, 1979); Michael J. Dash, *Literature and Ideology in Haiti, 1915–1961* (Totowa, NJ: Barnes and Noble, 1981); Leon-Francois Hoffman, *Le roman haitien: Ideologie et structure* (Sherbooke, CA: Editions Naaman, 1982); Gordon K. Lewis, *Main Currents in Caribbean Thought: The Historical Evolution of Caribbean Society in Its Ideological Aspects, 1492–1900* (Baltimore: John Hopkins University Press, 1983); Ulrich Fleishmann, *Ideyoloji ak reyalite nan literati ayisyen* (Port-au-Prince: Henri Deschamps, 1981).

9. Lucian W. Pye and Sidney Verba, eds., *Political Culture and Political Development* (Princeton: Princeton University Press, 1965), p. 16.

10. For an illustration of the first genre, see Erik H. Erikson, *Young Man Luther* (New York: W.W. Norton & Co., 1958); for the second, see Karl W. Deutsch, et al., *France, Germany and the Western Alliance* (New York: Charles Scribner's Sons, 1967); or Wendell Bell, *Jamaican Leaders: Political Attitudes in a New Nation* (Berkeley and Los Angeles: University of California Press, 1964).

11. See the works of Jean Price-Mars, the very sensitive interpretation done by Ghislain Gouraige, *La diaspora d'Haiti et l'Afrique* (Ottawa: Editions Naaman, 1974), and Auguste Viatte, *Histoire litteraire de l'Amerique francaise* (Paris: Presses Universitaires de France, 1954).

12. T. B. Bottomore, *Elites and Society* (London: Penguin Books Ltd., 1964), p. 93.

13. Gaetano Mosca, *The Ruling Class* (New York: McGraw-Hill, 1939), p. 53.

NOTES TO CHAPTER 1

1. See Henry Adams, *History of the United States during the Administrations of Jefferson and Madison* (New York, 1930) and cited in Rayford W. Logan,

The Diplomatic Relations of the United States with Haiti, 1776–1891 (Chapel Hill: University of North Carolina Press, 1941), p. 142. Adams commented: "The colonial system of France centered in Santo Domingo. . . . Of what use was Louisiana when France had clearly lost the main colony which Louisiana was meant to feed and fortify? . . . A year of war had consumed 50,000 men and money in vast amounts, with no other result than to prove that at least as many men and as much money would still be needed before any return could be expected. . . ."

2.   See Dantès Bellegarde et al. eds., *Morceaux choisis d'auteurs haitiens*, 2 vols. (Port-au-Prince: Imprimerie de Mme. F. Smith, 1904), 1: 10. Isaac later settled in Bordeaux where he died in 1854. Placide was incarcerated at Belle-Isle, while Toussaint died at the Fort de Joux, in the Jura mountains.

3.   In 1801, Toussaint promulgated a constitution that created a state of internal autonomy in Saint Domingue. His flag was a Negro's head on a white field. For details, see Alfred Nemours, *Toussaint Louverture fonde à Saint-Domingue la liberté et l'égalité* (Port-au-Prince: Imprimerie du College Vertiéres, 1945), p. 72–74.

4.   See Harold E. Davis, *History of Latin America* (New York: Ronald Press, 1968), p. 257. He argued that the Haitian Revolution was the French Revolution in America.

5.   See among others, Hubert Herring, *A History of Latin America*, 3rd ed. (New York: Alfred A. Knopf, 1968), p. 243. The economic production of Saint Domingue at the end of the eighteenth century surpassed that of the thirteen North American colonies and that of Hispanic America.

6.   See Davis, *History*, p. 257, and the books by Eric Williams, *Capitalism and Slavery* (Chapel Hill: University of North Carolina Press, 1944), C. L. R. James, *The Black Jacobins: Toussaint Louverture and the San Domingo Revolution*, 2nd ed. (New York: Vintage Books, 1963), and Aimé Césaire, *Toussaint Louverture: la révolution francaise et le problème colonial* (Paris: Présence Africaine, 1962).

7.   Charles A. Hale, *Mexican Liberalism in the Age of Mora, 1821–1853* (New Haven: Yale University Press, 1968), p. 61.

8.   Winston Churchill declared in 1938: " . . . our possessions of the West Indies, . . . gave us the strength, the support, but especially the capital, the wealth, at a time when no other European country possessed such a reserve, . . ." quoted by Eric Williams, *The Negro in the Caribbean* (Washington, D.C.: Associates in Negro Folk Education, 1942), p. 14.

9.   See Ida Greaves, "Plantations in World Economy," *Plantation Systems of the New World*, Social Science Monographs, 7 (Washington, D.C.: Research Institute for the Study of Man and the Pan American Union, 1959), p. 15. George L. Beckford, *Persistent Poverty: Underdevelopment in Plantation Economies of the Third World* (New York: Oxford University Press, 1972).

10.   See Douglas Hall, "Absentee-Proprietorship in the British West Indies, to about 1850," *Slants, Free Men, Citizens: West Indian Perspectives*, Lambros

Comitas and David Lowenthal, eds., (New York: Doubleday Anchor Books, 1973), pp. 105–35, and Dantès Bellegarde, *Histoire du Peuple Haitien, 1492–1952* (Port-au-Prince: Collection du Tricenquantenaire, 1953), p. 30. The latter described the absentee-landowners who were well-connected with the French haute-bourgeoisie, as a plague for Saint Domingue.

11. On the important question of "Creole culture," see Richard N. Adams, "On the Relation Between Plantation and 'Creole Culture,'" *Plantation Systems of the New World*, Social Science Monographs, 7 (Washington, D.C.: Research Institute for the Study of Man and the Pan American Union, 1959), pp. 73–82, including the subsequent comments by Remy Bastien and M. G. Smith. See also, James G. Leyburn, *The Haitian People* (New Haven: Yale University Press, 1941), pp. 86–87.

12. The social composition of the whites in the French Antilles led to the following description: the lords of Saint Domingue, the messieurs of Martinique, and the *bonnes gens* of Guadeloupe. The *petits blancs* "lesser Whites" belonged to an artisan urban grouping. Race prejudice forestalled the possibility of an alliance between that group and the colonial petite bourgeoisie against the propertied class.

13. See the excellent interpretative history by Gérard M. Laurent, *Contribution à l'histoire de Saint-Domingue* (Port-au-Prince: Imprimerie La Phalange, 1971), p. 47 *passim*.

14. The Haitian flag, created out of the French emblem in 1803, symbolized in the blue and the red the unity between the mulattoes and the blacks against the white element represented by the white center of the French tricolor.

15. Davis, *History*, p. 257.

16. Haitian historiography assumes unanimity at the time of independence; this view has never been seriously challenged. There was, however, an exodus, although it did not amount to the numbers and percentage that fled the United States upon its independence. Many *affranchis* who left Saint Domingue were so light-skinned as to pass easily for white. This led the French historian Auguste Viatte to describe Louisiana as a "mulatto culture."

17. It is estimated that 5 million out of the 27 million French depended upon Saint Domingue for their livelihood. See Robert I. Rotberg, "The Legacy of Haiti's First Revolution," mimeographed (Boston: Massachusetts Institute of Technology, n.d.). When viewing economic development in a worldwide perspective, a more conservative outlook would argue that healthy parts contribute to a healthy whole. Abstraction seems to be made, however, of the possibility for domination and exploitation of one part by another.

18. Bellegarde, *Peuple haitien*, p. 94.

19. Thomas Madiou, *Histoire d'Haiti*, 4 vols. (Port-au-Prince: Imprimerie J. Courtois. 1847–1904), 3: 143.

20. Albert Memmi, *The Colonizer and the Colonized* (Boston: Beacon Press, 1965), p. 119 *passim*.

21. See the argumentation of Clive Y. Thomas, "Bread and Justice: The Struggle for Socialism in Guyana," *Monthly Review* 28, no. 4 (1976): 29 and any of the works of Frantz Fanon.

22. See Ghislain Gouraige, *La diaspora d'Haiti et l'Afrique* (Ottawa: Editions Naaman, 1974), p. 125. Gouraige asserted that a Creole translation of official documents was originally provided for those acts directed at the people, an improvement over current practice.

23. On this subject, see Earl Griggs and Clifford Prator, eds., *Henry Christophe and Thomas Clarkson: A Correspondence* (New York: Greenwood Press, 1968).

24. Quoted by Maurice A. Lubin, "Les premiers rapports de la nation haitienne avec l'étranger," *Journal of Inter-American Studies* 10, no. 2 (1968): 282.

25. Griggs and Prator, *Christophe*, p. 52. Also see Logan, *Diplomatic Relations*, p. 226 for a view of the hysteria in the United States about Haitian independence.

26. Bellegarde, *Peuple haitien*, p. 134.

27. Ibid., pp. 179–82, 199–201. After Germany intervened on several occasions and exacted reprisals from Haiti, the United States refused to interfere after being asked to by Haiti.

28. *Register of Debates*, vol. 2, part 1, pp. 165–66, 330–32 cited in N. Andrew N. Cleven, "The First Panama Mission and the Congress of the United States," *The Journal of Negro History*, 13. no. 3 (1928): 237, 240.

29. Ibid.

30. Ibid., pp. 225–54.

31. Logan, *Diplomatic Relations*, pp. 64–67. Logan asserted, regarding the accord negotiated by Toussaint with the English: "The victory of Toussaint Louverture was as important to the United States as it was to Britain, for the United States was also determined not to become 'the slave of France'."

32. The debt was subsequently reduced to a more manageable sum of 60 million francs in 1838. See also Robert I. Rotberg, *Haiti: The Politics of Squalor* (Boston: Houghton Mifflin Company, 1971), p. 67.

33. Bellegarde, *Peuple haitien*, p. 132.

34. At that period, the cotton boom brought renewed proslavery sentiment in the United States. See Samuel Eliot Morison, *The Oxford History of the American People* (New York: Oxford University Press, 1965), p. 500 *passim*.

35. For further information on the religious history of Haiti, see Adolphe Cabon, *Notes sur l'histoire religieuse d'Haiti, de la révolution au concordat. 1789–1860* (Paris: Imprimerie des Orphelins-Apprentis, 1933); Harold Courlander, Rémy Bastien, and Richard P. Schaedel, *Religion and Politics in Haiti* (Washington, D.C.: Institute for Cross-Cultural Research, 1966); François Duvalier. *Mémoires d'un leader du tiers-monde* (Paris, Hachette, 1969); Cans Pressoir, *Le protestantisme haitien*, 2 vols. (Port-au-Prince: Imprimerie de la Société Biblique, 1945–46).

36. For instance, in the late nineteenth century, Senegal went from *comptoirs* to French communes; after World War II, the French colonies of the West

Indies acquired the status of *départements d'outre-mer.* The Gaullist *communauté francaise* answered the same imperative.

37. See Memmi, *Colonizer,* O. Mannoni, *Prospero and Caliban: The Psychology of Colonization* (New York: Praeger, 1956). and Frantz Fanon, *Black Skin, White Masks* (New York: Grove Press, 1967).

38. Raymond F. Betts, *Assimilation and Association in French Colonial Theory, 1890–1914* (New York: Columbia University Press, 1961), p. 10.

39. Dimitri George Lavroff, *La République du Senegal* (Paris: Librairie générale de droit et de jurisprudence, 1966), p. 23.

40. See Ruth Schachter, *French-Speaking West Africa in Transition* (New York: Carnegie Endowment of International Peace, 1960), p. 386–87.

41. Quoted by Betts, *Assimilation,* p. 45.

42. See L. Gray Cowan, et al., eds., *Education and Nation-Building in Africa* (New York: Preger, 1965), pp. 15 and 38. See also Ruth Schachter, "Political Leaders in French-Speaking West Africa," (Paper presented at the Second Annual Conference of the American Society of African Culture, New York, 26–29 June, 1959), p. 1. She stated: "Africans reasoned that to be effective their representatives had to be equipped to deal with the Europeans, their language and their institutions." Also see Gordon K. Lewis, *The Virgin Island: A Caribbean Lilliput* (Evanston: Northwestern University Press, 1972), p. 29 Lewis related the policy spelled out in the Danish Royal Edict of 1831, which granted to the free colored elements of the Virgin Islands the legal recourse of declaring themselves white on the basis of "good behavior." Lewis insisted that the policy was instituted to prevent a mulatto-black alliance as had occurred in Haiti at the end of the eighteenth century.

43. See Immanuel Wallerstein, "Elites in French-Speaking West Africa." *Journal of Modern African Studies* 3, no. 1 (1965): 1–33, cited in P. J. M. McEwan, ed., *Twentieth Century Africa* (New York: Oxford University Press, 1970), p. 71.

44. Because of the premium placed on Western-style education, a high school diploma may be sufficient to label an individual an intellectual. *Haute culture* becomes Western bourgeois behavior.

45. Edward Shils, "The Intellectuals in the Political Development of the New States," *Political Change in Underdeveloped Countries: Nationalism and Communism* ed. John H. Kautsky (New York: John Wiley & Sons, 1965), pp. 195–234.

46. Memmi, *The Colonizer,* p. 120.

47. See P. Bellegarde-Smith, "Race, Class and Ideology: Haitian Ideologies for Underdevelopment, 1806–1934," *AIMS Occasional Papers* no. 34 (1982).

48. See Amry Vanderbosch, "The Small States in International Politics and Organization," *The Journal of Politics* 26, no. 2 (1964): 293–312 and Annette Baker Fox, "Small State Diplomacy." Stephen Kertesz and M. A. Fitzsimmons, eds., *Diplomacy in a Changing World* (Notre Dame: University of Notre Dame Press, 1959). For the Caribbean scene, see the books by

Basil A. Ince, ed., *Contemporary International Relations of the Caribbean* (St. Augustine, Trinidad and Tobago, 1979), and Vaughan Lewis, ed., *Size, Self-Determination and International Relations: The Caribbean* (Mona, Jamaica: Institute of Social & Economic Research, 1976).

49. Jean-Jacques Dessalines, Proclamation du Géneral-en Chef au Peuple d'Hayti, (1 January, 1804) quoted by Madiou, *Histoire* 3: 105.

50. In a reverse fashion, this ploy is reminiscent of the United States foreign policy bluff illustrated in the 1823 Monroe Doctrine. One could already observe the use of defensive versus offensive diplomatic tools in the hands of large versus small powers.

51. In the first twenty years after independence was won, large sums of money and great efforts were expended erecting fortifications throughout the nation. Most of these forts can still be seen in Haiti.

52. Constitution of 1805, Article 36.

53. Griggs and Prator, *Christophe*, p. 277. The English translation is provided by Griggs and Prator on page 99.

54. Pétion was elected president of the Republic of Haiti, which comprised the West and South Departments; Christophe declared himself King of Haiti. His fiefdom consisted of the North, Northwest, and Artibonite Departments. The schism lasted fourteen years, until Christophe's death in 1820. Haiti was reunited under Pétion's successor, President Jean-Pierre Boyer.

55. See Paul Verna, *Pétion y Bolivar, cuarenta años (1790–1830) de relaciones haitiano-venezolanas y su aporte a la emancipación de hispanoamérica* (Caracas: Imprenta nacional, 1969).

56. Haiti would later intervene in favor of Dominican independence, accord political asylum to Cuban independence leaders, and favor the Greek insurrection against Turkey.

57. France and Haiti still refer to the whole island as Haiti, though it is subdivided into the Dominican and Haitian republics. In the 1930s the United States decided to adopt the name Hispaniola for the island, under protest from the Haitian government. The eastern part of the island of Haiti (or Hispaniola), whose association with France was consecrated by the 1795 Treaty of Basel, was an integral part of the French colony of Saint Domingue at the time that Haiti became independent. Santo Domingo, although Hispanic in character, was thus declared independent with the western part in 1804. At that time, the island was given its old Arawak name of Haiti by the victorious Haitians. The eastern part, however, remained in French hands, until reverting to Spanish rule in 1814, at the fall of Napoleon. The substitution of Haitian rule for continued Spanish domination was Haiti's preferred solution. That the Dominican question was ultimately tied to Haitian national security cannot be doubted. See Jean Price-Mars, *La République d'Haiti et la République Dominicaine: les aspects divers d'un problème d'histoire, de géographie et d'ethnologie*, 2 vols. (Port-au-Prince, Imprimerie Held [Suisse], 1953). Also see Pierre-Eugène

de Lespinasse, *Gens d'autrefois, vieux souvenirs* (Paris: Editions de la Revue
Mondiale, 1926). For a recent work on the Haitian domination of the
Dominican Republic by a Dominican historian, see Frank Moya Pons,
La dominación haitiana (Santiago, R. D.: Universidad Católica Madre y
Maestra, 1972). For an analysis of virulent and traditional anti-Haitianism
in the Dominican Republic, see Lil Despradel "Les étapes de l'anti-
haitianisme en République Dominicaine; le rôle des historiens," *Revue de
l'Institut de Sociologie* (Brussels), no. 1, 1973, pp. 135–60.

58. Quoted by German Arciniegas, *Latin America: A Cultural History* (New
    York: Alfred A. Knopf, 1967), p. 379.

59. See Logan, *Diplomatic Relations*, pp. 397–457, and Bellegarde, *Peuple haitien*,
    p. 197. There is presently renewed interest by the administrations of both
    Presidents Jean-Claude Duvalier and Ronald Reagan in that Haitian port.

60. See Myra Himelhock, "Frederick Douglass and Haiti's Mole St. Nicolas,"
    The Journal of Negro History 56, no.3 (1971): 161–80.

61. While flying toward Haiti in 1975 for research on this study, the author vig-
    orously protested the pilot's announcement that the aircraft was over Navasa,
    U.S. territory. Word came back from the cockpit that "the map said so." But
    who drew the maps? See Logan, *Diplomatic Relations*, pp. 361–62.

62. The United States intervened in Haiti, in 1857, 1859, 1868, 1869, 1876,
    1888, 1889, 1892, 1902, 1903, 1904, 1906, 1907, 1908, 1909, 1911,
    1912, 1913. See U.S. Navy Department Memorandum submitted to the
    United States Select Committee on Haiti and Santo Domingo, Senate
    Hearings, 1922, p. 63 cited in Harold P. Davis, *Black Democracy: The Story
    of Haiti* (New York: Biblio & Tannen, 1967), pp. 115, 125, and 313, and
    Hans Schmidt, *The United States Occupation of Haiti, 1915–1934* (New
    Brunswick, NJ: Rutgers University Press, 1971), p. 31.

63. Schmidt, *United States*, p. 246 n. 34.

64. William A. MacCorklc, *The Monroe Doctrine in its Relation to the Republic of
    Haiti* (New York: Neale Publishing Co., 1915), p. 25.

65. Testimony of the financial advisor at U.S. Senate Hearings, cited in Schmidt,
    United States, p. 43.

66. Ibid., pp. 32, 43 citing the Council of the Corporation of Foreign Bond-
    holders, *Forty-Second Annual Report*, 1915 (London: Wertheimer, Lea &
    Co., n.d.), pp. 375–76.

67. Arthur C. Millspaugh, *Haiti under American Control (1915–1930)* (Boston:
    World Peace Foundation, 1931), p. 22.

68. By which the bank agreed in 1914 to advance the Haitian government funds
    on a monthly basis rather than to maintain the old 1910 agreement whereby
    all government receipts were held by the bank until the end of the fiscal year.

69. The U.S. Minister to Haiti (M. R. Smith) to Secretary of State Bryan,
    Foreign Relations (June 1914), pp. 345–46, also quoted by Emily Green
    Balch, ed., *Occupied Haiti* (New York: Writer's Publishing Co., 1927),
    p. 15.

70. See Joseph Chatelain, *La Banque Nationale: son histoire ses problèmes* (Port-au-Prince: Imprimerie Held [Suisse], 1954), p. 105, and Bellegarde, *Peuple haitien*, p. 245. Also see Schmidt, *United States*, pp. 49–51.

71. Millspaugh, *Haiti*, p. 21: "The concession provided that the railroad company should issue bonds at the rate of $20,000 per kilometer of constructed track. The Haitian government guaranteed payment of 6% interest on these bonds and, from January 1, 1916, a payment of 1% on account sinking fund. The government was to make these payments only when the railroad, after meeting costs of operation and maintenance, was unable to pay all the interest and sinking fund charges. When profits reached 12% or more the state was to receive one sixth of all profits. The railroad property was to revert to the state on the expiration of the concession [in 1960]."

72. John H. Allen, "An Inside View of Revolutions in Haiti," *Current History* 32 (May 1930): 325–29.

73. Davis, *Black Democracy*, pp. 155–58.

74. Rotberg, *Haiti*, p. 115. Documentary evidence from United States archival sources reveal that detailed plans had been prepared for the invasion of Haiti, with the exact date left blank.

75. Davis, *Black Democracy*, p. 158.

76. Balch, *Occupied Haiti*, p. 20. Also, according to Lewis, *The Virgin Islands*, p. 351, in 1915 Washington was prepared to forcibly seize the Danish Virgin Islands in case Denmark refused to sell.

77. Mercer Cook, "Dantès Bellegarde," *Phylon* (Atlanta) 1, no. 2 (1940): 128. Sidney W. Mintz, "Introduction," in *The Haitian People* by James G. Leyburn, rev. ed. (New Haven: Yale University Press, 1966), p. xvii: "Eventual firm control by this force of weaponry, communications, and transport ended the era of presidential succession by invasion [from Northern insurgent forces], turned the army into the major locus of non-electoral, president-making power, and may have ended forever the possibility of an agrarian revolt against the central authority." Also see Davis, *Black Democracy*, pp. 169–70, who stated that the financial control of Haiti was the objective of the United States invasion of 1915.

78. Admiral H. S. Knapp, RADM, USN, to Secretary of the Navy Denby, "Supplementary Report on Haiti," (13 January. 1921) cited in Schmidt, *United States*, p. 142.

79. The Forbes Commission (1931) had bemoaned the fact that Americans with "strong racial prejudices" had been sent to Haiti. Quoted by Davis, *Black Democracy*, p. 280.

80. SD 838.00/2881, Grummon to Stimson, 29 August, 1930, quoted by Schmidt, *United States*, pp. 145–46.

81. Millspaugh, *Haiti*, p. 86.

82. The Protestant churches, being American directed, had an even easier time of it. They have since grown steadily and, being afflicted with a strong American social conservatism, serve well the aims of the United States policy

in Haiti which is to keep the country within the United States political orbit. This assessment is based on a recent trip to Haiti by the author.

83. Suzy Castor, *La ocupación norteamericana de Haiti y sus consecuencias, 1915–1934* (Mexico, D.F.: Siglo veintiuno editores s.a., 1971), p. 64. She cites the American evaluation of Catholic prelate, Mgr. Kerzusaii, from State Department, ADE/Document/838.00/1533, Division of Latin American Affairs: " . . . *habla en 1918 de la excelente cooperación entre la iglesia y la ocupación.*"

84. Ibid., p. 63.

85. Although considered "fully Haitian" by the American authorities, the Italian and Levantine merchants were discriminated against by the Haitian aristocracy, which preferred "more cultured" Northern Europeans for marriage. See Conclusion of this book for details.

86. Sténio Vincent, *En posant les jalons* 5 vols. (Port-au-Prince: Imprimerie de l'Etat, 1939–45), 1: 278–79.

87. Mintz, "Introduction," *The Haitian People*, p. xvii.

88. *Le choc* [The shock] is the title of a book by the major literary figure Léon Laleau, chronicling the events of the 1915 to 1918 period.

89. Harold E. Davis, "Trends in Social Thought in Twentieth Century Latin America," *Journal of Inter-American Studies* 1, no. 1 (1959): 65.

90. Schmidt, *United States*, p. 103.

91. Georges Anglade, *L'espace hatien* (Montreal: Les Presses Universitaires de l'Université du Québec, 1974), p. 33 *passim*. Anglade believed that the total number of dead had reached 50,000.

92. Dantès Bellegarde, *La résistance haitienne; récit d'histoire contemporaine* (Montreal: Editions Beauchemin, 1937), p. 67. American professor Raymond Leslie Buel quoted by Bellegarde, numbered the dead at 4,000 for the prison at Cap Haitien, and at 5,475 for the Chabert prisoner camp.

93. Castor, *Ocupación*, pp. 83–84.

94. United States Congress, Senate, *Report No. 794, Inquiry into the Occupation and Administration of Haiti and the Dominican Republic*, 67th Cong., 2nd sess. 1929, pp. 13–14, and 19.

95. Dantès Bellegarde was the only black to sit on the Administrative Council of that organization in 1940. See Chapter 3.

96. Balch, *Occupied Haiti*, pp. 126–27.

97. See Herbert J. Seligmann, "The Conquest of Haiti," *The Nation*, CSI, no. 2871, 1920, pp. 35–36.

98. Davis, *Black Democracy*, p. 220.

99. Rotberg, *Haiti*, p. 122.

100. Davis, *Black Democracy*, p.219.

101. Ibid., p. 224.

102. Ibid., p. 238

103. Ibid., p. 220.

104. Ibid., p. 224.

105. Millspaugh, *Haiti*, p. 89, citing *Hearings before a Senate Select Committee on Haiti and Santo Domingo*, 67th Cong., 1st sess., pursuant to S. Res. 112, p. 1504.

106. See, for instance, Ludwell Lee Montague, *Haiti and the United States, 1714–1938* (Durham: Duke University Press, 1940), p. 259.

107. Rotberg, *Haiti*, p. 120. President Philippe-Sudre Dartiguenave.

108. Ibid., pp. 125–26, citing a message of Secretary Josephus Daniels to President Franklin Delano Roosevelt.

109. See David Y. Thomas. *One Hundred Years of the Monroe Doctrine, 1823–1923* (New York: Macmillan, 1923), p. 254.

110. Schmidt, *United States*, p. 121.

111. Samuel Guy Inman, *Through Santo Domingo and Haiti: A Cruise with the Marines* (New York: Committee on Cooperation in Latin America, 1919), pp. 68–69.

112. Davis, *Black Democracy*, pp. 252, 320.

113. Ibid., p. 284.

114. Constitution of 1918, Article V.

115. Schmidt, *United States*, pp. 111–12, detailed plans of President Franklin D. Roosevelt's cousin, Henry L. Roosevelt, for colonizing La Gonáve and other Haitian offshore islands.

116. Richard P. Schaedel, ed., *Papers of the Conference on Research and Resources of Haiti* (New York: Research Institute for the Study of Man, 1969), p. 14.

117. Davis, *Black Democracy*, p. 274.

118. Ibid., p. 216.

NOTES TO CHAPTER 2

1. Darcy Ribeiro, *The Americas and Civilization* (New York: Dutton, 1971), p. 49.

2. See Francisco Garcia Calderón, "Las corrientes filosoficas en la America latina," in his *Ideas e impresiones* (Madrid: 1919), pp. 56–57, quoted by W. Rex Crawford, *A Century of Latin American Thought* (New York: Praeger, 1966), p. 8. Also see Jose Gaos, "Significación filosofica del pensamiento hispano-americano," *Cuadernos americanos*, 1943, pp. 63–86, Harold E. Davis, "Sources and Characteristics of Latin American Thought," *Topic* 20 (Fall 1970): 15. Professor Davis saw "notes of originality" rather than full-fledged innovations. For Latin American influences upon contemporary European thought in the eighteenth century, see German Arciniegas, *Latin America: A Cultural History* (New York: Alfred A. Knopf, 1967), p. 251.

3. Charles A. Hale, *Mexican Liberalism in the Age of Mora, 1821–1853* (New Haven: Yale University Press, 1968), p. 38.

4. The dosage of French, Spanish, and Anglo-American philosophical influence on Latin America is a subject for eternal debate. See for instance, Augusto Salazar Bondy, *Sentido y problema del pensamiento filosofico hispano-americano* (University of Kansas, Occasional Publications no. 16, 1969).

5. See for instance, Cesar Graña, "Cultural Nationalism: The Idea of Historical Destiny in Spanish America," *Social Research* 39 (1962): 395–418.
6. Luis Villoro, "The Ideological Currents of the Epoch of Independence," in *Major Trends in Mexican Philosophy*, ed. Mario de la Cueva et al. (Notre Dame: University of Notre Dame Press, 1966), p. 207.
7. Gabriel Debien, *Esprit colon et esprit d'autonomie à Saint-Domingue au XVIIIe siècle* (Paris: Larose, 1954), p. 14.
8. Ibid., p. 17.
9. See Chapter 4 for Bellegarde's view of Haiti as a French cultural province.
10. Gérard M. Laurent, *Contribution al histoire de Saint-Domingue* (Pon-au-Prince: Imprimerie La Phalange, 1971), p. 22.
11. Ibid., p. 39.
12. Dantès Bellegarde, *Histoire du peuple haitien, 1492–1952* (Port-au-Prince: Imprimerie Held [Suisse], 1953), pp. 35–36.
13. In Saint Domingue, those suspected of having some Negro blood were often harsher to blacks than were whites.
14. Laurent, *Contribution*, pp. 60–72, related the following incident: After peace was established temporarily in October 1791, between warring *affranchis* and whites, the latter insisted that the slaves who had given the former their military support not be granted the customary reward of freedom. Instead, the whites suggested that the slaves be put to death since they were, after all, the common enemy of both whites and *affranchis*. A compromise was achieved, and the slaves were deported to a desert island. Somehow, they were repatriated shortly to Saint Domingue and murdered to the last man.
15. Edner Brutus, *Revolution dans Saint-Domingue* (Paris: Editions du Panthéon, 1973), 1: 290.
16. Roger Dorsinville, *Toussaint Louverture, ou la vocation de la liberté* (Paris: R. Julliard, 1965), p. 38, quoted in Laurent, *Contribution* p. 54.
17. Debien, *Esprit colon*, p. 51. The letter was dated 24 August, 1791.
18. C. L. R. James, *The Black Jacobins: Toussaint L'Ouverture and the San Domingo Revolution* (New York: Dial Press, 1938), p. viii.
19. Aimé Césaire, *Toussaint Louverture: La révolution francaise et le problème colonial* (Paris: Présence Africaine, 1962), p. 180.
20. Eric Williams, *Capitalism and Slavery* (Chapel Hill: University of North Carolina Press, 1944).
21. This statement is relative, since the Haitian revolution is the most neglected of all major revolutionary movements.
22. For a Marxist interpretation, see Jean-Jacques Doubout, "Problème d'une période de transition: de Saint-Domingue à Haiti, 1793–1806," *La Pensée* (France), no. 174, (March-April 1974), pp. 67–80.
23. Ghislain Gouraige, *La diaspora d'Haiti et l'Afrique* (Ottawa: Editions Xaaman, 1974), p. 99.
24. Justin-Chrysostome Dorsainvil et al., *Manuel d'histoire d'Haiti* (Port-au-Prince: Procure des Frères de l'Instruction Chrétienne, 1949), p. 137.

25. See Davis, "Sources and Characteristics," p. 16: "This question of Indian and African influences has a key importance from the standpoint of the degree of autonomy in Latin American thought."
26. See Bellegarde, *Peuple haitien*, p. 71, and Arciniegas, *Latin america*, p. 251.
27. Bellegarde, *Peuple haitien* p. 111, quoting from the constitution of 1806.
28. Jacques Droz, *Histoire des doctrine politiques en France* (Paris: Presses Universitaires de France, 1948), p. 59.
29. See Leslie F. Manigat, *La politique agraire du gouvernement d'Alexandre Pétion, 1807–1818* (Port-au-Prince: Imprimerie La Phalange, 1962).
30. Dorsainvil, *Manuel*, p. 179.
31. See Simón Bolivar, "Message to the Congress of Bolivia," quoted by Lecuna and Bierk, *Selected Writings of Bolivar, 2*, pp. 596–606, quoted in Harold E. Davis, *Latin American Social Thought: The History of its Development since Independence, with Selected Readings* (Washington, D.C.: The University Press of Washington, D.C., 1961), p. 34. Bolivar stated:

    The President of Bolivia enjoys many of the powers of the American chief executive but with limitations that favor the people. For Bolivia, I have borrowed the executive system of the most democratic republic in the world.

    The island of Haiti, if you will permit the digression, was in a state of perpetual insurrection. Having experimented with an empire, a kingdom, and a republic, in fact every known type of government and more besides, the people were compelled to call upon the illustrious Pétion to save them. After they had put their trust in him, Haiti's destinies pursued a steady course. Pétion was made President for Life, with the right to choose his successor. Thus, neither the death of that great man nor the advent of a new President imperiled that slate in the slightest. Under the worthy Boyer, everything has proceeded as tranquilly as in a legitimate monarchy. There you have conclusive proof that a life-term President, with the power to choose his successor, is the most sublime inspiration amongst republican regimes.

32. The *affranchis* Ogé and Chavannes were put to death on the wheel, and quartered in February 1791. Julien Raimond led the struggle for *affranchis* rights in France proper. See Mercer Cook, *Five French Negro Authors* (Washington, D.C.: The Associated Publishers, 1943), pp. 3–37.
33. The Guyanese Marxist theorist Clive Y. Thomas argues that, even in the building of socialism which, by definition, is democratic and egalitarian, the totalitarian spirit inherited from the plantation economy and slavery seems almost too strong to be transcended. "Bread and Justice: The Struggle for Socialism in Guyana," *Monthly Review* 28, no. 4 (1976): 23–36.
34. Felix Boisrond-Tonnerre, *Mémoires pour servir à l'histoire d'Haiti* (Paris, 1851), Juste Chanlatte, *Le cri de la nature* (Paris, 1819), and *Histoire de la*

catastrophe de Saint-Domingue (Paris, 1924), among others. Also see Baron de Vastey, *Reflexion sur les noirs et les blancs* (Cap Henry, 1816), *Réflexions politiques* (Cap Henry, 1817), *Essai sur les causes de la revolution et sur les guerres civiles d'Haiti* (Cap Henry, 1819), among others. Julien Prévost, *Le machiavélisme du cabinet français* (Cap Henry, 1814), Guy-Joseph Bonnet, *Souvenirs historiques* (Paris, 1864), Joseph-Balthazar Inginac, *Mémoires* (Kingston, Jamaica, 1843).

35. Bellegarde, *Peuple haitien*, p. 141.
36. Dorsainvil, *Manuel*, p. 197.
37. Ralph L. Woodward, ed., *Positivism in Latin America, 1850–1900* (Lexington, Mass.: Heath, 1971), p. ix.
38. Leopoldo Zea, *Dos etapas del pensamiento hispano-americano* (Mexico, D. F.: Colegio de Mexico, 1949), p. 54.
39. Droz, *Doctrines politiques*, p. 73 and Alvin W. Gouldner, *The Corning Crisis of Western Sociology* (New York: Avon Books, 1970), p. 115.
40. Droz, *Doctrines politiques*, p. 69.
41. See Claude Nicolet, *Le radicalisme* (Paris: Presses Universitaires de France, 1957).
42. See Jean Touchard, *Histoire des idées politiques*, 2 vols. (Paris: Presses Universitaires de France 1959), 2: 580–83, and the conclusion of this work for Dantès Bellegarde's and liberalism's confusion of concepts.
43. Pradel Pompilus, et al., *Manuel illustré d'histoire de la littérature haitienne* (Port-au-Prince: Imprimerie Henri Deschamps, 1962), p. 33.
44. In 1804 pending review of claims, Haiti had nationalized all lands.
45. Dorsainvil, *Manuel*, p. 199.
46. See David Nicholls, "A Work of Combat: Mulatto Historians and the Haitian Past, 1847–1867," *Journal of Inter-American Studies and World Affairs* 16, no. 1 (1975): 15–38.
47. Thomas Madiou, *Histoire d'Haiti*, 4 vols. (Port-au-Prince: Imprimerie J. Courtois, 1847–1904), 1: 1.
48. Ibid., 4: vi.
49. Beaubrun Ardouin, *Etudes sur l'histoire d'Haiti*, 11 vols. (Paris: Debrozy et E. Magdeleine, Libraire-Editeur, 1854), 5: 184.
50. Ibid., 6: 344.
51. Ibid., 8: 467; 5: 102 (1958 edition). Toussaint is said to be "the blind instrument of metropolitan policy." Toussaint is considered practically a counter revolutionary, but not André Rigaud. Also see Henry Adams, 1, *History of the United States of America during the First Administration of Thomas Jefferson* (New York, 1962), p. 378: "[Toussaint] hated by the mulattoes with such vindictiveness as mutual antipathies and crimes could cause, he was liked by the whites rather because he protected and flattered them at the expense of the mulattoes than because they felt any love for him or his race."
52. Ardouin, *Etudes*, 3: 163–64.

53. Ibid., 1: 111, also cited in Auguste Viatte, *Histoire littéraire de l'Amérique francaise* (Paris: Presses Universitaires de France, 1954), p. 370.
54. Joseph Saint-Rémy, *Mémoires de Toussaint Louverture* (1853), pp. 8, 15.
55. Ardouin, *Etudes*, (1958 edition), 1: 17, also quoted by Nicholls, "A work of Combat," p. 26.
56. Beauvais Lespinasse, *Histoire des affranchis de Saint-Domingue* (Paris: Imprimerie Kugelmann, 1882), pp. 15–16.
57. For further analysis of these ideas, see Crawford, *Latin American Thought*, p. 4.
58. See Harold E. Davis, *History of Latin America* (New York: The Ronald Company Press, 1968), p. 360. Davis asserts: "Differences in political and social ideologies contributed to divisions within the oligarchy that prevented stable government."
59. Irene Collins, *Liberalism in Nineteenth Century Europe* (London: The Historical Association, no. 34, 1957), p. 4.
60. Ibid. See the entire essay for an excellent summary of the basis of liberalism.
61. It may well be that in Latin America this *rapprochement* was made easier by the fact that the elite constituted a small segment of the total population, blood related in many instances.
62. Hale, *Mexican Liberalism*, p. 8.
63. Hale, *Mexican Liberalism*, p. 153: "Though utilitarianism was applied broadly to political problems, it was not a theory of politics. Men of quite different political persuasions were utilitarians. . . ."
64. Quoted by German Arciniegas, "From Utilitarianism to Positivism," in *Positivism in Latin America, 1850–1900*, ed. Ralph L. Woodward (Lexington, Mass.: Heath, 1971), p. 5. Also see Donald M. Dozer, *Latin America: An Interpretative History* (New York: McGraw-Hill, 1962), p. 563 and John D. Mam, "Characteristics of Latin American Thought," in *Positivism in Latin America, 1850–1900*, ed. Ralph L. Wood ward (Lexington, Mass.: Heath, 1971), p. 8.
65. Leopoldo Zea, "Positivism," in *Major Trends in Mexican Philosophy*, ed. Mario de la Cueva, et al. (Notre Dame: Notre Dame University Press, 1966), p. 226. Auguste Comte, in his *Cours de philosophie positive*, wrote: "No legitimate order can be established nor last if it is not compatible with progress; no real progress can be efficaciously achieved if it does not tend, in the final analysis, to the inherent consolidation of order" [from the 46eme lecon].
66. Ibid., p. 228. Gabino Barreda was the minister of education under President Benito Juarez.
67. See Miguel Jorrin and John D. Martz, *Latin American Political Thought and Ideology* (Chapel Hill: University of North Carolina Press, 1970), pp. 124, 128.
68. See João Cruz Costa, *A History of Ideas in Brazil: The Development of Philosophy in Brazil and the Evolution of National History* (Berkeley and Los Angeles: University of California Press, 1964).

69. Arturo Ardao, "Assimilation and 'Transformation of Positivism in Latin America," *Journal of the History of Ideas* 24 (1963): 515–22. He slated peremptorily: "There was no intellectual interchange among our universities and cultural centers."

70. Thomas L. Skidmore, *Black into White: Race and Nationality in Brazilian Thought* (New York: Oxford University Press, 1974), p. 27.

71. On the subject of social thought and ideological politics, see Edward J. Williams, "Secularization, Integration and Rationalization: Some Perspectives from Latin American Thought," *Journal of Inter-American Studies* 5, part 2 (November 1973): 199–216.

72. See Davis, *History*, pp. 492–93.

73. Bellegarde, *Peuple haitien*, p. 189.

74. Jean Price-Mars, *Jean-Pierre Boyer-Bazelais et le drame de Miragoâne* (Port-au-Prince: Imprimerie de l'Etat, 1948), p. 24.

75. Ernest Trouillot, *Demesvar Delorme, le journaliste, le diplomate* (Port-au-Prince: Imprimerie Théodore, 1958), p. 41.

76. Jean Price-Mars in *Le Nouvelliste*, 10 February, 1931, cited by Trouillot *Demesvar Delorme*, pp. 43, 44, citing *Le Moniteur*, 7 September, 1867, no. 36.

77. Demesvar Delorme, *Les théoriciens au pouvoir* (Paris, 1870), pp. 182–83.

78. Jean Price-Mars in *La Relève* (1933), quoted by Jacques C. Antoine, "Literature: From Toussaint Louverture to Jacques Roumain," in *An Introduction to Haiti*, ed. Mercer Cook (Washington, D.C.: Federal Security Agency, 1948), pp. 93–94.

79. Baron de Vastey, *Reflexions politiques* (Cap Henry, 1817) quoted in Gouraige, *Diaspora*, pp. 52–53.

80. Ardouin, *Etudes* (1958 edition), 7: 9.

81. Frederic Marcelin, *Ducasse Hippolyte, son époque, son oeuvre* (Le Havre: Imprimerie A. Lemale, ainé, 1878), p. 52.

82. Ibid., p. 95. This situation is reminiscent of the French African elite member who, soon after independence, continued the custom of traveling to France, "on leave."

83. Max Wilson, interview held in Washington, D.C., 8 April, 1976.

84. On 22 and 23 September, 1883, seemingly under orders from President Salomon of the National party—he was an educated black who had married a French woman—the entire commercial district of Port-au-Prince was set on fire. This action was apparently in retaliation for an attempt at overthrowing the government by those who were called the "bourgeois." An eyewitness revealed that only two blacks were found to own property in the commercial district. See Catts Pressoir, *Le protestantisme haitien* (Port-au-Prince: Imprimerie de la Société Biblique, 1945), p. 294, Adolphe Cabon, *Mgr. Guilloux, deuxième archevêque de Port-au-Prince* (Port-au-Prince: Archeveché de Port-au-Prince, 1929), p. 482, and Alfred Jean, *Les journées du 22 et 23 septembre 1883* (Port-au-Prince: Imprimerie

A. P. Barthelemy, 1944). The author's grandmother, Cécile Bellegarde, often reminisced about these eventful days. She was then seven years old.

85. Louis-Joseph Janvier, *Les antinationaux* (Port-au-Prince: Editions Panorama, 1962), p. 78. Pierre Lafitte, king of bankers and the banker of kings, Guizot, and others, were ministers in the cabinet of the bourgeois-king Louis-Philippe, which marked the triumph of liberalism in France. See also, Touchard, *Idées politiques*, pp. 524 and 526; "If bourgeois life-style, as it appears for instance in the work of Balzac is quite diverse, bourgeois ideology is, in its ensemble, of a great unity: Gaudissart is not far, from the thought of Nucingen, and Lafitte recognizes himself in Béranger, as does Michelet."

86. Gouldner, *The Coming Crisis*, p. 114, and Touchard, *Idées politiques*, p. 668.

87. Dantès Bellegarde, *Ecrivains haitiens* Port-au-Prince: Société d'Editions et de Librairie, 1947), p. 124. On Firminism, also see Bellegarde, *Peuple haitien*, pp. 227–31.

88. See, Anténor Firmin, *Lettres de Saint-Thomas; études sociologiques, historiques et littéraires* (Paris: V. Giard et E. Brière, 1910), chap. 2.

89. Duraciné Vaval, *Histoire de la littérature haitienne ou l'âme noire* (Port-au-Prince: Imprimerie Aug. A. Héraux, 1933), pp. 299–300 and Dantès Bellegarde, *Un haitien parle* (Port-au-Prince: Chéraquit, Imprimeur-Editeur, 1934), pp. 125–26.

90. Dantès Bellegarde, *Pour une Haiti heureuse*, 2 vols. (Port-au-Prince: Chéraquit, Imprimeur-Editeur, 1927–29), 1: 24.

91. Ibid., p 22.

92. Max Wilson, interview held in Washington, D.C., 8 April, 1976.

93. Friedrich Heer, *The Intellectual History of Europe* (New York: Doubleday 1966), p. 281, considered the nineteenth century to extend from 1789 to 1945: "The nineteenth century came to an end amid the rubble of European cities at the end of the Second World War. It was, says Heidegger, 'the darkest of all centuries of modern times.'"

NOTES TO CHAPTER 3

1. Duraciné Vaval, *Histoire de la littérature haitienne ou l'âme noire* (Port-au-Prince: Imprimerie Aug. A. Héraux, 1933), p. 365.

2. W. E. B. Du Bois, *The Crisis* (April, 1926), p. 295.

3. Beatrice B. Berle and Travis B. Jacobs, eds., *Navigating the Rapids, 1918–1971: From the Papers of Adolf A. Berle* (New York: Harcourt Brace Jovanovich, 1973), p. 593.

4. Sidney W. Mintz, Introduction to *The Haitian People*, by James G. Leyburn (New Haven: Yale University Press, 1966), p. xiii.

5. Edner Brutus, *Instruction publique en Haiti, 1492–1945* (Port-au-Prince: Imprimerie de l'Etat, 1948), p. 463.

6. Léon Laleau, "Dantès Bellegarde, une célébrité, amie de la pénombre," *Conjonction* (Port-au-Prince), no. 118, July 1972, p. 89.

7. The author attempts to describe the appearance of Bellegarde's forebear as indicated from written or oral sources, without establishing a "racial" typology. The reader must remain alert that the social concept called race differs markedly in its definition and application in each of the great cultural areas of the world: it is no secret that the Anglo-American and the Latin versions of the same phenomena give rise to, oftentime, divergent social policies.

   It is possible for two light-skinned parents to produce a progeny that range from "pure" white to black appearance, with no two children *du même lit* ("from the same bed", i.e., "litter") alike.

8. Louise Boisson was literate. Dantès Bellegarde often related the story of Louise and Marie Boisson visiting President Geffrard at the traditional weekly open house, which was a feature of Haitian presidential politics, asking that Marie be sent to school. The president promised, but was overthrown before he could act on the request in 1867.

9. Simone Bellegarde Smith, interview, New Milford, Conn., 15 February, 1976.

10. Mercer Cook, "Dantès Bellegarde," *Phylon* (Atlanta): 1, no. 2 (1940), 1.

11. Charles MacKenzie, *Notes on Haiti, Made During a Residence in that Republic*, 2 vols. (London: Henry Colburn & Richard Bentley, 1830), 1: 10.

12. Simone Bellegarde Smith, to author, 13 December, 1975.

13. Jean-Louis Bellegarde seemed to have been a mere gardener at the Gardens. No further details were obtained: Dantès Bellegarde very seldom spoke about his father.

14. Dantès Bellegarde, *Pour une Haiti heureuse*, 2 vols. (Port-au-Prince: Imprimerie Chéraquit, Imprimeur-Editeur, 1927–29), 1: 3.

15. MacKenzie, *Notes on Haiti, Made During a Residence in that Republic*.

16. Bellegarde, *Haiti heureuse*, 1: 3.

17. Jean-Louis Bellegarde is said never to have married.

18. Jean-Baptiste Lesage Windsor Bellegarde and his friend Mirabeau Drice were in France on scholarships from the Haitian government.

19. Dantès Bellegarde, *Ecrivains haitiens* (Port-au-Prince: Société d'Editions et de Librairie, 1947), p. 292.

20. Both Argentine Bellegarde (Madame Foureau) and Dantès Bellegarde are buried in the family crypt in Port-au-Prince.

21. Bellegarde, *Haiti heureuse*, 1: 1–16, and *Dessalines a parlé* (Port-au-Prince: Société d'Editions et de Librairie, 1948), pp. 325–31.

22. Simone Bellegarde Smith, interview, New Milford, Conn., 15 February, 1976.

23. Decreed in 1816 for elementary education, and extended to all levels in 1879. See Constitution of 1816, Article 36, and Constitution of 1879, Article 30. Louis-Joseph Janvier, *Les constitutions d'Haiti, 1801–1885* (Paris: C. Marpon et E. Flammarion, 1886). Haiti was one of the first nations in history to have passed such laws.

24. Lycée National de Port-au-Prince, *Bulletin*, "Distribution solemnelle des prix, années scolaires, 1896–97" (Port-au-Prince: Imprimerie H. Chauvet, 1897).

25. Bellegarde, *Haiti heureuse*, 1: 205.

26. The fact that Dantès Bellegarde spoke only Creole in his preschool days was ascertained from Minutes, "Conseil Consultatif," Session of 13 October, 1950, p. 10.

27. Cuban independence leaders José Martí and Antonio Maceo also had visited Haiti. See Bellegarde, *Haiti heureuse*, 1: 288.

28. This would be the sixth, ninth, tenth, and thirteenth year of secondary education respectively; United States grade equivalency would be grossly misleading, especially since the French system of education tends to be ahead of the American system, particularly insofar as classical (liberal) studies are concerned. The end product is a baccalaureate.

29. Jean Bellegarde to author, 10 December, 1975.

30. Viviane Nicolas, conversations, Port-au-Prince, June and July 1975.

31. Simone Bellegarde Smith, interview, New Milford, Conn., 15 February, 1976.

32. Bellegarde practiced his trade but once. He defended a woman guilty of thievery, and kept her from going to jail on account of a child she was nursing. From the author's conversations with Bellegarde, 1960s.

33. See Adolphe Cabon, *Mgr. Alexis Jean-Marie Guilloux, deuxième archevêque de Port-au-Prince* (Port-au-Prince: Archevêché de Port-au-Prince, 1929).

34. *La Ronde* (1898–1902), was succeeded by *Haiti littéraire et sociale* (1905–07), *Haiti littéraire et scientifique* (1912–13), whose editor in chief was Dantès Bellegarde, and by *Haiti politique et littéraire* (1909–11).

35. For an analysis of the latter period, see Naomi Garren, *The Renaissance of Haitian Poetry* (Paris: Presence Africaine, 1963). She covers the period from 1923 to 1953.

36. Edmund Wilson, *Red, Black, Blond and Olive: Studies in Four Civilizations* (New York: Oxford University Press, 1956), p. 110, and Barbara Howes, ed., *From the Green Antilles: Writings of the Caribbean* (New York: Macmillan Co., 1966), pp. 147–48.

    Edmund Wilson wrote: "The literature of Haiti . . . is highly sophisticated and has a long and sound tradition behind it. Venezuela, it seems with about the same population as Haiti, has, exclusive of government documents, published less than two thousand volumes to Haiti's five thousand; and neither Argentina, with twenty million [inhabitants], nor Brazil, with forty-five million, again with the exclusion of official publications, printed twenty thousand volumes."

37. Pradel Pompilus, et al., *Manuel illustré de la littérature haitienne* (Port-au-Prince: Imprimerie H. Deschamps, 1961), p. 219.

38. Pètion Gérôme, *La Ronde June*, 1898.

39. Dantès Bellegarde, *La Ronde*, May, 1898.

40. Bellegarde, *Dessalines*, pp. 96–97.
41. Sténio Vincent was subsequently president of Haiti from 1930 until 1941.
42. Bellegarde, *Haiti heureuse*, vol. I, pp. 137–38.
43. Some of Dantès Bellegarde's earlier volumes were textbooks, written in collaboration with Sténio Vincent. See the Bibliography to this book, and also Bellegarde, *Haiti heureuse*, 1: 206–12.
44. Bellegarde, *Haiti heureuse*, 2: 3. Bellegarde admitted to paraphrasing a Polish author, no name given.
45. Ibid., 1: 224–26.
46. Ibid., 2: 6. There he met with Roger L. Farnham who became an important adviser on Haitian matters for the United States government; this, in part, led to the American occupation of Haiti in 1915.
47. Dantès Bellegarde, *Histoire du peuple haitien, 1492–1952* (Port-au-Prince: Imprimerie Held [Suisse], 1953), pp. 230, 240. President Oreste had been a professor of law and a parliamentarian for over twenty-five years before attaining the presidency.
48. Berthoumieux Danache, *Le Président Dartiguenave et les américains* (Port-au-Prince: Imprimerie de l'Etat, 1950), pp. 112–13.
49. Among others, see Brutus, *Instruction publique*, Rayford W. Logan, "Education in Haiti," *The Journal of Negro History*, October 1930, pp. 401–60, and Raymond Leslie Buell, *The American Occupation of Haiti* (New York: Foreign Policy Association, 1929).
50. Wilson, *Studies in Four Civilizations*, p. 76; Bellegarde is also discussed on pages 74–77, and 144.
51. Samuel Guy Inman, *Through Santo Domingo and Haiti: A Cruise with the Marines* (New York: Committee on Cooperation in Latin America, 1919), p. 75.
52. Brutus, *Instruction publique*, p. 468.
53. Ibid., p. 466. Brutus discussed that law in some detail.
54. See Robert I. Rotberg, *Haiti: The Politics of Squalor* (Boston: Houghton Mifflin Co., 1971), pp. 129–30.
55. Cook, "Dantès Bellegarde," p. 128.
56. Logan, "Education in Haiti," p. 450, author's comment in brackets. Also see Buell, *American Occupation*, and Bellegarde, *Haiti heureuse*, 2: 215–17, and 250–67.
57. Logan, "Education in Haiti," pp. 459–60. Also see Carl Kelsey in *Annals of American Academy*, March 1922, p. 180.
58. See Basil Matthews, "The Continuing Debate: Washington vs. Du Bois," *W. E. B. Du Bois: A Profile*, ed. Rayford W. Logan (New York: Hill & Wang, 1971), pp. 183–209. See also John Hope Franklin, *From Slavery to Freedom: A History of Negro Americans*, 3rd ed. (New York: Alfred A. Knopf, 1967), p. 390 passim., and William Z. Foster, *The Negro People in American History* (New York: International Publishers, 1954), pp. 408–18.
59. Cook, "Dantès Bellegarde," p. 128.

60. Bellegarde, *Haiti heureuse*, 2: 75.

61. Ibid., pp. 75, and 60–61.

62. For further evaluation of Dantès Bellegarde's actions while at the ministry, see Brutus, *Instruction publique*, pp. 489–90, *Le Nouvelliste*, 3 July, 1919, and *Le Matin*, 4 July, 1919.

63. Roger N. Baldwin (founder of the ACLU) to author, 7 April, 1975.

64. President Dartiguenave to Dantès Bellegarde, 22 March, 1922: "I have always considered and will continue to consider that having spontaneously given you the mission of representing Haiti in France was the most handsome action of my government."

65. Ghislain Gouraige, *La diaspora d'Haiti et l'Afrique* (Ottawa: Editions Naaman, 1974), p. 14.

66. Léon-Gontran Damas, interview, Washington, D.C., 25 May, 1975.

67. This policy was also pursued with vehemence in the Dominican Republic under President Rafael Leónidas Trujillo y Molina.

68. Dantès Bellegarde was thus able to avoid much of the unpleasantness created by racial discrimination that was shown other Haitian diplomats accredited to the United States. As an example, Bellegarde was able to live in Washington hotels, while Jean Price-Mars was forced to reside at the Haitian chancery. See Mercer Cook, interview, Washington, D.C., 19 February, 1975

69. Rotberg, *Haiti*, p. 110.

70. "Dantès Bellegarde Dies in Haiti . . . ," *The New York Times*, 16 June, 1966.

71. The Haitian government failed to take advantage of the situation Bellegarde had tried to create, according to Cook, "Dantès Bellegarde," p. 129.

72. Jules Meulemans, "M. Bellegarde quitte Paris," *La Revue diplomatique*, 31 December, 1922.

73. President Dartiguenave to Dantès Bellegarde, 20 August, 1921.

74. Dantès Bellegarde to Secretary of State Barau, 24 April, 1923 (addressed from Rome, Italy). The expenses amounted to $234.81 in U.S. dollars and were never reimbursed, on orders from American officials.

   This is the same financial advisor, John A. McIlhenny (1919–22), who reported to Franklin D. Roosevelt (who relished it) that he was fascinated by the robust minister of Agriculture [Dantès Bellegarde]: "I couldn't help saying to myself that that man would have brought (U.S.) $1,500 at auction in New Orleans in 1860 for stud purposes." Cited in Hans Schmidt, *The United States Occupation of Haiti, 1915–1934* (New Brunswick, N.J.: Rutgers University Press, 1971), pp. 110–11, quoting from Roosevelt, "Trip to Haiti and Santo Domingo, 1917," unpublished travel diary.

75. Dantès Bellegarde, *Au service d'Haiti: Appréciations sur un haitien et son oeuvre* (Port-au-Prince: Imprimerie Théodore. 1962), p. 67. Sir Eric Drummond was appraised of the situation and showed sympathy for Haiti's financial dilemma.

76. Cited in *La Suisse*, 22 September, 1921, and quoted by Bellegarde, *Au service d'Haiti*, p. 68.

77. Pedro Rossello, *Les précurseurs du Bureau International d'Education* (Geneva: Bureau international d'Education, 1943), p. 155.

78. William G. Carr, *Only by Understanding*, Headline Series (New York: Foreign Policy Association, 1945), pp. 36–37.

79. UNESCO, *XVIIIe conférence internationale de l 'instruction publique* (Paris: Publication No. 166), quoted by Bellegarde, *Au service d'Haiti*, p. 72.

80. See Rayford W. Logan, *The Operations of the Mandate System in Africa* (Washington, D.C.: The Foundation Publishers, 1942), and Raymond Leslie Buell, *International Relations* (New York: Holt & Co., 1929).

81. *Le Journal de Genève* 9 September, 1922.

82. See Minute 31 Record of the Third Assembly, Plenary Meetings, also quoted by Buell, *International Relations*, pp. 365–66, and Paul Fauchille, *Traité de droit international public* (Paris: Rousseau & Cie., 1926), 1A: 818.

83. Cablegram by Paul S. Mowrer. A copy was sent to Dantès Bellegarde by its author. Also quoted in Logan, *The Operation of the Mandate*, p. 477.

84. Philip Noel Baker [Nobel Peace Prize, 1959] to Dantès Bellegarde, 10 October, 1921. Dantès Bellegarde confided to Rayford W. Logan that he had been promised a seat on the PMC at the first vacancy. See Logan, *The Operation of the Mandate*, p. 477.

85. Jules Meulemans, "Haiti à la Société des Nations," *La Revue diplomatique* 31 October, 1922.

86. Buell, *International Relations*, p. 367.

87. Jessie Fauset, "Impressions of the Second Pan-African Congress," *The Crisis*, 23, no. 1 (1921): 16, 17.

88. W. E. B. Du Bois, in *History of the Pan-African Congress*, ed. George Padmore (Manchester, England: Hammersmith Bookshop, 1945), p. 21. A good survey of the development of Pan-Africanism is given in George Padmore, *Pan-Africanism or Communism* (New York: Doubleday Anchor, 1972).

89. W. E. B. Du Bois, "Manifesto to the League of Nations," *The Crisis*, 23, no. 1 (1921): 18.

90. See Francis L. Broderick, *W. E. B. Du Bois: Negro Leader in a Time of Crisis* (Stanford, Calif: Stanford University Press, 1959), p. 131.

91. See Harold R. Isaacs, "Pan-Africanism as 'Romantic Racism'," in *W. E. B. Du Bois: a Profile*, ed. Rayford W. Logan (New York: Hill & Wang, 1971), p. 213.

92. Fauset, "Impressions," p. 17.

93. Elliot M. Rudick, *W. E. B. Du Bois: Propagandist of the Negro Protest* (New York: Atheneum, 1969), p. 224.

94. See Harold Cruse, *The Crisis of the Negro Intellectual* (New York: W. Morrow & Co., 1967), especially pages 115–46.

95. Padmore, *Pan-African Congress*, p. 21.

96. Bellegarde, *Dessalines*, pp. 23–24.

97. W. E. B. Du Bois to Dantès Bellegarde, October 1925.

98. Bellegarde, *Au service d'Haiti*, p. 184.

99. Dantès Bellegarde, *La résistance haitienne; récit d'histoire contemporaine* (Montreal: Editions Beauchemin, 1937), pp. 135–49.
100. See Schmidt, *The United States*, p. 128, and Rotberg, *Haiti*, p. 129.
101. Hyalmar Branting, "Rapport au Conseil," quoted by Bellegarde, *Au service d'Haiti*, pp. 125–26.
102. Ibid., and "Resolution du Conseil 12.VI.24-P.V.C. XXIX," p. 909.
103. See Georges Ottlik, ed., *annuaire de la Société des Nations, 1920–1927* (Geneva: Librairie Payot et Cie., 1927), pp. 634–38.

    The Haitian government sought to remove Bellegarde from the commission because he planned to investigate employment conditions, which had been described as close to slavery, of Haitian peasants on American-owned sugar plantations in Cuba.
104. "24è. Congrès Universel de la Paix," *Le Nouvelliste* 9 and 11 November, 1925.
105. *The New York Times*, 4 July, 1924.
106. Dantès Bellegarde, *Un haitien parle* (Port-au-Prince: Chéraquit, Imprimeur-Editeur, 1934), p. 220. The title of the speech was, "Les Etats-Unis et l'Amérique latine à la Société des Nations."
107. Ibid., p. 214.
108. "Haitian Assails Us at League Meeting," *New York Times* 12 September, 1930.
109. Cook, "Dantès Bellegarde," p. 132.
110. *La Liberté*, 14 September, 1930, passage quoted and translated by Cook, "Dantès Bellegarde," p. 132.
111. President Vincent to Dantès Bellegarde, 30 January, 1931.
112. Bellegarde, *Au service d'Haiti*, p. 179.
113. Ibid., p. 180. Some discussion on the matter was also held in Havana in 1940 and at Chapultepec in 1945.
114. Private correspondence between Paul Claudel and Dantès Bellegarde, Bellegarde Collection, at Port-au-Prince, Haiti.
115. Bellegarde, *Peuple haitien*, p. 296.
116. NAACP Secretary Walter White to Dantès Bellegarde, 13 November, 1933.
117. George Abel, "Haitian Minister Startles Diplomats with Resignation; Dramatic Announcement Made at Pan American Governing Board Meeting; Resents U.S. Financial Administration," *Washington Daily News* 2 November, 1933, p. 38.
118. Jean Arcille, *L'homme libre* (Paris), 23 December, 1922.
119. Max Wilson, interview, Baltimore, Maryland, 13 February, 1975.
120. Secretairie d'Etat aux Relations Extérieures [Haitian foreign Ministry], "Instructions Spéciales à la Délégation Haitienne à la Conférence de Lima," Confidential, Port-au-Prince, 25 October, 1938, pp. 3–4. Also see Secretairie d'Etat aux Relations Extérieures, *La République d'Haiti dans la politique intéramericaine* (New York: Fisher Press, 1939).
121. At the creation of the International Court of Justice, the candidacy of American jurist James Brown Scott had been supported by the Haitian

delegation at the League and by the Haitian government. See the American Institute for International Law, *Proceedings of the Eight Scientific Congress* (Washington, D.C.: 1941), pp. 200, 205, 210, 223.

122. See Société Haitienne d'Etudes Scientifiques, *Travaux du Congrès International de Philosophie* (Port-au-Prince: Imprimerie de l'Etat, 1946).

123. Bellegarde, *Peuple haitien*, p. 321.

124. Ibid., p. 328.

125. Commission Politique Spéciale, Compte-Rendu analytique, Nations-Unies (January 5, 1952), p. 13 in the papers of Dantès Bellegarde, Port-au-Prince, Haiti.

126. Dantès Bellegarde to Ralph Bunche (marked "confidential,") 25 June, 1953. Also see H. Santa Cruz, D. Bellegarde, and H. Laugier, U.N. Commission on the Racial Situation in the Union of South Africa, *Reports* I, II, U.N. Doc. A/2505 & A/2505/Add. 1, p. 166–January 1954 (GAOR, 8th Sess. suppl. no. 16) and A/2719, 2nd Report (agenda item 23 (IX)), p. 121–October 1954 (GAOR, 9th Sess. suppl. no. 16, appended special statement by D. Bellegarde, UN A/AC70/SR43. The commission met at the Palais des Nations (Geneva) in more than forty-three formal meetings.

127. Dantès Bellegarde to Jean Bellegarde, 19 February, 1957; Jean Bellegarde to Dantès Bellegarde, 21 February, 1957.

128. The family did not take too kindly to that suggestion in the midst of the political turmoil, fearing the possibility of exile or assassination at the end of the ordeal.

129. Based on the personal memories of the author and Leslie F. Manigat, *Haiti of the Sixties: Object of International Concern; a Tentative Global Analysis of the Potentially Explosive Situation of a Crisis Country in the Caribbean* (Washington, D.C.: The Washington Center of Foreign Policy Research, 1964), and Jean and Suzanne Comhaire-Sylvain, "Urban Stratification in Haiti," *Social and Economic Studies* (Jamaica) 8, no. 2 (1959): 179–89.

130. Thence came the idea that the United States was manipulating Négritude for its own ideological ends as preferable to a socialist alternative in Haitian society.

131. See Colbert Bonhomme, *Révolution et contre-révolution en Haiti de 1946 à 1957* (Port-au-Prince: Imprimerie de l'Etat, 1957), and Clément Célestin, *Compilations pour l'histoire*, 4 vols. (Port-au-Prince: Imprimerie Théodore, 1958–1960).

132. Mintz, Introduction, p. xiii.

133. See Jules Blanchet, *Peint par lui-même ou la résistance de M. Bellegarde* (Port-au-Prince: Imprimerie Valcin, 1936), and Henock Trouillot, *M. Dantès Bellegarde, un écrivain d'autrefois* (Port-au-Prince: Imprimere Théodore, 1957).

134. Bellegarde, *Dessalines*, pp. 141–42.

135. Mercer Cook and Max Wilson, in interviews with the author, agreed that the criticism leveled against Dantès Bellegarde was often the result of envy.

136. The author found a front page of Dantès Bellegarde's intended autobiography, containing but two short paragraphs.
137. Auguste Viatte to the author, 8 March, 1975, and 4 December, 1975, and Laleau, "Dantès Bellegarde," p. 90. See also, Jean Price-Mars, "La position d'Haiti et de la culture française en Amérique," *Journal of Inter-American Studies* 8, no. 1 (1966): 44–53.
138. *Le Monde Nouveau* 25 January, 1931, quoted by Cook, "Dantès Bellegarde," p. 126.
139. Laleau, "Dantès Bellegarde," p. 89.
140. Bellegarde, *Haiti heureuse*, 1: 10–11.
141. Henri Béranger, in an address at Port-au-Prince, 29 December, 1935, said that *Haiti est le phare avancé de la latinité en Amérique.*
142. Chef du Protocole, (Ministry of Foreign Affairs) "Cérémonial des Funérailles Nationales de Monsieur Dantès Bellegarde. . . ." Port-au-Prince, 16 June, 1966.

NOTES TO CHAPTER 4

1. Pétion Gérome, *La Ronde*, 1 June, 1898.
2. Some of the participants were German Arciniegas, W. E. B. Du Bois, Henri Laugier, Thomas Mann, Jose Nucete-Sardi, Fernando Ortiz, Jules Romains, Alfonso Reyes, among others. See Comisión Nacional de Cooperación Intelectual de Cuba, *Lista de Participantes a la platica de La Habana*, 23–26 November, 1941.
3. Dantès Bellegarde, in *El Universal* (Caracas) 12 October, 1944.
4. See Gabriel Debien, *Esprit colon et esprit d'autonomie à Saint-Domingue au XVIIIe siècle* (Paris: Larose, 1954).
5. Jean Touchard, *Histoire des idées politiques*, 2 vols. (Paris: Presses Universitaires de France, 1959), 2: 451.
6. See Robert R. Palmer, *The Age of Democratic Revolution: A Political History of Europe and America, 1760–1800*, 2 vols. (Princeton: Princeton University Press, 1959–64), 1: 267, Louis Hartz, *The Liberal Tradition in America* (New York: Harcourt, Brace, Jovanovich, 1955), p. 11, both were quoted by Charles A. Hale, *Mexican Liberalism in the Age of Mora, 1821–1853* (New Haven: Yale University Press, 1968). See in particular, chapter 6 of the latter work, pp. 188–214. Also see Robert Nisbet, "The Social Impact of the Revolution," *Wilson Quarterly* 1, no. 1 (1976): 93–107.
7. See Rayford W. Logan, *The Diplomatic Relations of the United States with Haiti, 1776–1891* (Chapel Hill: University of North Carolina Press, 1941), p. 25.
8. See Dantès Bellegarde, *Histoire du peuple haitien, 1492–1952* (Port-au-Prince: Imprimerie Held [Suisse], 1953), p. 62.
9. Alvin W. Gouldner, *The Coming Crisis of Western Sociology* (New York: Avon Books, 1970), p. 115.
10. Touchard, *Idées politiques*, 2: 390.

11. See A. Cuvillier, *Sociologie et problemes actuels*, 2nd ed. (Paris: Vrin, 1961), especially chapter 2, "Sociologie et théorie du droit."

12. Touchard, *Idées politiques*, 2: 407.

13. Ibid., p. 383.

14. Jacques Droz, *Histoire des doctrines politiques en France* (Paris: Presses Universitaires de France, 1966), p. 62.

15. Cesar Grana, *Bohemian Versus Bourgeois* (New York: Basic Books, 1964), p. 107.

16. Léon-Gontran Damas, interview, Washington, D.C. 25 May, 1975.

17. Dantès Bellegarde, *Pages d'histoire* (Port-au-Prince: Chéraquit, Imprimeur-Editeur, 1925), p. 23. The statement was based on a lecture Bellegarde gave in 1903.

18. Bellegarde, *Peuple haitien*, p. 7.

19. Pradel Pompilus et al., *Manuel illustré d'histoire de la littérature haitienne* (Port-au-Prince: Imprimerie H. Deschamps, 1961), p. 546.

20. Bellegarde, *People haitien*, p. 8.

21. The author's conversations with Dantès Bellegarde in the 1960s. Also unkind remarks were heard regarding the marriage of two anthropologists, one foreign, the other Haitian: "He wanted to study her no doubt."

22. Dantès Bellegarde, *Dessalines a parlé* (Port-au-Prince: Société d'Editions et de Librairie, 1948), p. 356.

23. Ibid., p. 355.

24. Bellegarde, *Dessalines*, p. 356.

25. *Encyclopaedia of the Social Sciences* (Macmillan Co., 1937), 5, 6: 223–24. Fichte opposed the state and emphasized society as a counterweight, and ended with a synthesis between universalism and individualism. In fact, he combated the notion of Pan-Germanism: "Fichte declared that it was infinitely more important for the Germans to develop their national culture whose support was society than to dominate by external victories obtained by their state. Since he urged that the national genius be realized in the objective and unpersonifiable community and not in the will of a state, there was nothing aggressive about Fichte's nationalism; it harmonized with his cosmopolitan ideal of humanity—in which all nations were to collaborate in original ways—and with his pacifism." He created an ideal that was anti-individualistic liberalism and anti-state socialism, and his intellectual heirs were Proudhon and Lassale.

26. Bellegarde, *Dessalines*, p. 358.

27. Ibid., p. 310.

28. Gaetano Mosca and Gaston Bouthoul, *Histoire des doctrines politiques depuis l'antiquité* (Paris: Payot, 1955), p. 335.

29. Hale, *Mexican Liberalism*, p. 1 similarly commented upon the study of his topic: "When I told him [Mexican scholar] that I was having difficulty assessing . . . the prevailing Mexican interpretations of liberalism, he responded with a knowing smile: 'Si, todavía hay mucha pasión en eso . . . ;'

for despite the lapse of a century, post independence thought and policy is not a subject to be treated dispassionately."

30. Edmund Wilson, *Red, Black, Blond and Olive: Studies in Four Civilisations* (New York: Oxford University Press, 1956), pp. 76–77.

31. Commission de Revision des Programmes de l'Enseignement Secondaire, "Plan de Réforme Scolaire," *Bulletin* du Département de l'Instruction Publique, September 1906.

32. Dantès Bellegarde, *Pour une Haiti heureuse*, 2 vols. (Port-au-Prince: Imprimerie Chéraquit, Imprimeur-Editeur, 1927–29), 1: 29, and *Dessalines*, p. 324.

33. See note above for the first mentioned work, and Dantès Bellegarde, *La Résistance haitienne; récit d'histoire contemporaine* (Montreal: Editions Beauchcmin, 1937).

34. Bellegarde, *Peuple haitien*, pp. 25–26.

35. Ibid., p. 96.

36. Dantès Bellegarde, *La nation haitienne* (Paris: J. de Gigord, Editeur, 1938), p. viii.

37. Bellegarde, *Peuple haitien*, p. 27 and *Pages d'histoire*, p. 25.

38. Bellegarde, *Peuple haitien*, pp. 36–37.

39. Mosca and Bouthol, *Doctrines politiques*, pp. 305–6.

40. Alfred L. Kroeber, "The Superorganic," *American Anthropologist*, April-June 1917, p. 186, quoted by John S. Haller, *Outcasts from Evolution: Scientific Attitudes of Racial Inferiority, 1859–1900* (New York: McGraw-Hill, 1975), p. 98. See also Droz, *Doctrines politiques*, p. 84 who paraphrased Auguste Comte: "L'humanité se compose de plus de morts que de vivants."

41. Bellegarde, *Peuple haitien*, pp. 34, 38, 40, 42, 66.

42. Bellegarde, *Peuple haitien*, p. 52.

43. Anténor Firmin quoted by Bellegarde, *Nation haitienne*, p. 68.

44. Bellegarde, *Peuple haitien*, p. 90. Common belief has it that the Spanish never introduced color distinctions as stringently as did the French in their American possessions. A high colonial official in Saint Domingue declared in 1724, in reference to Santo Domingo: "If one does not take care, the French will become as their Spanish neighbors three-fourths of whom are of mixed blood." Quoted in Bellegarde, *Peuple haitien*, p. 36.

45. Nathaniel S. Shaler, "European Peasants as Immigrants," *Atlantic Monthly*, May 1893, p. 649. Also see Pierre L. van den Berghe, *Race and Rarism: A Comparative Perspective* (New York: John Wiley & Sons, 1967).

46. William John McGee, "Trend of Human Progress," *American Anthropologist* 1 (July 1899): 401–7, quoted by Haller, *Outcasts from Evolution*, pp. 105, 107.

47. There are severe critiques of pluralism, both Marxists and non-Marxists. For a new pluralism that, contrarily to the original, hinges on economic and social exploitation of one human group by another and that is overwhelmingly West Indian in derivation, see, for instance, Leo Kuper and M. G. Smith, eds., *Pluralism in Africa* (Berkeley and Los Angeles: University of California Press, 1971).

48. Gouldner, *The Coming Crisis*, pp. 136 and 111. He has posited that much of mainstream Western European and North American scholarship in social science was developed as a response to the gains of Marxism.
49. Ibid., p. 114.
50. Frédéric Burr-Reynaud, "Coopération interaméricaine," *La Phalange*, 7 September, 1943.
51. Bellegarde, *Peuple haitien*, pp. 36–37
52. Bellegarde, *Pages d'histoire*, p. 55.
53. Dantès Bellegarde, *Haiti et ses problèmes* (Montreal: Editions Bernard Valiquette, 1941), p. 11, and *Nation haitienne*, p. 35.
54. Bellegarde, *Haiti et ses problèmes*, p. 37.
55. Ibid., p. 12, and *Nation haitienne*, p. 348.
56. Dantès Bellegarde, "Troisième entretien sur la littérature haitienne," unpublished manuscript, lecture given 30 November, 1953. The author will return to this definition later.
57. Bellegarde, *Haiti et ses problèmes*, pp. 20, 38. Bellegarde agreed with Justin-Chrysostome Dorsainvil that Haiti was 80 percent the product of racial admixtures.
58. Ibid., p. 22.
59. Ibid., p. 24.
60. Until the United States occupation in 1915, there seems to be little evidence that Haitian students were sent to U.S. universities.
61. Haller, *Outcasts from Evolution*, p. 153. See also, Edward J. Pfeifer, "The Genesis of neo-Lamarckism," *Isis*, 56 (1965): 156–57, and George W. Stocking Jr., "Lamarckism in American Social Science, 1890–1915," *Journal of the History of Ideas* 13 (1962): 239–56.
62. Bellegarde, *Haiti et ses problèmes*, p. 16.
63. Bellegarde, *Nation haitienne*, p. viii.
64. Ibid., pp. 344–45.
65. Henri Béranger, in a speech delivered in Port-au-Prince, 29 December, 1935.
66. See Jean Price-Mars, "La position d'Haiti et de la culture francaise en Amérique," *Journal of Inter-American Studies* 8, no. 1 (1966): 44–53.
67. Dantès Bellegarde, "Haiti, centre de culture francaise en Amérique," unpublished manuscript, text of a lecture given in Havana, Cuba, in November 1941.
68. Bellegarde, *Haiti et ses problèmes*, p. 41, and *Dessalines*, pp. 154–62, also, p. 164, where Bellegarde compared Négritude to Hitlerian racism.
69. Jean Price-Mars, "La position d'Haiti et de la culture francaise en Amérique," *Culture Française* (Paris), no. 4 (October 1956), p. 53.
70. Leopold Sedar Senghor, "Discours de Reception," Congrès Constitutif du Parti de la Fédération Africaine, Dakar, 1959.
71. Auguste Viatte, *Histoire littéraire de l'Amérique française* (Québec: Presses Universitaires Laval, 1954), p. 452 and Ghislain Gouraige, *Histoire de la littérature haitienne* (Port-au-Prince: Imprimerie Théodore, 1960), p. 480.

72. George Padmore, *History of the Pan-African Congress* (Manchester: Hammersmith Bookshop, 1945), p. 20.

73. Elliot M. Rudwick, *W. E. B. Du Bois: Propagandist of the Negro Protest* (New York: Atheneum, 1969), pp. 222–23.

74. Ibid., pp. 232–33.

75. Bellegarde, *Haiti et ses problèmes*, pp. 7, 256, 272. For Bellegarde, fascism, nazism, and sovietism were three facets of a same reality.

76. Ibid., p. 9. *Le petit Larousse* (1967), p. 781 defines *phalange* as "1. Greek battle formation; . . . 3. a fascist political grouping."

77. Dantès Bellegarde to the United States Ambassador to Haiti, Gerald A. Drew, 1959.

78. See the conclusion for further analysis. At no time did "Négritude" imply separate black development or isolation. The Anglophonic variant, "Africanism," à la Nkrumah, may have had such notions, since it was wedded to a geographical expression (Africa), but the term *Négritude*, evolving out of the Francophonie group that adopted a universalisée outlook, never did acquire that meaning. These two terms have often led to confusion. In brief, the criticism leveled at "Négritude" by such writers as Ezekiel Mphahlele is a misrepresentation of the tenets of the concept. See for instance, E. Mphahlele, ed., *African Writing Today* (Baltimore: Penguin Books, 1967), pp. 247–63.

79. Bellegarde, *Peuple haitien*, p. 36, *Dessalines*, pp. 168–69, and *Nation haitienne*, p. 346.

80. For instance, see Rudwick, *W. E. B. Du Bois*, pp. 214–15, 218, 222–23, 224: "Both he [Diagne] and Gratien Candace . . . told delegates . . . about the good fortune of being 'Black Frenchmen.' One British observer noted that the English-speaking delegation referred to themselves as 'We Negroes,' while the French representatives always described themselves as 'We Frenchmen.'" Also see, 232–33, and Francis L. Broderick, *W. E. B. Du Bois: Negro Leader in a Time of Crisis* (Stanford: Stanford University Press, 1959), p. 131.

81. Bellegarde, *Hati et ses problemes*, p. 17.

82. Bellegarde, *Dessalines*, p. 199.

83. Bellegarde, "Troisième entretien," family archives.

84. See Jean Price-Mars, "La culture haitienne," lecture at the Société Haitienne d'Etudes Scientifiques, 20 January, 1939.

85. Célimène loved a mulatto officer named Chancy who committed suicide as a result of this affair. Pétion, reputed to have been a misogynist, never married, although he carried on a lifelong affair with Joute Lachenais. Upon Pétion's death, Joute Lachenais became President Boyer's mistress, and may have married him while they were both in exile in Jamaica, shortly before her death. President Boyer is buried at Père Lachaise, in Paris.

86. Characterization drawn from Emma Bovary, in Gustave Flaubert, *Madame Bovary* (1857); marginal notes made by Dantès Bellegarde in Jean Price-Mars,

Formation ethnique, folklore et culture du peuple haitien (Port-au-Prince: V. Valcin, Imprimeur, 1939), pp. 144–45.

87. Bellegarde, *Un haitien parle*, pp. 262–79, *Dessalines* p. 182 and also Mercer Cook, interview, Washington, D.C., 19 February, 1975.
88. Albert Memmi, *The Colonizer and the Colonized* (Boston: Beacon Press. 1965), p. 88.
89. Ibid., p. 125.
90. Ibid., p. 126.
91. See the critical study of Henock Trouillot, *Dantis Bellegarde, un écrivain d'autrefois* (Port-au-Prince: Imprimerie Théodore, 1957).
92. Ghislain Gouraige to the author, 26 December, 1975.
93. Haller *Outcasts from Evolution*, p. vi.
94. Gouldner, *The Coming Crisis*, p. 69.
95. Bellegarde, *Haiti heureuse*, 1: 35.
96. Ibid., p. 27 and *Dessalines*, p. 322.
97. Hale, *Mexican Liberalism*, p. 157.
98. Bellegarde, *Haiti heureuse*, 1: 47.
99. Ibid., p. 50.
100. Ibid., p. 51.
101. Ibid.
102. Dantès Bellegarde, "Education pour la paix et le bien-être social," *Journal of Inter-American Studies* 1, no. 1 (1959): 6. Bellegarde's statement of education was originally made in 1920, and repeated in 1948. See *Dessalines*, pp. 209–10.
103. Donald Atwell Zoll, *Twentieth Century Political Philosophy* (Englewood Cliffs, N.J.: Prentice-Hall, 1974), p. 89.
104. Gouldner, *The Coming Crisis*, p. 114.
105. Ibid., p. 115 and Droz, *Doctrines politiques*, p. 73: "Le Libéralisme est une pure doctrine de classe."
106. African socialists can be said to be dealing with this issue, or at least have that potential, as they are not bound by an exclusive Western viewpoint and as they draw from traditional African thought on social organization.
107. Bellegarde, "Education pour la paix," pp. 3 and 6.
108. Bellegarde, *Haiti et ses problèmes*, pp. 14–15.
109. Bellegarde, *Dessalines*, p. 301.
110. Ben-Ami Scharfstein, *Roots of Bergson's Philosophy* (New York: Columbia University Press, 1943), pp. 101, 137. Bergson is quoted as saying: "To us French people this question seems paradoxical. We are so completely assimilated. . . . I believe the Jewish question will be solved when the Jewish people will have attained equal rights in the countries where they have been persecuted. And the sooner that is attained the better for the Jews of course, and also for the countries where they live."
111. Bellegarde, *Dessalines*, pp. 306–7.

NOTES TO CHAPTER 5

1. See for instance, Aimé Césaire, *Discourse on Colonialism* (New York: Modern Reader, 1972), Frantz Fanon, *The Wretched of the Earth* (New York: Grove Press, 1963), *Black Skin, White Masks* (New York: Grove Press, 1967), Albert Memmi, *The Colonizer and the Colonized* (Boston: Beacon Press, 1965), O. Mannoni, *Prospero and Caliban: The Psychology of Colonization* (New York: Praeger, 1956). All these seminal works are from Francophonie authors.

2. See Dantès Bellegarde, *La nation haitienne* (Paris: J. de Gigord, 1938), p. 306.

3. See Durkheim, *Les formes élémentaires de la vie religieuse,* (Paris: Félix Alean, 1912), and also Guy Lafrance, *La philosophie sociale de Bergson* (Ottawa: Editions de l'Université d'Ottawa, 1974), particularly pp. 41–42.

4. Dantès Bellegarde, *Dessalines a parlé* (Port-au-Prince: Société d'Editions et de Librairie, 1948), p. 281.

5. Quoted by Jean Touchard, *Histoire des idées politiques*, 2 vols. (Paris: Presses Universitaires de France, 1959), 2: 383.

6. *Le petit Larousse*, 1967, pp. 761, 690.

7. Touchard, *Idées politiques*, p. 435.

8. Voltaire and Montesquieu, among others, saw themselves as universalists and cosmopolitan in their tastes. Their teachings, however, led to increasing nationalism in the following century. See the analysis of Touchard, *Idées politiques*. pp. 435–36.

9. Rayford W. Logan, interview, Washington, D.C., 21 November, 1975.

10. Friedrich Heer, *The Intellectual History of Europe*, vol. 2, *The Counter-Reformation to 1945* (New York: Doubleday & Co., 1966), p. 281 described the nineteenth century as extending from 1789 to 1945

11. A different illustration of the same phenomenon at the international level would be President John Kennedy's decision to harness the forces of nationalism in the United States interest by supporting Angolan Holden Roberto against more radical leadership. See the article by Azinna Nwafor, "The Liberation of Angola," *Monthly Review*, February 1976.

12. Jean Price-Mars having been one of the first Haitians to come to the "African" in Haitian popular culture can thus be considered a nationalist.

13. See Dantès's views earlier expressed on Treitschke and Fichte.

14. In an article, Zbigniew Brzczinski had argued that "egalitarianism" rather than "liberty" is the key objective of Third World nations, inferring disapproval of that goal. See "America in a Hostile World," *Foreign Policy,* Summer 1976. The question one raises is whether liberty can exist at all in the midst of economic inequalities.

15. Dantès Bellegarde, *Pour une Haiti heureuse* 2 vols. (Port-au-Prince: Imprimerie Chéraquit, 1927–29), 1: 9.

16. Ghislain Gouraige, *La diaspora d'Haiti et l'Afrique* (Ottawa: Editions Naaman, 1974), p. 102.

17. Bellegarde, *Dessalines*, p. 176.

18. Georges Sylvain in *La Ronde*, 15 May, 1901, also quoted by Bellegarde, *Dessalines*, p. 177.

19. Dantès Bellegarde, *Haiti et ses problèmes* (Montreal: Editions Bernard Valiquette, 1941), p. 40. Bellegarde nonetheless argued: "Scientifically, Haitian racism is not 'better' justified than Hitlerian racism. Historically, it is explicable. Our racism—to speak like Mr. Jeremie—has been 'defensive' rather than 'aggressive.' Today, as yesterday, no hatred of foreign peoples inspire it. But Haiti has been and still often is faced with the worst calumnies and the most insulting accusations."

20. Bellegarde, *Dessalines*, p. 323.

21. Ibid.

22. Dantès Bellegarde, *Au service d'Haiti: Appréciations sur un haitien et son oeuvre* (Port-au-Prince: Imprimerie Théodore, 1962), p. 62.

23. Cited in Brian Weinstein, "Francophonie: Language Groups in World Politics," unpublished manuscript, International Studies Association, Washington, D.C., 1973, p. 1.

24. Benjamin L. Whof and Edward Sapir, in *Language Thought and Reality: Selected Writings of Benjamin Lee Whof* ed. John B. Carroll, (Cambridge: Massachusetts Institute of Technology, 1956), quoted by Weinstein, "Francophonie," p. 2.

25. Dantès Bellegarde, "Le créole haitien, patois français," *Formes et Couleurs* (1954), n.p. 26. Ibid.

27. Anténor Firmin, *M. Roosevelt, président des Etais-Unis et la République d'Haiti* (Paris: Pichón et Durand Auzias, 1905) also quoted by Bellegarde, *Dessalines*, pp. 263 and 271.

28. Dantès Bellegarde, *Histoire du peuple haitien, 1492–1952* (Port-au-Prince: Imprimerie Held [Suisse], 1953), p. 120.

29. Bellegarde, *Haiti et ses problèmes*, p. 67.

30. Ibid., pp. 61–69. Haitian Creole is a language with an African syntax and a vocabulary derived mostly from French. Bellegarde never did accept this evaluation as valid.

31. Ibid., p. 61.

32. Minutes, Conseil Consultatif, Session of 13 October, 1950, p. 37.

33. Bellegarde, *Dessalines*, pp. 99–100.

34. Ibid., pp. 101, 109, (italics in original).

35. Dantès Bellegarde to Secretary of State Abel Léger, Washington, D.C., 23 June, 1931.

36. Bellegarde, *Dessalines*, pp. 106, 273.

37. Ibid., p. 109. Bellegarde's allies and friends were, among others, Roger Baldwin (founder of the ACLU), Adolf A. Berle, Jr. (President Roosevelt's "brain trust"), Ernest Gruening, Walter White (NAACP), the historian Raymond Leslie Buell, and the jurist James Brown Scott.

38. Quoted by Bellegarde, *Dessalines*, p. 317.

39. Ibid., p. 109.
40. Ibid., pp. 18–19.
41. Ibid., p. 20.
42. Richard Hofstadter, *Social Darwinism in American Thought* (New York: A Braziller, 1959), p. 151.
43. Bellegarde, *Haiti et ses problèmes*, pp. 252–53.
44. Ibid., p. 254.
45. Dantès Bellegarde, "Rapport," Quatrième Réunion Consultative des Secrétaires d'Etat des Relations Extérieures d'Amérique, Washington, D.C., 26 March 7 April, 1951, p. 6.
46. Bellegarde, *Haiti et ses problèmes*, p. 258.
47. Ibid., p. 259, *Au service d'Haiti*, p. 180, *Un haitien parle* (Port-au-Prince: Chéraquit, Imprimeur-Editeur, 1934), p. 255.
48. Bellegarde, *Haiti et ses problèmes*, p. 263.
49. Touchard, *Idées politiques*, p. 404.
50. Bellegarde, *Haiti et ses problèmes*, p. 263.
51. Ibid., p. 264.
52. Ibid., pp. 271, 282.
53. Bellegarde, *Un haitien parle*, p. 179–80.
54. Ibid., p. 181.
55. Ibid., p. 182.
56. Ibid., pp. 183, 185. On page 187, Bellegarde supported Puerto Rican independence in these words: "Puerto Rico is rich, but Puerto Ricans are poor. All its wealth is in the hands of American companies. Its small farmers have practically vanished, and its workers know today the misdeeds of the harshest capitalistic regime."
57. Ibid., p. 183.
58. Bellegarde, *Dessalines*, p. 27.
59. Dantès Bellegarde, "An Inter-American Economic Policy," *Annals of the American Academy of Political and Social Sciences* 150 (July 1930): 186.
60. Ibid.
61. The same benefits accrued to the United States during and after World War II. Between 1939 and 1945, the United States GNP went from $91 billion to $166 billion, "the most phenomenal such occurrence in world history," according to Walter Arnold, "A Cold Eye on the Home Front," *Saturday Review*, 10 July, 1976, p. 54.
62. Bellegarde, "Economic Policy," p. 187 (italics in original).
63. Bellegarde, *Un haitien parle*, p. 189.
64. Bellegarde, "Economic Policy," p. 189 and *Dessalines*, p. 83.
65. Bellegarde, *Un haitien parle*, p. 190.
66. Ibid., pp. 191–92, citing from the proceedings of the Third Pan-American Commercial Conference (1927), p. 43 *passim*.
67. "Dantès Bellegarde Dies in Haiti," *New York Times*, 16 June, 1966.
68. Bellegarde, "Economic Policy," p. 190.

69. Bellegarde, *Un haitien parle*, p. 195.
70. Bellegarde, *Dessalines*, pp. 286–87.
71. Ibid., pp. 86–88, *Un haitien parle*, p. 192, "Economic Policy," p. 191. An American businessman declared to Bellegarde at the Third Pan-American Commercial Conference: "We businessmen know that from an economic standpoint, imperialism is a failure." Bellegarde took the statement at face value.
72. Bellegarde, *Un haitien parle*, pp. 125–26. Bellegarde suggested that European peasants be allowed to immigrate to Haiti to preach by their example. Also see *Dessalines*, pp. 226–27: "The basis of the political, economic, and social organization of Haiti is the rural *section* [administrative subdivision]. Inherent is a biological truth on which modern medicine has established its most recent therapeutic methods: in order for the organism to defend itself, the cell must be strong . . ."
73. Bellegarde, *Un haitien parle*, p. 70 and *Dessalines*, p. 223.
74. Bellegarde, *Un haitien parle*, pp. 119–20 and *Dessalines*, pp. 411–17 where he related plans for credit associations for the peasantry, and of efforts to lure the petite bourgeoisie to agriculture. He also described the formation of an "intellectual-proletariat" consisting of unemployed or underemployed lawyers, teachers, doctors, and small merchants.
75. Bellegarde, *Un haitien parle*, p. 7, from a speech given originally in 1907.
76. Bellegarde, *Haiti et ses problèmes*, p. 194.
77. Bellegarde, *Un haitien parle*, p. 7, and *Dessalines*, p. 402.
78. Bellegarde, *Un haitien parle*, pp. 91–92.
79. Ibid., p. 90 and *Dessalines*, p. 64.
80. Bellegarde, *Un haitien parle*, p. 136.
81. Ibid., p. 70, and *Dessalines*, p. 223.
82. Bellegarde, *Un haitien parle*, p. 92.
83. Ibid., pp. 138, 140, and *Dessalines*, p. 125.
84. Bellegarde, *Un haitien parle*, p. 175, *Dessalines*, pp. 65–66, and *Haiti et ses problèmes*, p. 160.
85. Bellegarde, *Un haitien parle*, p. 175.
86. Ibid., p. 176.
87. Ibid.
88. Minutes, "Assemblée Constituante," 1950.
89. Bellegarde, *Haiti heureuse*, 2: 60–61.
90. Bellegarde, *Un haitien parle*, pp. 176–77.
91. Dantès Bellegarde, "La quatrième réunion consultative des Ministres des Relations Extérieures d'Aménque," *Journal of Inter-American Studies*, 4, no. 1 (1962): 3.
92. Ibid., pp. 2, 4.
93. Bellegarde, *Un haitien parle*, pp. 176–77.
94. Ibid., p. 176, and *Dessalines*, p. 64.

95. Bellegarde, *Haiti heureuse*, 1: 282, and *Peuple haitien*, p. 206.
96. Bellegarde, *Dessalines*, pp. 60 and 68.
97. Ibid., p. 56.
98. Ibid., p. 422.
99. Ibid., pp. 59, 88–89, *Un haitien parle*, p. 174, *Haiti heureuse*, 1: 128.
100. Bellegarde, *Haiti heureuse*, 1: 31–86.
101. Bellegarde, *Dessalines*, p. 204.
102. Bellegarde, *Haiti heureuse*, 1: 33.
103. Ibid., p. 42 *passim*. This was part of a debate that occurred at the turn of the century between the proponents of Anglo-Saxonism and the French forces as to the proper path for Haiti's modernization. See the works by Fleury Féquière, Alfred Auguste, and Seymour Pradel, "Les deux tendances," *Haiti littéraire et scientifique* 5 March, 1912.
104. See Alvin W. Gouldner, *The Coming Crisis in Western Sociology* (New York: Avon Books, 1970), pp. 125–34. Also see Norman and Jeanne MacKenzie, *The Fabians* (New York: Simon & Schuster, 1977).
105. Bellegarde, *Un haitien parle*, p. 125.
106. Bellegarde, *Dessalines*, p. 311.
107. Bellegarde, *Nation haitienne*, p. 307.
108. Dantès Bellegarde, "Education pour la paix et le bien-être social," *Journal of Inter-American Studies* 1 (1959): 6–7, *Dessalines*, p. 210, *Haiti heureuse*, 1: 284–85.
109. Bellegarde, *Nation haitienne*, p. 306.
110. It is the same reasoning that assigns guilt to individuals for their fate, absolving the system of responsibility, a conclusion that is inevitable in any social theories that would emphasize "individualism."
111. Bellegarde, "Education pour la paix," p. 7.
112. Bellegarde, *Dessalines*, p. 31.
113. Bellegarde, *Un haitien parle*, p. 71.
114. Bellegarde, *Dessalines*, p. 209.
115. Bellegarde, "Education pour la paix," p. 8.
116. Bellegarde, *Dessalines*, pp. 213–14.
117. Ibid., p. 201.
118. Bellegarde, *Nation haitienne*, p. 308.
119. Ibid., p. 312.
120. George Galloway, *Religion and Modern Thought* (Edinburgh: T. & T. Clark, 1922), quoted by Bellegarde, *Nation haitienne*, p. 312.
121. Bellegarde, *Nation haitienne*, p. 311.
122. Ibid., p. 310, *Haiti et ses problèmes*, pp. 95–96.
123. On the Vodou religion from which popular Haitian social thought can be extracted, see the work by the Haitian scholar, Laennec Hurbon, *Dieu dans le vaudou haitien* (Paris: Payot, 1972), among others.
124. Bellegarde, *Dessalines*, p. 202.

125. Bellegarde, *Haiti heureuse*, 1: 285. Italics mine. This author's experience in those schools maintained by the Roman Catholic hierarchy was that of a scarcely disguised racism on the part of many priests and nuns.
126. Bellegarde, *Haiti et ses problèmes*, p. 97.
127. Ibid., p. 98, and *Dessalines*, p. 203.
128. Bellegarde, *Haiti et ses problèmes*, p. 99.
129. Bellegarde, *Peuple haitien*, pp. 205–06.
130. Bellegarde, *Hati heureuse*, 1: 271–72.
131. See Cesar Grâna, *Bohemian Versus Bourgeois* (New York: Basic Books, 1964), p. 107.
132. Bellegarde, *Haiti heureuse*, 1: 9.
133. See Gouldner, *The Coming Crisis*, p. 115, Touchard, *Idées politiques*, p. 404, and Jacques Droz, *Histoire des doctrines politiques en France* (Paris: Presses Universitaires de France, 1966), p. 69.
134. Compte-Rendu, Congrès Philosophique, "Entretiens et discours sur la paix et l'éducation," Saturday, 30 September, 1944, p. 19.
135. Wladimir Weidle, *Le Mois*, September 1937, p. 153 quoted by Bellegarde, *Haiti et ses problèmes*, p. 165. Italics are Bellegarde's.
136. Bellegarde, *Dessalines*, p. 214.
137. Ibid., p. 206.
138. Ibid., pp. 423–24.
139. Dantès Bellegarde, "Notes sur l'éducation des femmes" (1906), unpublished manuscript.
140. Clothilde de Vaux was Auguste Comte's female companion who was enshrined by him after her death. This great reverence for womanhood was a primary factor in positivism, but it must be noted that sexism (and racism) was increasing throughout the nineteenth century.
141. Dantès Bellegarde was raised by his mother and her sister, and his first major intellectual influence was that of a paternal aunt, Argentine Bellegarde.
142. Bellegarde, *Nation haitienne*, p. 304. For the state of women's education under Bellegarde's tenure at the ministry, see *Haiti heureuse*, 1: 183–86.
143. Bellegarde, *Nation haitienne*, p. 305.
144. Minutes, "Assemblée Constituante," session of 15 November, 1950, pp. 1 and 4.
145. Ibid., pp. 6 and 7.
146. Ibid., p. 7.
147. In Haiti, the feeling about Bellegarde's "vanity" remains strong. He did collect nearly all that was ever written about him internationally, and he was quick to relate the lavish praise he had received. The author, however, remembers Bellegarde as a man of unsurpassed humility in his daily relationships with others.
148. Bellegarde, *Haiti heureuse*, 1: 55.
149. Bellegarde, *Dessalines*, pp. 365–66.
150. Ibid., pp. 368–70.

151. Bellegarde, *Un haitien parle*, p. 8.
152. Dantès Bellegarde, "Souvenirs de 1906, notes pour conférences," unpublished manuscript, p. 14.
153. Ibid., p. 18.
154. Ibid., p. 20. Bellegarde added this humorous passage: "One must believe that the genius of the race is truly powerful, since Schopenhauer and Hartmann, like two good bourgeois, contracted marriages and procreated: history does not tell us if they loved their wives."
155. Ibid., p. 22.
156. Ibid., pp. 1 and 2.
157. Ibid., p. 12.
158. Ibid., pp. 13–14.

NOTES TO CHAPTER 6

1. See the argument about Haitian regionalism in Georges Anglade, *Atlas critique d'Haiti*, (Montreal: ERCE & CRC, 1982).
2. Bureau of the American Republics, "Haiti," *Bulletin* No. 62 (Washington, D.C.: Government Printing Office, 1893), pp. 71–75, 49.
3. Ibid., pp. 66–67.
4. Ibid., p. 67.
5. Ibid., pp. 47–48: "Owing to the too frequent occurrence of insurrection and revolution from 1843 to 1888, there was a constantly increasing tendency on the part of persons born in Haiti partly of foreign origin or educated abroad, to seek foreign nationality, the French law affording this facilities [*sic*] which might result in making a considerable portion of the educated and well-to-do natives foreigners, but this tendency has recently been somewhat abated." The author notes that after the political events of 1946 and 1957 which produced large exile groups, consisting largely of members of the bourgeoisie, this tendency toward dual (or more) citizenship seems to have been resurrected.
6. Emile Luders had been found guilty in a court of law, and on appeal, of assaulting a Haitian policeman while the latter was attempting; to arrest a thief who had taken refuge in Luders's commercial establishment.
7. Dantès Bellegarde, *Histoire du peuple haitien*, (Port-au-Prince: Imprimerie Held [Suisse], 1953), pp. 199–201.
8. No studies on ethnic groups forming the Haitian nation have ever been undertaken by sociologists as far as can be ascertained by this author.
9. American interventions occurred in 1857, 1859, 1868, 1869, 1876, 1888, 1889, 1892, 1902, 1903, 1904, 1905, 1906, 1907, 1908, 1909, 1911, 1912, and 1913, before the final occupation which lasted from 1915 until 1934.
10. Dantès Bellegarde, *Pour une Haiti heureuse*, 2 vols. (Port-au-Prince: Cheraquit, Imprimeur-Editeur, 1927–29), 2: 3.
11. Levantine and Italian merchants seemed to have been actively pro-American in 1915. Schmidt, *United States*, pp. 36 and 41 argued that direct American

investments in Haiti were minimal: "Foreign investments in Haiti in 1915 consisted of $21.5 million owed to French bondholders as the result of the 1875, 1896, and 1910 loans, and United States investments in 1913 amounted to $4 million, as against $220 million in Cuba."

12. Jonathan Brown, *The History and Present Condition of St. Domingo* (Philadelphia: William Marshall & Co., 1837), 2: p. 286: "The tables are not exactly turned upon a white adventurer in the country, for he is not viewed with the contempt which is visited upon the African in other countries: but he is respected as a superior being, feared as a tyrant, and hated as the natural enemy of the negro race."

13. Jacques C. Antoine, interview, Washington, D.C., 20 May, 1975.

14. Alfred Nemours, *Ma campagne francaise* (Port-au-Prince: Imprimerie de l'Abeille, 1919), p. 261.

15. Herbert Spencer, "The Comparative Psychology of Man," *Popular Sáence Monthly* 8 (January, 1876): 260–61, 266, and John Haller, Jr., *Outcasts from Evolution: Scientific Attitudes of Racial Inferiority, 1859–1900* (New York: McGraw-Hill, 1971), p. 126.

16. In 1915, Haiti's literacy rate was estimated at about 3 percent. This fact alone seems to explain United States reliance on mulattoes for high governmental positions, since they were the overwhelming majority in the educated sector. But the Americans seemed to have preferred the "simple" and unpretentious black peasant to this elite, and this, not in a fit of egalitarianism. United States authorities in Haiti ended up massacring tens of thousands of Haitian peasants involved in guerrilla warfare against the United States Marines.

17. Ali A. Mazrui, "From Social Darwinism to Current Theories of Modernization," *World Politics*, 21, no. 1 (1968): 82.

18. To use Rayford W. Logan's phrase in reference to the emergence of the Pan-African movement, "The Historical Aspects of Pan-Africanism, 1900–1945," *Pan-Africanism Reconsidered*, ed. The American Society of African Culture (Berkeley and Los Angeles: University of California Press, 1962), p. 37.

19. See Dimitri G. Lavroff, *Ia République du Sénégal* (Paris: Librairie générale de droit et de jurisprudence, 1966), p. 23 who argued that these metropolitan individuals are those who had advocated assimilation.

20. See the argument of Albert Memmi, *The Colonizer and the Colonized* (Boston: Beacon Press, 1965), p. 29 *passim.*

21. Francis P. Walters, *History of the League of Nations*, 2 vols. (London: Oxford University Press, 1952), p. 147.

22. For instance, see Camille Lhérisson, *De la responsabilité des élites dans la société moderne* (Port-au-Prince: Imprimerie de l'Etat, 1947).

23. John Ciardi, "Manner of Speaking," *Saturday Review*, 21 August, 1976, p. 52.

24. Ghislain Gouraige to author, 26 December, 1975.

25. Cesar Graña, *Bohemian Versus Bourgeois* (New York: Basic Books, 1964), p. 107.

26. Bellegarde asked for cooperation between social classes for a strong Haiti. See Dantès Bellegarde, *Haiti et ses problèmes*, (Montreal: Editions Bernard Valiquette, 1941), p. 262.

27. Dilia Vieux argued that most of Haiti's nineteenth-century social thinkers were members of the petite bourgeoisie. Interview, Washington, D.C., 23 August, 1976.

28. Harold E. Davis, *History of Latin America* (New York: Ronald Press, 1968), p. 491.

29. Jacques Droz, *Histoire des doctrines politiques en France* (Paris: Presses Universitaires de France, 1966), p. 86.

30. Harold J. Laski, *The Rise of Liberalism: The Philosophy of a Business Civilisation* (New York: Harper & Brothers Publishers, 1936), p. 273.

31. Ibid., p. 276.

32. Saint-Simon, *Vues sur la propriété et la législation*, ed. Rodriges (1832), p. 255, quoted by Laski, *Rise of Liberalism*, p. 277.

33. Laski, *Rise of Liberalism*, pp. 277–78.

34. See Gordon K. Lewis, *The Virgin Islands: A Caribbean Lilliput* (Evanston: Northwest ern University Press, 1972), p. 29 who related Danish official policy that awarded the mulatto "aristocracy" with the legal means to declare their entire family "white" based on their good social behavior over time.

35. For instance, see Dantès Bellegarde, *La nation haitienne* (Paris: J. de Gigord, 1938), p. 306.

36. Jean Touchard, *Histoire des idées politiques*, 2 vols. (Paris: Presses Universitaires de France, 1959), 2: 518.

37. Jacques C. Antoine, interview, Washington, D.C., 20 May, 1975 and Max Wilson, interview, Washington, D.C., 8 April, 1976.

38. Davis, *History*, p. 498.

39. Jacques C. Antoine, interview, Washington, D.C., 20 May, 1975.

40. Bellegarde would diplomatically declare in public that, after all, French was English badly pronounced; in private, he held the opposite view, based on the English language's heavy reliance on Norman-French and Latin- and Greek-derived words for its "educated" speech, rather than the more "primitive" Saxon words.

41. Jacques C. Antoine, interview, Washington, D.C., 20 May, 1975.

42. See Arturo Ardao, "Assimilation and Transformation of Positivism in Latin America," *Journal of the History of Ideas*, 24 (1963): 517, Thomas E. Skidmore, *Black into White: Race and Nationality in Brazilian Thought* (New York: Oxford University Press, 1974), p. 27.

43. Similarly, "in Haiti, Africa manifests itself through an ensemble of perceptions, of representations, of reflexes, of psychological particularities, of forms of religious alienation. . . . which are translated in Vodou, in artisan skills, in the cultivation of crops, in folklore. . . . and in other manifestations of

the sensitivity and of the psychic life of the people which are the results of a long process of cultural *métissage* and syncretism." Rene Depestre, "Jean Price-Mars et le mythe de l'orphée noir ou les aventures de la négritude," *L'Homme et la Société* (Paris), no. 7, January-February 1968, p. 174.

44. We are told that in China there is a power struggle between Left, Right, and moderate factions: all three, however, seem steeped in Marxism-Leninism.

45. In contrast, Bellegarde's *compere*, W. E. B. Du Bois, "flipped" and "flopped" so often on so many issues that scarcely anyone knows where he stood, according to Rayford W. Logan, interview, Washington, D.C., 21 November, 1975. This author does not agree with this overly severe judgment of Du Bois.

46. Robert J. Alexander, *Communism in Latin America* (New Brunswick, N.J.: Rutgers University Press, 1957), pp. 296–97 argued that Estimé's government represented a short period of democratic government in Haitian history since it allowed several political parties to be formed, legalized the Haitian Communist party, and fostered the development of an embryonic trade-union movement.

47. Hénock Trouillot, *M. Dantès Bellegarde, un écrivain d'autrefois* (Port-au-Prince: Imprimerie Théodore, 1957), pp. 23–24.

48. See the biographical data on Dantès Bellegarde in *Grand Larousse encyclopédique*, vol. 2 (1960), p. 48.

49. Ghislain Gouraige to the author, 26 December, 1975.

50. See Bellegarde, *Peuple haitien*, p. 36.

51. Rayford W. Logan, interview, Washington, D.C., 21 November, 1975.

52. Jacques C. Antoine, interview, Washington, D.C., 20 May, 1975.

53. Auguste Viatte, *Histoire littéraire de l'Amérique francaise* (Paris: Presses Universitaires de France, 1954), p. 452, wrote that Gérard de Catalogne is the only theoretician to have followed Bellegarde's lead. Gerard de Catalogne was a gifted social thinker at the extreme right of the political spectrum who approved of fascism and defended Franco, Salazar, Vargas, and Mussolini (up to the invasion of Ethiopia by Italy). See his *Notre Révolution*, 3 vols (Motreal: Editions Bernard Valiquette, 1941–44).

54. Historically, positivism aimed at checking the excesses of liberalism, and attempted to put order and stability back into European politics.

55. Davis, *History*, p. 500.

56. "Ronde": children holding hands in a circle, singing while turning.

57. René Laloue, *Histoire de la poésie française* (Paris: Presses Universitaires de France, 1970), p. 107. Paul Claudel, (1868–1955), was Bellegarde's colleague in Washington, D.C. in 1931–1933, and so was Pierre Uval, of Vichy frame, whom Bellegarde had known well in the 1920s.

58. Dantès Bellegarde, *Haiti et ses problèmes* (Montreal: Editions Bernard Valiquette, 1941), p. 164. On the other hand, Alexander Solshenitzin has argued that Marxism was Western, therefore alien and not applicable to the Soviet people.

59. The Haitian writer Jacques Roumain and Dantès Bellegarde's son-in-law, Max Hudicourt, were cofounders of the Parti Socialiste Populaire, Haiti's Marxist party in 1930. Hudicourt was assassinated shortly after his election to the Senate in 1946. Both he and Roumain had come from the ranks of the aristocracy. Also see Alexander, *Communism*, pp. 296–98.

60. Aimé Césaire, *Cahier d'un retour au pays natal* (Paris: Présence Africaine, 1960), p. 46.

61. For instance, see Bellegarde, *Peuple haitien*, pp. 155, 192.

62. Dantès Bellegarde, "Troisième entretien sur la littérature haitienne," unpublished manuscript of lecture given on 30 November, 1953, p. 2. Cacos were revolutionaries from the North of Haiti while *Piquets* were their southern brethren.

63. See Harold E. Davis, "Trends in Social Thought in Twentieth Century Latin America," *Journal of Inter-American Studies* 1, no. 1 (1959): 65.

64. See Fernando Salmerón, "Mexican Philosophers of the Twentieth Century," *Major Trends in Mexican Philosophy*, ed. Mario de la Cueva et al. (Notre Dame: University of Notre Dame Press, 1966), p. 248 *passim*.

65. See the arguments based on the colonial past, made regarding Caribbean political authoritarianism, in Clive Y. Thomas, "Break and Justice: The Struggle for Socialism in Guyana," *Monthly Review* 28, no. 4 (1976): 23–35.

66. Georges LeFèvre, "Le quinzième convive," *L'Intransigeant* (Paris) 28 March, 1922. Not even the French people were able to accomplish such feats as Bellegarde described: a recent survey has revealed that the French stop reading literature altogether upon leaving high school. In order to change the tide, the French government was offering several classical novels as a gift to couples upon marriage, strengthening two ideals at once.

67. Touchard, *Idées politiques*, p. 522.

68. Charles A. Hale, *Mexican Liberalism in the Age of Mora, 1821–1853* (New Haven: Yale University Press, 1968), p. 177.

69. American Republics, "Haiti," pp. 47–48.

70. Depestre, "Jean Price-Mars et le mythe," p. 175.

71. Ibid.

72. Leopold Sedar Senghor, *Prose and Poetry*, ed. John Reed and Clive Wake (London: Oxford University Press, 1965), pp. 57–59. Kwame Nkrumah changed his mind over time.

73. Dantès Bellegarde, *Un haitien parle* (Port-au-Prince: Chéraquit, Imprimeur-Editeur, 1934), p. 7 and *Dessalines aparlé* (Port-au-Prince: Société d'Editions et de Librairie, 1948), p. 252.

74. Dantès Bellegarde reported with pride to the author, on several occasions, the following anecdote: Upon entering Notre Dame basilica for a Te Deum and on his way to his assigned seat in the diplomatic corps section, he was stopped by a member of the Academic Française gently pulling at his sleeve. The French writer asked him to sit with the *académiciens*, because his place as a Francophonic writer of renown was with them.

75. Quoted by William T. Fontaine, "Philosophical Aspects of Contemporary African Social Thought," *Pan-Africanism Reconsidered*, ed. The American Society of African Culture (Berkeley and Los Angeles: University of California Press, 1962), p. 247. Also see Aimé Césaire, *Discourse on Colonialism* (New York: Monthly Review Press, 1972).

76. Bellegarde, *Dessalines*, p. 115 *passim*.

77. Auguste Viatte to the author, 8 March, 1975.

78. Auguste Viatte to author, 8 March, 1975: Viatte stated that Price-Mars had never intended that Vodou replace Roman Catholicism, nor did he advocate that Creole replace French as the official language.

79. Ghislain Gouraige to author, 26 December, 1975.

80. Bellegarde, *Un haitien parle*, p. 183.

NOTES TO EPILOGUE

1. John Updike, in "The Cultural Situation of the American Writer," *(Washington Star*, Calendar, 26 September, 1976, pp. 1 and 5) argued that the United States writer shares in the affluence of his society; even a minor author finds ready translation throughout the world due to the political importance of the United States. He adds: "In contrast, the Danish, or Dutch, or Turkish writer needs great genius to escape the parish of his native language and reach an international audience."

2. See Robert I. Rotberg, "The Legacy of Haiti's First Revolution," unpublished manuscript, Massachusetts Institute of Technology, Boston, n.d.

3. This would include those adhering to the dependency and world systems models as will Marxism in its infinite variety.

4. Emile Nau, *Le Républicain*, 1 October, 1836, quoted by Auguste Viatte, *Histoire littéraire, de l'Amérique francaise* (Paris: Presses Universitaires de France, 1954), p. 360.

5. Jacques Maritain, *Man and the State* (Chicago: University of Chicago Press, 1951), p. 8.

6. Gordon Lewis, *The Virgin Islands: A Caribbean Lilliput* (Evanston: Northwestern University Press), pp. 84 and 111.

7. Dilia Vieux, interview, Washington, D.C., 21 February, 1975.

8. See the principal thesis of Edward J. Williams, "Secularization, Integration and Rationalization: Some Perspectives from Latin American Thought," *Journal of Inter-American Studies* 5, pt. 2, (November 1973): 199–216.

9. Dantès Bellegarde, *Au service d'Haiti: Appréciations sur un haitien et son oeuvre* (Port-au-Prince: Imprimerie Theodore, 1962), p. 222.

10. Dantès Bellegarde, *Histoire du Peuple haitien* (Port-au-Prince: Imprimerie Held [Suisse], 1953), p. 30. He described absenteeism as a plague for Saint Domingue.

11. Olavo Bilac, *Gazeta de noticias*, 8 September, 1907, quoted by Skidmore, *Black into White: Race and Nationality in Brazilian Thought* (New York: Oxford University Press, 1974) p. 93.

12. Jacques Droz, *Histoire des Doctrines politiques en France*, (Paris: Libraire Presses Universitaires de France), p. 45.

13. See H. Hoetink, *The Two Variants in Caribbean Race Relations: A contribution to the Sociology of Segmented Societies* (London: Oxford University Press, 1967), p. 181 *passim.*

14. See Alvin W. Gouldner, in *The Coming Crisis of Western Sociology* (New York, Avon Books, 1970), p. 125, argued that the violence of the French Revolution had traumatized the English and sealed the merger. But it appears to this author that the English had already shown great propensity for merging bourgeois and aristocratic elements. The War of the Roses in the sixteenth century is a case in point.

15. Harold E. Davis, *History of Latin America* (New York: Ronald Press, 1968), p. 362.

16. Harold A. Bierck Jr., ed., *Selected Writings of Bolivar* (New York: The Colonial Press, 1951), 1: 110, quoted in Davis, *History*, p. 362.

17. Celso Furtado has argued that the Haitian agrarian reform of 1807 had resulted in a higher standard of living for the Haitian peasantry than existed in the remainder of Latin America throughout the nineteenth century. See Vera Rubin and Richard P. Schaedel, eds., *The Haitian Potential: Research and Resources of Haiti* (New York: Teachers College Press, 1975), p. xiii.

18. Beaubrun Ardouin, *Etudes sur l'histoire d'Haiti*, 11 vols. (Paris: 1854, and Port-au-Prince: Imprimerie de l'Etat, 1958), 7: 9.

19. Walter Rodney, *How Europe Underdeveloped Africa* (Washington, D.C.: Howard University Press, 1974), p. 114.

BIBLIOGRAPHY

BOOKS BY DANTÈS BELLEGARDE

Bellegarde, Dantès; Ménos, Solon; Duval, Amilcar; and Sylvain, Georges. *Auteurs haitiens: Morceaux choisis; précédés de notices biographiques*, vol. 1: *Poésie*, vol. 2: *Prose*. Port-au-Prince: Imprimerie de Mme. F. Smith, 1904.

Bellegarde, Dantès, and Vincent, Sténio. *L'Ecolier haitien*. Namur, Belgique: A. D. Wesmel-Charlier, 1911.

———. *L'Année enfantine d'histoire et de géographie d'Haiti*. 1st ed. Bruxelles: Société Anonyme Belge d'Imprimerie, 1913. 3rd ed. rev. Bruxelles: Imprimerie Puvrez, 1939. 6th ed. rev. Port-au-Prince: Imprimerie de l'Etat, 1947.

———. *Haiti et les Etats-Unis devant la justice internationale*. With English translation by Charles M. Depuy. Paris: Librairie de Paris-Livres, 1924.

———. *Pages d'histoire*. Port-au-Prince: Imprimerie Chéraquit, 1925.

———. *Pour une Haiti heureuse*. Vol. 1 *Par l'education;* Vol. 2; *Par l'education et le travail*. Port-au-Prince: Chéraquit, Imprimeur-Editeur, 1927 and 1929.

———. *L'Occupation américaine d'Haiti: Ses conséquences morales et économiques*. Port-au-Prince: Chéraquit, Imprimeur-Editeur, 1929.

———. *Un haitien parle*. Port-au-Prince: Chéraquit, Imprimeur-Editeur, 1934.

———. "Haiti and Her Problems, Four Lectures." *The University of Puerto Rico Bulletin*, series 7, no. 1 (September 1936).

———. *La nation haitienne*. Paris: J. De Gigord, Editeur, 1938.

———. *La résistance haitienne: L'Occupation américaine d'Haiti*. Montréal: Editions Beauchemin, 1937.

———. *Haiti et ses problèmes*. Montréal: Editions Bernard Valiquette, 1941.

Bellegarde, Dantès, and Cook, Mercer, eds. *The Haitian-American Anthology: Haitian Readings from American Authors*. Port-au-Prince: Imprimerie de l'Etat, 1944.

———. *Ecrivains Haitiens: Notices biographiques et pages choisies*. Port-au-Prince: Société d'Editions et de Librairie, 1947.

———. *Dessalines a parlé*. Port-au-Prince: Société d'Editions et de Librairie, 1948.

———. *Lectures haitiennes*. Port-au-Prince: Editions Henri Deschamps, 1950.

———. "Haiti et son peuple." *Ensayos sobre la Historia del Nuevo Mundo*. Instituto Panamericano de Geografía e Historia, Comisión de Historia,

Estudios de Historia 4 publicación num. 118. Mexico, D.F.: Talleres de la Editorial Cultura, 1951, pp. 195–231.

———. *Haiti et son peuple.* Paris: Nouvelles Editions Latines, 1953.

———. *Histoire du peuple haitien (1492–1952).* Collection du Tricinquantenaire de L'Indépendance d'Haiti. Lausanne, Suisse: Imprimerie Held S.A., 1953.

———. *Au service d'Haiti: Appreciations sur un haitien et son oeuvre.* Port-au-Prince: Imprimerie Théodore, 1962.

———. *La nación haitiana.* Santo Domingo: Sociedad Dominicana de Bibliofilos, Inc., 1984.

SELECTED WORKS BY DANTÈS BELLEGARDE

L'Instruction publique en Haiti. Port-au-Prince: Imprimerie Nationale, 1908.

Conférence sur la situation agricole. Port-au-Prince: Imprimerie Nationale, 1917.

"France et Haiti." Speech given at the reception of the Comité Haitien de l'Alliance Française, 5 May, 1918. *Bulletin du Comité Haitien de l'Alliance Française* (Port-au-Prince): 21–41.

"Haiti under the Rule of the United States." Translated by Rayford W. Logan. *Opportunity* (December 1927): 22–25.

Préface *La Famille des Pitite-Caille,* by Justin Lhérisson. 2nd ed. Paris: Typographie Firmin-Didot et Cie. (1929): 5–10.

"An Inter-American Economic Policy." *The Annals of the American Academy of Political and Social Science* 150 (July 1930): 186–91.

"L'Amérique latine à la Société des Nations." *Revue de l'Amérique latine* (Paris) 20, No. 107 (November 1930): 414.

"La République d'Haiti et la Belgique." *Bulletin périodique,* no. 104 (February 1937): 73–78.

"The Haitian Nation." In *The Negro in the Americas,* edited by Charles H. Wesley. Washington, D.C.: The Graduate School for the Division of Social Sciences, 1940.

"The Organization of Inter-American Solidarity." Translated by Mercer Cook. *Phylon* l, no. 4 (1940): 327–35.

"Projet d'université haitienne." Paper presented to the Commission Haitienne de Coopération Intellectuelle, Port-au-Prince, 1940.

"Pétion et Bolivar." *Revue de la Société d'Histoire et de Géographie d'Haiti* 12, no. 43 (October 1941): 1–13.

"Haiti, centre de culture francaise en Amérique." Speech given at the American Conference of National Commissions of Intellectual Cooperation, Havana, 15 November, 1941. Port-au-Prince: Imprimerie La Phalange, 1942.

"President Alexandre Pétion." *Phylon* 2, no. 3 (1941): 205–13.

Speech. *Diario das Sessoes de Terceira Reuniao de Consulta dos Ministros das Relacoes Exteriores das Repúblicas Americanas.* Rio de Janeiro 1, no. 14 (30 January, 1942): 3–14.

"Genève et une Société des Nations américaines." Translated into Spanish by Jesus de Galindez. *Anales de la Universidad de Santo Domingo,* (March 1942): 110–24.

"The Epic of Haiti." *Tomorrow*, (March 1943): 11–14.

"Discours de Dantès Bellegarde." *Revista da Academia Brasileira de Letras*, 63 (January–June 1942): 44–67.

"What is the Color of Freedom." *The Pan American: Magazine of the Americas* (New York) 4, no. 1 (April 1943): 19–21.

"Alexandre Pétion, A Pioneer of Pan Americanism." Translated by Mrs. W. Geter Thomas. *Bulletin of the Pan American Union*, (May 1943): 245–52.

"Un haitien parle. . . de deux grands haitiens." *Cahiers d'Haiti* (August 1943): 7.

"Haiti's Voice at the Peace Table." *Opportunity*, no. 4 (1943): 154.

"Quatre grands panaméricains." *Cahiers d'Haiti* (February 1944): 22–28.

"Jose Martí et la race noire." *Cahiers d'Haiti* (June 1944): 10–13.

"Armand Thoby et l'Affaire Batsch." *Horizons; Revue politique, littéraire et scientifique* (Saint-Marc, Haiti), no. 33, 34, 35 (April, May, June 1944), pp. 731–738.

"Haiti et la Paix." *La république francaise* (New York), May 1945, pp. 16–18.

"Christian Haiti." *An Introduction to Haiti*, edited by Mercer Cook. Washington, D.C.: Office of Education, 1950.

"Pétion: Pioneer of Pan-Americanism." In An Introduction to Haiti, edited by Mercer Cook. Washington, D.C.: Office of Education, 1950.

"The Start of the Road." In An Introduction to Haiti, edited by Mercer Cook. Washington, D.C.: Office of Education, 1950.

"Whites in Black Haiti." In An Introduction to Haiti, edited by Mercer Cook. Washington, D.C.: Office of Education, 1950.

"France et Haiti." *Culture française*, no. 3 (July 1953): 14–22.

"A Haitian Speaks on Race Relations in South Africa." Speech given at Palais des Nations, Geneva, 3 October, 1953. *Journal of Human Relations* (Spring 1954): 23–31.

"Les grands hommes de la révolution haitienne." *Projection* (Port-au-Prince), Special Edition (July 1954): 5–17.

"Le créole haitien, patois français." *Panorama: Revue américaine de culture interaméricaine*, no. 11 (1954): 56–63.

"Mass Education in Latin America." Institute of International Education, *News Bulletin* 30, no. 7 (April 1955): 19.

"Education pour la paix et le bien-être social." *Journal of Inter-American Studies* 1, no. 1 (January 1959): 1–9.

"La quatrième réunion consultative des ministres des relations extérieures d'Amérique." *Journal of Inter-American Studies* 4, no. 1 (January 1962): 1–21.

SELECTED BIBLIOGRAPHY

André, Jacques. "Deux aspects du sous-developpement d'Haiti, commerce extérieur et réforme agraire." *Frères du Monde* (Bordeaux, France) Special Edition, "Haiti Enchainée," nos. 43–44 (1966): 10–24.

Anglade, Georges. *Atlas critique d'Haiti*. Montréal: ERCE & CRC, 1982.

———. *L'Espace haitien*. Montréal: Presses de l'Université du Québec, 1974.

Arciniegas, German. *Latin America: A Cultural History.* New York: Alfred A. Knopf, 1967.

Ardao, Arturo. "Assimilation and Transformation of Positivism in Latin America." *Journal of the History of Ideas*, 24 (1963): 515–22.

Ardouin, Beaubrun. *Etudes sur l'histoire d'Haiti.* 11 vols. Paris: Debrozy et E. Magdeleine, Librarie-Editeur, 1853–60.

Auguste, Jules; Denis, Clément; Bowler, Arthur; Dévot, Justin; and Janvier, Louis-Joseph. *Les détracteurs de la race noire et de la République d'Haiti.* Paris: C. Marpon et E. Flammarion, 1882.

Balch, Emily Green, ed. *Occupied Haiti.* New York: The Writer's Publishing Co., 1927.

Bastide, Roger. *Les Amériques noires: Les civilisations africaines dans le nouveau monde.* Paris: Payot, 1967.

Bastien, Rémy. "The Role of the Intellectual in Haitian Plural Society." In *Social and Cultural Pluralism in the Caribbean.* New York: Research Institute for the Study of Man, 1959.

Bastien, Rémy, and Courlander, Harold. *Religion and Politics in Haiti.* Washington, D.C.: Institute for Cross-Cultural Research, 1966.

Beer, George Louis. *African Questions at the Paris Peace Conference.* New York: Macmillan Co., 1923.

Bellegarde-Smith, Patrick. "Class Struggle in Contemporary Haitian Politics: An Interpretative Study of the Campaign of 1957." *Journal of Caribbean Studies* 2 (1981): 109–27.

———. "Haitian Social Thought in the Nineteenth Century: Class Formation and Westernization." *Caribbean Studies* 20 (1980): 5–33.

———. "Race, Class, Ideology: Haitian Ideologies for Underdevelopment, 1806–1934." *AIMS, Occasional Papers* 32 (1982).

Betts, Raymond F. *Assimilation and Association in French Colonial Theory, 1890–1914.* New York: Columbia University Press, 1961.

Blanchet, Jules. *Peint par lui-même, ou la résistance de M. Dantès Bellegarde.* Port-au-Prince: V. Valcin, Imprimeur, 1937.

Blanchet, Paul. "Sur la tombe de Dantès Bellegarde." *Le Nouvelliste*, 17 June, 1966.

Blassingame, John W. "The Press and American Intervention in Haiti and the Dominican Republic, 1904–1920." *Caribbean Studies* 9 (1969): 27–43.

Bonhomme, Colbert. *Révolution et contre-révolution en Haiti de 1946 à 1957.* Port-au-Prince: Imprimerie de l'Etat, 1957.

Bourguignon, Erika. "Haiti et l'ambivalence socialisée: Une reconsidération." *Journal de la Société des Américanistes* 58 (1971): 173–205.

Brading, D. A. "Creole Nationalism and Mexican Liberalism." *Journal of Inter-American Studies and World Affairs* 15, no. 2 (May 1973): 139–90.

Breem, Camille. "La société haitienne: Amalgame incohérent ou société structurée?" *Frères du Monde* (Bordeaux, France) special edition, "Haiti Enchainée," nos. 43–44 (1966): 25–38.

Brown, Jonathan. *The History and Present Condition of St. Domingo.* 2 vols. Philadelphia: William Marshall & Co., 1837.

Brutus, Edner. *Instruction publique en Haiti, 1492–1945.* Port-au-Prince: Imprimerie de l'Etat, 1948.

Buell, Raymond Leslie. *The American Occupation of Haiti.* New York: Foreign Policy Association, 1929.

Cabon, Adolphe. *Notes sur l'histoire religieuse d'Haiti de la révolution au concordat, 1789–1860.* Paris: Imprimerie des Orphelins-Apprentis, 1933.

Carr, William G. *Only by Understanding.* Headline series, no. 52. New York: Foreign Policy Association, 1945.

Carter, George E. "Traditional African Social Thought." In *Pan-Africanism Reconsidered*, edited by American Society of African Culture. Berkeley and Los Angeles: University of California Press, 1962.

Castor, Suzy. *La ocupación norteamericana de Haití y sus consecuencias, 1915–34.* Mexico: Ediciones siglo veintiuno, 1971.

Catalogne, Gérard de. *Haiti à l'heure du tiers-monde.* Port-au-Prince: Editions du Nouveau Monde, 1964.

———. *Notre révolution.* 3 vols. Montréal: Editions Bernard Valiquette, 1941–44.

Célestin, Clément. *Compilations pour l'histoire.* 4 vols. Port-au-Prince: Imprimerie Théodore, 1958–60.

Césaire, Aimé. *Discours sur le colonialisme.* Paris: Présence Africaine, 1955.

———. *Toussaint Louverture: La révolution francaise et le problème colonial.* Paris: Présence Africaine, 1962.

Chatelain, Joseph. *La Banque Nationale,* son histoire, *ses problèmes.* Port-au-Prince: Imprimerie Held, Switzerland, 1954.

Chomsky, Noam, and Herman, Edward. *The Washington Connection and Third World Fascism.* Boston: South End Press, 1979.

Cleven, N. Andrew N. "The First Panama Mission and the Congress of the United States." *Journal of Negro History* 13, no. 3 (July 1928): 225–54.

Collins, Irene. *Liberalism in Nineteenth Century Europe.* London: The Historical Association, no. 34, 1957.

Cook, Mercer. "Dantès Bellegarde." *Phylon* 1, no. 2 (1940): 125–35.

———. "The Writings of Dantès Bellegarde." *Books Abroad*, University of Oklahoma, 25, no. 3 (1949): 292–94.

Cooper, Daniel B. "The Withdrawal of the United States from Haiti, 1928–1934." *Journal of Inter-American Affairs* 5 (1963): 83–101.

Cordova-Bello, Eleazar. *La independencia de Haití y su influencia en Hispanoamerica.* Caracas, 1967.

Costa, Joao Cruz. *A History of Ideas in Brazil: The Development of Philosophy in Brazil and the Evolution of National History.* Translated by Suzette Macedo. Berkeley and Los Angeles: University of California Press, 1964.

Crahan, Margaret E., and Knight, Franklin W., eds. *Africa and the Caribbean: The Legacies of a Link.* Baltimore: John Hopkins University Press, 1979.

Crawford, William Rex. *A Century of Latin American Thought.* Cambridge: Harvard University Press, 1944.

———. "The Concept of Freedom in Latin America." In *Freedom and Reform in Latin America,* edited by Frederick B. Pike. Notre Dame: Notre Dame University Press, 1959.

Cruse, Harold. *The Crisis of the Negro Intellectual: From its Origins to the Present.* New York: William Morrow & Co., 1967.

Cueva, Mario de la; Leon-Portilla, Miguel; O'Gorman, Edmundo; Gallagos, Rocafull, José M.; Moreno, Rafael; Villoro, Luis; Zea, Leopoldo; and Salmeron, Fernando. *Major Trends in Mexican Philosophy.* Translated by A. Robert Caponigri. Notre Dame: University of Notre Dame Press, 1966.

Curtin, Philip D. ed. *Africa and the West: Intellectual Responses to European Culture.* Madison: University of Wisconsin Press, 1972.

———. *Two Jamaicas: The Role of Ideas in a Tropical Colony, 1830–1865.* New York: Atheneum, 1975.

Damas, Léon-Gontran. "Price-Mars: The Father of Haitianism." In *Négritude: Essays and Studies,* edited by Albert H. Berrian and Richard A. Long. Hampton, VA: Hampton Institute Press, 1967.

Danache, Berthoumieux. *Le Président Dartiguenave et les américains.* Port-au-Prince: Imprimerie de l'Etat, 1950.

Dash, J. Michael. *Literature and Ideology in Haiti, 1915–1961.* Totowa, NJ: Barnes & Noble, 1981.

Davis, Harold E. "The History of Ideas in Latin America." *Latin American Research Review* 3, no. 4 (1968): 23–44.

———. *Latin American Thought: A Historical Introduction.* Baton Rouge: Louisiana State University Press, 1972.

———. "Sources and Characteristics of Latin American Thought." *Topic: A Journal of the Liberal Arts,* no. 20, "Themes in Latin American Culture" (Fall 1970): 12–20.

———. "Trends in Social Thought in Twentieth Century Latin America." *Journal of Inter-American Studies* 1, no. 1 (January 1959): 57–71.

Davis, H. P. *Black Democracy: The Story of Haiti.* Rev. ed. New York: Biblo & Tannen, 1936.

Debien, Gabriel. *Esprit colon et esprit d'autonomie à Saint-Domingue au XVIIIe siècle.* 2nd ed. Paris: Larose, 1954.

Decraene, Philippe. *Le panafricanisme.* Paris: Presses Universitaires de France, 1970.

Delorme, Demesvar. *Les théoriciens au pouvoir.* Paris: H. Plon, 1870.

———. *Réflexions diverses sur Haiti.* Paris: E. Dentu, 1873.

Depestre, René. *Bonjour et adieu à la négritude.* Paris: Editions Robert Laffront, 1980.

———. "Jean Price-Mars et le mythe de l'orphée noir ou les aventures de la négritude." *L'Homme et la société* (Paris), nos. 7–8 (January-March 1968): 171–81.

Despradel, Lil. "Les etapes de l'antihaitianisme en République Dominicaine: Le rôle des historiens." Université de Bruxelles, *Revue de l'Institut de Sociologie*, no. 1 (1973): 135–60.

Dévot, Justin. "Considérations sur l'état mental de la société haitienne: L'organisation des forces intellectuelles." *Revue occidentale* 26, no. 6 (1902): 305–40.

———. *Cours élémentaire d'instruction civique et d'éducation patriotique*. Paris: F. Pichon, 1894.

———. *La nationalité et son influence quant à la jouissance et à l'exercise des droits*. Paris: F. Pichon, 1893.

———. *La prévision scientifique*. Paris: V. Giard et E. Brière, 1904.

Dorsainvil, J. C., et les Frères de l'Instruction Chrétienne. *Manuel d'histoire d'Haiti*. Port-au-Prince: Les Frères de l'Instruction Chrétienne, 1949.

Doubout, Jean-Jacques. "Problèmes d'une période de transition de Saint-Domingue à Haiti, 1793–1806." *La pensée* (France), no. 174 (March-April 1974): 67–80.

Dozer, Donald M. *Latin America: An Interpretative History*. New York: McGraw-Hill, 1962.

Droz, Jacques. *Histoire des doctrines politiques en France*. Paris: Presses Universitaires de France, 1966.

Duvalier, François. *Mémoires d'un leader du tiers-monde*. Paris: Librarie Hachette, 1969.

Fanon, Frantz. *Peau noire, masques blancs*. Paris: Editions de Seuil, 1952.

———. *Les damnés de la terre*. Paris: Francois Maspero, Editeur, 1961.

Fauset, Jessie. "Impressions of the Second Pan-African Congress." *Crisis* 23, no. 1 (November 1921).

Fernandes, Florestan. *The Negro in Brazilian Society*. New York: Atheneum, 1971.

Féquière, Fleury. *L'education haitienne*. Port-au-Prince: Imprimerie L'Abeille, 1906.

Firmin, Anténor. *De l'égalité des races humaines: Anthropologie positive*. Paris: Cotillon, 1885.

———. *Lettres de Saint-Thomas: Études sociologiques, historiques et littéraires*. Paris: V. Giard et E. Brière, 1910.

———. *M. Roosevelt, Président des Etats-Unis et la République d'Haiti*. Paris: F. Pichón et Durand Auzias, 1905.

Fleischmann, Ulrich, *Idéyoloji ak réyalité nan literati ayisyèn*. Geneva: Koleksion, 1981.

Fontaine, William T. "Philosophical Aspects of Contemporary African Social Thought." In *Pan-Africanism Reconsidered*, edited by the American Society of African Culture. Berkeley and Los Angeles: University of California Press, 1962.

Fordham, Monroe. "Nineteenth Century Black Thought in the United States: Some Influences of the Santo Domingo Revolution." *Journal of Black Studies* 6 (1975): 115–26.

Fowler, Carolyn. *A Knot in the Thread: The Life and Work of Jacques Roumain.* Washington, D.C.: Howard University Press, 1980.

Fox, Annette Baker. "Small State Diplomacy." In *Diplomacy in a Changing World,* edited by Stephen Kertesz and M. A. Fitzsimons. Notre Dame: University of Notre Dame Press, 1959.

Francisque, Edouard. *Perspectives du développement économique en Haiti.* Port-au-Prince: Imprimerie Deschamps, 1968.

Franklin, John Hope. *From Slavery to Freedom: A History of Negro Americans.* 3rd ed. New York: Alfred A. Knopf, 1967.

Gallagher, Idella J. *Morality in Evolution: The Moral Philosophy of Henri Bergson.* The Hague: Martinus Nijhoff, 1970.

Gaos, José. "Significación filosófica del pensamiento hispanoamericano." *Cuadernos americanos* (Mexico) 2 (1943): 63–86.

Gardiner, Robert K. A. "Race and Color in International Relations." *Daedalus* (Spring 1967): 296–311.

Garrity, Monique P. "The Assembly Industries in Haiti: Causes and Effects." *Journal of Caribbean Studies* 2 (1981): 25–37.

Genovese, Eugene D. *The World the Slaveholders Made: Two Essays in Interpretation.* New York: Random House, Vintage Books, 1969.

Gossett, Thomas F. *Race: The History of an Idea in America.* New York: Schocken Books, 1963.

Gouldner, Alvin W. *The Coming Crisis of Western Sociology.* New York: Equinox Books, 1970.

Gouraige, Ghislain. *La diaspora d'Haiti et l'Afrique.* Ottawa: Editions Naaman, 1974.

———. *Histoire de la littérature haitienne, de l'independence à nos jours.* Port-au-Prince: Imprimerie Theodore, 1960.

Graña, Cesar. *Bohemian versus Bourgeois.* New York: Basic Books, 1964.

———. *Cultural Nationalism: The Idea of Historical Destiny in Spanish America.* Berkeley: Latin American Monograph Series, reprint no. 172, Center for Latin American Studies, Institute of International Studies, University of California Press, n.d.

Griggs, Earl, and Prator, Clifford, eds. *Henry Christophe and Thomas Clarkson: A Correspondence.* New York: Greenwood Press, 1968.

Gunder Frank, Andre. *Lumpenbourgeoisie, Lumpendevelopment: Dependence, Class and Politics in Latin America.* New York: Monthly Review Press, 1972.

Guy, Alain. "Le bergonisme en Amérique Latine." *Caravelle,* University of Toulouse (1963): 121–39.

Hale, Charles A. *Mexican Liberalism in the Age of Mora, 1821–1853.* New Haven: Yale University Press, 1968.

Haller, John S., Jr. *Outcasts from Evolution: Scientific Attitudes of Racial Inferiority, 1859–1900.* Chicago: University of Illinois Press, 1971.

Hanna, Thomas, ed. *The Bergsonian Heritage.* New York: Columbia University Press, 1962.

Heinl, Robert D., and Heinl, Nancy. *Written in Blood: The Story of the Haitian People, 1492–1971.* Boston: Houghton Mifflin, 1978.

Henriquez Ureña, Pedro. *A Concise History of Latin American Culture.* Translated with supplementary chapter by Gilbert Chase. New York: Praeger, 1966.

Herskovits, Melville J. *Life in a Haitian Valley.* New York: Anchor Books, 1971 [1937].

Himelhock, Myra. "Frederick Douglass and Haiti' Mole St. Nicolas." *Journal of Negro History* 41, no. 3 (July 1971): 161–80.

Hoetink, H. *The Two Variants in Caribbean Race Relations: A Contribution to the Sociology of Segmented Societies.* Translated by Eva M. Hooykaas. London: Oxford University Press, 1962.

Hofstadter, Richard. *Social Darwinism in American Thought.* New York: G. Braziller, 1959.

Honorât, Jean-Jacques. *Enquête sur le développement.* Port-au-Prince: Imprimerie Centrale, 1974.

———. *Le manifeste du dernier monde.* Port-au-Prince: Imprimerie Deschamps, 1980. Hurbon, Laennee. *Culture et dictature en Haiti: L'imaginaire sous contrôle.* Paris: L'Harmattan, 1979.

———. *Dieu dans le Vaudou haitien.* Paris: Payet, 1972.

Ince, Basil A., ed. *Contemporary International Relations of the Caribbean.* St. Augustine: University of the West Indies, 1979.

Inman, Samuel Guy. *Through Santo Domingo and Haiti: A Cruise with the Marines.* New York: Committee on Cooperation in Latin America, 1919.

Isaacs, Harold R. "Pan-Africanism as 'Romantic Racism'." In *W. E. B. Du Bois: A Profile,* edited by Rayford W. Logan. New York: Hill & Wang, 1971.

James, C. L. R. *The Black Jacobins: Toussaint L'Ouverture and the San Domingo Revolution.* New York: Random House, Vintage Books, 1963.

Janvier, Louis-Joseph. *Les constitutions d'Haiti, 1801–1885.* Paris: C. Marpon et E. Flammarion, 1886.

———. *L'égalité des races.* Paris: G. Rougier et Cie., 1884.

———. *La République d'Haiti et ses visiteurs 1840–1882.* Paris: Marpon et Flammarion, Librarie-Editeur, 1883.

Jones, Edward A. "Phylon Profile XX: Dantès Bellegarde, Miracle of Haiti." *Phylon* 11, No. 1 (1950): 16–22.

Jordan, Winthrop D. *White over Black: American Attitudes toward the Negro, 1550–1812.* Chapel Hill: University of North Carolina Press, 1968.

Jorrín, Miguel and Martz, John D. *Latin American Political Thought and Ideology.* Chapel Hill: University of North Carolina Press, 1970.

July, Robert. *The Origins of Modern African Thought: Its Development in West Africa during the Nineteenth and Twentieth Centuries.* New York: Frederick Praeger, 1967.

Labelle, Micheline. *Idéologie de couleur et classes sociales en Haiti.* Montréal: Presses Universitaires de Montréal, 1978.

Lacerte, Robert K. "Xenophobia and Economic Decline: The Haitian Case, 1820–1843." *Americas* (1981): 500–515.

Lacombe, Robert. *Histoire monétaire de Saint-Domingue et de la République d'Haiti jusguén 1874.* Paris: Larose, 1958.

Lafrance, Guy. La *Philosophie sociale de Bergson; sources et interprétation.* Ottawa: Editions de l'Université d'Ottawa, 1974.

Laleau, Léon. "Dantès Bellegarde, une célébrité, amie de la pénombre." *Conjonction* (Port-au-Prince), no. 118 (July 1972), pp. 88–94.

Laski, Harold J. *The Rise of Liberalism: The Philosophy of a Business Civilization.* New York: Harper & Brothers Publishers, 1936.

————. *The State in Theory and Practice.* New York: Viking Press, 1970.

Laurent, Gérard M. *Contribution à l'histoire de Saint-Domingue.* Port-au-Prince: Imprimerie La Phalange, 1971.

Lefebvre, Georges. *The Coming of the French Revolution.* Princeton: Princeton University Press, 1947.

Lefebvre, Georges; Guyot, Raymond; and Sagnac, Philippe. *La révolution Francaise.* Paris: Presses Universitaires de France, 1952.

Lemoine, Maurice. *Sucre Amer, esclaves d'aujourd'hui dans les Caraibes.* Paris: Nouvelle Société des Editions Encre, 1981.

Lespinasse, Beauvais. *Histoire des affranchis de Saint-Domingue.* Paris: Kugelmann, 1882.

Lespinasse, Pierre-Eugène, de. *Gens d'autrefois, vieux souvenirs.* Vol. 1. Paris: Editions de la Revue Mondiale, 1926.

Le Vine, Victor T. "The Trauma of Independence in French-Speaking Africa." *Journal of Developing Areas* 2 (January 1968): 211–24.

Lewis, Gordon K. *Main Currents in Caribbean Thought: The Historical Evolution of Caribbean Society in its Ideological Aspects, 1492–1900.* Baltimore: Johns Hopkins University Press, 1983.

Lewis, Vaughan, ed. *Size, Self-Determination and International Relations: The Caribbean.* Mona: Institute of Social and Economic Research, 1976.

Leyburn, James G. *The Haitian People.* New Haven: Yale University Press, 1966.

Lhérisson, Camille. *De la responsabilité des élites dans la société moderne.* Port-au-Prince: Imprimerie de l'Etat, 1947.

Logan, Rayford W. *The Diplomatie Relations of the United States with Haiti, 1776–1891.* Chapel Hill: University of North Carolina Press, 1941.

————. "Education in Haiti." *Journal of Negro History,* (October 1930): 401–60.

————. "The Historical Aspects of Pan-Africanism, 1900–1945." In *Pan-Africanism Reconsidered,* edited by American Society of African Culture. Berkeley and Los Angeles: University of California Press, 1962.

————. "The Operation of the Mandate System in Africa." *Journal of Negro History* 13 (1928): 423–77.

Lowenthal, David. "Race and Color in the West Indies." *Daedalus,* (Spring 1967): 580–626.

Lubin, Maurice A. "Les premiers rapports de la nation haitienne avec l'étranger." *Journal of Inter-American Studies* 10, no. 2 (April 1968).

———. "Ou en sommes-nous avec l'élite intellectuelle d'Haiti?" *Journal of Inter-American Studies* 3, no. 1 (January 1961): 121–31.

Luc, Jean. "Connaissance sensible et connaissance rationnelle dans les luttes politiques haitiennes." *Nouvelle Optique* 1, no. 2 (May 1971): 7–34.

———. *Structure économiques et lutte nationale populaire en Haiti.* Montréal: Nouvelle Optique, 1976.

Lundhal, Mats. "A Note on Haitian Migration to Cuba, 1890–1934." *Cuban Studies* 12 (1982): 22–36.

Macaulcy, Zachary. *Haiti ou renseignements authentiques sur l'abolition de l'esclavage et ses résultats à Saint-Domingue et à la Guadeloupe avec des détails sur l'état actuel d'Haiti et des noirs émancipés qui forment population.* Paris: Chez L. Hachette, 1835.

MacCorkle, William A. *The Monroe Doctrine in Its Relation to the Republic of Haiti.* New York: Neale Publishing Co., 1915.

MacKenzie, Charles. *Notes on Haiti, Made During a Residence in That Republic.* 2 vols. London: Henry Colburn and Richard Bentley, 1830.

MacLeod, Murdo J. "The Haitian Novel of Social Protest." *Journal of Inter-American Studies* 4, no. 2 (April 1962): 207–21.

Madiou, Thomas. *Histoire d'Haiti.* 4 vols. Port-au-Prince: Imprimerie J. Courtois, 1847–48, and Imprimerie J. Verrollot, 1904.

Magloire, Auguste. *l'erreur révolutionnaire et notre état social.* Port-au-Prince: Imprimerie Le Matin, 1909.

Malval, Marc E. *La politique financière de la République d'Haiti depuis 1910.* Paris: Baron, 1932.

Manigat, Charles; Moise, Claude; and Ollivier, Emile. *Haiti: Quel développement?* Montréal: Collectif Paroles, 1975.

Manigat, Leslie F. *L'Amérique latine au XXe siècle, 1889–1929.* Paris: Editions Richelieu, 1973.

———. *Haiti of the Sixties, Object of International Concern.* Washington, D.C.: The Washington Center of Foreign Policy Research, 1964.

———. *La politique agraire du gouvernement d'Alexandre Pétion, 1807–1818.* Port-au-Prince: Imprimerie La Phalange, 1962.

———. "La substitution de la prépondérance américaine à la pré pondérance francaise en Haiti au debut du XXème siècle." *Revue d'histoire moderne et contemporaine* 14 (1967): 321–55.

Mannoni, O. *Psychologie de la colonisation.* Paris: Editions du Seuil, 1950.

Marcelin, Frédéric. *Choses haitiennes: Politiques et littérature.* Paris: Imprimerie Kugelmann, 1896.

———. *Ducas-Hippolyte: Son époque, ses oeuvres.* LeHavre: Imprimerie A. Lemale aine, 1878.

———. *Une evolution nécessaire.* Paris: P. Taillefer, 1898.

————. *Propos d'un haitien.* Paris: Imprimerie Kugelmann, 1915.

Markovitz, Irving Leonard. *Leopold Sédar Senghor and the Politics of Négritude.* New York: Atheneum, 1975.

Marshall, Dawn I. *The Haitian Problem: Illegal Migration to the Bahamas.* Mona: Institute of Social and Economic Research, 1979.

Martz, John D. "Characteristics of Latin American Political Thought." *Journal of Inter-American Studies* 8, no. 1 (January 1966): 54–74.

Mathon, Alix. "Effeuillement de pages inédites: Quand Dantès Bellegarde parle." *Le nouvelliste,* 8 August, 1973, p. 1.

Mazrui, Ali A. "From Social Darwinism to Current Theories of Modernization." *World Politics* 21, no. 1 (October 1968): 69–83.

Meier, August. *Negro Thought in America, 1880–1915.* Ann Arbor: University of Michigan Press, 1963.

Memmi, Albert. *Portrait due colonisé précédé du portrait du colonisateur.* Paris: Editions Buchet/Chastel, Correa, 1957.

Menos, Solon. *l'affaire Luders.* 2nd ed. Port-au-Prince: Imprimerie J. Verrolot, 1898.

Métraux, Alfred. *Voodoo in Haiti.* New York: Schocken Books, 1959.

Millet, Kethly. *Les paysans haitiens et l'occupation américaine, 1915–1930.* Montréal: Collectif Paroles, 1978.

Millspaugh, Arthur C. *Haiti under American Control, 1915–1930.* Boston: World Peace Foundation, 1931.

Mintz, Sidney W. *Caribbean Transformations.* Baltimore: Johns Hopkins University Press, 1983.

Montague, Ludwell Lee. *Haiti and the United States, 1714–1938.* Durham: Duke University Press, 1940.

Mosca, Gactano. *The Ruling Class.* Edited by Arthur Livingston. New York: McGraw-Hill, 1939.

Nemours, Alfred. *Histoire militaire de la guerre d'independence de Saint-Domingue,* vol. 1. Paris: Berger-Levrault, Editeurs, 1925.

————. *Sur le choix d'une discipline, l'anglo-saxonne ou la francaise.* Cap Haitien: Imprimerie La Conscience, 1909.

————. *Toussaint Louverture fonde à Saint-Domingue la liberté et l'égalité.* Port-au-Prince: Imprimerie du College Vertieres, 1945.

Nicholls, David. *From Dessalines to Duvalier: Race, Colour and National Independence in Haiti.* Cambridge: Cambridge University Press, 1979.

————. "A Work of Combat: Mulatto Historians and the Haitian Past, 1847–1867." *Journal of Inter-American Studies and World Affairs* 16, no. 1 (February 1975): 15–38.

Nicolas, Hogar. *L'occupation américaine d'Haiti: La revanche de l'histoire.* Madrid: Industrias Gráficas España, 1956.

Nisbet, Robert A. *Social Change and History: Aspects of the Western Theory of Development.* London: Oxford University Press, 1969.

Padmore, George. *Pan-Africanism or Communism?* Anchor Books. New York: Doubleday & Co., Inc., 1971.

Bibliography 257

Pan American Union and the Research Institute for the Study of Man. *Plantation Systems of the New World*; Papers and Discussion Summaries of the Seminar Held in San Juan, Puerto Rico. Social Science Monographs 7. Washington, D.C.: Pan American Union, 1959.

Pascal-Trouíllot, Ertha. *Statut juridique de l'haitienne dans la législation sociale.* Port-au-Prince: Imprimerie des Antilles, 1973.

Pfeifer, Edward J. "The Genesis of Neo-Lamarckism." *Isis* 56 (1965): 156–67.

Pierre-Charles, Gérard. *L'économie haitienne et sa voie de développement.* Paris: Editions G.-P. Maisonneuve & Larose, 1967.

Pompilus, Pradel, and the Frères de l'Instruction Chrétienne. *Manuel illustré d'histoire de la littérature haitienne.* Port-au-Prince: Imprimerie Henri Deschamps, 1961.

Pressoir, Catts. *Le protestantisme haitien.* 2 vols. Port-au-Prince: Imprimerie de la Société Biblique, 1945–46.

Price, Hannibal. *De la réhabilitation de la race noire par la République d'Haiti.* Port-au-Prince: Verrolot, 1900.

Price, Richard, ed. *Maroon Societies: Rebel Slave Communities in the Americas.* Baltimore: Johns Hopkins University Press, 1979.

———. *First Time: The Historical Vision of an Afro-American People.* Baltimore: Johns Hopkins University Press, 1983.

Price-Mars, Jean. *Ainsi parla l'oncle: Essais d'ethographie.* Paris: Imprimerie de Compiegne, 1928.

———. *Une étape de l'évolution haitienne.* Port-au-Prince: Imprimerie La Presse, 1929.

———. *Formation ethnique, folklore et culture du peuple haitien.* Port-au-Prince: Imprimerie V. Valcin, 1939.

———. "La position d'Haiti et de la culture francaise en Amérique." *Journal of Inter-American Studies* 8, no. 1 (January 1966): 44–53.

———. *La République d'Haiti et la République Dominicaine: Les aspects divers d'un problème d'histoire, de géographie et d'ethnologie.* 2 vols. Lausanne: Imprimerie Held, 1953.

———. *La vocation de l'élite.* Port-au-Prince: Imprimerie Edmond Chenet, 1919.

Renaud, Raymond. *Le régime foncier en Haiti.* Paris: Levilón et Cie., 1934.

Ribeiro, Darcy. *The Americas and Civilization.* Translated by Linton Lomas Barrett and Marie McDavid Barrett. New York: E. P. Dutton and Co., 1971.

Rossello, Pedro. *Les précurseurs du Bureau International d'Education.* Genève: Bureau International d'Education, 1943.

Rotberg, Robert I. *Haiti: The Politics of Squalor.* Boston: Houghton Mifflin Company, 1971.

Rubin, Vera, and Schaedel, Richard P., eds. *The Haitian Potential: Research and Resources of Haiti.* New York: Teachers College Press, 1975.

Rudwick, Elliot M. *W. E. B. Du Bois: Propagandist of the Negro Protest.* New York: Atheneum, 1969.

Sagax, Pierre. "Une géohistoire à problèmes." *Frères du monde* (Bordeaux, France), Special Edition, "Haiti enchaînée," no. 43–44 (1966), pp. 40–56.

Saint-Méry, Moreau de. *Description topographique, physique, civile, politique et historique de la partie francaise de l'île de Saint-Domingue.* 2nd ed., vol. I. Paris: Edité par L. Guerin et Cie., 1875.

Salazar Bondy, Augusto. *Sentido y problema del pensamiento filosofico hispano-americano.* Occasional publications no. 16. Lawrence: University of Kansas Press, 1969.

Scharfstein, Ben-Ami. *Roots of Bergson's Philosophy.* New York: Columbia University Press, 1943.

Schmidt, Hans. *The United States Occupation of Haiti, 1915–1934.* New Brunswick: Rutgers University Press, 1971.

Schoelcher, Victor. *Colonies étrangères et Haiti: Résultats de l'émancipation anglaise.* Vol. I. Paris: Pagnerre, Editeur, 1843.

Secrétaire d'Etat des Relations Extérieures. *La République d'Haiti dans la politique interaméricaine.* New York: Fisher Press, 1939.

Singer, Marshall R. *Weak States in a World of Powers: The Dynamics of International Relationships.* New York: The Free Press, 1972.

Skidmore, Thomas E. *Black into White: Race and Nationality in Brazilian Thought.* New York: Oxford University Press, 1974.

Société Haitienne d'Etudes Scientifiques. *Travaux du Congrès International de Philosophie consacré aux problèmes de la connaissance.* Port-au-Prince: Imprimerie de l'Etat, 1946.

Spitzer, Leo. *The Creoles of Sierra Leone: Responses to Colonialism, 1870–1945.* Madison: University of Wisconsin Press, 1974.

Stocking, George W., Jr. "Lamarckism in American Social Science, 1890–1915." *Journal of the History of Ideas* 23 (1962): 239–56.

Stremlau, John J., ed. *The Foreign Policy Priorities of Third World States.* Boulder, Colo.: Westview Press, 1982.

Sylvain, Georges. *Dix années de luttes pour la liberté, 1915–1925.* 2 vols. Port-au-Prince: Editions Henri Deschamps, 1925, 1959.

Thomas, David Y. *One Hundred Years of the Monroe Doctrine, 1823–1923.* New York: Macmillan Co., 1923.

Tocqueville, Alexis de. *l'ancien régime et la révolution.* Edited by J. P. Mayer. Paris: Gallimard, 1952.

Touchard, Jean. *Histoire des idées politiques.* 2 vols. Paris: Presses Universitaires de France, 1959.

Trouillot, Ernst. *Demesvar Delorme, le journaliste, le diplomate.* Port-au-Prince: Imprimerie Théodore, 1958.

Trouillot, Hénock. *M. Dantès Bellegarde, un écrivain d'autrefois.* Port-au-Prince: Imprimerie Théodore, 1957.

Turnier, Alain. *Les Etats-Unis et le marché haitien.* Washington, D.C., 1955.

Tyson, George F., Jr., ed. *Toussaint Louverture.* Englewood Cliffs, N.J.: Prentice-Hall, 1973.

Union Patriotique d'Haiti. "Memoir." *The Nation* (New York) 25 May, 1921.

United Nations, Educational, Scientific, and Cultural Organization. *Race and Science.* New York: Columbia University Press, 1961.

U.S. Congress. Senate. Inquiry into Occupation and Administration of Haiti and the Dominican Republic. S. Rep. 794, 67th Cong., 2nd sess., 1922.

Valdman, Albert. "Créole et français en Haiti." *French Review* 49, no. 2 (December 1975): 174–85.

Vanderbosch, Amry. "The Small States in International Politics and Organization." *Journal of Politics* 26, no. 2 (May 1964).

Vastey, Pompée Valentin, Baron de. *An Essay on the Causes of the Revolution and Civil Wars of Hayti.* Translated by W. H. M. B. in 1823. New York: Negro University Press, div. of Greenwood Press, 1969.

Verna, Paul. *Pétion y Bolivar: Cuarenta años 1790–1830 de relaciones haitiano-venezolanas y su aporte a la emancipación de hispanoamerica.* Caracas: Imprenta nacional, 1969.

Viatte, Auguste. *Histoire littéraire de l'Amérique française*, Paris: Presses Universitaires de France, 1954.

———. "Le Livre d'Or de la culture francaise à son excellence M. Dantès Bellegarde." *Culture française,* no. 4 (October 1954), pp. 3–5.

Vincent, Sténio. *En posant les jalons.* 5 vols. Port-au-Prince: Imprimerie de l'Etat, 1939–45.

Wallerstein, Immanuel. "Elites in French-Speaking West Africa." *Journal of Modem African Studies* 3, no. 1 (1965): 1–33.

Walters, Francis P. *History of the League of Nations.* 2 vols. London: Oxford University Press, 1952.

Whitaker, Arthur P., ed. *Latin America and the Enlightenment.* New York: Appleton-Century Co., 1942.

Williams, Edward J. "Secularization, Integration and Rationalization: Some Perspectives from Latin American Thought." *Journal of Latin American Studies* 5, part 2 (November 1973): 199–216.

Williams, Eric. *Capitalism and Slavery.* New York: Capricorn Books, 1944.

Wilson, Edmund. *Red, Black, Blond and Olive, Studies in Four Civilizations: Zuñi, Haiti, Soviet Russia, Israel.* New York: Oxford University Press, 1956.

Wolff, Robert Paul. *The Poverty of Liberalism.* Boston: Beacon Press, 1968.

Woodward, Ralph Lee, ed. *Positivism in Latin America, 1850–1900: Are Order and Progress Reconcilable?* Lexington, Mass.: D.C. Health & Co., 1971.

Yacono, Xavier. *Les étapes de la décolonisation française.* Paris: Presses Universitaires de France, 1971.

Yepes, Juan del Pozo. "La guerra de independencia desde el punto de vista socio-logico." *Journal of Inter-American Studies* 4, no. 2 (April 1962): 273–91.

Zea, Leopoldo. *The Latin American Mind.* Norman: University of Oklahoma Press, 1963.

Zoll, Donald Atwell. *Twentieth Century Political Philosophy.* Englewood Cliffs, N.J.: Prentice-Hall, 1974.

REFERENCES TO DANTÈS BELLEGARDE IN NEWSPAPERS AND PUBLICATIONS

COMPILED FROM THE D. BELLEGARDE MANUSCRIPT COLLECTION, PORT-AU-PRINCE, HAITI

L'Action Catholique, Quebec
Aesculape, Paris
The Afro-American
Ahora, Caracas
The Annals of the American Academy of Political & Social Science
Les Amitiés Catholiques Francaises, Paris
Amsterdam News, New York
Anales de la Universidad de Santo Domingo
Les Annales de Médecine Haitienne, Port-au-Prince
Aux Ecoutes, Paris
Bulletin de l'Assemblée des Nations Unis
Bulletin de la Chambre de Commerce d'Haiti, Port-au-Prince
Bulletin Religieux de Haiti, Port-au-Prince
Bulletin de la Société Historique Franco-Américaine, Boston
Les Cahiers d'Haiti, Port-au-Prince
Comoedia, Paris

Conjonction, Port-au-Prince
Correspondance Universelle, Paris
Le Courrier de la Plata, Buenos Aires
The Crisis, New York
Culture Française, Paris
La Démocratie Sociale, Guadeloupe
Le Devoir, Montreal
Le Droit, Ottawa
El Universal, Caracas
The Evening Star, Washington, D.C.
Le Figaro, Paris
France-Amérique Magazine, Paris
Le Gaulois, Paris
La Gazette de Lausanne
The Geographical Review, New York
Haiti Journal, Port-au-Prince
Haiti-Sun, Port-au-Prince
Headway, London
The Hispanic American Historical Review
L'Homme Libre, Paris
Imperium, Paris
L'Information, Paris
L'Intransigeant, Paris

Le Leune République, Paris
Le Journal des Débats, Paris
Le Journal de Genève, Geneva
Journal of Inter-American Studies
The Journal of Negro History
Journal Officiel, League of Nations
La Liberté, Lyon
La Liberté, Paris
Listin Diario, Santo Domingo
Le Matin, Paris
Le Matin, Port-au-Prince
Le Monde Nouveau, Paris
Le Moniteur, Port-au-Prince
La Nacion, Santo Domingo
Le National, Port-au-Prince
The New Republic
The New York Times
Le Nouveauté, Port-au-Prince
Opportunity, New York
Outbound, London
La Paix par le Droit, Paris
Paris-Midi, Paris
Paris-Sud et Centre Amérique, Paris
Pax, Paris
Le Petit Journal, Paris
Le Petit Parisien, Paris
La Petite Revue, Paris

La Phalange, Port-au-Prince
Phylon, Atlanta
The Pittsburg Courier
The Plain Dealer, Cleveland
La Poste, Port-au-Prince
La Prensa, Lima
Le Progrès, Lyon
Relations, Montreal
Revista Nacional de Cultura, Caracas
La Revue des Ambassadeurs, Paris
Revue de l'Amérique Latine, Paris
La Revue Diplomatique, Paris
La Revue Hebdomadaire, Paris
Revue de l'Histoire des Colonies Francaises, Paris
Le Salut Public, Lyon
Stella, Cap-Haïtien
Le Temps, Paris
Le Temps, Port-au-Prince
Temps-Revue, Port-au-Prince
Le Travailleur, Worcester, Massachusetts
The Washington Daily News, Washington, D.C.
The Washington Post, Washington, D.C.
The Washington Tribune, Washington, D.C.

INDEX

Bellegarde, Dantès (*continued*)
  Eighth Pan-American Conference
    (Lima, 1938) and, 81–82
  on elites, 144, 155
  on family, 146
  family of, xvii, 55–59, 198
  Firmin and, 51
  on French language and culture in
    Haiti, 96, 102, 104, 121–24,
    128–29, 140, 155–56, 163, 169–70
  génération de la Ronde, la, and, 59–61
  German-Haitian commission and, 61
  Haitian Chamber of Commerce and,
    74
  on Haitian foreign policy and
    reputation, 124–25
  on Haitian Revolution, xix–xx, 6, 80,
    180
  on Haitian society, 114–15, 136–37
  historical works by, 92–102
  importance and reputation of, xv–xvi,
    xvii, xxii–xxv, 54–55, 62–63, 85–88
  individualism and, 148–50
  International Bureau of Peace and, 26
  internationalism and, xxi
  League of Nations and, xxiii, 42, 69–72,
    73–75, 76–77, 127, 129
  lecture by, 185–97
  liberalism and, 134–36, 154–60,
    162–64, 166–67, 169–72
  on literature and politics, 89
  on love, 146, 149–51
  McIlhenny on, xi–xii, xiii
  on nation and state, 94, 108, 118–20,
    169
  nationalism and, 60, 118–19, 144, 166
  official portrait of, *x*
  Oreste and, 23
  Pan-Africanism and, xxiii, 71–74,
    75–76, 106–7
  Pan-American Union and, 78
  Pan-Americanism and, xxiii, 78,
    126–29, 127, 185–86, 190–91,
    195–97
  on patriotism, 118–20, 144, 146
  on peace, 117–18, 127–28, 186–91
  positivism and, 103–4, 110–12,
    125–26, 146, 166–67
  Price-Mars and, xx, 86, 91, 105–6, 165,
    173–74

  on race and racial exploitation, 96–109,
    155–56
  on religion and Christianity, 140–43,
    144–46, 149–50, 155, 169
  retirement and death of, 86–88, 173
  on role of government, 133–36, 141
  on socialism and Marxism, 82, 106–7
  on tradition and opinion, 111
  on United States, 120–21, 123, 126,
    128–29, 130–32, 154, 192–94
  utilitarianism and, 111–12
  on Vodou, 141–43
  on women and women's rights, xviii, 57,
    146–48
Bellegarde, Fernande, xvii–xviii, 58
Bellegarde, Jean, 58
Bellegarde, Jean-Louis (DB's father), 55,
  56
Bellegarde, Jean-Louis de (DB's
  grandfather), 56
Bellegarde, Jeanne, 58
Bellegarde, Marie, xvii–xviii, 58
Bellegarde, Simone, 58
Bellegarde, Windsor (DB's half-brother),
  56, 61
Benedict XV, Pope, 67
Bentham, Jeremy, 39, 53, 111–12
Benton, Thomas Hart, xii–xiii, 9
Béranger, Henri, xxi, 88
Béranger, Pierre-Jean de, 42
Bergson, Henri, xxi, 52–53, 115, 137, 143,
  158
Berle, Adolf A., Jr., 54, 113–14, 157,
  232n37
Biassou, Georges, 37–38
Bilac, Olavo, 180
Bilbao, Francisco, 182
Blanchet, Albert, 78
Blanchet, Paul, xxiii
Boas, Franz, 103
Bogota Conference (1948), 78
Boisrond-Tonnerre, Félix, 38
Boisson, Jules, 55
Boisson, Louise, 55
Boisson, Marie (DB's mother), 55, 57
Boisson, Marie-Noëlle, xviii
Boisson, Pétion, 55
Bolívar, Simón, 9, 16–17, 38–39, 40, 181,
  185–86
Bolivia, 40

Bellegarde on, 96, 102, 104, 121–24,
140, 163, 169
Delorme on, 49
Firmin on, 51
role of, xxi–xxii, 7, 38–39, 86, 116–17,
163
French Revolution, 4, 11–12, 90, 99, 143,
281
Fresnel, Jacques-Ignace, 55, 108
Frost, Robert, 159
functionalism, 100, 101
Furtado, Celso, 28

Galloway, George, 142
Garvey, Marcus, 73, 171
Geffrard, Fabre-Nicolas, 10, 43, 58, 168
génération de la Ronde, 59–61, 110,
155–56, 165, 167, 182
génération de l'Occupation, 155–56, 167,
182
Germany
African colonies and, 71
Bellegarde on, 192–93
economic interests in Haiti and, 19, 61,
153–54
League of Nations and, 188
Nazism in, 135
Gérome, Pétion, 59–60, 89
Gobineau, Arthur de, 99
Goodhue, Abbot, 195
Gouldner, Alvin W., 101, 110, 113, 138
Gouraige, Ghislain
on Bellegarde, 110, 159, 165, 174
on colonial "dislocation," 37
on Creole language, 205n22
on Haitian foreign service, 67
on Price-Mars, 165
Graña, Cesar, 91, 144, 159
grands blancs, 98–99
grands seigneurs, xix, 4–5
Grasse, Count de, 185
Great Britain, 89–90, 192–93
Grenada, 179
Gruening, Ernest, 78–79, 157, 232n37
Guerrier, Philippe, 43
Guesde, Jules, 138

Haiti
American economic interests in, 19–20,
80–81, 154
anticlericalism in, 143

bourgeois revolution (1843) in, 42–43
conservatism in, 31–40
cultural assimilation and, 12–14
educational system in, 6, 10–11, 57,
58–59, 61, 64–66, 116–17, 146
foreign policy and, 7–10, 14–18, 68,
152–54
France and, 68, 89–90, 132
German interests in, 19, 61, 153–54
historians in, 43–45
international image of, xiii–xv
liberalism in, 16–17, 31–33, 41, 42, 45,
48, 53, 144
origins of social thought in, 32–38
plantation economy in, 2–4, 15
positivism in, 48–53, 97–101
race and racial prejudice in, 36–37, 108
romanticism in, 43, 46–47, 51, 60
society in, 4–6, 98–99, 136
trauma of insignificance and, 175–84
use of term, 207n57
utilitarianism in, 53, 101
See also French language and culture in
Haiti; Haitian Revolution; Roman
Catholic Church in Haiti; Saint
Domingue (French colony)
Haiti et ses problèmes (Bellegarde), 106, 144
Haiti littéraire et scientifique (journal),
219n34
Haiti littéraire et sociale (journal), 219n34
Haiti politique et littéraire (journal), 219n34
Haitian Chamber of Commerce, 74
Haitian language, 123–24
Haitian People, The (Leyburn), 169
Haitian Revolution
affranchis and, xviii–xix, 4–6, 15, 37
cultural dimension of, 10–14
economic dimension of, 2–4
international dimension of, 7–10
political dimension of, 6–7
silencing of, xii–xiii
social dimension of, xviii–xx, 4–6
social thought and, 32–38
Hale, Charles A., 2, 31, 46, 170
Haller, John S., Jr., 110
Hantos, Elemer, 129–30, 191
"Harbingers of Communism" (Bellegarde),
145
Harding, Warren G., 28
Hartmann, Karl Robert Eduard von, 150
Hayne, Robert Y., 9

CPSIA information can be obtained
at www.ICGtesting.com
Printed in the USA
LVHW091354230119
604958LV00001B/43/P

9 780826 522226